PRAISE FOR RIAN MALAN'S *MY TRAITOR'S HEART*

"A scorching exposé . . . Malan has taken truth-telling to the most grueling degree imaginable."—*San Francisco Chronicle*

"This book grabs you by the throat and will not let go. It is mesmerizing. It will profoundly alter whatever you have felt about South Africa—and mankind."—Peter Maas

"One of the most exhilarating books to come along in years. . . . Malan's overview is so thorough and compelling that you can hardly bear the pain of it. But his writing is so awesome you wish it would never end."—*Details*

"An unimaginably good book . . . I cannot recommend this book too highly to all who wish to think of themselves as conscious, and who are still willing to bear the burden of conscience. *My Traitor's Heart* is a book that will *change* your mind."—Jim Harrison

"The raw, heartbreaking cry that sounds from *My Traitor's Heart* . . . gives the routine violence of apartheid an unbearable reality."—*Vanity Fair*

"This is a great swirling devil of a book and it is equal in every way to its vast subject—the black and white country of the heart."—Don DeLillo

"A beautifully written book . . . Malan makes us better understand what has happened and what yet needs to be done."—*Houston Chronicle*

"A book that speaks with eloquence . . . It condemns with uncompromising moral persistence the racism underpinning white South African society, but never resorts to simple stereotyping, naïve liberal cant, or easy outs. It is an honest book by an honest man."—*Chicago Sun-Times*

"Passionate, informed, and compelling."—Richard Price

"Malan is bent on uncovering another level altogether of South African life, and he does so beautifully. . . . He sharply expands our understanding of his strange, strange country's complexities."
—William Finnegan, *The New York Times*

"Eloquent, sometimes almost shrill, but never glib . . . Malan loves his country even as he mourns its history, loves his family even as he deplores the society they helped create."—*Newsweek*

"*My Traitor's Heart* is a book with many things to teach us. . . . A seeker of the truth, [Malan] takes us along in this excellent book as he discovers the complexities of his troubled land."—*USA Today*

"A parable of terror and beauty . . . the stuff of tragedy, acted out in blood."
—James Dickey

"An honest and complicated contribution to a centuries-old discourse on colonialism."—*The Village Voice*

"Malan proves himself a masterful writer, perhaps because he is so obviously honest and writing from the heart."—*The Oregonian*

"One of the most coldly realistic yet compassionate accounts of contemporary South Africa. . . . Malan's colloquial tone gives this heartfelt confession of his fears, contradictions, hopes, and love a compelling immediacy."
—*Kirkus Reviews*

"Malan is singularly well placed to tell the tale of how his country closed its eyes to the march of history."—*New York*

"This is not just another book about South Africa. It is the corrosive, self-doubting, anguished, courageously brash testimony of a young Afrikaner appalled by the intellectual and emotional dishonesty involved in taking on the stance of liberal or radical white freedom fighter."
—*The Christian Science Monitor*

"Malan's book raises hard questions about race that most white leftists both in and outside of South Africa have preferred not to face."—*The Nation*

"Although Mr. Malan's true-life tales are as ironic and uncanny as Isak Dinesen's stories, his voice ultimately offers no distractions and almost no consolation, and this book becomes an act of human patriotism in the face of evil choices."—*The New Yorker*

"*My Traitor's Heart* is the thoughtful and thought-provoking account of a man who has come to terms with his country. It is not merely a parable of terror; it is a candle that has been lit to light the obliterating darkness."
—*The Star* (Minneapolis)

MY TRAITOR'S HEART

MY TRAITOR'S HEART

HEART

A SOUTH AFRICAN EXILE
RETURNS TO FACE
HIS COUNTRY, HIS TRIBE,
AND HIS CONSCIENCE

RIAN MALAN

GROVE PRESS
New York

Excerpt from *Foe* by J. M. Coetzee. Copyright © J. M. Coetzee, 1986. All rights reserved. Reprinted by permission of Viking Penguin, a division of Penguin Books USA, Inc.

Published simultaneously in Canada
Printed in the United States of America

Library of Congress Cataloging-in-Publication Data

Malan, Rian.
My traitor's heart : a South African exile returns to face his
country, his tribe, and his conscience / Rian Malan.
ISBN: 978-0-8021-3684-8
1. Malan, Rian. 2. Malan, Rian—Family. 3. Malan family.
4. South Africa—Exiles—Biography. 5. Huguenots—South Africa—Biography.
6. South Africa—Exiles—Genealogy. 7. Huguenots—South Africa—Genealogy.
I. Title.
CT1929.M35A3 1990   929'.2'0968—dc20   89-15169

Design by Laura Hammond Hough

Grove Press
an imprint of Grove/Atlantic, Inc.
841 Broadway
New York, NY 10003

Distributed by Publishers Group West
www.groveatlantic.com

10 11 12 13 14   10 9 8 7 6

For the forgotten legions of the South African center, for my parents, and for Creina, who took the enormous risk of trusting me.

BOOK I

LIFE IN THIS STRANGE PLACE

How do I live in this strange place?

> —*BERNOLDUS NIEMAND, from the*
> *Boer reggae song "Reggae Vibes Is Cool"*

I'm burned out and starving to death, so I'm just going to lay this all upon you and trust that you're a visionary reader, because the grand design, such as it is, is going to be hard for you to see. I know you're interested in my ancestors, so I guess I should begin at the very beginning. I am a Malan, descendant of Jacques Malan, a Huguenot who fled the France of Louis XIV to escape being put to the sword for his Protestant faith. He sought refuge among the Dutch, only to be put aboard ship in 1688 and sent to the Dark Continent, to the rude Dutch colony at the Cape of Good Hope. Jacques the Huguenot was the first Malan in Africa. In the centuries since, a Malan has been present at all the great dramas and turning points in the history of the Afrikaner tribe.

Jacques tamed the Cape and planted vineyards. His sons built gracious gabled homesteads in the lee of Table Mountain. His grandson Dawid the Younger ran off to the wild frontier in 1788, where he fought the savage Xhosa and took part in Slagtersnek, the first Afrikaner rebellion against the British.

Hercules, son of Dawid the Younger, led the third wave of Voortrekkers into the heart of Africa. In February 1838 he sat in the kraal of the great king Dingaan, watching a huge Zulu army wheeling back and forth on the plain. The sun glinted off thousands of spears. Feet thundered in unison. Clouds of dust rose into the sky. And then Dingaan cried, "Kill the wizards," and Hercules and his seventy companions were murdered—stakes driven up their anuses, skulls smashed with stones, and their bodies left on a hill for the vultures.

Once the killing was done, King Dingaan pointed, and his army set off for the north at a run. They ran all day and most of the night, and it was still dark when they fell on the main Trekker party. The attack was unexpected. Men were disemboweled, women mutilated, and the brains of small children dashed out on wagon wheels. In all, 530 Trekkers died that dawn, in a place we still call Weenen—the Place of Weeping.

In the aftermath, the survivors drew their wagons into a circle on the bank of a nameless river and made ready for the final battle. On its eve, they laid hands on the Bible and swore a covenant with Jehovah: If he granted them victory over the heathen, they would hold true to his ways forever.

5

A Malan was there—Jacob Jacobus Malan, brother of the fallen Hercules. As the sun rose on December 16, he saw something amazing: rank upon rank of Zulu warriors sitting silently on their haunches, waiting for the mist to rise. Two hours later, the river was red with black blood, and it was no longer nameless: It was Blood River. Mountains of Zulus lay dead on the battlefield, but not a single Boer was slain. It was surely a miracle, a sign that God's will was ours.

So we remember Jacob Jacobus Malan and still honor his solemn covenant. We also remember his sons Jacobus and Hercules, who survived the Zulu wars, dragged their covered wagons over the mountains, and smashed the black tribes on the high plain. There, on conquered land, they established Boer republics, where white men were free to rule blacks in accord with their stern Jehovistic covenant.

In 1881, Hercules Malan the second sat on an African hilltop watching another seminal event in the white tribe's bloody saga—the Battle of Majuba, turning point in our first war against the British. Kommandant Malan's soldiers were an undisciplined rabble of farm boys and graybeards, but they could drop a buck at a thousand yards, and every bullet counted. The redcoats were annihilated, and the British retired to lick their wounds. A few years later, however, gold was discovered on our land, and they came after us in earnest. In that next war—the Second War of Freedom—our forces were outnumbered nine to one. The largest army yet assembled on the planet rolled across our frontiers and occupied our towns. We fought on, though. A Malan was there, too: General Wynand Malan, the bravest of the brave, leader of a guerrilla band that ranged deep into enemy territory. To crush our resistance, the British scorched the earth and put Afrikaner women and children in concentration camps, but General Malan fought on to the bittersweet end, taking a bullet on the war's very last day.

In the aftermath, we became a backward peasantry, despised by our British bosses and betters. But we rose again, with yet another Malan at the fore—Daniel François Malan. His Afrikaner National Party came to power in 1948, vowing to throw off the imperial British yoke and devise a final solution for the "native question." This final solution was apartheid, a gridlock of more than a hundred laws designed to keep blacks and whites forever separate and to ensure, not at all coincidentally, that blacks remained in their God-ordained place, hewers of wood and drawers of water, forever and ever.

This fate was unacceptable to blacks, so they rose against us in earnest in 1976, in a rebellion that has never really ceased since. In this era, too, the destiny of the tribe is in the hands of a Malan—General Magnus Malan, minister of defense. There are those who say it is he who truly controls the country, through the awesome power of the white military, and through a network of secretive paramilitary entities called Joint Management Centers. In these troubled times, the name Malan is often heard on the lips of black comrades, in the chanted litany of those who will die when the day comes. I see them at the township rallies, thousands upon thousands of them, running to and fro in tight formation. Their feet thunder in unison. Their faces glisten with sweat and excitement. Dust rises. They cradle imaginary AK-47s in their arms, and chant, *"Voetsek,* Malan!" Fuck off, Malan! Fuck off! Fuck off! And then they wheel in formation and thunder away to the far side of some dusty township stadium, leaving me poised on a cusp of history.

There is only one war here, you see, the war that was and is and yet will be. I don't know how it will end, but I can tell you where it began. It began in the 1780s, on the eastern frontier of the old Cape Colony, and a Malan, inevitably, was there.

I found him in the national archives in Cape Town, buried in the index underneath a cryptic "M." The entry referred to a trial held in 1788, but the felon's name was not revealed. He was just M. It was the only entry of its kind. I thought, here lies some secret, some truth long obscured, so I asked to see the records of this two-hundred-year-old trial. The story they revealed was myth made flesh, the destiny of a nation embodied in the fate of a single man.

On the outskirts of Cape Town, beside a four-lane freeway, stands a pair of whitewashed pillars and an imposing wrought-iron gate. Behind the gate, in a grove of oak and chestnut trees, lies the homestead Vergelegen, one of the finest remaining examples of an architectural style called Cape Dutch. The house is achingly lovely to the eye, a symphony of whitewashed walls, flowing gables, dark thatch, wooden shutters and huge yellowwood doors that open on the cool gloom of tiled interiors. Two centuries ago, it was the home of one Dawid Malan, the man behind the M.

Dawid Malan was born in 1750, son of Dawid the Elder and grandson of Jacques the Patriarch. At the age of twenty-four, and by virtue of a shrewd marriage to his cousin Elizabeth, he became master of Vergelegen, then the finest estate in the entire Cape Colony. Vergelegen stood at the foot of the

Hottentot's Holland Mountains, a day's horseride from the shores of Table Bay.

In Dawid's time, the Cape was already a tame, orderly place. Lions and elephants were a fading memory, and the yellow-skinned Hottentot tribes living there when whites first came had long since been driven off or turned into servants and herders. From his rooftop, Dawid would have looked out upon a breathtaking tableau of vineyards, golden wheat fields, whitewashed farmhouses, and purple mountains. In the distance, at the foot of Table Mountain, stood a great stone castle flying the flag of the mighty Dutch East India Company. Under its ramparts lay a bustling wharf where merchantmen bound for the Spice Islands of the Orient took on fresh food, water, and wine.

Above the castle, on the slopes of the mountain, stood a city of great beauty. Cape Town struck one early visitor as a place of "elegant and capacious dwellings," inhabited by people of "general intelligence and cultured politeness." Travelers were invariably astonished to discover so charming and civilized a settlement in such an unlikely place. In Cape Town, the gentry sported powdered wigs and danced the minuet in the castle's ballroom. They built schools and churches, employed learned pastors and pedagogues. They had heard of Rousseau and Voltaire, and there were even some Free Thinkers among them. Cape Town was a tiny outpost of Europe, an enclave of the Enlightenment at the foot of the Dark Continent.

In this community, in the year 1788, Dawid the Younger was a citizen of great substance. As master of Vergelegen, he was a rich man, owner of a score of slaves, twice that many horses, and more than fifty thousand vinestocks. His father was a candidate for a seat on the citizen's council that advised the Dutch governor on matters of policy; his uncle, an elder of the Dutch Reformed Church. Dawid himself was a colonel in the Burger Dragoons, the citizens' militia. He had an upstanding wife, four young children, and a neighbor named Jurgen Radijn.

Radijn was a German, a mercenary who had recently retired from the service of the Dutch East India Company and settled on an estate called Harmonie. Among Radijn's many possessions was a slave girl named Sara, who gave birth that year to a son. Her master would normally have taken pleasure in this increase in his human flock, but this child was a half-breed, and that meant money out of his pocket: The children of slave and Christian had to be baptized, educated, and eventually freed, and Sara's child, by the look of it, had surely been fathered by a Christian. Radijn was incensed. Someone had been tampering with his brood stock, so to speak. He demanded the man's name, but Sara refused to answer. She swore to don a man's clothing and run away if a hand was laid upon her, then turned her face to the wall. Under the circumstances, there was little Radijn could do but keep a close watch on the errant girl and make sure that she remained henceforth chaste.

Late one night, Radijn's wife was awakened by the barking of dogs. She looked outside and saw a shadow stealing across the courtyard below her window. She waited. A while later, two shadowy figures came out of the dark and disappeared into the door of the slave quarters. This was the moment Mother Radijn was waiting for. She gathered up her nightdress and tiptoed after them. In the slave quarters, she lit a taper and held it aloft. Sara was lying in her cot, feigning sleep. Mother Radijn was not fooled. She summoned the intruder forth. At that, a white man crawled out from under Sara's bed and stood up, naked save for his stockings. It was Dawid Malan, master of Vergelegen. "Mother Radijn," he said lamely, "this is not what you think it to be."

For masters to sleep with slaves was not unheard-of, but it was done discreetly, furtively. It was a breaking of caste and, worse yet, a violation of Calvinist piety. So there was a minor scandal when Malan's philandering first came to light, but it was nothing compared with what was to come. Dawid seemed obsessed with the slave girl, and refused to give her up. He took to lurking around Harmonie's homestead, trying to catch a glimpse of her. He waylaid Radijn's slaves in the fields and begged them to carry secret messages to her. It was outrageous. In the court case in which these doings were subsequently aired, witness after witness stepped forward to tell of their shock at Malan's behavior, and of the dire warnings of God's punishment they had issued to him. Dawid scorned their advice, and his conduct became the talk of the colony. His wife kicked him out of her bed, the Church shunned him as a fornicator, and Radijn, in a final effort to put an end to the shameful affair, took the child from Sara's breast and sent her to live with Jan de Vos, keeper of tolls on a distant mountain pass. De Vos was instructed to keep Sara indoors at all times, and Dawid Malan at bay.

The toll-keeper tried, but he had to leave his home from time to time. One day, a slave informed de Vos that something curious had happened while he was away. A white man had crept into his cottage, spoken to Sara, and then slipped quietly away. Who was it? The slave had no idea.

On the night of August 11, Dawid Malan rose from his bed and crept into Vergelegen's stables. He saddled two horses, loaded them with provisions, powder, and shot. And then he rode out into the night and started climbing the pass that led over the Hottentot's Holland Mountains and away from Cape Town. In his day, the pass was just a rough track that wound tortuously up the hillside, following a path worn centuries earlier by herds of migrating antelope. Near the stone cottage of the toll-keeper, Malan whistled like a bird, and a woman materialized out of the darkness. Sara mounted Dawid's spare horse, and they rode on up the pass together.

It was a long and grueling climb, so dawn was probably breaking by the time they reached the mountain's crest. If his eyes were keen, Dawid might have seen a frenzied scurrying between the tiny farmhouses far below. Finding two horses missing, Elizabeth Malan had broken into her estranged husband's bedroom and discovered his bed unslept-in. She galloped over to Harmonie, tears streaming down her face, and told Jurgen Radijn, who instantly dispatched a rider to check on Sara's whereabouts. She, too, was gone; her guardian, the toll-keeper de Vos, was out on the mountainside with his flintlock and his dogs, searching for the spoor. Radijn's messenger wheeled and rode off to raise the alarm. The fugitives had to make haste.

Ahead of Dawid and Sara lay a cool, high plain called Overberg, the land beyond the mountains. They pushed on across it, riding as hard as they could. On the third day of their flight, an inquisitive militiaman barred their way, and Malan was forced to give a false name, and a false account of himself. He claimed to be Jan Nortjé of Cape Town, and introduced his dark-skinned companion as his wife. After that, they avoided farms and settlements, although a sharp-eyed widow spotted them as they skirted the town of Goudini. Beyond Goudini lay the Breede River. In Dutch, *breede* means "broad," and there was only one way to cross such a river—by ferry.

The ferryman, one Abraham Finnerholm, was surprised to see a well-horsed white gentleman on his landing. Such gentry seldom passed his way. Finnerholm couldn't help asking his name. "I am Jan Nortjé," said the stranger. The ferryman asked his business, but the traveler gave no reply. All this was most unusual. The details lodged in the ferryman's memory, and when the pursuers galloped up to his landing a few days later he was able to give them an unmistakable description of Dawid Malan and the missing slave girl.

Beyond the ferry, Dawid and Sara drew away from the Cape, where nature was benign. The landscapes across which they now crawled were arid, and empty. The green grass of the Cape gave way to dust and rocks and thorns. The ridges above them were lined by spiny aloes, each as tall as a man, a watchful sentinel against the sky. They were drawing closer to the frontier, to Africa. There were few people, no permanent settlements. After about two weeks of hard riding, they came to a wild canyon cut deep into the earth by a muddy brown river. This was the Great Fish River, the Cape Colony's outermost frontier. Ahead lay the howling wilderness, full of wild beasts and hostile savages; behind, the scaffold for Dawid Malan, death by strangulation for his runaway slave lover.

Dawid's first life was over; he must have known he would never return to the Cape. The Dragoons were on his trail, but they would turn back short of the frontier and return to the castle with the evidence they had gathered. A trial would be held, and Malan found guilty in absentia of stealing a slave. The Council of Justice would issue a decree banishing him from the Dutch colony forever. His disgraced father would disown him, the authorities strip him of his rank in the burger cavalry, and his bitter wife attempt to have him declared dead. He had sacrificed everything for the love of a black woman.

That was quite something, I thought, a Malan forfeiting his birthright and all his worldly goods for the sake of a black slave—staggering, in light of the humiliations Dawid Malan's descendants would later inflict on their half-breed brothers and sisters. In a century to come, Afrikaners would claim that the so-called colored people were spawned in dockside brothels by seafaring white rabble, certainly not by Malans and their pious Calvinist ilk. It was a Malan, the dour and bloodless Daniel François Malan, who rose in Parliament to promulgate the laws that made it a crime for blacks to sleep with or marry whites. The same Malan stripped Dawid and Sara's colored descendants of their right to vote, evicted them from white suburbs, and chased them out of white schools. No wonder this tale had been buried in the archives, the trail to it obscured by that cryptic M. The honorable Daniel François was linked by blood, and even love, to the colored people he so cruelly scorned.

Those moldering court documents made it clear that Dawid's feeling for Sara was no mere fit of lust. Dawid was an educated man. He knew the law. He must have calculated his losses before saddling his horses, and known the price he would pay. Yet he went ahead with it, stole away with a black slave girl to brave an uncertain future in a terribly dangerous place. To go that far, he must have loved Sara, and that love must surely have opened his heart to other black people. So it seems fair to say that Dawid Malan left the Cape a racially enlightened man. And then he crossed the river and disappeared into Africa, where he was transformed, as all white men who went there were transformed.

I shall tell you the details of that transformation in due course, but first we must consider the nature of the wilderness into which Dawid and Sara had fled. In maps of the time, the territory behind the Great Fish River was shown as a void. Nobody really knew what was out there, save wild beasts and savages and wild white men in animal skins. It was a place of nightmarish harshness, hot and dry, with meager, shallow soils and, in places, grass so sour that cattle balked at eating it. It was stricken by periodic droughts and hailstorms, infested with lions and leopards. Huge swarms of locusts darkened its skies and crossed its rivers on bridges of their own dead. Migrating antelope flowed across it in herds so huge that they took days to pass a single point.

The white men along and beyond the frontier lived as nomads, moving from place to place as the grazing wore out. They were simple to the point of idiocy, naming each feature of the landscape for its characteristics: the Great Fish River, the Broad River, the Snow Mountains, the River of Elephants. They were desperately poor, ragged, and mostly illiterate, and their Dutch was degenerating into the vulgar dialect that would later be called Afrikaans. They lived by the gun, and according to the Old Testament. Its tales of tribes wandering in the desert spoke to them, and so did its notions of an eye for an eye and a tooth for a tooth.

Since straying from the Dutch-ruled colony a century earlier, these nomadic Boers had extracted many teeth. At first, the country they moved into was populated by yellow-skinned races that disintegrated in the face of white advance. Those Hottentot not wiped out by smallpox were made servants; and as for the stone-age Bushmen, they were regarded as dangerous vermin. The Bushmen saw no distinction between domestic cattle and wild game and preyed on both alike, so they were hunted like wild dogs, and if caught, slaughtered; no one was spared save those women and children who might be tamed and put to work as chattel. It was cruel, but then the Bushmen themselves had the cruel hearts of beasts of prey. They would hack a limb off a living cow and eat it before the bellowing animal's eyes. Once the Bushmen had tasted the white man's retribution, they began to retaliate in kind. A Boer who didn't kill one when he had the chance was likely to collect a poison arrow from behind a rock, or find his family butchered when he returned from hunting.

And so the Bushmen were dying out, retreating into the deserts and mountains, but the blame for their sad fate did not rest with the white men alone. Others persecuted them, too. These were the Xhosa, the magnificent and warlike African tribe that was migrating slowly down the east coast toward the Cape even as the Boers advanced to meet them. Like the Boers, the Xhosa had driven the weak before them, and had never met a foe sufficiently powerful to contain them. In 1778, the Boers and Xhosa came face to face along the Great Fish River. Both races owned vast herds of cattle, and that alone doomed them to clash. The fact that the Xhosa were savage and heathen in white eyes merely made it easier for whites to kill them.

The Xhosa had no writing and few tools, not even the wheel. Their incomprehensible tongue is full of strange clicks. They went naked save for a fringe of beads and a cloak of animal hide. They daubed their bodies with red clay, and traded cattle for wives. They worshiped their ancestors and blamed illness and misfortune on witches, who were routinely smelled out and put to a hideous death. They left their old to die in the bush, bled the vaginas of young girls to cool their lust, and twirled thorn twigs up the rectums of ailing babies to bleed the bad blood out of them. In the words of an Englishman named Steadman who hunted and explored beyond the frontier in the early nineteenth century, the very sight of the Xhosa produced in a white man "the most appalling sensations."

On the other hand, early travelers were scarcely more complimentary of the Boers who inhabited the void beyond the Great Fish River. Most concluded that they were sliding back toward barbarity, each generation growing wilder than the last. When a stranger came among them, they swarmed over him like curious savages, fingering his fancy European clothing, gaping in awe at his modern guns and possessions, asking childlike questions. The Boers, observed the botanist Lichtenstein, were rendered "no less laughable than dangerous" by their "ignorance and crude conceptions." As to how the Boers felt about him, the record is silent. Very few of them could read or write.

And so white men squared off against the Africans, and in 1779 the war began—a war without end, a war that just *was,* and still is, for what started then is still not finished today. The Xhosa rustled cattle, and the Boers' bloody reprisals usually turned into outright raids of plunder. Capturing Xhosa cattle, one white frontiersman noted, was easier than breeding your own. On both sides, men died in droves, but the black bodies were always stacked deeper, because the white men had guns. Their strategy was to ride within range of the Xhosa, fire a volley, and gallop off before the sprinting warriors were close enough to hurl their spears. It was an ignoble form of warfare, but then the Boers could ill afford casualties: There were scarcely five hundred able-bodied white men and boys on the frontier in the 1780s, ranged against a hundred thousand Xhosa. Neither side was strong enough to win an outright victory, so the line of battle swept back and forth across the Great Fish River for decades.

There were many such frontiers in the world at that time, but this one was unlike most others. All the Dutch really wanted of Africa was the land they could see from the battlements of Cape Town Castle. They had no imperial ambitions, no interest in the interior. Dutch governors seldom sent military expeditions to help the beleaguered frontiersmen. Instead, they sent bailiffs to collect the "lion and tiger" tax, the "pontoon" tax, and the quitrent on farmland. Most Boers resented paying taxes to a government that did little or nothing for them, so the taxmen invariably returned to the castle empty-handed. At one stage, there was talk of dispatching troops to tame the frontiersmen and seize their taxes. It came to nothing, though. The governor was warned that if he sent soldiers, the Boers would kill half of them, salt their corpses and send them home with the survivors, "as earnest of what they would do to any authority that should dare interfere with them."

So the frontiersmen struggled on alone. In 1793, they drove the Xhosa out of the Zuurveld, a buffer zone separating black from white. Two years later, a British fleet sailed into Simon's Bay, captured Cape Town Castle, and raised their flag over the Cape Colony. The Xhosa took advantage of the ensuing disarray to pour across the frontier in force, looting and pillaging all the way to Mossel Bay, almost three hundred miles to the south. More than half the Boer farms on the border were abandoned or destroyed. In the following decade, the Boers pushed the front line back across the Great Fish River. In 1811, the Xhosa reoccupied the buffer zone. It went on like that for almost sixty years.

This then was the maelstrom into which Dawid Malan and Sara vanished in August 1788. Elsewhere in the world, great upheavals were taking place, new orders coming into being. In America, democracy was twelve years old. The French were poised to topple Louis XVI in the name of liberty, equality, and fraternity. It was the Age of Enlightenment, but Dawid and Sara seemed to disappear into darkness.

I spent months in the Cape Town archives, reading the yellowed annals of those times, searching for clues to their fate. At first I found none, just chronicles of hatred received and hatred applied, of raids and reprisals and bloodshed. And then I started reading the chronicles of Slagtersnek, the first Boer rebellion against the British. Around 1806, the British installed a magistrate on the frontier, ordering him to impose upon it the rule of law. As the British conceived it, that meant justice for all, not only for white men. To the Boers, the very idea was abhorrent. Their concept of relations between master and servant, or Christian and heathen, arose from the Old Testament's most stern and unforgiving passages. Read selectively, the Old Testament provided divine justification for the way they lived and the cruelties they inflicted on the dark-skinned heathen: "a whip for the horse, a bridle for the ass, and a rod for the fool's back." The Boers found succor in such stern Old Testament injunctions. They found the New Testament less palatable, however, and some of them seemed to disregard everything in the Bible save the bit about stern punishment.

One such frontiersman was Frederik Bezuidenhout, a shameless fornicator who had a white wife, a black concubine, and a house full of half-breed children. Like many of his neighbors, Bezuidenhout was less a pious Calvinist than a creature of Africa, where the strong eat and the weak are eaten— or beaten, as the case may be. In 1815, Bezuidenhout whipped a Hottentot shepherd named Booi. After the flogging, Booi took up his goods and vanished. A few weeks later, a horseman rode out to serve a summons on Bezuidenhout. Booi had been to see the British magistrate in Graaff Reinet and laid a charge against his white master.

The Boers did not accord servants, heathens, and blacks generally the right to do such a thing. When Bezuidenhout heard why the horseman had come, he "flew up, with fists swaying to and fro," uttering "curses and invective" and declaring that he would sooner die than answer such a summons. The British magistrate ordered him arrested, but that was easier said than done. Bezuidenhout inspired "general dread" in the hearts of more civil men, and the magistrate's *veldkornets,* his sheriffs, were too scared to set foot on his land. The stalemate dragged on for months, making the mighty British Empire look foolish and ineffectual. In the end, the magistrate had to dispatch troops to bring Bezuidenhout in.

True to his word, Bezuidenhout holed up in a cave with his musket and opened fire on the redcoats, who slew him with a bullet in the heart. His death ignited a smoldering anti-British sentiment among the frontier Boers. In the Boer view, British missionaries and administrators were siding with

15

the enemy, interfering with their right to chastise and slaughter the dark-skinned heathen as they deemed necessary. The frontiersmen swore drunken vengeance over Bezuidenhout's coffin and, once it was laid to rest, rose up against the British. The rebellion that followed heralded the start of another war that continues to this day—the war of words and moral recrimination between Boers and other white men. In military terms, the Slagtersnek uprising was an utterly futile affair, soon put down by British troops. In the aftermath, the ringleaders were rounded up and put on trial in the town of Uitenhage.

And that is where Dawid Malan resurfaced—among the race-hating white savages in the dock, on trial for high treason. The man who abandoned his birthright for the love of a black woman had become what would one day be called a white supremacist, willing to die rather than accord black people equality before the law. According to evidence laid before the court, it was Malan who penned the rebels' insolent communiqués. He set the paper on the saddle of a horse and scrawled upon it with a quill pen. When the writing was done, the illiterate rabble peering over his shoulder asked, "Is it proper?" As a learned man, he was a figure of influence among the rebels. Indeed, the prosecutor singled Malan out as a man "of the most dangerous sort"—one of a triumvirate of white barbarians "who have never submitted to any authority, who have been the greatest part of their lives among savages, and are men of the most depraved morals."

I cannot tell you what became of Sara in the intervening twenty-seven years; she simply disappeared from the records, and her resurrected lover now had a white woman at his side, and a brood of strong white sons. Nor can I tell you what befell Dawid Malan in the void, what caused his heart to turn. All I know is that he was one man when he crossed the river into Africa and another when he reappeared, and that his transformation paralleled the transformation of his entire tribe, for that was what the Boers had become in their isolation: They had become Afrikaners, the white tribe of Africa, arrogant, xenophobic, and "full of blood," as the Zulus say of tyrants. They had their own language, their own customs and traditions, and a myth to light their way, a mystic Christian mission on the Dark Continent. They spoke of themselves as bearers of the light, but in truth they were dark of heart, and they knew it, and willed it so.

The Afrikaners lived in isolation, but rumors and fragments of ideas reached them from the outside world, borne by deserters and outlaws and missionaries. They heard of the American Revolution, and of the new philosophies sweeping Europe—of the Jacobin doctrine of liberty, equality, and fraternity, of Rousseau's concept of the Noble Savage, and of the Enlightenment, the civilized reinterpretation of the Scriptures upon which all this was based. They did not like what they heard. To them, such ideas invited a degree of moral introspection that could make men weak and doubtful. On the frontier, it was an eye for an eye, and then an arm for an arm, and a leg for a leg, or so the Boers believed, and who is to say they were wrong? There was nothing in the Xhosa's history of expansion and conquest to suggest that they were any more willing to love than the white man. *Bloed roep om wraak. Siyabiza igazi wetho.* That was a saying on both sides of the frontier. It means, "Spilled blood calls for vengeance." In such a place, or so the Boers believed, a weak and doubtful man would soon be a dead one.

And so, when rumors of the Enlightenment penetrated their wilderness, the Afrikaners considered them, consulted their Bibles and preachers, and finally reached a consensus: These new ideas presented a threat to their survival, and should be suppressed—not only in the world at large, but in their own hearts. Soon, many Afrikaners were calling themselves Doppers, after the little metal caps with which they snuffed out candles. They called themselves Doppers because they were deliberately and consciously extinguishing the light of the Enlightenment, so that they could do what they had to do in darkness.

There are many truths about Afrikaners, but none so powerful and reverberant as this willful self-blinding. It was the central act in our history, or so it seems to me. The men of Dawid Malan's generation were the first true Afrikaners; they were the mold, and all who followed were cast in it. They snuffed out the light, and we have lived ever since in darkness. We shit on the altars of Western enlightenment and defy the high priests who would have us behave in accordance with its moral tenets. It was so; it is so.

Dawid Malan was spared the gallows and died in 1824, but his spirit lived on. His sons' Great Trek of 1838 was essentially a flight from the light, from the enlightened policies of the British. The Voortrekkers drove into the heart of the Dark Continent, where no light penetrated at all, and there, on conquered land, they set up Boer republics in which blacks were ruled in accordance with the Dopper principle. There was apartheid by another name in those republics, and apartheid of sorts in the era of British dominion.

After Daniel François Malan came to power in 1948, there was apartheid in earnest, but it was really nothing new. It was the same old Dopper principle, disguised in the language and strategies of twentieth-century totalitarianism.

It seems to me, looking back on history, that all of South Africa's agony is rooted in Dawid Malan's ancient act of self-blinding. The Dopper spirit survived the centuries and finally blossomed in apartheid, and we are eating its poisonous fruit to this day. The Dopper spirit manifests itself in everything my tribe has done to dark-skinned people: in repression and censorship, pass laws and job reservation; in the disfranchisement of our colored brothers and the razing of District Six; in the Sharpeville massacre and bloody Soweto uprising; in detention without trial and interrogation by torture; in the death of Steve Biko and the jailing of Nelson Mandela; and finally, in 1985, in the shooting of black schoolchildren in township streets. It all leads back, in the end, to Dawid Malan and a law formulated on the far bank of the Great Fish River two hundred years ago: You have to put the black man down, plant your foot on his neck, and keep him that way forever, lest he spring up and slit your white throat.

What would you have me say? That I think apartheid is stupid and vicious? I do. That I'm sorry? I am, I am. That I'm not like the rest of them? If you'd met me a few years ago, in a bar in London or New York, I would have told you that. I would have told you that only I, of all my blind clan and tribe, had eyes that could truly see, and that what I saw appalled me. I would have passed myself off as a political exile, an enlightened sort who took black women into his bed and fled his country rather than carry a gun for the abominable doctrine of white supremacy. You would probably have believed me. I almost believed myself, you see, but in truth I was always one of them. I am a white man born in Africa, and all else flows from there.

Socialism has done an invaluable service to humanity, and not the least to Christianity itself, by turning its searchlight on the evils of the existing system. We hope and pray that Christianity and socialism may be so guided in their future development that the deep yearning, the widespread movements, and even the passions and the violence of the age may prove to be but the birthpangs of a better social world.

—*DANIEL FRANÇOIS MALAN, architect of apartheid*

I was born in 1954, a member of the tribe that upheld Dawid Malan's legacy, a citizen of the country ruled by it, and son of a man who believed in it all. And yet, if you'd put it to my father that he believed blacks had to be kept down lest they leap up and slit white throats, he would have insisted that he thought nothing of the sort. He would have told you that his faith lay in something called grand apartheid, the overarching ideology that promised to make white South Africans and all their nine subject African tribes "separate but equal" in separate nation-states. In favor of this schema, he would have offered some fairly sophisticated arguments revolving around the awesome power of ethnocentricity and the apparent failure of the integrationist solution everywhere from Ireland to Armenia, from Chicago to Nigeria. My father had an uncanny ability to discern a moral basis to apartheid. In fairness to him, there was one, in the beginning, but it was betrayed in the year of my birth.

Soon after coming to power, in 1948, the government of Daniel François Malan set up a commission to establish what would be required to turn South Africa's bitterly poor and crowded tribal homelands into free and economically viable Bantustans. The Tomlinson Commission tabled its report in 1954, and it must have made disheartening reading for true believers in ethical apartheid. It said that vast tracts of farmland would have to be expropriated from whites and turned over to blacks. It called for massive investments in infrastructure, education, and industry. It concluded that it would cost at least a billion English pounds over the coming decade to make apartheid work—ten times more than the Malan government had planned to spend. This was far too high a price to pay for good intentions, of course, so the Tomlinson Report was buried. After that, separate but equal became an empty slogan, and apartheid was just another variant of the ancient Afrikaner doctrine of keeping blacks down.

Ah, but I knew nothing of such things in the year of my birth. When my eyes opened, I found myself in a split-level suburban house surrounded by similar houses, in a white suburb much like any other white suburb anywhere else in the Western world. My father worked for Total, the French oil company, and my mother taught at a school for the mentally retarded. Mr. Prior, who lived next door, worked for Volkswagen, and Mrs. Pretorius across the street was a primary-school principal. Our house had three levels. My mother, father, brother, and I lived in the top two stories, and the black servants lived at the bottom, next to the garage. I had two living grandmothers, and two dead grandfathers, who were pictures on the wall. One grandfather was wearing a broad ceremonial sash and topcoat and twirling his handlebar mustache. The other grandfather was sitting at a desk, brooding and smoking. His name was Stephanus Jacobus Malan, and he had died the year I was born.

Stephanus Jacobus Malan was said to have been a melancholy man. He had a smattering of education, rare for an Afrikaner of his era, and was known to quote Shakespeare and sing snatches of opera in his more buoyant moods. Mostly, though, he was melancholy. He would come home after work and shut himself into his study to drink brandy and read. There was always a cigarette in his mouth. He didn't puff it, just let it dangle there, burning slowly, the smoke trailing up his cheek and over his squinting eye. After fifty years, the stream of smoke left an indelible yellow streak across his face. In the photograph, it looked as though someone had slashed his cheek with a knife.

Stephanus was the bookkeeper in a dusty sheep town called Calvinia, which lay in the semidesert Great Karroo—three hundred miles north of Cape Town and south of almost nothing. There were no blacks in Calvinia, only Afrikaners, "Boer Jews," "Hottentots," sheep, dust, and locusts. My grandfather married a Steenkamp, daughter of Piet Steenkamp, whose farm was almost as big as some European countries. They had five children, of whom my father, born in 1920, was the second eldest.

My grandfather Stephanus was a SAP—a supporter of General Jan Smuts's South African Party, which was in power at that time. General

Smuts was that rare creature, a reasonable Afrikaner, an internationalist and a philosopher. He was also a segregationist and white supremacist, of course. Everyone was. Even the Communist Party deferred to Dawid Malan's legacy and organized under the slogan "Workers of the world unite and fight for a white South Africa." In any event, my grandfather was a SAP, but Calvinia was no SAP town. It was the parliamentary seat of Dr. Daniel François Malan, leader of the Afrikaner National Party.

Dr. Malan passed himself off as a full-blooded Afrikaner nationalist, but his credentials were dubious. He sat out the Boer War in Holland, where he was a student, and later returned to South Africa with a head full of exotic philosophies. In many ways, Malan was a classic early-twentieth-century intellectual, a utopian social engineer inclined to speak of socialism as a "passionate and imperious demand for justice," a "moral force" more powerful than "the fury of the storm." He was also a Calvinist, though, so he resolved the conflicts between Marx and God in God's favor, and wound up a national socialist of a uniquely Afrikaner ilk.

After his return from Europe, Daniel François became a minister in the Dutch Reformed Church and later, a politician. He was a pale man with soft white flesh, soft white hands, and weak eyes. Like most social engineers, he was somehow cold and bloodless, more comfortable with books and theories than human beings. He apparently remained celibate until late middle age, and his belated marriages—first to M. M. Van Tonder, and then to Maria Louw, a niece of my grandmother's—had less to do with love than with his need to cut an acceptable figure on the political hustings, or so the cynics said. Malan's National Party was bent on ousting General Smuts and his English-speaking chums, and D.F. himself was applying his rather formidable intellect toward a "scientific" and final solution for the native question.

Dr. Malan's 1938 election campaign caused a rift among his Calvinia cousins. D.F. was blood—a second cousin to my grandfather and married to my grandmother's niece besides—but Stephanus Malan did not allow that to sway his judgment. In his eyes, D.F. was something of a clown, but my schoolboy father, Adriaan, thought otherwise. He had been all the way to Cape Town and seen District Six, the sprawling colored slum above the docks. District Six was the reputed lair of whores, drunken sailors, and knifemen. He shuddered at the thought of going in there, and concluded that separation of the races was probably a good idea. There was a solid segregationist plank in the National Party's platform, so Adriaan Malan threw his support to D.F., in defiance of the rest of the family.

The Nats stood for segregation, but Smuts's SAP also stood for segregation. Since there was little to choose between the parties on that score, it was clear that their differences would have to be resolved by violence, in accordance with Boer political tradition. It was a very rough campaign. The Nats started it, breaking up a SAP rally with their fists. In retaliation, the SAPs swore that Dr. Malan would never speak in Calvinia again. The Nats picked up the gauntlet and organized a rally in Calvinia's town hall. When Dr. Malan arrived, a riot broke out, and he had to beat a strategic retreat to the home of one Schalk Pienaar. The SAPs gave chase. Malan's supporters armed themselves with sticks and prepared to defend their cowering candidate.

Just then, a distant bell rang, and school let out. My barefoot, eighteen-year-old father and his barefoot friends came running through the dusty streets and arrived on the scene just as the confrontation was coming to a head. The SAPs were parading up and down outside Pienaar's house, carrying their candidate, a certain Dr. Loek, on their shoulders. Dr. Loek was waving a blown-up photograph of a prominent Nat leader borne aloft like a hero on the shoulders of some black men. This was intended to show that the Nats were actually soft on blacks. If they truly favored segregation, how come they had such ardent black supporters?

"The Nats are *kafferboeties!*" cried Dr. Loek of the SAP. A *kafferboetie* is a "brother of blacks"—a nigger-lover, if you will. It was a grave insult, but Dr. Loek was so sallow of complexion that he could have passed for a light-skinned black man himself. A Nat lady pointed an angry finger at him. "Who are you to talk!" she shrieked. "You black Abyssinian!"

After this exchange, a fight was inevitable, and the Nats and SAPs joined battle. In the ensuing melee, my father struck his first blows for the National Party, and one of his friends, finding his shoes squishy with blood, discovered a stab wound in his buttocks. The battle was inconclusive, but Dr. Malan was so shaken by the SAPs' show of force that he moved to a safer constituency, where he was easily reelected. Ten years later, he became prime minister and started shoveling blacks around like cement in the name of his apartheid doctrine.

I tell you this story because it was the centerpiece of my Afrikaner political heritage. My father was a man of few words, and disinclined to waste those he spoke on philosophical dispute with small boys. When I was old enough to understand these things, I often asked my father how he came by his political convictions, and why he supported apartheid. His invariable answer was, "We have no choice. We must make it work." One day, though, I caught him in an expansive mood, and he came out with that story. I was taken aback by its farcical tenor. It was hard to imagine my old man fighting SAPs in the street, but then his transfiguring passion was lost to me too.

In my father's youth, in the twenties and thirties, race wasn't the central issue in white South African politics. Afrikaners of his generation were less concerned about keeping blacks in their place than tearing down the Union Jack, resurrecting the lost Boer republics, and uplifting the *volk* from its poor white penury. As my father saw it, his own SAP father was something of a collaborator, a lackey of the English king. My father did not quote Shakespeare, and he had no love for the British Empire. It was the British, after all, who had invented concentration camps, using them to crush Afrikaner resistance in a war still remembered with great bitterness.

In 1939, Adriaan Malan went off to the University of Stellenbosch, crucible of Afrikaner nationalism. The campus was seething with radicalism. Student nationalists wanted nothing to do with the looming war in Europe, and when it broke out, many joined the *Ossewa Brandwag,* or Oxwagon Sentinel, an extremist sect virulently opposed to South Africa's entry into World War II on the British side. My father joined up too. For several melodramatic months, he was a virtual terrorist, attending clandestine midnight meetings on the university's rugby fields or climbing "like a baboon" into the surrounding mountains, to plot sabotage of the British war effort and guerrilla war against the traitor Smuts.

In Stellenbosch, the Boer rebel cadres merely talked about such things, but their comrades in Johannesburg actually did them—blew up a police station and a power pylon or two. At that point, the *Brandwag* started falling into disrepute, becoming so nakedly fascist and Germanic that even Dr. Malan denounced it. At that, my father quit the organization, and his career as a terrorist came to an end. Beyond that point, he more or less withdrew from active politics, although he always marched in step with the *volk,* subscribed to Afrikaans magazines and newspapers, and voted for the National Party.

After graduating from Stellenbosch, he became a teacher of mathematics at a high school in Queenstown, where he met my mother. She was a jolly-hockey-sticks headgirl type, the school's lively mistress of gymnastics. It was a most unlikely love affair. My mother was English-speaking, my father a real Afrikaner who stumbled and stuttered in the British tongue. They were an "interracial couple," in the newspaper usage of the day, but they fell in love and married anyway—an act of tribal treachery on both their parts, given the lingering bitterness between Briton and Boer. After the wedding, my father returned to Stellenbosch, earned a second degree, and emerged a personnel manager. My brother Neil was born in 1952, and I in 1954, and we lived in a triple-story house on Penelope Avenue, in a Johannesburg suburb called Blairgowrie.

Having married an Englishwoman, my father had little choice other than to embrace a doctrine known as "broader South Africanism," which held that it was time for the English and Afrikaners to let bygones be bygones. Ours was a "dual-medium" household. My brother and I spoke English at school, Afrikaans at home. Dinner began with grace, and concluded with a reading from the Bible. On Sunday mornings, my mother slicked down my hair with Brylcreem and put on my Davy Crockett tie, and we went to the Afrikaner church, the Dutch Reformed Church, where dreary sermons were preached and dirges sung. After church, there was Sunday school, where we studied the *katkisasieboek*—the heavy gray tome of Calvinist catechism. The book was full of solemn warnings about idolatrous Catholicism and heathen Judaism, but it made no mention of the *swart gevaar*, the black threat. It was not necessary. The legacy of Dawid Malan was taken for granted.

We lived in the city, but every year or so we'd go on a pilgrimage into the heartland, into Afrikanerdom. It started in Calvinia, where my grandmother, the widow of Stephanus Jacobus, lived in an old-age home. My father had converted her from a SAP to Nat, and she became a party stalwart in her old age, always turning out to flip pancakes for the apartheid-supporting faithful at National Party rallies. She was a nice old lady. She smothered me in the lavender-smelling folds of her huge bosom and pressed treats on me—pancakes with cinnamon and sugar, and *koeksisters*, twists of deep-fried dough saturated with golden syrup.

From Calvinia we trekked south to the Sandveld, where my Uncle Ben farmed sheep on the shore of a cold gray sea. It was a barren and lonely place, the Sandveld, charged with an ominous and forbidding power. Ben's farmhouse stood all alone in a desolate, dun-gray landscape, shuttered against the harsh light, the heat and drifting sand. The house was dark and gloomy inside, the heavy Victorian furniture sinister under dust drapes never removed unless the Calvinist *dominee* was due to visit. At dusk, an old crone in a long black dress came hobbling across the sand dunes to fetch food at the kitchen door. She was a *bywoner,* one of Ben's white vassals, too old to work now and living out her life as the master's pensioner. Her name was Tannie Jeanette, and she terrified me. She had hairy warts on her face and a hunchback, and I took her for a witch. She once bought a portable radio from the Jewish peddler who made the rounds of those lonely farms. When the peddler returned, months later, Tannie Jeanette tried to claw his eyes out, claiming he'd sold her a radio that spoke only English. She had never owned a radio before. She didn't know it could be tuned.

There was an Afrikaner for you. Almost all of us were that way, three or four generations ago. In fact, everyone on Ben's farm was a throwback in some sense or other. The Mongolian cheekbones of the brown-skinned shepherds recalled the Hottentots, a race long extinct. Ben's speech was haunted by the *brei*—a roll of the *r* that harked back to French, a language unspoken in South Africa for almost two centuries, and his white *bywoners* spoke an archaic dialect called High Dutch.

Indeed, the *bywoners* themselves were archaic. There were three of them in all, Tannie Jeanette and men named Nic and Evert. They were unlike any other whites I had ever met, standing in virtually the same feudal relation to their master as the brown shepherds. They lived in bare rooms whose whitewashed walls were hung with the skins of trapped animals. The men often went barefoot, wore beards that hung to their chests, and sawed through the throats of kicking sheep on a bluegum stump in the yard of the farmhouse. They were the last of their kind, but then Ben's way of life was dying, too. It seldom rained on the Sandveld, so he drank from a brackish well. His wife cooked on one of those old cast-iron stoves with balled claw feet and lighted her house with paraffin lamps. At night, they slept under karosses made of jackal skins.

I think Uncle Ben was happy in the nineteenth century, but his wife Millicent aspired to better. She wanted tiled bathrooms, pop-up toasters, eye-level electric ovens and other trappings of white civilization. She was my father's youngest sister, and very beautiful, with raven hair and skin as dark as a Spaniard's. She was stern, pious and prone to fits of shrieking: at children, at Ben, at the ragged colored girls who slaved over the cast-iron stove in her kitchen. Ben, on the other hand, was a quiet, goodnatured fellow. He smoked a pipe and wore khaki shorts. There were lines around his eyes from squinting at the sun, and he seldom felt the urge to speak.

His farm was big and trackless, and he traveled it in a prototypical beach buggy, an old car stripped down to its engine and steel skeleton. It took half a day to cross the farm, and Ben always brought his rifle along in case he saw a buck for the pot, or a lynx; the lynx took lambs, so he shot them on sight. In the far corner of his land there lay a *vlei,* a marsh that was home to one of Africa's largest breeding colonies of flamingo. As we drew near, the sound of the engine startled the birds into flight, and there would be streaks of pink and gray across the sky, as if the sun was rising at noon.

At day's end, we drove over the sand dunes to watch the gray-green Atlantic breakers rolling onto a lonely, windswept beach. There was always a gale on that beach. It picked up sand and blasted it at your legs, and it stung so sharply it made you want to cry. Sometimes a defense-force Shakleton flew by at rooftop height, patrolling against the Russians. Ben knew they were out there, lurking, because a Russian lifejacket had once washed ashore on the beach. The Russians were the enemy. That was already known. Ben's only son grew up to be a professional soldier, and went off to fight Russia's Cuban surrogates in darkest Africa. His daughter also joined the army, and married a very famous South African soldier indeed—Captain Wynand du Toit, shot and captured by Cubans in 1985 while trying to blow up Gulf Oil's installations in Angola.

When we returned to the farmhouse in the evening, the brown shepherds would be lined up in the courtyard, tin beakers in their hands, waiting for their "tot"—their daily ration of *vaaljapie,* a crude white wine that came from a town two hours' drive to the south. Ben kept the stuff in a stack of leaky old barrels, in a room where the sandy floor had remained damp with wine for generations. As the door of the wine room swung open, the pungent smell of *vaaljapie* permeated the yard, and everyone's mood seemed to lighten. The tired shepherds drew their daily tumblerful and settled down along the walls of the barn, talking softly. Sometimes I sat with them. The wall at my back was still warm from the sun, golden dust hung in the air, and the evening was filled with the heady fragrance of cheap wine. It was the best time of day on that farm. When I went back twenty years later, the farmhouse was empty and abandoned, its shutters flapping in the wind. Ben was dead, his wife had moved into a condo, and all the *bywoners* and brown shepherds had vanished. But I picked up a handful of dust in the old wine room, and it still smelled of *vaaljapie.*

From the Sandveld we traveled inland to Nieuwoudtville, home of

Tannie Aletta, my father's elder sister. Her husband, Jooste, was a sergeant in the South African Police. They lived in the stone police station. When we visited, they put us in the whites-only section of the adjoining jailhouse, where we slept under rough blankets on bare wooden bunks. This seemed very exciting to me. I shivered deliciously at the thought that my bunk might once have harbored a murderer or bank robber. I once asked my aunt if this was at all likely. "Oh no," she said, "it's very quiet here. There has never been a murder here. It's only the coloreds who kill each other."

Nieuwoudtville lay at the foot of the Bokkeveld Mountains, high and dry and sometimes very cold at night. Through the barred window of my cell, I saw a dusty street, a post office, a general-dealer store, a church, and distant mountains. The town was a speck in a vast ocean of arid scrub and dust. Its emptiness was frightening. Even more frightening were my cousins, tough little fellows with brush-cut hair who ran barefoot over thorns and played rugby to maim on fields of dust and stone. They called me *Rooi Jan,* or Red Rian, a play on my name that embodied a scornful reference to the Boer term for a foreigner who turned pink and peeling in the blazing African sun. They were barbaric little tribesmen, those cousins of mine. I was always relieved when we moved south to Clanwilliam, where my uncle Etienne taught farmers' sons in the village boarding school.

My uncle Etienne was a gregarious fellow, darkly handsome, with a flashing gold tooth in his easy smile. Decades later, I opened a book called *The Super-Afrikaners* and discovered his name in it. In fact, both my father's brothers were in it. They were both *Broederbonders,* members of the Brotherhood, the secret society of Calvinists and apartheid zealots that constituted the spine of the Afrikaner power structure. The prime minister, his cabinet, most Afrikaner MPs, and all senior civil servants were Brothers. The Brotherhood's invisible hand controlled the state broadcasting corporation, the censor board, the police, the education system, and probably the army too. The Brotherhood was a sinister organization, ruthlessly dedicated to the aggrandizement of Afrikaner power and the imposition of doctrinal purity on South African minds.

Even in retrospect, my Oom Etienne seems a most unlikely Brother. He had none of the trappings—no Mercedes Benz with tinted windows, no lucrative government contracts, and no secret bank accounts bulging with the profits from crooked land deals, at least as far as I know. My Oom Etienne even had a sense of humor, not a quality for which Brothers were known. He owned a movie projector, and when we visited, he'd show us

Laurel and Hardy shorts or Al Debbo's lunatic Boer farces. He had a Wag-nerian passion for rugby, but as for apartheid, I never heard him mention the word.

And that was Afrikanerdom for me. Those pilgrimages marked me, to be sure, but they were not enough to make me a true Afrikaner. Even my father failed in that. I was always sceptical or disdainful of those things that lay closest to the Afrikaner heart. I used to stare up into the eaves of the church while the *dominee* droned on, wondering how on earth God tolerated such boredom. I flinched when the brush-cut Boerboys came in for the tackle, and struggled to breathe in the oppressive Calvinist atmosphere of their homes. I was intimidated by the immensity of the landscapes in which they lived, and horrified when they shot wild animals out there.

Once, crossing Ben's farm in his buggy, we flushed an aardvark on the sun-blackened plain. Aardvark were harmless and inedible, but Ben was tired of breaking axles in their burrows, so he gave chase. The creature disap-peared down a hole in the ground. Ben leapt from the buggy, rifle in hand. The aardvark was trying frantically to dig its way out of sight. Ben put a bullet or two into its scrambling hindquarters before it dragged itself around a bend. He shrugged and climbed back in the buggy, but I was traumatized for weeks by the thought of that wounded creature, dying slowly in its dark tomb. It was an unworthy reaction for a Boer, but I was never much of a Boer anyway.

I didn't even enjoy playing war with my brush-cut cousins. They always wanted to play Boer War, and stalk imaginary British invaders around the outbuildings and barns of various farms. It seemed a stupid and backward game to me. I came from Johannesburg, you see, and my imagination had already been colonized by foreign influences. In Jo'burg, we always fought the Japs or Jerries, like the heroes in Hollywood movies or imported war comics.

Johannesburg lay in Africa, but that was more or less incidental. Johan-nesburg had skyscrapers, smart department stores, cinemas, and theaters. It was part of a larger world. There was no TV in my boyhood, because the Brotherhood feared it would cause what Mao termed "spiritual pollution." We had radio, though, and all the characters in the boys' serials were British or American. Randy Stone was the night-beat reporter in an American city. Ricky Roper, the Sunrise Toffee Junior Detective, lived in an ambiguous someplace where everyone had BBC accents. Chuck drove a cab in Brooklyn. Mark Saxon came from outer space, but even his world seemed more immediate than Afrikanerdom to me.

I mean, I didn't realize *Reader's Digest* was a foreign magazine until I was at least ten. I have no recollection at all of the Sharpeville massacre, in which sixty-nine black people were shot dead while protesting against the pass laws; only the vaguest memory of Nelson Mandela's trial and jailing. I remember the day John F. Kennedy died, though. It was a Saturday morning in South Africa. I was helping my father in the garden when Mrs. Pretorius came scurrying across the street to say President Kennedy had been shot. She'd just heard it on the radio. My mother gasped, clasped her hand over her mouth and said, "Shame." My Afrikaner father shook his head regretfully.

Even he was somehow detribalized—by education, by urbanization, maybe just by inclination; all that was left in him of the mythic Afrikaner was the peasant cast of his features and an instinctive desire to plant things. He was an Afrikaner Nationalist and a supporter of apartheid, but above all he was a personnel manager, and his overriding preoccupations were insurance, the mortgage, the garden, the car, the family, and the job. The shelves of his study were lined with American tomes on management and motivation. He even bought *I'm O.K., You're O.K.*, thinking it might be useful in his line of work. He subscribed to *Die Huisgenoot,* to be sure, but he also got *Time* and *Life* and *National Geographic.* Those American magazines brought news of a world that seemed infinitely more alluring than my own—a world where people a few years older than me were growing their hair long, smoking dope, and rioting in the streets.

In 1967 or thereabouts, *Life* carried a story about a Frenchman named Regis Debray who went off to Bolivia with one Che Guevara. Their mission was to help oppressed Indians in their fight for freedom. I gathered from the text that Che was a disreputable something called Communist, but he cut a pretty dashing figure in the pictures, with his long black hair, combat boots, beard, and beret. I thought, whoa, Communism, that's for me. The plight of Bolivia's Indians seemed rather similar to the wretched lot of the blacks in my own backyard, so I put two and two together, and bingo, I was the Just White Man, champion of the downtrodden, sworn foe of racism, and ardent proponent of Communism, whatever that was supposed to be.

No, that's not all there was to it; there was more to it than that. I'd better go back to the beginning and see if I can dredge it up.

* * *

In my childhood, there were always Africans in our backyard. We called them natives. They lived in cold, dark rooms with tiny windows. They put their beds on stacks of bricks, so that the mattresses stood waist-high to a grown man. This was to thwart a ground-hugging, night-prowling gremlin called the *tokoloshe*. The natives' quarters smelled of Lifebuoy soap, red floor polish, and *putu*, the stiff corn porridge that is the staple food of Africa. Natives cooked my meals, polished my shoes, made my bed, mowed the lawn, trimmed the hedge, and dug holes at my father's direction. They ate on enamel plates and drank out of chipped cups with no handles, which were known as the boy's cup or girl's cup and kept separate from the rest of our china. They spoke broken English or Afrikaans, wore old clothes, had no money and no last names. That was all it was really necessary to know about them.

On Thursdays, their day off, many natives donned Crusader robes of blue or green and tied white sashes across their chests. They took up their staves and shepherd's crooks and set forth for the nearest stretch of undeveloped land, where they sang and danced in circles around fires. There was a place near our home called the Dip, a steep valley that separated the suburbs of Victory Park and Parkhurst. Looking down into the Dip on Thursday afternoons, you saw at least a dozen columns of smoke and a dozen rings of dancing Zionists. The drums of Africa were beating in the humdrum heart of white suburbia, but that sound made virtually no impression on me as a child. I never asked Zionists who they were worshiping, and why. I never made a point of finding out what the *tokoloshe* looked like and whether he might get me, too. Natives put their beds on bricks, Zionists danced on Thursdays, and thunderstorms washed streaks of red African earth into the streets. These were signs of Africa, but almost all of us were blind to them.

Some natives lived in white backyards, and some lived elsewhere— over those hills, beyond the mine dumps, beyond the industrial wastelands, in a desolate and despairing place called Soweto. On winter evenings, the acrid smoke of cooking fires came drifting over the horizon from that direction. Otherwise, you wouldn't have known there were a million natives living there, in regimented ranks of boxlike cement houses that marched over the horizon in all directions.

Some of our servants had homes and families in Soweto, and we sometimes dropped them off there on Saturday afternoons. They were actually "from" somewhere else, though, some faraway place where natives lived in mud huts and kept cattle. We drove through such places when we went away on holiday, singing "She'll Be Coming 'Round the Mountain" or Afrikaans songs about baboons and angry farmers. We saw the mud huts and the cattle, as well as children dancing for coins in the roadside dust. My mother waved at everyone she saw and encouraged us to wave, too. The blacks always waved back.

My mother was very fond of the natives—good natives, at any rate, the ones with shining, open faces and friendly smiles. She didn't like coloreds much, and sometimes said nasty things about Greeks, Portuguese, or Afrikaners. Sometimes she wasn't even sure about the natives. "They'd still be in mud huts if it weren't for us," she'd snap. "What did they do to build this country? Just dug where we said dig." But that was only when she was cross with them, or cross with me, when I was in my Communist phase and wont to rant about their miserable lot. Mostly she loved natives, and they loved her.

She and our girl Lena were always chatting over the sink in a language known as Fanagalo, half Zulu, half pidgin English. They'd tut-tut sympathetically over each other's children's diseases, and gossip about the neighbors. Lena would say, this madam pays her girl only ten rand a month, that one gives no paid holiday. My mother would say, "Shame," or cluck her tongue disapprovingly. It's a little harder to say how my father really felt about natives. He was a slow, grave man, quite shy, and often lost in abstraction. His dealings with blacks tended to be awkward and formal, as though he didn't know quite what to say, but this was true of all his human dealings. My old man was not one to jive and scintillate. He once remarked that he would never want to work under a black man, but his opinions on race were otherwise quite moderate, his unshakable faith in the doctrine of "separate but equal" notwithstanding. He forbade the use of the word "kaffir" in our house, and instructed my brother and I always to say "please" when issuing orders to the servants.

Apart from the natives in our backyard, the ones I knew best worked for my mother's brother John, who lived in the small Free State town of Parys. Parys was like a Mark Twain novel for me. It lay in a ring of low hills, and through it flowed a slow brown river, overhung with willows, full of fish to catch and islands to explore. In the older parts of Parys, houses were set directly on the street, giving the town a vaguely European flavor. At sunset, gnarled old Boers in floppy hats would come out into the cool evening air and sit on their porches, talking about the Boer War and watching the sparrow hawks circling in the sky above. Once a week, water came running down the roadside furrows, and my granny would lead it into her backyard to irrigate her corn, tomatoes, and peaches, which she grew in abundance and canned for storage in her fragrant pantry. At night, when the rain drummed like thunder on the tin roof and I was warm in bed, it was the best place in the whole world to be.

As for my Uncle John, he was a heroic figure. He had fought in World War II, in the western desert, and had a scar on his knee to prove it. His house was full of spectacular war loot: an Iron Cross, a Jerry helmet, and a braided Jerry officer's whip. There were empty shell casings alongside the fireplace and empty Sten gun cartridges on the mantelpiece. He also had a record of Scottish martial music called *Tartan on the Veld,* for which I developed a most disloyal and unpatriotic passion. It opened with the sound of the artillery barrage at the battle of El Alamein. You heard the cannon crumping and the machine guns rattling, and then you heard the thin skirl of bagpipes sounding the infantry charge, and shivers of glory ran down your spine.

My uncle owned a shop and employed lots of boys. His boss boy was Paul, except you said it "Pole," because the natives in Parys spoke Afrikaans. Paul was big and strong and had an open, honest face that was always creased with a smile. He was a good native. The same could not be said of Mathibes, who scowled and drank too much. Mathibes was said to be "cheeky," but he was very clever with his hands, knew welding and soldering and how to make change, so he was put up with—respected, even.

On Saturday mornings my uncle took some bills out of his hand-cranked cash register and sent me down to the butcher to buy *boerewors,* a long coil of raw sausage that came wrapped in bloody brown paper. At one o'clock, my uncle shouted, *"chila,"* African for knock off. The boys closed the doors, and we all trooped into the shop's yard, which was full of machinery and gutted old trucks. The boys made a fire. We put the *wors* on a blackened old plowshare, and while it sizzled my uncle gave each of his boys a bottle of Castle beer and a wage packet. Then we stood around the fire, eating the *wors* with our fingers. I wouldn't exactly say my Uncle John was a liberal, but he had a way with natives. He understood some of their language, joked with them, shook their hands—he *saw* them, whereas most whites didn't.

So there was always laughter and good feeling around that fire. Mathibes scowled and made cynical remarks, but even his heart wasn't in it. If I asked nicely, he would sometimes give me a slug of his beer, as if I were a real man. Goddamn it, remembering those Saturdays makes me cry. It was all so simple then.

When the *wors* and the beer were finished, we loaded up the truck with big bottles of propane gas. My uncle and Paul got in front; my brother and I climbed on the back with the boys. We turned left on Dolf Street, drove past the railroad station, over the bridge, and into the location where the natives lived. Here and there, you saw a facade decorated with geometric tribal designs, but most of the houses were the same color as the rutted roads—gray, like Free State mud. We drove all around the location, dropping the boys off one by one and delivering gas to the homes of my uncle's customers. I stood up behind the cab with the wind in my face. Many of the blacks we passed knew my uncle, so they smiled and waved and yelled, *"Baas John, Baas John."* I waved and shouted right back. I felt like a war hero, like a little white prince.

Maybe it was the love of a prince for his loyal subjects, and conditional upon their remaining loyal and subservient, but I loved natives anyway. The first one I loved was Johannes, our garden boy before I went to school. Johannes looked after me while my mother was away teaching. I followed him everywhere. When he was tired, I made him come inside and sit in my father's armchair. I made him put his feet up and served him tea. Ah, yes—a revealing choice of word. I was only five years old, but already I was giving orders. I *made* Johannes accept my gestures of love. Was I any more to him than a bossy white child? I don't know, because he went away, or we went away, and James eventually came in his place. James taught me to play Zulu walking guitar, and then he went away, too, and along came Piet.

Piet was a squat, ugly Tswana. He drank and smoked *zol*—dope—but he had spirit, and big dreams. He once bought some rabbits and made a pen for them on the compost heap behind the shed. He was going to breed and butcher them to make some money. It was a secret from my father, but he let me in on it. One day our dog got into the pen, and that was the end of the rabbits. Another time, Piet bought one of those motor tricycles with a box on the back, the kind delivery boys drove. He was going to fix it up and make a business taking things home to Pietersburg for other natives, but he never could get it going. Piet and I spent hours lying shoulder to shoulder in the dirt between the peach trees in my father's garden, shooting rats in the hedge with my pellet gun. He bought beer for me when I was too young to be drinking legally, and scored the first *zol* I ever smoked. When Phillip Nel and his gang were sitting on my chest, beating me, it was Piet Maribatse who pulled them off. Piet was my good friend. Hey, what can I say; I loved him.

I loved them all, indiscriminately: Lena, Johannes, Piet, James, Betty, Miriam, Miriam's children and teeming grandchildren, the other Piet, who worked next door, the waiters in the hotel down the road, John's boys—all of them. Loving natives was a very good investment. I learned that at the very beginning, and it remains true to this day. If you were friendly, they lit up and laughed and returned your love a hundredfold. It seemed so easy and ordinary to love them then. Maybe we are all that way in the beginning. Maybe we just grow out of it, or are taught otherwise. When I was a little older, I began to notice that many whites around me felt otherwise about blacks.

By then, we were living in Linden, a predominantly Afrikaans suburb of Johannesburg. All the houses in Linden were square and tin-roofed, set exactly in the middle of one-acre plots with a garage on the side, a lawn out front, and some fruit trees in the back. Linden was infested with Broederbonders and Dutch Reformed ministers, but that wasn't why my father found it congenial. He liked it because the garden was so big; it offered scope. My old man was always happiest in his garden, wearing short pants and a funny hat and up to his elbows in muck. So he sunk a borehole, put a swimming pool in the back, and filled the front yard with neatly regimented flower beds. A very Afrikaans garden it was.

In Linden, there were Afrikaners to the left, Afrikaners to the right, and Afrikaners to the fore. The ones across the street were most interesting. They were all Smits, a whole row of houses full of Smits. On the corner was a slovenly woman whose son, Stoffel, sometimes played with me. Next door to Stoffel was Smit the sportsman, who went to the races several times a week, and in the next house down, Mr. Justice Smit of the Supreme Court. Judge Smit was famous, among other reasons, for presiding over the trial of John Harris, the white idealist who blew up Johannesburg's railroad station in the early 1960s. Judge Smit sent him, among many others, to the gallows.

Judge Smit had some strange habits. Every now and then, he filled his trunk with brandy and beer and hailed one of his tattooed, ducktailed nephews. The judge and the greaser drove to a dismal industrial region south of the city and parked on the banks of a slow, scummy river. They watched the river flowing by, the smoke rising from the steelworks, and drank until they could no longer sit up straight, or so Stoffel told me. In mitigation, I should mention that this usually happened after the judge sentenced someone to death. Still, it was typical Smit behavior. They were all *goms,* or rednecks—common, in my mother's prim Victorian estimation. On Friday nights they'd get drunk, and there'd be cars with twin-cam engines and furry dashboards revving up in the road, women screaming, men cursing and once, guns going off in the air.

In any event, the point about the Smits is that some of them weren't very nice to natives. When they wanted one, they yelled, "Come here" in the tone of voice you might use with a dog. Or one of the women would stick her peroxided head out the front door and shriek, *"Stoffel, waar's die boy? Laat die boy die kar skoonmaak!"* (Stoffel, where's the boy? Tell the boy to clean the car!) And Stoffel, who was barely twelve, would swagger over to the boy and tell him to wash the car, make it nice and clean now, understand? The boy was really a grown man, but he was a native, so he had no choice but to lower his sullen head and obey.

That sort of thing rankled me. I had an entirely uncalled-for internal struggle about it and decided that calling a boy "boy" to his face was rude and that I would henceforth call a boy "sir" if I didn't know him. I didn't like the way Stoffel talked to boys, and I didn't really like Stoffel, either. One day we were playing in the garden, and he said, "These kaffirs must all go back to kaffirland." I said, "This is kaffirland." He was taken aback, and so was I. Where did that come from?

So Stoffel and his clan were otherwise, which in white South Africa means mean-spirited. So was Mr. Greyvenstein, who was reputedly nasty to his garden boy, and Mrs. Greef, who locked up her grocery cupboards so that her girl couldn't pilfer sugar. In fact, most whites were to some degree otherwise. It wasn't that they beat or whipped blacks; it was the way they talked to them. Many years later, when I lived in Los Angeles, I heard LAPD officers using the same bullying tone of voice, the same body language. A cop told me it was called "command presence" and taught at the academy. It was the tone of voice you used to exact instant and unquestioning obedience.

In Linden, that was a common language of interracial communication. The Portuguese who ran the greengrocery on the corner used it, and so did the Greek who owned the Soft Serv ice-cream store in the arcade. One

Sunday afternoon, I was hanging around in his shop when an albino came in. The Greek started taunting him, saying, "You're a white kaffir, aren't you, a white kaffir, hey?" The albino was hurt and humiliated, but he put on a brave face, slapped his coin on the counter, and demanded service. The Greek just laughed and called him more names. I was hurting for the freak, so I huffed and puffed and looked the Greek in the eye. "You're the white kaffir," I said. Then I turned and ran, because I thought he might hit me.

No, I'm lying. I mustn't lie anymore. I stood there watching, with that retort running through my mind. I thought, Say it, say it, but I didn't, because I was scared. I just stood there seething.

I am trying to explain why I became a "Communist," and this is all part of it. I suppose it would make more sense if I could testify to gruesome and bloody acts of cruelty and repression, but it wasn't that way in Linden. In Linden, apartheid atrocities were something you read about in the English newspapers, which gave the impression that the state was in the hands of some profoundly warped men. Instances of warp were legion. Some drunken white would beat a "cheeky" black to death and leave the dock with six months suspended. A sallow little schoolgirl whose hair was suspiciously kinky was summoned before a tribunal of apartheid experts, judged a half-breed, and kicked out of her whites-only school. Some colored fishermen once drowned in a storm because they were scared to put ashore on a whites-only beach. Once or twice in my childhood the police swept through Linden in the dead of night, knocking on the doors of servants' quarters, hunting blacks without passes. If they caught one, he or she was carted off in a police truck and usually jailed for thirty days. This never happened to any of our natives, though, and I never saw a black physically abused save once.

One afternoon, on my way home from school, I heard screams in the distance. A black youth came sprinting down the hill toward me with several white men and a shrieking woman on his heels. The fugitive had apparently snatched her purse. About ten yards from me, the black man tripped and went sprawling across the pavement. In an instant, the whites were on him. They pulled him to his feet, punched him twice in the face, and then dragged him away to the police station.

This was the first time I had witnessed such violence. I mean, I had seen the ducktailed white battlers kicking one another in the face outside the Linden Hotel Bar on Friday nights while their bouffant-hairdoed wives and girlfriends screamed in the Chevy, but I had never seen a black man struck.

I reacted like a proper liberal. I was appalled. All my sympathy lay with the black, because he seemed an underdog. That is how I was. I was a sentimental little fellow who liked natives and thought it a pity that they were so poor and that so many whites were nasty to them. In their wretchedness, they seemed rather similar to those Bolivian Indians in *Life* magazine, so I thought, okay, if Che can do it, so can I, and I became a "Communist." After that, I took to mooning around in my bedroom after school, delivering imaginary speeches to the United Nations or writing letters to the editor about the plight of black South Africans.

When I was in the ninth or tenth grade, an Indian revolutionary named Ahmed Timol "fell" to his death from a tenth-floor window while undergoing interrogation by the secret police. Ahmed Timol was the twelfth man on the list of detainees who'd died suspiciously in the custody of the secret police, falling somewhere between the Islamic imam who "fell down a flight of stairs" and Steve Biko, who "struck his head on a bench" during a "fight" with his interrogators. Something sinister was obviously afoot, so I wrote a letter to *The Star,* Johannesburg's dominant daily, expressing my Afrikaner's dismay over the manner in which Timol died, and my Afrikaner's insistence on a thorough and impartial inquiry.

In those days, an Afrikaner with a conscience was still something of a novelty, even if he was only fourteen. A day or two later, my letter appeared at the head of the letters-to-the-editor page, under a huge headline reading, "An Afrikaner Speaks Out." At the bottom, in bold type, it said "—Rian Malan, Linden."

It was a day of delirious triumph for me, largely because my childish scribblings had been accorded such adult weight and dignity. Mrs. Pretorius, the neighbor, rang up to congratulate me. Two schoolteachers called to commend me. My Uncle John called from Parys, chuckling, "Ho, ho, ho, what's all this, then?"

Toward evening, my father came home, poured himself a whiskey, and sat down to read the afternoon papers. My father supported apartheid, moderately, and didn't mind moderate criticisms of it. In his eyes, it was a sensible solution to the problems of a multiethnic society—the only solution. It wasn't perfect, but you couldn't change things overnight. He truly believed apartheid's central lie, its promise to create a world in which blacks and whites were separate but equal, and he was incapable of seeing the suffering it was inflicting meanwhile. In some ways, he was a wise and compassionate man—wise enough, several years later, to talk a friend of mine down from a bad acid trip. In other ways, he was completely blind. It seemed very strange to me.

He paged through *The Star*'s news and business sections, scanning the headlines, and came at last to the letters page. He read my letter and let the paper fall to his lap. He took off his glasses and gave me a dirty look. I thought he was about to offer his standard argument, which ran thus: The secret police know more than you do. If they lock somebody up, there must be a reason for it; and if they say Timol fell, he surely fell. But he didn't say that. He just said, "What gives you the right to call yourself an Afrikaner?" Then he lifted the paper and turned to the sports page.

One summer night, a few years after my conversion to "Communism," I donned dark clothing and slipped out of my sleeping father's house to strike a blow against apartheid. My fellow conspirators were waiting on the wall of Emmarentia Dam. Anton wore John Lennon glasses, read Dostoyevsky, and considered himself to be on a higher spiritual plane than the rest of us. He was the mastermind of this escapade. Robin was already out of school. He had curly, shoulder-length hair and girls thought he looked just like Marc Bolan, the English rock star. I was sixteen, pimply and anguished. I suggested that we blacken our faces with mud so as to flit through the sleeping suburbs unseen, but Anton vetoed the proposal. He didn't want to dirty his new cowboy boots scrambling around on the shore of the dam. So we scrapped that precaution and we set off as we were, the weapon tucked under Anton's denim jacket.

The year was 1971. It was the eleventh anniversary of the Sharpeville massacre, the eighth of Mandela's incarceration, and the fifth of the inauguration of our stern Calvinist ruler, Balthazar Johannes Vorster. It was the apogee of the apartheid era. All across the country, government trucks were moving into so-called "black spots," black settlements inside "white" South Africa, where no blacks were allowed to be. The sight of such settlements offended the mad scientists of apartheid. The blacks had to go. They had to get onto the trucks and cross the border of the nearest Bantustan, where they could be separate but equal. Three million blacks were moved that way, dumped on the barren homelands, and often left to starve, in triumphant culmination of Daniel François Malan's cold-blooded logic.

We were vaguely aware that the forced removals were underway, but they were not on our minds that night. We were talking about UFOs, as I recall. Our friend John claimed to have seen one hovering over our very suburb, so we were on the lookout for more. It was a mild night, and we were stoned, as usual, so we didn't mind that it was two in the morning before we came across a vast embankment of virgin concrete where the deed could be done on an appropriate scale. Robin stood on the pedestrian bridge and kept chips for the fuzz. I stood on the corner in case they came the other way, and Anton wielded the spray can. Our subversive slogan was the title of an American soul hit, but we'd never heard James Brown sing it. The Brotherhood would never have allowed us to hear a song entitled "Say It Out Loud, I'm Black & I'm Proud." We had read about it in *Time.*

If you'd chanced upon us that morning and asked us what we thought we were doing, we would probably have said we were into the concept of just war and supported the struggle of the people against the tyranny of the rockspiders, crunchies, hairybacks, ropes, and bloody Dutchmen. Those were the names by which we referred to Afrikaners. I was an Afrikaner, too, but I was a member of a subspecies known as the detribalized krantz athlete—that is, a Boer who'd somehow become a liberal or whatever and thrown himself into the struggle against apartheid. I'm not sure how spray-painting the title of a James Brown song on a wall in a lily-white neighborhood was supposed to harm the hairybacks, but that wasn't very important anyway. We believed that apartheid was stupid and vicious, but we also believed that growing our hair long undermined it. We believed Tolkien's hobbit books were founts of pure wisdom, and that drugs raised one's spiritual quotient.

As teen rebels, we considered ourselves among South Africa's oppressed. If you asked why, we probably would have talked about school. Robin went to a private school, but both Anton and I had been inmates of whites-only government schools, where we were "forced," in the earliest grades, to color in pictures of Dirkie Uys, the twelve-year-old Voortrekker who sacrificed his life in a futile attempt to save his father during an epic battle against the Zulus in 1838. Later, we were taught that history began in 1488, when a Portuguese navigator first rounded the Cape. We were likely to point to such things as proof that the rockspiders were giving us lies for truth and trying to wash our brains with "Christian nationalism."

There was an element of truth in that, but we had more compelling reasons to hate the system. We hated it because it made us lop off our sideburns at the ear lobe, caned us if we misbehaved, and forced us to wear military uniform on Fridays, when we spent the first hour of the school day marching around the rugby field as part of something called youth preparedness. The cadet uniform featured short khaki pants and a silly cap that made you look ridiculous in front of the girls, who didn't have it so easy themselves. While we marched, they were inspected by women teachers, to make sure that their skirts hung demurely to the knee and that their undies conformed to regulation. In our eyes, there was an unmistakable link between such fascism and the larger workings of apartheid, between short-back-and-sides haircuts and pass raids, between the banning of *Playboy* and forced removals, between corporal punishment and the mysterious deaths of black dissidents in detention. Those totalitarian bastards stopped at nothing. They banned Sunday sport, forbade movies on the Sabbath, and wouldn't even play the Beatles on state radio after John Lennon claimed to be more popular than Jesus. That was why they had to be overthrown.

So we were into toppling Vorster, but we were also into ending the Vietnam War and scrapping the draft. We knew what was what and what was cool, because we read about it in *Time* and *Life*. Carlos Castaneda was cool, and so were Tolkien, Hermann Hesse, *The Greening of America*, campus revolt, and the Black Panthers. Our heads were full of hand-me-downs from the great white mother culture, ideas that we copied from foreign books and movies and magazines in the way other teenagers copied hairstyles or fashions. I had a picture of Che on my wall, alongside one of Frank Zappa and one of Danny the Red hurling cobblestones at riot police in Paris in May '68. The person I most admired in the entire world was Anton's older brother, Leon, a student leftist in the SDS tradition. Leon was always cloaked in a duffle coat and an aura of conspiracy. He demonstrated against apartheid on Jan Smuts Avenue. He owned a tattered copy of *Rolling Stone*, the only one I'd ever seen, and he was a close personal friend of "Franco," a political cartoonist whose seditious work appeared in the local student newspaper. Franco's most notorious cartoon showed a toddler peering down into a toilet and asking, "Are you the Prime Minister?"

Most of my schoolmates were into the Beatles and bubble gum, but my circle had more sophisticated tastes, thanks to Leon's civilizing influence. It was Leon who turned us on to Bob Dylan. I bought all Dylan's old records and painted his name in psychedelic letters on my schoolbag. I knew the words to all his generational war songs: "The Lonesome Death of Hattie Carroll," "Oxford Town," "The Times They Are A-Changin'," "Only a Pawn in Their Game," and "Masters of War." I also knew the words to "We Shall Overcome" and "Marchin' to the Freedom Band" by heart. In contrast, I doubt that any of us could so much have as hummed the melody of "Nkosi Sikalel' iAfrika"—"God Bless Africa"—the black African national anthem. Don't think we weren't into black culture, though. We were heavily into black culture. We dug soul, reggae, and the blues, too, and we even smoked dope, a mostly black habit, supposedly.

I was thirty before I discovered that many Africans thought dope-smokers were losers and fuck-ups. In my teens, everyone knew that all "Afs" smoked dope. That was why they were so wise. They sat up there in the hills, you know, smoking *zol,* watching the sun rise and set, just being cool and in touch with nature and all that. We were plastic; they were real. It was a time when silly ideas were rampant everywhere in the West, and we did our best to keep up. Americans and Europeans had their Hindu gurus; we had our wise old Afs. Once, on an unsupervised camping trip in the Drakensberg Mountains, some friends and I had a passing encounter with such a wise one—an old, yellow-eyed *kehla* who sold us some *zol* and invited us to sit down for a smoke outside his hut. It was a moment of profound, almost religious significance. We were at great pains to hold the pipe right and not cough as we drew the raw, searing smoke into our lungs. A real African did not cough when he "bust" a pipe; everyone knew that.

And there we sat, zonked, the white sons of personnel managers, art dealers, and brain surgeons, utterly oblivious to the squalor and misery around us, rocking back and forth on our haunches and thinking, Ah, so this is what it's really like to be one of them; pretty cool. We couldn't talk to the old one, of course, because we learned useless languages at school, like German, or dead ones, like Latin. Instead, we communed silently. We could tell just from the old one's vibe that he was a head, as we would have said.

Vibes were an inarticulate tongue, but it really didn't matter. This was a symbolic encounter anyway. It was hip to be into black culture, so we got into it in much the same way that we got into bell-bottom pants. In white Johannesburg, black culture was inclined to mean James Brown and James Baldwin, not the culture of that old black man in the mountains or the black people in our back yards. They didn't really count, because they were inscrutable Africans and, worse yet, "local." Almost all things South African were tawdry and third-rate, except notional noble savages and maybe Herman Charles Bosman, who wrote witty short stories about simple backcountry Boers. People from "overseas" were celebrities in their own right, just for being from there. Culture was also something that came from there, even if it stopped in Salisbury on the way.

In my thirteenth year, there came from the north a blues band, the first-ever heard in South Africa. They were long-hair white boys from the rebel colony of Rhodesia, where Ian Smith was holding out for a thousand years of white rule. They were the Otis Waygood Blues Band. I heard the blues, and I saw the light. I slaved in a bakery, folding boxes, until I had the money for an electric guitar, and then we started our own blues band. Ferreira blew that blues harp, Malan tried to make his guitar cry like B.B. King, and Van de Vyfer strummed the chords. We got us a bass and drummer, learned some Howlin' Wolf numbers and some Sonny Boy Williamson tunes, and there we were, Boerboys, wailin' and hollerin' about Negro trouble and sufferin' at garage parties in the segregated white suburbs of John Vorster's South Africa. *And nobody laughed at us.*

Isn't that absurd? Nobody laughed. We were utterly oblivious to the irony of it, which says something significant about those English-speaking, bourgeois northern suburbs. They were in South Africa, but somehow not really of it. The rest of the country was a racist Calvinist despotism, but the northern suburbs were liberal, permissive, governed by the ruling philosophical orthodoxies of the West.

My ninth-grade English teacher, Mrs. Hunter, had a short story published in *Harper's* or *The Atlantic Monthly*. She read it aloud to the class. It was about an innocent black youth beaten up on a Jo'burg street by some white thugs who suspected him of picking pockets. When the story was finished, Mrs. Hunter asked, "What is the highest virtue of civilization?" and I raised my hand.

"Tolerance," I said.

"Very good, Rian," she replied.

I liked Mrs. Hunter and did my best to please her, putting some strong language in my essays. In one, I was on an imaginary mission in Bolivia, fighting to free the Indians. "I was filled with revolutionary fervor," I wrote, "burning with desire to fight against imperialism, colonialism, and many other evils." Mrs. Hunter gave me high marks and appended an approving remark: "Good ideas, well expressed."

And that was a government school, a "Nazi youth camp," in our scathing estimation. A year or so later, I somehow conned my conservative father into sending me to a liberal private school called Woodmead. I promised to reform and work hard, but all I really wanted to do was grow my hair. The headmaster of my new school espoused the progressive educational theories of Britain's A. S. Neill, founder of the "free school" Summerhill, and the progressive politics of Alan Paton's defunct Liberal Party, which had espoused one-man, one-vote democracy. Mr. Krige invited Soweto headmasters to address the student body and sent us off to play cricket against a black school in Swaziland. A few years later, he was the first private-school headmaster to defy the law and integrate his school.

At Woodmead, everyone's parents were rich; everyone's parents were left-liberal. Hugo's mother, Nadine Gordimer, wrote novels about the horrors of apartheid. Brenda's father, David Goldblatt, photographed them. David's father, Dr. Neville Proctor, later demolished the state's lies at the inquest into Steve Biko's death. As president of the Student Council, I organized fund drives for black education and closed the school cafeteria in solidarity with the Reverend Barry Wrankmore's epic anti-apartheid hunger strike. In the northern suburbs of Johannesburg, such actions were not necessarily evidence of moral grit and courage. We liked to think of ourselves as brave opponents of tyranny, but the secret police weren't particularly interested in us. Indeed, my worst fear was that someone might stake out a position to the left of mine, or do something more radical than what I was doing. It was at least partly for that reason that I slept with a black woman when I was sixteen.

It was a Thursday night, maid's night off in the white suburbs. I had a friend named Ivan who lived in the stockbroker suburb of Saxonwold, where every second house was mock Tudor and the streets named for the forests of old England. Every Thursday night, our band practiced in Ivan's garage, and black servants came from all around to drink and dance to our music. It was sometimes noisy and riotous, but Ivan's parents didn't mind. They were "Progs," partisans of the tiny pro-black Progressive Party, which had one seat in parliament and supported democratic principles.

One night, a black woman among the dancers took a liking to me. She came and stood right in front of me, bumping and grinding drunkenly. She was wearing her maid's uniform, a plain blue housedress, and a headscarf known as a *doek*. She had a generous behind and thighs like tree-trunks, and seemed very old indeed—at least twenty-five if not older. When we took a smoke break Ivan's gardener came over to say, "That woman, she wants the big one." That was me.

I was a virgin, but this was not something one admitted. Pretending sophistication in sexual matters was crucial to preserving face. So I couldn't say, hey, *nooit,* never, I've never done it with anyone. And I certainly couldn't say, are you crazy? She's black. That was what I was thinking, but I could never have said it, because I was a social democrat or whatever. I umm'd and ah'd and drew manfully on my cigarette and finally said, "Thanks anyway, but I don't really feel like it tonight." At this, my chinas started taunting me for being chicken, and it suddenly became a question of face. So I shrugged and arranged an assignation.

After practice, I set off on foot down Abbotswold Road, swept along by a gang of jeering, sniggering teenage boys. Whenever I stopped, they joshed and jeered, so I had to keep going. We came to a big white house. My mates decamped outside under a streetlight, and I slunk down the dark alley that led to the servants' quarters, moving on tiptoe, because what I was about to do was unlawful.

I tapped on an iron door and the black woman opened it, wearing a satin nightgown. A candle was burning in the room behind her. The cement floor was bare, the walls adorned only by a picture of a blond Jesus, his blue eyes spaniel with compassion. A lace-covered table stood at her bedside, and on it a mirror, some cheap trinkets, and a bottle of skin-lightening cream. The room smelled of all the things I associated with servants—red floor polish, *putu,* and Lifebuoy soap. Even her bed was waist-high on bricks, to thwart the *tokoloshe.* I took off my clothes and clambered onto it, and then I was in her arms, overpowered by the smell of her, and terrified, utterly terrified. I couldn't talk to her because we had few words in common. I didn't know what to do. I recoiled at the thought of French-kissing her, but I did it anyway, because I was a social democrat, and I did not want to insult her. And then I pulled up the nightie and instants later it was over. I rolled off and asked, "Was I good? Am I big enough?" She said yes. She was very kind.

For years after, I offered this incident as the ultimate proof of my anti-apartheid bona fides, of my triumph over my Afrikaner conditioning. It was nothing of the sort. I came out of that room laughing nonchalantly, but at heart I was stricken with guilt. In my fevered racist imaginings, I was quite sure she'd given me the pox, or had turned me in to the police. It was a nightmare, but I dared not say so out loud. Instead, at school the next day, I casually mentioned that I had taken a black lover. My chinas were impressed. This was a truly staggering defiance of the rockspider tyranny. I sat there smiling modestly, praying that no one would ask her name. I didn't know it, you see.

The only black person I really knew, at the age of sixteen, was Mrs. Miriam Tshabalala, our servant. Lena had retired by then, and my friend Piet Maribatse was dead. He had moved on to another gardening job, where he was set to work felling trees. One struck his head as it came down. He went into his room, complaining of a headache, and never came out again. So Miriam was the only black person in my life. She had no idea of her birth date, but she was already old when she came to work for us. She wore spectacles for knitting and sewing, and, as I saw on those rare and startling occasions when she was bareheaded, her stubbly peppercorn hair was flecked with gray. She could not read or write, and spoke very little English. When she was pleased, she clapped her hands and said, "Happy-happy." When she was angry, she stamped her foot and said, "Hau!" She was plump and shapeless, walked with a waddle, and seemed to sag, the downward slope of her shoulders following the downward curve of her mouth. She was not defeated, just resigned. Her life had been hard. She had endured.

Miriam was a Catholic, but she still feared the *tokoloshe* and slept with her bed on bricks. Whenever there was misfortune or illness in her family, she suspected witchcraft. The witches must have been active, because Miriam's life was full of unbearable woe. She gave birth to five children, but only two survived to adulthood. Her husband deserted her, leaving her to bring up Elizabeth and Ephraim on her own. Ephraim developed epilepsy and could never work. In Soweto, epilepsy was often mistaken for possession by demons. Whenever Ephraim "fell down," as Miriam put it, onlookers would stone him, to stop his diabolical writhings. By the time he shambled into our lives, Ephraim was so fucked up it was hard to look at him. One leg dragged, he could barely talk, and his face was all asymmetrical where the bones had been smashed in.

As for Elizabeth, she married a rotter who abandoned her with six young children and no means of support. Miriam and Elizabeth tried their best, but they had a very hard time of it. The boys cut school, and the girls—well, the eldest put on a little weight after her thirteenth birthday, and next thing a baby popped out of her. There were several more babies after that, sliding out between the legs of startled schoolgirls, all fathered by hit-and-run seducers, born into a family where there was too little food, less money, and no hope. Things never got better for Miriam and her family; they just seemed to sink deeper and deeper into the mire.

Miriam's clan lived in Soweto, but they paid periodic visits to our white suburb. Those weekends are among the sweetest memories of my childhood. I trundled Miriam's grand- and great-grandchildren around the garden in a wheelbarrow. I taught them to swim in our swimming pool, and to ride on my bicycle. I led processions of dapper little black boys to the corner store, and squandered my pocket money on great feasts of candy and cake.

I loved Miriam and her family, and dare to presume they loved me back, and yet there was something symbiotic about our relationship: Its essential condition was that they were victims and I their putative savior. I used to spend hours lecturing Miriam about the evil of apartheid, as if this was something she didn't know. I told her I was fighting for her with all my teenage might. She was never very impressed, but those discussions left me feeling very good about myself.

One afternoon, I swore Miriam to secrecy and drew her attention to the front page of *Rapport,* an Afrikaans Sunday paper. On it was a photograph of a roadside embankment, disfigured by a monumental graffito, six feet tall, forty yards long, and bracketed, come to think of it, by twin sets of the hammer-and-sickle. Miriam was illiterate, so I read the slogan to her: "Say It Out Loud, I'm Black & I'm Proud." I beamed proudly. I think I expected her to say thank you, but she just snapped, "Ah, *suka,* " and walked away.

"Suka" means "get lost."

Maybe she didn't understand. Maybe she understood all too well.

Ah, my friend, do I seem poisoned with cynicism? I try not to be. It's just that I'm trying to fight my way out from under an ages-old accretion of myth about the world I grew up in. An African boyhood? An Afrikaner boyhood? I don't think so. Looking back, the strangest thing about my African childhood is that it wasn't really African at all. It was a more or less generically Western childhood, unfolding in generic white suburbs where almost everyone subscribed to *Life* and *Reader's Digest,* and to the generic Western verities they upheld. Our heads turned to the north like flowers to the sun, toward where the great white mother culture lay. Our imaginary lives were rooted there, not in this strange place, where Zionists danced on Thursdays and rain washed the red earth of Africa into the streets.

In our imaginations, painting "I'm Black & I'm Proud" on a wall was an entirely logical act of subversion. In the real South Africa, it was pointless. That embankment lay in a lily-white neighborhood where few blacks would see it and few who did could read it. In a day or two, the wall was sandblasted clean, and the grim mechanics of apartheid ground on regardless. The sole result of the entire effort was to boost our sense of self-righteousness.

That was the common outcome of most political undertakings in Johannesburg's predominantly English, predominantly liberal northern suburbs. In the northern suburbs, most whites disapproved of apartheid and were free to say so more or less openly. The intelligentsia denounced it, the English newspapers condemned it, and most people—my Afrikaner father and sundry others excepted—voted against it in elections. The hard men who ruled the country simply ignored us, because we were too few to make a difference. The northern suburbs were like a glass-bottomed boat, adrift on a violent and mysterious sea. We could peer down into the depths and see strange life-forms—twisted Calvinists, cold-blooded apartheid zealots, dancing Zionists and suffering, inscrutable Africans—but we remained tourists of sorts, warm and safe in our comfortable berths. So long as we stayed in our proper place, the hard men left us to our own devices. If we stepped overboard, though, anything could happen. There were killer sharks down there.

It was hard to know exactly where the line was, but spraying a James Brown song title on a lily-white suburban wall apparently carried us across it. According to the caption under *Rapport*'s photograph of our handiwork, the Security Police were investigating. Not the juvenile delinquency squad, or the vandalism squad, but the heavyweight political enforcers themselves. It was absurd. In such a country, it was not entirely illogical to think that growing your hair undermined the state. It may be true that my various "blows" against apartheid were callow acts of self-aggrandizement, but worse was true of the hard white men who ran the country. They really were cruel and twisted, and one thing was certain: I was not willing to carry a gun for them.

After high school, white boys were supposed to report for military service, the most dreaded rite of a white boy's passage. Not mine, though; not if I could help it. I was determined that the army would not have me. The South African Defence Force was run by mean hairybacks who toughened you up to keep blacks down. They forced you to leopard-crawl from horizon to horizon, or run around the Namib desert carrying telephone poles—a notorious torture known as pole PT.

I considered myself above such indignities, of course, but my stated reasons for avoiding the call-up were political. I was a white leftist, and white leftists did not serve in apartheid's army, especially not in 1975. There had been a revolution in Portugal the previous April, and the new Portuguese government was about to set its African colonies free. That raised the specter of bitterly hostile black Marxist governments in neighboring Angola and Mozambique, and that, in turn, raised the specter of regional war. If there was to be a war, I knew which side I wanted to fight on: the other side.

Meanwhile, I had parents to oblige. I was doing odd jobs here and there, attending some university classes, playing in rock and roll bands, and, for a while, prospecting for copper in Namibia. None of it led anywhere in particular. My despairing parents insisted I make something of myself, so I applied for a newspaper job.

Next to joining the underground, journalism was the most honorable calling for a white leftist, and besides, there was a certain overlap between the two professions. As a journalist, you could do propaganda for the cause, and you could always dabble in revolution on the side. In that era, as in this, whites picked up for running guns or joining Communist plots almost invariably turned out to have been newspaper reporters at some point or other. The paper to work for was the *Rand Daily Mail*, Johannesburg's cocky morning daily, but the *Mail* wasn't hiring, so I applied to *The Star* instead. *The Star* was the city's afternoon paper, and the largest daily in Africa.

The Star summoned me to take a test. I answered a general-knowledge questionnaire and wrote a mock report of a "terrorist" attack in the Kruger National Park. I guess my scribblings passed muster, because I was called back for an interview. A panel of white editors interrogated me across a conference table. They posed some probing questions, and then asked whether I had ever written a letter to the editor. "Yes," I said, "I wrote a letter protesting the death of Ahmed Timol." The editors exchanged glances, as if to say, Aha, here's our boy. I think that's why they hired me, and sent me upstairs to the Argus Group's Cadet School.

The Argus Group was South Africa's premier newspaper chain. It owned dailies in Johannesburg, Durban, Cape Town, Bloemfontein, and Pretoria, plus the weekly *Sunday Tribune*. Those were its white possessions. It also owned *The World*, Soweto's black daily; *The Cape Herald*, a semiweekly for Cape coloreds; and *The Post*, an Indian paper. Each year, every outpost of the group's far-flung empire recruited one or two aspiring hacks and sent them to Johannesburg, to be trained in the crafts of typing and shorthand and the allied art of writing succinct prose.

This here is a picture of my graduating class. That's me in the fore-

ground, shaking hands with René de Villiers, the retired eminence of South
Africa's liberal editors, but the interesting thing about this photograph is the
background. Consider the faces of my fellow cadet reporters. There are four
white men, four white women, and four "blacks"—two black Africans, one
Indian, and one colored man. To your outsider's eye, it might seem an almost
perfect affirmative-action tableau, with its precise symmetries of race and
gender. The Argus Group was a liberal institution, genuinely committed to
the Western ideals of equal opportunity and affirmative action.

This was South Africa, though. There were about seventeen million
blacks out there, plus two million colored people and 750,000 Indians. If
they were all allowed in, the white liberals would have been swamped, and
that was too high a price for good intentions. So they opened the doors
just a crack. According to the mathematics of affirmative action, there
should have been at least eight Africans in our class of twelve, not just
Mthobi and Mike, but I was thankful anyway. I had been on the side of the
blacks for more than a decade, but Mthobi and Mike were the first real
black men I ever met. By real, I mean men who assumed three dimensions
in my white eyes and culture; black men who spoke perfect English,
looked me in the eye, told me to shut up about this, reconsider that, or
siddown and have a beer.

Indeed, I have much for which to thank *The Star*—an introduction to
real black men and to my one true calling, a close look at how the country
worked, a two-year deferment of military service, and last—and least of
all—a salary. The pay was $120 a month, but it was enough to afford a flat
of my own. My Belgian girlfriend, Joji, and I moved into a block called
Sandringham in the suburb of Berea. It was a dank, verminous place. Plaster
flaked off the walls, and paint peeled from the ceilings. Green slime oozed
out of the ancient water faucets and welled up out of the shower drain. The
rent was $15 a month.

In my parents' shocked view, the flat was a *krot*, a "cave." In my circle,
it was a fashionable address, a liberated zone of sorts. Almost all the inhabitants of Sandringham were social or political deviants. I lived in number 2.
There was a *Rand Daily Mail* reporter in number 1, a future anti-apartheid
filmmaker in number 3, and a banned person upstairs. His name was Garth,
and he had been a trade union organizer until the secret police silenced him.
A banned person could not engage in political activities or be quoted by the
media or even attend gatherings of more than two or three persons. I forget
the precise terms of Garth's banning order, but he had a tendency to slink

away when third or fourth parties joined a conversational knot. It was safer that way. You never knew who was watching, or working, for "them."

Garth had a wife and newborn baby. He also had a sister named Faye, who lived in a cottage in the backyard with her boyfriend, Blair. Faye is in the African National Congress these days, in its military wing, but back then she was just a radical feminist with ambitions. Blair was one of those desperately earnest, tortured whites who couldn't handle South Africa at all. Faced with an army call-up, he ran away to Europe, where he joined the external wing of Swapo—the Southwest African People's Organization, a terrorist organization in the eyes of the South African authorities. As it turned out, he couldn't handle exile either, so he came home and fell into the hands of the military police, who threw him into detention barracks and finally into Ward 30 at Voortrekkerhoogte Military Hospital. I knew Ward 30 well. It was the psychiatric ward. Several of my friends ended up there, trying to fake their way out of uniform. It was full of bush-mad hard cases and brutalized gays, raving acid casualties and suicidal liberals. Blair wasn't deranged, but he soon learned the tricks. He was discharged as insane, whereupon he became a reporter. So did Faye.

Blair and Faye were my good friends. I was going to be their best man, but Faye called off the wedding, claiming fresh insights into the manner in which marriage perpetuated capitalist patriarchal structures. Blair barely seemed to notice. He was a mystic, a Marxist visionary with a wild beard and eyes that burned in torment in deep holes in his skull. He and I spent our evenings endlessly harrowing the same old bone, the bone of what was to be done.

We were all socialists, of course. In a country like South Africa, with its brutal disparities in wealth, socialism had the logic of gravity. As far as we were concerned, all men of good faith were socialists. The capitalist democracies were the scourge of the earth. Business stood condemned by its own crass profit motive. The wealth of Western industrialized countries was the fruit of neocolonialist exploitation of the Third World. And as for white South Africa, it was infected with greed and racism and had to be destroyed. Toward this end, Blair was planning to form a Marxist study group, but all we ever did was get drunk on cheap red wine and sleep with each other's girlfriends, in deference to the Bolshevik free-love tradition. No, that's not true; we once visited Red China's embassy in Botswana, hoping to be recruited. They didn't even offer us tea.

Blair also worked for *The Star.* Our corporate slogan—*"The Star* tells it like it is"—was emblazoned across billboards and bus shelters all over town, and I guess the paper tried to live up to it. Its editorials were critical of apartheid, so many blacks saw it as an ally. African women would wrap themselves in blankets and sit in the lobby in mute suffering, waiting for a chance to tell their troubles to some white reporter whose intervention might save them. A black breadwinner had died, and his survivors were being evicted from their township house and "endorsed out" to the homelands. A black husband had been picked up without a pass and had disappeared. The *baas* had cheated them on their wages, or they'd signed a hire-purchase contract they didn't really understand to buy a lounge suite they couldn't afford. That was very common, that one: Respectable white businessmen made fortunes gulling deposits out of blacks and repossessing and recycling the goods once they missed a payment, which was often inevitable. Sometimes they couldn't afford schoolbooks or school fees, or they were just hungry and out of work and thought we could help.

My first assignment was to cover the magistrates' courts, which lay within walking distance of *The Star*'s offices on the west side of downtown. The magistrates sat in an imposing stone courthouse with wide marble corridors, but they tried mostly petty cases—shoplifting, drug offenses, assault, muggings, prostitution, car theft, and burglary.

A magistrates'-court reporter seldom made the front page, but the assignment had its moments. South Africa was reputed to have the highest crime rate in the "free world," and most of the alleged perpetrators were black. To my socialist eye, crime seemed a just mechanism of redistribution. Apartheid and capitalism gave, and black criminals took away. There was so much petty crime in Jo'burg that *The Star* had to be selective. The news desk was not interested in magistrates'-court stories unless there was an unusual angle, which usually meant that whites were involved. In our copy, we always designated race with a capital letter. A White woman would lose her bag to a Black purse-snatcher. That was too commonplace to make the paper. A White burglar, on the other hand, might merit a story, but his Black counterpart not, unless he was mastermind of a Black burglary ring.

On slow days, I often sat in on black trials anyway, just for interest's sake. The state provided a defense in capital cases, but otherwise indigent blacks were on their own, and the odds were against them. Some couldn't read and had no idea of the contents of statements to which they affixed their *x*. Others didn't understand white languages and struggled to follow the proceedings through interpreters. They couldn't really comprehend what witnesses were saying against them, and the be-robed white man on the bench couldn't really make out their rebuttals. Sometimes they made long, impassioned speeches, at the end of which the black interpreter would turn to the court and say, "He says he didn't do it, your honor." Many black accused were clearly guilty; many simply despaired of proving their innocence, hung their heads, and trooped off to do their time. I have never understood why Justice should be blind; she should be clear-eyed. In those courts, she was indeed blind, and less just for it.

So I spent eight hours a day in the magistrates' court, and at night, I jolled. I haven't said much about ordinary life, have I? It's strange how obsessed we South Africans are with race. To hear me talk, you'd imagine there was no more to life than being white or black and coping with the relevant consequences. It wasn't really that way. I was fixated on apartheid, to be sure, but I was equally agonized about acne and premature ejaculation. Sometimes the racial conundrum sat in my brain like a gnarling, malevolent octopus, but at others it was very remote, as remote as the threat of earthquakes in Los Angeles. We all knew disaster was coming, but we didn't know when. Meanwhile, we ate, drank, and jolled.

The *jol*—say "jawl"—was a very important South African concept, connoting kamikaze debaucheries. It was a Cape colored street term, but all races used it, making it one of the pathetically few things we had in common. Divided we stood, united we jolled. Blacks jolled to obliterate their dismal present; whites to blot out the uncertain future. The word is essentially untranslatable, but any tattooed gangster from the colored slums could define its essential ingredients: *drank, dagga, dobbel en vok*—"drink, dope, dice and fucking."

I spent most of my youth jolling. *Jol* is both verb and noun, and a jol can take many forms. If you were brave, you could jol to a shebeen in Soweto, and have a jol once you got there. You could jol to Zoo Lake on a Sunday afternoon to laze on the greensward, watching blacks jive to the music of transistor radios, and you could jol to Swaziland. Swaziland was a free black country, six hours' drive east of Johannesburg. It was a peaceful tribal kingdom, ruled by an absolute monarch, King Sobhuza. There was no racial tension in Swaziland. The countryside was green and fertile, the people well fed and friendly. As you crossed the Swazi border, some huge and dark shadow seemed to lift from your shoulders. Swaziland was a balm for the mind of racially tormented South Africans. I grew deliriously light-headed the instant I set foot in it, and not just from smoking *zol.*

You could buy *zol* on almost any roadside in Swaziland. A finger cost ten cents, an arm five rand, and it was very strong. We stuffed it into the jagged maw of a broken bottle-neck and smoked it in the African manner, holding the pipe in clasped hands and drawing in great billowing clouds of smoke. Then we put Dollar Brand on the tape player, and set forth on voyages of discovery in my old green Peugeot. Dollar was a black jazz pianist from Cape Town, and his "Mannenberg" was the song of those times— twenty-two intoxicating minutes of wailing African saxes and shifting township rhythms.

Swaziland's back roads were crude, and I often had accidents on them. It was in the benign nature of the place that we would always come out laughing. One afternoon, I put the Peugeot's nose into a ditch. We dug it out, but I was so goofed that I reversed the rear end into the ditch on the far side of the road. At that moment, a laughing tribesman leapt out of the bush, quoting Yeats: "Things fall apart; the center cannot hold." He was a mission boy, and spoke with a BBC accent. The car was firmly stuck, so we sat down and laughed at it. Then we made another pipe. I got out my guitar and taught our black samaritan to sing "Da-Doo-Ron-Ron," and there we were—some Boers, a Swazi, a Muslim from the Cape and two girls, dancing and singing in the dust of an African roadside. It was a moment of utterly blinding exultation, and all the more precious because it was so rare, so rare.

In my life, those moments seemed to come mostly when I was stoned. Maybe it was my imagination, but being stoned seemed a Switzerland of the mind to me. All of a sudden, it didn't really matter whether you and blacks really understood each other. You could just laugh. It was good enough. The best times I had with blacks were when we were smoking together. Indeed, the ritual of buying the stuff was one of the few activities that brought me face-to-face with a black man who had to be dealt with as an equal. Black dope dealers were suspicious of whites, so you had to tune them in *tsotsi-taal,* the half-Afrikaans patois of the streets; you had to *gooi* (give) the double-horned devil's hand sign and *charf* (say), *"Level with the gravel, ek sê."* And then, if the dealer smiled, you had a black brother in conspiracy, bonded to you in mutual terror of the police. It lasted no more than a minute or two, but it was something to hold onto.

Until I became a reporter, those furtive encounters with dope-dealing *skollies* in alleys were just about the only contact I had with blacks, other than servants. I had a head full of grandiose political theories, all revolving around blacks and my putative brotherhood with them, but I was completely bereft of black friends. I yearned for black friends, to make it all real, and in the end I was given some. Their names were Mike, Fanyana, Khulu, and Langa, and they were reporters on *The Star*'s Soweto edition. Fanyana was a man of kingly proportions—tall, broad, and muscular—and staggeringly good-looking, a giant with the smooth round face and saucerlike eyes of a child. Langa was older, a veteran reporter with a grizzled beard and liver trouble. And Mike—Mike was a spiv, a sharp dresser and quick as a card-sharp in mind and movement. I liked Mike because he didn't give a fuck. He was an absolute nihilist and cared about nothing, least of all the honorary whiteness of his well-paid white-collar job. He'd say, "I'm just a boy around here," as in garden boy, or kitchen boy, and stare you in the eye, you white liberal, as if daring you to contradict him.

I didn't. Maybe that's why we got on. It was clean and cutting between us, utterly without sentiment. There was an unspoken rule that we would not talk politics, except to make cynical jokes about it. We talked about boxing, soccer, the bosses, music, sex, booze, gangsters, but not politics. If we had talked politics, I would have had to creep and crawl and beg forgiveness for what my people were doing to his. I would have turned into a worm, and Mike into a cripple, a victim. So we kept it hard and unsentimental. He called me *boertjie*, "little Boer," and I—no, I didn't call him kaffir; I just grinned his insults away. If I had, though, I think he would have roared with laughter. Like most politicized blacks in that era, he was a Biko man, into black consciousness, black pride. Maybe that's why he was so clean and hard, so determined not to be pitied or patronized. I don't know. We didn't talk about it.

Mike was my friend, but he didn't trust me, not an inch. Almost everything I knew about him and his background was scavenged, dropped by him in passing and stashed away in my memory, bit by bit, never adding up to much. His grandfather was a farm laborer in the Free State; his father, a driver in Johannesburg. He won all sorts of academic prizes at Soweto's Orlando High and had a brother, Martin, who was somehow involved in the underground. One day Martin slipped over the border and disappeared into exile. A week or so later, the secret police kicked down the door of Mike's father's house in Orlando West, looking for the fugitive brother. Mike once acted out the ensuing scene for me, darting from one side of his father's kitchen to the other, cackling like a maniac, playing now a loutish white cop, now himself, standing at attention in the corner, rigid with terror, saying "Yes, sir. No, sir" like a schoolboy. At one stage, the cop was going through the kitchen cupboard, scattering utensils while Mike watched in silence. The cop looked up and barked, "Don't look at me! I'll shoot you! Don't look at me!"

Mike's father was an immensely dignified old man who treated white visitors with equanimity. I wish I could say the same for my parents. I once took Mike home with me. Having an educated black in the house was a big event for my parents and visiting aunt. They were determined to make a good impression. They sat Mike down in the lounge. My mother brought out her best china, and put the kettle on while I ran upstairs to search for something in the room that had once been mine. When I came back down, my aunt was perched uneasily on the edge of her chair, *talking to Mike in pidgin*—in the childlike English of illiterate black servants. "You like it sugar?" she asked. "How many spoon sugar you like?" As I entered, she looked up at me with a vapid smile on her face and said, "Wouldn't the boy like a biscuit?"

It was best, under the circumstances, to meet on neutral ground. But where was that? After work, most white reporters got pissed over the road in the bar at the Elizabeth Hotel, but we couldn't do that. Oh, we tried it once, white Mike (another reporter) and Langa and I, but there was a little scene. The owner was sorry but he stood to lose his license, would we please go. After that, we walked down to Solly Kramer's bottle store after the day's last deadline, bought whiskey and six-packs of Lion or Castle and carried them up to a disused canteen on the fourth floor of *The Star*'s office building, where we sat around Formica tables that shimmered with neon, drank out of paper cups, and smoked Lexingtons till the whole room fogged up. Sometimes we played dice, blowing on the stones for luck and incanting lucky rhymes—"lucky five, staying alive, lucky seven, going to heaven"—and hurling them down with a great flourish and a cry of *tsa!* And sometimes we played informer-informer.

There was surely a secret-police informer in our newsroom, perhaps even among us. I was a prime suspect, of course, being a Malan, but I was so obvious not even the Boers would be so stupid. Or would they? You never knew. Maybe they were smart enough to use a man like Don Mattera, a colored poet who edited copy in a Nigerian dashiki and preferred to be called Bra Zinga, his name from the days when he led a township gang. Don was under a banning order, but he was so free in his talk of revolution you sometimes wondered whether he was trying to lure you out.

Was it Harry Mashabela? Probably not. They'd already had Harry, used him up, and spat him out. He'd been a state witness in a Communist Party pamphlets case, and now he wouldn't meet your eye and wore a neck brace that said, They made me do it. Was it John Horak, who weaseled around in safari suits, poking his nose into sensitive corners? Possibly. Or maybe it was someone at this very table, a black man with a wife and kids to support, always short because he pissed away his wages in the shebeens. Such an *oke* could use a little extra on the side. I'd suggest that, and eyes would go darting around the table, each man eyeing the next over the rim of his beer can and thinking, yes, oh yes indeed; but then someone would laugh, and we'd all laugh, and it'd be okay again.

And so we'd sit there until late at night; and as the levels in the bottles sank, it became easier and easier to believe that we were truly brothers. This was the second empirical property of racial tension: It went up in dope smoke, and it also dissolved in alcohol. Drunkenness was also Switzerland.

Few of the brothers had cars, so I'd sometimes drive them home to Soweto. They'd take me inside to meet their wives, who were by now in nighties and face cream and radiating disapproval. They'd pour me one for the road, and we'd exchange soul handshakes and fraternal hugs, and then I'd be back in the battered Peugeot, driving home, and I'd be thinking, There is something *profoundly* fucking wrong with a system that makes kaffirs of these my brothers. I'd think, *Fuck* white South Africans, and all they have wrought, and fuck their army, whose summons to service I had been dodging since I was eighteen. I wasn't going to carry a gun for them. I'd run away, join the other side, and come back to blow them all up.

It was two or three in the morning, and we were standing in a dark garden, waiting for a sound. My companion was a nervous, chain-smoking white woman in a nightgown and hair curlers. She lived in a working-class neighborhood in south Johannesburg, under the walls of a grimy old police station. She'd just gone to bed when she first heard the scream. It started loud, trailed off into choking sobs and then silence. Five minutes later, it came again. And again, five minutes after that. At first, the howling was merely irritating, because the woman couldn't get to sleep. After an hour, though, she'd been unnerved by the thought of what might be causing it. So she'd called *The Star*, where I was working the night shift, and I'd driven out to investigate. And now we were standing under the walls of the police station, waiting.

In due course, the scream came again. It was coming from inside the police station, and it sounded as though they were killing someone in there, slowly. I wanted to block my ears, but the woman clapped her hand over her mouth and looked at me with frightened eyes. She expected me to do something, so I walked around to the front of the station, where a wan, blue light burned, and pounded on the door. Nobody answered. I shouted. Nobody came. I tried the door; it was locked. There were no lights on inside the building, not that I could see. There was nothing I could do. The woman and I smoked a few more cigarettes. In a while, the screaming stopped, and I went back to the office. I left a note asking the day shift to look into it, but that was just to cover myself. It wasn't a story. It was just one of those South African things.

After six months in the courts, I had been appointed *The Star*'s crime reporter, a job usually reserved for someone who had the common touch— who spoke fluent Afrikaans, that is. Most English South Africans had some Afrikaans, but their accents betrayed them as *soutpiels*—"salt dicks." A *soutpiel* was an Englishman with one foot in South Africa and the other in England—a straddle so broad that his cock dangled in the sea. Most policemen, on the other hand, were rocks, or Afrikaners, and rocks were not all that fond of *soutpiels,* especially those who worked for the disloyal English press. So the crime reporter slot usually went to someone like me, a rock-spider who could speak the tongue and had some cultural affinity with Boers. Afrikaner policemen were sentimental about their rural past. Even if they worked in skyscrapers, looking out on tar and concrete, they liked talking about the rains, rugby, and prospects for the forthcoming harvest.

I could pass as a Boer on the telephone, but I was less convincing in person, perhaps because the cops could see in my eyes that I wasn't truly one of them. Almost every day brought a moment when my eyes threatened to give me away. Still, I developed a good contact in the so-called ghost squad, a plainclothes unit that patrolled downtown Jo'burg on the lookout for pickpockets and knifemen. They shadowed a likely black suspect, and when he struck they usually shot him dead. My china on the ghost squad often called me when he killed someone, hoping that we would dash out and photograph him standing over the body like a trophy hunter. What was I supposed to say? If I'd told him he was a bloodthirsty fucking savage, he would never have called me again. So I just looked away when he started boasting, hoping that my eyes would hold their secrets.

South African policemen tended to be very firm in their support of the government and its apartheid policies. Next to rugby and rain, the subject they most loved to discuss was the unfair and hypocritical way in which the rest of the world was ganging up on us over apartheid. I couldn't afford to alienate them, so I always sighed and shook my head and said "ja-nee," a Boer phrase that means "yes-no" and comes in handy when nothing else comes to mind. If I wrote anything critical about the force, it appeared without a byline.

Someone once leaked me an "ethnographic" manual used as a textbook in the police training college. It was a nasty little book, full of comically malevolent racial characterizations. It proceeded from the assumption that Aryans generally behaved themselves. Indians, on the other hand, were "the advanced guard of countries trying to rid themselves of their surplus population," and an "unhygienic health menace" to boot. Jews were sly and cunning, inclined toward "fraud, embezzlement and swindling." Greeks and Portuguese were hot-blooded and prone to crimes of passion. And as for the Bantu, they were "primitive" and likely to resort to violence at the slightest provocation. "They do not think in an abstract way," said the manual. "This is reflected in the way they count. Their way of thinking is full of contradictions. They cannot talk logically." A black man was childlike, and needed firm but kindly guidance from his white "guardian and superior." My piece laid out these assertions and wondered, somewhat ingenuously, whether this might be why relations between police and blacks were so sour.

In the Vorster era, such insolence was not tolerated. The response of the commissioner of police was characteristic. He didn't defend the book, or apologize for it, or promise to investigate, or yank it out of circulation. He called for the traitor's head. He ordered *The Star* to identify the writer so that measures could be taken. The editor held firm, and the storm blew over.

As it turned out, that was one of the few blows I got to strike for the cause in my years as a crime reporter. For the most part, I was too busy covering the endless churning of the great redistribution machine—bank robberies, holdups, muggings, and murders. Around Easter 1976, I wrote something a little out of the ordinary, a series about illegal-gambling bosses and their friends in the police vice squad. It was well received, so the news desk set me to work on an "exposé" of child homosexual prostitution. This was a novel vice in a puritanical country, and a white vice to boot, which made it a high-priority story—at least as high as anything that happened in Soweto.

Earlier that year, pupils at several Soweto schools had gone out on strike against the imperial Afrikaner government. Urban blacks reviled Afrikaans as the language of the oppressor, and most black schools chose English as their medium of instruction. The Vorster government felt slighted. It didn't want its Bantu vassals becoming Anglicized, so it decreed that certain school subjects would henceforth be taught in Afrikaans. It didn't matter that many teachers and pupils could barely speak the language, or that their textbooks were in English. The Vorster government ignored petitions and turned away deputations, so the students called a strike. So what? It was a black issue, an inside-page story. *The Star*'s white readers were presumably much more eager to read about perverse goings-on in the dead of night in the vast, echoing concourse of Johannesburg railroad station.

The concourse was deserted after midnight, and lonely gay men threw long shadows as they stalked rent boys across its floodlit floor. In the early weeks of June 1976, I spent my nights lurking in the station, observing these eerily beautiful courtship rites and plying sad young runaways with coffee and doughnuts. I had dispensation to go into work late in the mornings. On the morning of June 16, I arrived in the newsroom around 10:30, just in time to catch the tea trolley on its midmorning round. I was sipping my first cup of tea and reading the morning papers when Harry Mashabela burst through the door to announce the end of an era.

Harry was black, but at that moment his face was gray, and his white shirt was spattered with blood. He'd been in Soweto covering a march. High-school pupils had taken to the streets with placards denouncing the Afrikaans-language decree. A few stones were thrown, and the police opened fire, killing two young boys and wounding untold others. Harry loaded some of the injured in a staff car and rushed them to Baragwanath Hospital, which lay on the outskirts of the township. When he looked back, Soweto was already exploding. The schools and government installations were destroyed first. Then the mob turned on anything associated with the white economic structure, burning trucks, delivery vans, shops, and banks. The tinder had been accumulating for generations, and once it caught the conflagration was unstoppable.

I stayed on the telephone all day, trying to keep track of casualties, but it was impossible. Soweto was in a state of anarchy. The police were trapped inside their stations, all roads blocked by mobs and barricades of burning tires. Everything was burning. Toward sunset, I went out into the streets of Jo'burg, and it was as though the world had ended. There were no people, no cars, no city sounds. The black work force had rushed home to Soweto as news of the trouble spread, and whites were cowering behind locked doors, waiting. We all knew this was coming, you see; we knew it in our bones. A day would come when the blacks would rise up and surge through the city, and we'd all wind up on the roofs of our burning American-dream split-levels, begging the baying horde for mercy.

The outcome hung in the balance for thirty-six hours. The police had been taken by surprise, but they pulled themselves together, moved heavy reinforcements and armored vehicles into the townships, and put the rebellion down at a terrible cost in lives. When the fires finally died down several months later, there were four hundred black corpses, or five hundred, or seven hundred, and the police were firmly back in control. Newspapers proclaimed that the situation had returned to normal, but there was no longer any such thing. South Africa's psychic landscape had been transformed. Blacks saw that they had shaken the white power structure to its very foundations, and they suddenly had hope. The tide of history had turned.

After June 16, a dozen black suppliants were steered to my desk each day. They'd press a dirty scrap of ruled exercise-book paper into my hand. On it would be written the name of a missing person—a son, usually. I was supposed to help find him, but there was nothing I could do. I just wrote a note on the newspaper's stationery and sent them off on the usual pilgrimage: police headquarters to Diepkloof Prison to Modder B Prison to the morgue, where they often found what they were looking for. Sometimes the grieving parents would return to say, But he was well and strong when they arrested him, and now the nostrils have been ripped off his face; his bones are broken and his body is full of contusions. How can this be? I couldn't tell them. I didn't know. I couldn't find out. But I couldn't help wondering as I did my rounds inside the Blue Hotel.

The Blue Hotel was police headquarters, a blue-trimmed office block called John Vorster Square. Every fortnight or so, I parked my car outside the Blue Hotel, walked around the back and into the underground parking garage. In a corner of that garage was an elevator, a special elevator, with padded walls and only one button on its control panel. You pushed the button, and it took you nonstop to the tenth floor, headquarters of the Witwatersrand Division of the Security Police, the secret police. On the tenth-floor landing, a man in a bullet-proof glass booth looked you over and pressed a button that spun a steel turnstile, and then you were walking down a corridor that gleamed with fluorescence, on your way to pay a courtesy call on the colonel. Every now and then, you passed an open office door, and maybe glimpsed a frightened black suspect handcuffed to a bench. Your eyes might meet, but not for long, because you didn't really want to see, and besides, this was no place for shows of empathy. There were cannibals here. This was the floor from which Ahmed Timol had "fallen" to his death six years earlier. This was the haunt of the notorious "Nails" van Zyl, a cop who supposedly nailed the foreskins of obstinate suspects to the interrogation desk. This was where rebellious blacks were beaten, shocked, suffocated in wet canvas bags, and forced to stand naked on bricks for days on end.

On one such visit, I had just stepped into the secret elevator when a car drew up at the door and disgorged three men. Two were plainclothes white cops with short hair and neat mustaches wearing cheap jackets that gaped at the stomach and trousers that showed too much sock. The third was a black man in a black hood. The cops dragged him toward the lift. They were a little taken aback to find it already occupied, but it was too late, so they got in with me. The door closed, and the elevator started rising. The black man's shirtfront was drenched with blood. I couldn't think of anything to say, and the white cops avoided my eyes. There was no sound, save the gurgling of blood in the prisoner's ruined mouth. At the tenth floor, the doors opened, the turnstile turned, and the cops hustled their quarry out of my life. No, this wasn't a story either. It was just another of those South African things.

In my time, the chief of the Witwatersrand Division of the Security Police was Colonel Coetzee, later revealed to be the great Boer spymaster, running agents in the very hearts of the exiled liberation movements. He was a portly, courtly fellow, very dapper in his expensive dark suits. He sported a Clark Gable mustache and seemed to regard himself as something of a ladies' man, and an erudite conversationalist to boot. A glass case in his office was crammed with banned books—Marx, Engels, Althusser, and so on. The colonel was particularly interested in Trotsky. He was preparing a doctoral thesis on Trotsky. He assumed I was a leftist of some sort, perhaps because I worked for the English press, perhaps because he'd read the report of my own "interrogation."

The secret police had intercepted a letter to my friend Robin, who was living in London. In it, I went on at length about how much I hated my job and what brutal swine the police were, but they didn't seem to care what I had said about them. They were interested only in this observation: "Meanwhile, underground, Maoist cells are plotting in deadly earnest." What did I mean by that? What did I know? I explained that the remark was sarcastic, so they let me go.

For whatever reason, Colonel Coetzee was always eager to engage me in ideological debate. In a country where almost anyone who opposed apartheid was considered a Communist, his line was very sophisticated. "These Marxists claim they're fighting for freedom," he'd say, "but what freedom is there under a dictatorship of the proletariat?" Stuff like that. I think he hoped I would argue, but I was so nervous that I always agreed with him, no matter what he said. I just wanted to get out of there, before my eyes betrayed me. I must have been a terrible disappointment.

By and by, Colonel Coetzee would ring a bell, and a black constable would appear carrying a tray. On one occasion, the door to an adjoining office opened, and Colonel Swanepoel joined us for afternoon tea. Swanepoel's gray hair was cropped like a Prussian's. His face was a bloodred morass of broken veins—hence his nickname Rooi Rus, the Red Russian. Swanepoel was a man who gave off great blasts and gusts of energy. His movements were rapid and agitated, his speech a jackhammer in your face. It seemed an ongoing struggle for him to control himself. He was so right wing that he thought his own government, the most right wing in the world, was infiltrated by Reds.

He was also world famous. Colonel Swanepoel's exploits as chief interrogator of the Security Police had been discussed at the United Nations. His alleged cruelties had made him a one-man propaganda liability, so his superiors transferred him to the office next to Coetzee's, to do God knows what. He was soon to be sent to the border, where he enhanced his reputation still further as a member of a notorious counterinsurgency unit called Koevoet—the Crowbar. Koevoet was once accused of searing the flesh off Swapo suspects on the red-hot exhaust pipes of armored cars. That lay in the future, though. For the moment, the Red Russian was sipping tea with the liberal English press and not liking it at all.

This was just after the fall of South Vietnam, around the time of the U.S. Senate's Church hearings. Senator Church's revelations about poisoned cigars for Fidel and other CIA plots had caused a furor, and President Carter was clearly bent on reining in the agency. Britain's MI5 had long since been infiltrated by pink nancyboys, and now the CIA was having its teeth pulled, too. In the colonel's opinion, this was proof of Western decadence. "The West is a spent force," growled Swanepoel. "It has lost its blood." In fact, all white nations save the Afrikaners and Israelis had lost their blood, and would shortly wind up on the trash heap of history.

Swanepoel got so worked up about Jimmy Carter and the Church hearings that you could almost hear him sizzle. He was quivering with rage, his florid face pulsating as he spilled his tea in the saucer. "They're cutting off their own balls!" he bellowed, glaring at me as though it were my fault. I sat there nodding my head, agreeing frantically, spilling tea in my own quaking lap. "*Ja-nee,* Colonel," I said. "You certainly have a point there, Colonel."

At such moments I'd close my eyes and think, This is not my life. This is too weird to be true. Is this me, this Afrikaner who says yes-no to cold-blooded colonels? If so, who was drinking with the black brothers last night? Or was that me the night before, tripping on acid in a white slum flat, watching the grains in the floorboards turn into revolutionary armies that fought battles across a darkling plain while Dollar Brand played saxophone on the turntable and Faye danced around me with closed eyes, dreaming of bearded guerrillas?

That word *yaw.* It's an aeronautical term, isn't it, a word to describe the shuddering of an aircraft in a dive too steep and fast for its design, an aircraft that's shaking itself to bits? I was yawing in that time, going too fast, propelled by fuels too volatile between points immeasurably distant from one another. It was too far from Sandringham to the Blue Hotel, too far from the canteen where I drank with the brothers to the house of my Afrikaner father. He wanted me to do my duty and put on a uniform for my country. I had been dodging military service since I was eighteen, and now I was twenty-two and running out of options. They wanted me in June, infantry, Walvis Bay, and this time there was no way out. I either reported for duty or left South Africa forever. It was not an easy decision. I got drunk most nights rather than think about it, and then I lay down under my naked light bulb, watching shadows stirring on the wall and listening for footsteps in the alley outside. I was waiting for something.

On almost any night in 1977, all the lights in number 2 would have been blazing, and a spent record spinning endlessly on the turntable. Malan would have been passed out in his clothes on a mattress on the bedroom floor. He would probably have looked shabby and disheveled, with ballpoint ink all over his hands and face, and drifts of cigarette ash in his lap. He would almost certainly have been wearing his brown leather jacket, the lining of its pockets rent by the barrel of the pistol he had recently taken to carrying. Oh, and the knife—we mustn't forget the knife. It would have been imbedded in the floorboards near his head, within easy reach, in case he woke up from one of his thrashing nightmares and discovered that the apocalypse was finally underway.

What form did those nightmares take? Once, I would not have told you, but now I may as well.

Maybe I should never have become a reporter, especially not a reporter who worked the police beat. Maybe I should have been a dentist, like my mother wanted, and stayed in the white suburbs, cosseting my illusions and plodding blindly toward the light, like the other white liberals. If I'd done that, I might never have left South Africa. Instead, I took a job that put me in contact with people most white liberals never met, and took me to places they never saw. Many of those places were the scenes of crime, and many of the crimes were murder. That was my job; I waded chin-deep through gore. Almost every day, I tucked my spiral-bound notebook in my pocket and ventured forth to study the way South Africans killed each other.

South Africa wasn't like other countries when it came to murder. Elsewhere in the world, murder was just another function of ordinary social relationships. In the vast majority of cases, murderers killed someone they knew—wives, bosses, fellow drunkards, rivals in business or love. In South Africa, it wasn't like that. In South Africa, you could be walking down the street, minding your own business, when white trash boiled off the back of a passing pick-up and kicked your head in, simply because your skin was black.

On the other hand, you could be white and lying in bed at night, counting your blessings, when a black came through the window and sank a knife into your chest—not because you were white, necessarily, but because you had something he wanted, while he had nothing at all. It wasn't really a racial murder, but then again it was, because the black murderer's destitution was to some large extent a consequence of the color of his skin. To my socialist eye, such killings seemed telling little parables of Marxism in action, skirmishes in the great class war. I had a theory to contain and explain them, but there was a third category of resonant killing for which I had no theory at all.

Consider, if you will, this newspaper photograph. It was taken inside an ordinary Soweto house—a cement hut, really, with an asbestos roof and three tiny rooms—in a zone of Soweto called Naledi. There are three people in the picture: an elderly black woman wrapped in a blanket and her two small grandchildren. Mrs. Christina Ramathlape is displaying the shattered door of a clothes wardrobe, and telling an invisible reporter how it got that way.

Her story began with the theft of a battery from a car that was parked outside her house. Suspicion fell on her son, Jeremiah. The boy knew nothing about the stolen battery, but nobody believed him. One night, the car's owner and several of his friends came pounding on Christina's door, looking for her son. As they burst in, the boy crept into a wardrobe and pulled the door shut behind him. The intruders somehow sniffed him out, though, and smashed the cupboard open with an ax, as I could plainly see. Then they grabbed Jeremiah, put a belt around his neck, and dragged him away screaming.

They took him to a house diagonally across the street. Christina followed. She stood outside in the dark, listening to her son's screams. She threw stones on the roof, but she was too scared to go inside. She couldn't call the police, because there were no telephones in Soweto. After a while, the screams stopped, and she went home, hoping that the boy would soon be released, whipped but none the worse for his ordeal. Jeremiah didn't show up the next day, however, nor the next. In fact, she hadn't seen him since. Eventually, she wrapped herself in a blanket and joined the throng of victims and suppliants in *The Star*'s waiting room.

In itself, the abduction was just another of those South African things. There was an unusual angle, though, in that Mrs. Ramathlape claimed that the men behind the kidnapping were Makgotla—members of a tribal vigilante movement that had recently been dispensing rough justice in the townships, administering public floggings to suspected thieves and adulterous women. Now that was a story. That is why I was there, looking at the ax-splintered cupboard and other evidence. After taking down the details, I drove to the nearest police station and reported the abduction to its white commandant. He promised a prompt investigation.

A week later, I went back to Soweto to see what had developed. It was midafternoon, but Mrs. Ramathlape's house was locked up tight, all the curtains drawn. I knocked on the door. Someone peeped out from behind a curtain, and I heard heavy objects and furniture scraping across the floor. The door opened a crack, and I slipped through. It was dark inside, and reeked of shit and urine. Old Mrs. Ramathlape and her grandchildren had been barricaded inside the house for almost a week. The day after my first visit, she told me, detectives had moved through the neighborhood, asking questions about her missing son. They had no sooner gone than a crowd surrounded her house and tried to break down the door. It was a steel door, and it withstood the mob's battery, so they poured paraffin under it and tried to burn her out. She managed to smother the flames before they did serious damage. As soon as night fell, she tried to slip away, but the house was being watched. She and the children had been barricaded inside ever since. They had no water, no food, and no toilet.

I took the children to my car. Their tiny hands clung to mine like vices, and their eyes were wide with fear. I returned to the house to help their grandmother, who was gathering her possessions into a bundle. Meanwhile, a crowd of blacks was gathering on the far side of the street. Some of the men were armed with fighting sticks and *sjamboks*—whips—and I didn't like the look of them. My guts knotted in dread. Just as we were about to leave, they crossed the road and surrounded the car.

Their leader, a wiry man with yellow eyes, came up to me and said, "You can't take this woman away. This woman is *skaberash*"—she is a drunken whore. "Give her," he said, "give her." I gave him my shit-eating grin, saying brother this, brother that, not nice to harm a woman and children. It didn't help. I couldn't speak his language, and he barely understood mine. And besides, I doubt he was amenable to talk of justice and fair play, anyway. He lost control of himself at the mere sight of Mrs. Ramathlape, yelled and gesticulated and tried to push past me so he could lay into her with his whip. The children started screaming. I pushed their grandmother into the car, locked the door behind her, and leapt into the driver's seat. I started the engine, but the mob's leader planted himself in front of the hood and started performing some sort of primordial war dance, gyrating and grunting and smiting the dust with his whip. I gunned the engine threateningly. He leapt aside and froze in a crouch, with the whip raised high in the air. He looked like a gargoyle. Only his impenetrable yellow eyes followed us as we moved off down the road.

Such incidents left me with grave misgivings. Misgiving was part of my life, Soweto being part of my crime reporter's beat. Almost every day, I wrote a story or saw something that inspired misgiving. As far as *The Star* was concerned, crimes perpetrated by blacks against other blacks were just more of those South African things. It was the paper's practice to lump all Soweto crime into a single, essentially statistical story. I once wrote a lead that ran, "In what Soweto police described as a quiet weekend, only eleven people were murdered and nineteen stabbed"—something like that. A copy editor had the good taste to put a blue line through it.

So we didn't print the grisly details, but white cops rubbed my nose in them anyway. As a representative of the liberal English press, I was presumably in need of stiff doses of brutal reality, and whenever I toured Soweto's police stations, I was given one. The cops would say, "Ah, here's Malan. Come here, Malan; here's a nice case for you. Nine men raped this woman; then someone jumped the queue, and the tenth *ou* got stabbed in the back while he was on top of her. Then they all started fighting with knives, so we've got a murder, nine rape charges, and six stabbings on our hands." Or, "Come into the morgue, Malan; we've got something to show you." Once, the body on the tray was that of a ten-year-old black child, the victim of what headline writers called a *"muti* slaying"—a voodoo killing. The boy's fingers, eyes, liver, heart, and genitals had been cut out, to be used in some sorcerer's brew. "How do you like that?" guffawed one of my guides. "That's how your black friends behave."

These killings were fairly common, but this was the first such corpse I'd seen, and its empty eye sockets haunted my dreams for months. In my imagination, Soweto came to resemble Europe in the Dark Ages, a place where humble people barricaded their doors at darkness and trembled through the night while werewolves howled outside. It was not an entirely fanciful vision. Soweto was a charnel house. Its murder rate was four or five times higher than New York's. Its trains were infested with *tsotsis,* young gangsters who immobilized their victims with a sharpened bicycle spoke in the thigh, and then made off with their cash or packages. On Friday nights, pay nights, wolf packs of gangsters lay in wait for incoming trains, and picked off the breadwinners on their way home from the station.

Every now and then, a white liberal or academic weighed in with an op-ed piece about black crime, attributing it all to adverse social conditions. I wrote such pieces myself. Here's one—a review of a criminological study, in which I resoundingly trash racist assumptions about innate black criminality and explain Soweto's crime rate in terms of apartheid-induced poverty, overcrowding, frustration, and nihilism. There was a drastic shortage of houses and schools in Soweto. There were no cinemas, no bars, no hotels, no modern shopping centers, few recreational facilities, and no electricity. The place was a giant labor barracks, grimly utilitarian, and intentionally so. The mad scientists of apartheid *wanted* urban blacks to be miserable. They wanted blacks to get out of white South Africa, to go to the homelands. Soweto was one big apartheid atrocity. I said that, and believed it, but my own words did nothing to dilute the apprehension I felt whenever I set foot in that grim black city.

In my memory, it is always winter in Soweto; the setting sun is an orb of cold orange in a gray sky, and gray smoke is drifting across a desolate gray landscape. The houses are gray; their asbestos roofs are gray; the wastelands are strewn with gray ash and rubble. The roads are clogged with morose men streaming home from the railroad station in cast-off gray overcoats. As I flash past, they register white skin; their mouths form silent words, and something leaps into their eyes—maybe just recognition; maybe something else. It was hard to be sure. At such moments, I'd shudder and thank God I was inside the steel exoskeleton of a fast car.

After dark, it was even worse. The night seemed full of sinister shadows. It was easy to get lost, easier still to wander into a ditch. Late one night, I drove into a morass of mud around a communal tap and couldn't get out again. The roar of my engine and the shriek of my spinning wheels drew a crowd, and before I knew it the car was surrounded by *tsotsis* in baggy chinos, their skulls shaved to the nub and riven with glistening scar tissue. I was terrified. One tapped on the window. I rolled it down and flashed my shit-eating grin. "I want to know," the *tsotsi* said mockingly, "what the *baas* is going to give me."

"A few kind words?" I said. "A little encouragement?"

He laughed. "I like your jacket," he said. "If I want your jacket, I can have it."

This was certainly true. He and his comrades exchanged glances, as if to coordinate their next move, and I floored the accelerator. The wheels caught, and I went fishtailing out of there, drenched with sweat and weak with relief.

I was always relieved to leave Soweto, to see the lights of white Johannesburg looming up ahead—always. Once I was back in the world of light, the fear would dissipate, and I'd be ashamed of myself, to think that my own psyche was riddled with irrational racist phantasms. And yet, whenever I returned to Soweto the fear fell in behind me, and dogged me like a shadow. I loved blacks, and yet I was scared of them. I was scared of them, and yet I loved them. It was a most paradoxical condition. One minute, you'd be harrowed with guilt and bleeding internally for your suffering black brethren. The next, you'd recoil in horror from the things they did, and from the savage latencies that seemed to lie buried in their hearts. You yawed between extremes. Sometimes you completed the round trip in just fifteen minutes.

One lunchtime, my source in the ghost squad called me from a down-town phone booth. It was soon after the riots of June '76, and Johannesburg was so tense it was hard to breathe. Soweto was mourning its many hundred martyrs, and a political detainee named Wellington Tshazibane had just "hanged himself" while in the custody of the secret police. Rumors of Götterdämmerung were sweeping the white suburbs. Some whites had heard that tomorrow was kill-a-white day. Others had it on good authority that black maids were being incited to poison the master's morning tea. Whenever my telephone rang, some white paranoiac came on the line to pass along another rumor. Children were being butchered on their way to school. A black mob was marching on Roodepoort. Terrorists had blown up Rose-bank. Then the phone rang again, at lunchtime, and a voice said, "There's a kaffir running amok in the streets. He's shouting, 'Africa! Africa!' and chopping whites' heads off with an ax." This time it was for real. The axman was avenging Soweto's slaughtered innocents.

A photographer named Noel Watson and I leapt into a car and rushed to the scene. When we got there, a few white pensioners who couldn't run fast enough were bleeding on the pavement, and a knot of plainclothes cops was bundling a black suspect into a car. Noel shot a few pictures, and then we raced off after the police. I was thinking, Well, this is how it is, and how it will always be. If your skin was white and fate had placed you in that axman's path, all the good you'd ever said, thought, and done would not have saved you. It's us or them, I thought; it's primordial, primeval.

I was still thinking along those lines as we drew up outside the Blue Hotel. And then a black man fell out of the sky. He came flying through a fifth-floor window, landed at our feet in a spray of glass, and lay there like an upturned tortoise, feebly waving his arms in the air. I ran over and knelt beside him, but I didn't know what to do; his body was all broken, blood was oozing from his mouth, and I was afraid to touch him. Just then, a shiny black boot entered my field of vision. I looked up, and there stood the divisional commissioner himself, Brigadier Visser, his shoulders encrusted with gold braid and a little smile playing about beneath his handsome mustache. He stirred the black man with his toe. *"Ja,"* he told me, "this is the Bantu who was hitting people with an ax. He just dived out the window."

"Ja-nee, Brigadier," I said. "Yes-no."

So what did you do at the end of such a day? You went down to Solly Kramer's for another bottle of whiskey, and up to the fourth floor with the brothers to drink the paradox away. Sometimes it just wouldn't go, though. On the night of the axman's rampage, the air around our Formica table was dense with thoughts unspoken, and unspeakable. I couldn't exactly say, Listen, brothers, on the basis of today's events, it occurs to me that the Boers might be right—that if we don't keep you blacks down, you'll all rise up and come after us with axes, screaming, "Africa! Africa!" And they, too, had to mask their feelings. How could they fail to empathize with the axman? I was white, but even I had an inkling of the rage that surely drove his ax through white skulls. Was I really on their side? Were they on mine? Or did we meet like soldiers in no-man's-land, exchanging cigarettes and hand-shakes on Christmas Day? It sometimes felt that way. When the whiskey was finished, we always returned to our own psychic trenches, to vastly different and possibly irreconcilable worlds: Mike to his single room in Soweto, and I to my slum flat, where I lay down on my mattress in a wintry bleakness of spirit to think things over.

I thought a lot about the riots of June '76, and about Dr. Melville Edelstein, the only white civilian to die in them. Edelstein was a sociologist, a liberal who had recently published a book entitled *What Young Africans Think.* It was deeply sympathetic to the black point of view, and uncannily prescient. Edelstein warned that black youths were angry and that a storm was building inside them. He foresaw many things clearly, but not the way in which the storm would consume him. On the morning of June 16, he was doing research at a clinic in Soweto. When rioting broke out, police advised all whites to leave, but Edelstein and another man stayed. Edelstein was not scared; he knew which side he was on. When the mob came, he walked out to greet it, and they stomped him to death. He was white.

Seeing this, Edelstein's companion thought his time had come too. He locked himself into a tiny storeroom, put his back to the wall, both legs against the door, and braced himself. The ululating horde threw itself against the door, but it held. Then a window shattered above his head, and broken glass rained down upon him. A dozen black arms came through the window, groping for his face like the tentacles of an octopus. Just when he thought he was done for, he heard helicopters coming, and machine guns rattling, and then he fainted.

Ja-nee. So many things died in the course of those three bloody days, but the one I most selfishly mourned was the disintegration of a fantasy—of my dream of myself as the Just White Man leading blacks to the barricades. In the eyes of the mobs of June, I saw little but indiscriminate rage and nihilism, and I feared it might consume me too.

There were so many of them, and they were so poor and hungry, so primitive, so wounded and angry. Their numbers were exploding, their anger mounting, their demands growing more and more urgent, and less easily appeased. I used to watch the morose, sullen mass of them trudging past my office window at five o'clock, heading for the End Street bus terminal, an endless throng of them, a gray army of black men, and I'd say to myself, It's just a matter of time. I knew who I was waiting for as I lay drunk on my mattress, and what dreams awaited when I fell asleep.

I dreamed, one night, that my entire family, all the Malans in creation, were living in a huge bare tree on the banks of a broad and mighty river. The tree stood on a vast dry plain, flat and featureless, like the Karroo, and overhung with a feeling of inescapable doom and dread. The world was about to end. Three giant waves would come down the river and sweep away every last vestige of our world.

The sky was a baleful yellow. I looked upstream, to where the river meandered over the shimmering horizon, and saw tiny boats scattering for cover. The flood was coming. As I watched, a huge brown wave loomed over the horizon and came rumbling slowly across the plain, so high and broad it was as if a range of mountains was bearing down upon us. The terror was like a falling nightmare, and then the wave broke over our heads and we were deep under the dark water, clinging desperately to our branches. After an eternity, the water subsided and we could see the sky again. An aunt and some brush-cut cousins had been torn off their perches and washed away.

The second wave took my grandmother, and by then our situation was desperate. The raging waters had churned the plain into a muddy swamp and eroded a deep hole at the foot of our tree, leaving our roots dangling in thin air. Unless we built a dyke to divert the third and final wave, we were surely doomed. So my father and I floundered out into the mud and started clawing at it with our bare hands, but the mud was heavy and unyielding. It sucked at our feet and clung obstinately to our fingers. No matter how desperately we tried, we made no headway at all. It was hopeless.

The river was growing turbulent, roaring louder and louder, starting to heave and roll and break into standing waves. It was too late. I looked at my Afrikaner father; he was staring upstream, with an "oh, shit" look in his eyes. So was my mother. She was standing on a bough high above me, with that baleful yellow light playing across her face, her gray hair streaming out behind her in the wind of a gathering storm. The last wave was coming, and we were about to be obliterated.

We are betrayed by what is false within.

—GEORGE MEREDITH

And that, my friend, is why I ran away. I ran away because I was scared of the coming changes, and scared of the consequences of not changing. I ran because I wouldn't carry a gun for apartheid, and because I wouldn't carry a gun against it. I ran away because I hated Afrikaners and loved blacks. I ran away because I was an Afrikaner and feared blacks. You could say, I suppose, that I ran away from the paradox.

How do you render a paradox? I just don't seem able to get it down right, and yet I know it in my mind. On the beach near where I live today, a rocky promontory presents a square, blunt face to the sea. At high tide, a big wave sometimes charges the cliff, climbs halfway up it, then turns and rushes back to the sea. Twenty yards out, it meets the incoming wave, and they defeat one another in a great clash of spray. Both waves simply disappear, and for a few moments the sea lies still and hissing. It is that state of . . . quandary that I am trying to describe, but I can't get it; I can only feel it.

And that is how it has been all my life, from the moment my eyes first opened. It was quite clear, even to a little boy, that blacks were violent, and inscrutable, and yet I loved them. It was also clear that they were capable, kind, and generous, and yet I was afraid of them. The paradox was a given in my life, part of the natural order of things. It was only later, when I was old enough to be aware of what was happening around me that the paradox started eating me. I'd been born into an agony of polarization and felt I had to commit myself one way or the other. I couldn't just stand there, paralyzed by the paradox.

So I fell into the habit of saying that I loved blacks, and I sided with them against my own people. I did my best to act accordingly, but in truth, I was always riddled with doubt. The instant I stepped beyond rhetoric and into bed with a black woman, I felt as though I had broken a very law of nature, and yet, thinking such thoughts, I was simultaneously stricken by another shame and disgust, a traitor's shame, the shame of discovering that I was capable of harboring such ideas. Because I truly did love them.

You want to know my true position in the revolution? Look at this photograph, which comes from *Die Vaderland,* an Afrikaans daily. Those are my outstretched arms, and those are my cheekbones, jutting out over the layout artist's crop line. This picture was taken in July or August 1976, just after the riots of June. Soweto's students had the temerity to board trains and come into white Johannesburg, where they paraded through the streets with their placards. The Boers fell on them, of course. That snarling white traffic cop with a whip in his hand is trying to get at this black teenager here in the left-hand corner, and that's me in the middle, with arms akimbo and spiral-bound notebook between my teeth, trying to keep them apart. Trying to make them stop it. That was my position—in the middle, skewered by the paradox. It was a stupid position to be in, and untenable. In South Africa, you had to be true to one side or the other, but I belonged to neither, and that is why I ran away.

As I shook Mike's hand for the last time, he said, "So you're leaving us to the Boers' mercy, hey *boertjie?*" Langa said, "You're doing the right thing. Don't come back." Miriam wept and said, "Why are you going? You a good somebody." At the airport, my Afrikaner father said, "You have given nothing to this country. You have just taken, and now you are running away."

And then I got on a plane, and ran away.

I'd sworn not to inflict further disgrace on my long-suffering father by applying for political asylum as a draft dodger, so I roamed Europe for a few years, prodded onward by the unsympathetic immigration services of half a dozen countries. Canada didn't want me either, so I wound up in the United States in 1979, with no money and no working papers. I washed dishes, picked crops, sold my blood, rode freight trains and Greyhounds, cowering in bus-station toilets during stopovers for fear that *la migra* would nail me. No, I'm not whining. It was great adventure, and besides, I considered myself a socialist. I imagined that I was finally seeing the sole of the boot as it ground the working man down. I was certainly as low as you can go. There came a day when I had no money at all, not a cent. I was stranded on the side of a highway in the Cascades in Washington State, all alone on a continent on which I knew nobody, with nowhere to go and little hope of getting there before dark . . .

Anyway—my bit part in the great drama of American immigration isn't really at issue here. Suffice it to say that I ended up in Los Angeles, where I landed a job writing rock and roll reviews for a small music magazine. Being illegal, and wary of the immigration police, I published my scribblings under a nom de plume. I, Malan, an Afrikaner secretly beset by all manner of racist equivocations, called myself Nelson Mandela. It was meant as a tribute, but still: such staggering effrontery, and no one to take offense. The ESTians who owned the magazine mistook the word for *mandala,* but they saw where I was coming from; if I wanted to call myself a Buddhist meditation cycle, they were willing to grant me my space. In Los Angeles in 1979, the only people who seemed to have heard of Nelson Mandela were members of the Revolutionary Communist Party, who called up to invite me for a beer. They took me for a kindred spirit, which indeed I was, although I found their sectarian enthusiasm for Albania somewhat baffling.

Indeed, many things about America puzzled the socialist in me. The U.S. was the world's most advanced capitalist country, and yet there seemed to be no classes in it, and no class consciousness. After a year or so, it dawned on me that Marx had been wrong about a thing or two, and I fell in with the great mass of Russians, Chinese, and Eastern Europeans who were turning away from the Marxian dream in despair and disillusion. I had come to America imagining it to be a rather diabolical place, belly of the capitalist beast, but in the end I became something of an American myself. I got a green card, and I got some good stories. I came to see a certain tawdry glory in American democracy, and a clean and pleasing logic in the workings of free markets. I even learned to say "wadder" instead of "waw-tuh," and "assk," not "arsk," but I never stopped yearning for South Africa, or wrestling with the question of exactly whom I had betrayed.

Several candidates stepped forth to make claims on my conscience. I had betrayed the memory of my dead friend Piet, and all my promises to Miriam and her grandchildren. I had betrayed the brotherly spirit of *The Star*'s fourth-floor canteen. I had betrayed my tribe, whose cause I understood in my blood, and I had betrayed my Afrikaner father. And finally, I had betrayed myself.

It struck me, after a few years in exile, that I had thrown away something very precious by leaving South Africa. Maybe it was just nostalgia, but in my memory my former life seemed somehow charged with meaning. Every day had been a battle against howling moral head winds. I had lived amidst stark good and evil, surrounded by mystery and magic. There was a witchdoctor in the servants' quarters, and Zionists danced around fires outside the window. Nothing in America could ever compare with so powerful a set of intoxicants. In America, my soul was desiccated. There was nothing to do but get drunk, get laid, and make money, and no hope that there would ever be more to it than that. I used to lean against walls at parties, demoralized beyond uplift, asking Americans what the point was, what larger significance they saw in their lives. They seldom had answers.

And so I found myself yearning for South Africa. I yearned for the reckless jol, for rutted dirt roads and lonely farmhouses; for the clank of a windmill, the sound of Afrikaans, clouds towering over the Karroo; for the peculiar quality of African light, harsh and piercing; for the smell and look of Johannesburg after rain; and for my Uncle Ben's farm, the memory of which twisted in my heart like a knife, for its loneliness and foreboding, and the blackened plain on which it stood. I longed for Wicks bubble gum, radio serials, Mrs. H. S. Ball's homemade chutney, biltong, Lion beer, a pipe of Durban poison; and for the bikini girl on the back page of the *Sunday Times,* over whom I jerked off in the suffocating Calvinist stillness of Jo'burg Sunday afternoons. I longed for Parys, with its slow, brown river and its mysterious islands, and for its black location, through which I once rode like a little white prince, and even for the endless harrowed waiting. I yearned to sit again with anguished socialists over mugs of tea in cold slum kitchens, talking politics, for even then, at your lowest and most miserable, life was a larger stage and you were on it, playing your allotted part. I often wished I'd stayed at home, or that I could go back, but I couldn't; I might have been jailed as a draft evader. All I could do was go down to the nearest South African consulate and read its copy of *The Star.*

As the years passed, the South African conflict headed inexorably toward a conclusion foreseen thirty years earlier by Alan Paton. "By the time we turn to loving," he said, "they will have turned to hating." Four months after I ran away, Steve Biko died in the hands of the secret police. In the aftermath, his network of Black Consciousness organizations was crushed, all its leaders banned or jailed, and two Biko-supporting newspapers shut down. The time of black hating drew closer.

And then Pieter Willem Botha came to power. I wouldn't accuse Botha of loving blacks, but he was certainly more reasonable than any of his predecessors. One of Botha's first moves in office was to scrap the grand apartheid blueprint, which called for all blacks to be removed eventually from "white" South Africa. He recognized blacks as permanent residents of white cities and granted them the right to own houses and property in the townships. He permitted the rise of a real black opposition and allowed the hostile trade unions to organize openly. His predecessors banned *Guess Who's Coming to Dinner* for its favorable portrayal of blacks; Botha put Bill Cosby on state TV. He rescinded some of the more odious apartheid laws and offered a vote of sorts to the coloreds and Indians, hoping to make them allies in the struggle against blacks. He started pouring money into black education and easing restrictions on black enterprise, hoping to create a black middle class as a bulwark against revolution. To pay for all this, he taxed white South Africa till it bled. In the first several years of his rule, black income rose five-fold, while white income barely kept pace with inflation. To whites who whined, P.W. had this to say: "Adapt or die."

Adapt or die. That struck me as the strangest phrase I had ever heard in the mouth of an elected leader. It sounded like the choice you'd offer a deadly enemy while holding a knife to his jugular, not a politician addressing his constituency. To someone who had grown up under the imperial Calvinist tyranny of Verwoerd and Vorster, Botha looked a virtual liberal. In the eyes of the *Los Angeles Times,* he remained a white supremacist. The *Los Angeles Times* was right, of course, but so was I. Revolutions don't break out in times of intense oppression. They come during periods of reform and liberalization. P.W. Botha allowed black South Africans a little freedom of speech, organization, and action, and they responded according to the law of revolutions: As soon as he gave them an opening, they flew at his throat.

The first township to explode was Sebokeng, which went up in September 1984. Botha was forced to send in the army to quell that uprising, but the trouble spread to adjoining townships. Soon, all the townships in the industrialized Vaal Triangle were in flames, and then the fires spread to the Eastern Cape, to the cities of Port Elizabeth and Uitenhage, and into the country districts. Relatively minor issues like rent hikes or corporal punishment in schools sparked mass demonstrations which turned into battles between black youths and heavy-handed policemen whose concept of effective crowd control was a bullet between the eyes. The martyrs were buried at mass funerals, which turned into new demonstrations, which resulted in further casualties, more mass funerals, and still more bloodshed. The uprising became a fire storm, a cyclone of violence that threatened to engulf the entire country.

South Africa's agony made riveting cinema. Black youths danced like dervishes against skies of smoke and fire. Police came trundling over the horizon in nightmarish war machines, bristling with guns and helmets. You must have seen it on television—the hissing whips, the snarling white faces, the bloody welts on black skin; the savage shotgun volleys and the crumpled black bodies in the streets. It was on the evening news, night after night, for months on end. The toll of martyrs rose into the hundreds and finally the thousands, and South Africa was suddenly an issue, a searing hot one. Rock stars and celebrities sacrificed themselves on the police line outside South Africa's Washington embassy. Apartheid became the talk of the talk shows. Mock Sowetos arose on college campuses all across America. Worldwide, thirty anti-apartheid movies went into development.

As the distant uprising gathered momentum, discreet little ads started appearing in the classified sections of South African newspapers, offering "visa assistance" or the services of international house-moving concerns. In South Africa, 1985 was a boom year in such trades. Several American immigration lawyers hung up shingles in Johannesburg's northern suburbs, and for those who couldn't afford their services, there were several best-selling paperbacks with titles like *Leaving South Africa*. The subject was on many white minds. The white power structure was under assault, and the townships were on fire. The economy was sick, the price of gold was falling, and the rand had lost two-thirds of its value almost overnight. The militant black unions were demanding huge raises, and striking if they didn't get them. And now there was talk of sanctions. The good old days were clearly over. The time had come to abandon the sinking ship.

And so there came a time when you could go into the nicer parts of LA, the whitest of white middle-class suburbs, and find the air thick with Johannesburg accents—the nasal whine of Highlands North on this side, the plummy ripeness of Saxonwold on that. White South Africans loved Los Angeles. Its weather was sunny and its bland suburbs were not so very different from those they'd left behind. Many pitched up in Beverly Hills or West LA, burdened with moneybags and full of talk about how they'd fought apartheid, loved the blacks, and stood up to the Afrikaner tyranny for as long as they could stand it. I'd look at them and think, Fuck, there's me eight years ago, lying through my teeth.

Indeed, there was me to this day. You could still count on Malan for a glib denunciation of apartheid or a telling vignette about someone else's racist backwardness. Now that everyone knew what townships were, and what happened in them, these commodities were suddenly in demand. In an odd parody of my youth, South Africans became minor celebrities just for being from there. Magazines asked you to write about the uprising. People sought your opinion on it. Strangers even invited you to dinner, just to hear you talk about it.

One such dinner party took place in New York, around Easter, 1985. The host was a left-liberal lawyer, overflowing with love for the Sandinistas and enthusiasm for the nuclear freeze. His politics were impeccable, as were the politics of his guests. South Africa's foreign minister, Roelof "Pik" Botha, had been on TV the previous evening, talking about the nebulous "power-sharing" deal his government was offering its black subjects and warning of dire consequences if they dared reject it. "We'll fight to the very last drop of blood," he swore. My fellow Americans were shocked by such extreme language. Between courses, our host asked, "What's wrong with that man?" and I rose to sing for my supper.

I could have told the truth, I suppose, but the raw facts of the matter were as remote and irrelevant to most Americans as the fact that gravity bent light. In their imagination, South Africa was a distant place where everything was simple—a country adrift from its continent, populated by caricatural white villains and black victims. They thought the struggle was a replay of their own civil rights movement, and who was I to disillusion them? I didn't. I said the easy and obvious things, the things they expected to hear. I told them about Boer colonels who sputtered comically at the thought of Jimmy Carter, about little girls banished from white schools for having suspiciously kinky hair. By the time I was done, they were shaking their heads knowingly over white South Africa's racist backwardness, and I was counting my silver. My thirty pieces of silver.

I didn't tell the truth because I couldn't. It had nothing to do with politics, you see. It had to do with Africa, and the ancient mysteries of race; with the strange forces that put me to bed with a gun and a knife and eventually sent me scurrying out of my country like a coward. The entire subject was so deeply taboo that even dreams imposed silence on me.

In one dream, I was at a black-tie banquet in some great capital. The room was full of diplomats, ambassadors, mandarins of high government and distinguished correspondents. They were making speeches about my country, about all the bloodshed. I was burning to say something. It was very important. I knew why these terrible things were happening, and I also knew the antidote, the formula of understanding and healing that was suddenly blossoming in my mind like a miracle. Eventually someone asked, "Is there anyone here from the ANC?" and I, a Boer, raised my hand. I strode up to the podium, trembling with urgency. I leant into the microphone. I opened my mouth. And then my brain went dead, and I was struck dumb. There were no words for what I wanted to say. They were lost, banned, forbidden. By whom? By the high priests of Western culture. Does that make any sense to you?

As 1985 rolled on, the procession of South African images across my television screen grew increasingly grim, and the dreams came more and more frequently. One night, Boer cops would be whipping black schoolchildren on my TV, and I'd feel it was somehow my fault. The next, a township mob would burn a "sellout" alive in my living room, and I'd thank God I was on the far side of the planet. All the old misgivings would well up in my heart, and the old civil war break out in my brain. Part of me would say, You're twisted, Malan, you're poisoned with racism. The other would counter, Screw you; I'm just a realist. In the midst of all this, a letter arrived from Soweto, penned in a childlike hand. It was from Miriam Tshabalala, my family's beloved retainer. She couldn't read or write, so one of her children must have scribed it for her. Miriam was retired by now, and living in a house my father had bought for her in Diepkloof, one of Soweto's worst war zones. This is what she had to say:

"Now I can see the End of the Earth is coming. You cants walk at Night. I can say at about 8 o'clock we are afraid of soldiers shooting at us. I can't explain for you. Such a long time I am afraid, but the only thing is that God is here. Pray for God don't forget before you sleep."

Ja-nee, South Africa, *ja-nee.* I had been running for eight years, and I had run to the far side of the planet, but I hadn't outrun the paradox. It still had its claws in my brain. I had been running all my life, and each flight left me weaker, more diminished, more deeply dishonored. Each time I opened my mouth to speak about South Africa, I betrayed myself again. I always said the obvious things, the easy things, always presented myself as the Afrikaner dissident, too noble to carry a gun for apartheid. This did wonders for my political reputation, but nothing at all for the millions of Miriams. I was without honor: as an Afrikaner, as a liberal, as a reporter, and as a human being.

It might be hard for you to understand this, being an outsider, but South Africa holds the souls of its sons and daughters in an almost inescapable grasp. History cast all of us in a strange and gripping drama, but I had deserted the stage. I had no idea what my role was, and felt I would never be whole unless I found out. I would live and die in LA and be buried under a tombstone that read, "He Ran Away." People would ask, who was Malan? Ah, a South African. And what did he stand for? He never really knew.

It seemed to me, looking back, that my life had been somehow out of balance ever since my days as a police reporter. It was the most humble of newspaper jobs, but it took me to all those extraordinary places—to police stations where men screamed in the dead of night, to tea with cold-blooded colonels, into mortuaries to see eyeless black corpses, and down a street where a black man ran amok with an ax, crying, "Africa! Africa!" I didn't learn about the paradox by living in South Africa's white suburbs; I learned about it on the police beat. The job put me in a position to ask the right questions, the questions that cut to the very darkest heart of the matter, but I'd been too cowardly to wait for answers. Instead, I ran away.

I would have had to go home even if I sold real estate for a living, but I didn't; I typed. So I typed a book proposal and sent it to a New York publisher. I delayed leaving for several months because I was afraid of being jailed as a draft dodger, but in the end I just entrusted my fate to the hope that they'd forgotten me, and stepped aboard a plane. "To live in Africa," said Hemingway, "you must know what it is to die in Africa." That made sense to me. I was going home to be a crime reporter again, to seek a resolution of the paradox of my South African life in tales of the way we killed one another.

BOOK II

TALES OF
ORDINARY MURDER

And you must know this law of culture: two civilizations cannot know and understand one another well. You will start going deaf and blind. You will be content in your civilization surrounded by the hedge, but signals from the other civilization will be as incomprehensible to you as if they had been sent by the inhabitants of Venus. If you feel like it, you can become an explorer in your own country. You can become Columbus, Magellan, Livingstone. But I doubt that you will have such a desire. Such expeditions are very dangerous, and you are no madman, are you?

—RYSZARD KAPUSCINSKI, *The Emperor*

I found myself haunted by an impression I myself would not understand. I kept thinking that the land smelled queer. It was the smell of blood, as though the soil was soaked with blood.

—CARL JUNG, *upon arriving in Africa*

Exile is a sweet thing to end, even if you come from a troubled country like South Africa, or maybe especially if you come from South Africa. There is something in the air there that the Boer poet Breytenbach called "heartspace and the danger of beauty." In some way that I can't really capture, it is a function of all the hatred and horror, all the broken hearts and the blinding hope of a healing, sometime, someday. They say that junkies sometimes put themselves through the cold sweats and sickness of withdrawal just so they can start anew, and experience that wild rush of intoxication to the brain as if for the first time. Coming home was like that.

When I got off the plane during a brief stopover in Johannesburg, the first thing I saw was a gang of blacks pushing luggage around on a trolley. They were just ordinary black workmen, blank and inscrutable, chattering in an incomprehensible tongue, but I was transfigured by the sight of them. I just stood there staring, cursing myself for the tears running down my cheeks. It was so stupid. I was overwhelmed by the most absurd of things— the sound of Afrikaans, the sight of a Boer in a safari suit with a comb in the back of his socks, the face of Jan van Riebeeck on a South African bank note. My eyes blurred at the sight of Table Mountain, at the foot of which the first Malan had settled three centuries earlier. I found myself crying in the fur of two yapping mongrels that accompanied my mother to Cape Town's D. F. Malan Airport to fetch me, and even over my Boer old man, who sat in his easy chair that first night, explaining in his painfully sincere and Christian fashion that in spite of what the newspapers said, the Great Afrikaner Reform was still on track, and things would turn out well in the end.

For all I knew, he was entirely right. When I looked out the window, all I saw was gray fog and drifting rain. I had come home at the tail end of winter. Cold winds were sweeping in from the South Atlantic, bringing mist and rain and seas that broke heavily over the breakwater outside Cape Town harbor. It looked pretty grim out there, but worse was to come. The rest of the country was burning, wracked by riots and civil strife, but Cape Town somehow remained relatively peaceful. On the fifth day after my return, the weather cleared up. On the seventh, the Reverend Allan Boesak of the

United Democratic Front called a march on Pollsmoor, the prison where Nelson Mandela was being held. The police blocked the route with armored cars. Some kids threw stones. The police opened fire. People were killed, and the Cape townships exploded.

After the seventh day, every day was bloody. If I stood on the lawn outside my father's condominium and looked south, I could see smoke in the sky above the killing grounds—the bleak, windswept salt flats where the blacks lived, and where few white men dared go. Next morning, there would be pictures of it on the *Cape Times* front page—huge, full-color pictures, full of chilling detail: armored cars trundling across the killing grounds like medieval war machines, looming so huge they blotted out half the sky; masked black teenagers hurling petrol bombs; seething throngs of blacks, rivers of them, surging through the streets, unstoppable, uncontrollable, and the sky behind them filled with flames and black smoke. The mood of the white city was shot through with dread and foreboding. When I walked in the streets, I found it hard to look black people in the eye. Maybe it was my imagination, maybe it was just me, but whites seemed constantly to be looking to the sky for flames, smoke, or signs, or searching the horizon for the rampaging mobs for which they had so long been waiting.

I had seen this all before, in 1976, but now I seemed to be seeing it for the first time, and finally understanding it, especially its impact on the white psyche. Whites seemed to draw fearfully into themselves, closing their hearts to Africa, blinding their eyes to the suffering out there on the salt flats. In my Marxist days, I would have said that the force causing these peristaltic convulsions was class struggle, the mundane drama of having, not having, and wanting; but now it seemed a woefully inadequate explanation, much too small and dispassionate to explain the awful fury of white repression. It could not explain . . . this, for instance: this picture from the *Cape Times* of a shirtless twelve-year-old with his back to the camera, displaying the whip welts on his brown skin. Why did they do that to him? In furtherance of their class interests? Bullshit. They did it because he was black, and had to be kept down. They did it because they were scared of him. This was the law and legacy of Dawid Malan. We were keeping them down lest they leap up and slit our white throats.

There were armored cars on the highway as I drove away from Cape Town, taking a route that many whites were too scared to drive after dark for fear of bricks in their windshield. I was driving an ancient Mercedes, a veritable tank, chosen because it was cheap and immune to stones. I was wearing shades, and listening to Art of Noise on the headphones. My boots were Italian, and my leather jacket came from New York. I might have appeared a modern man, and yet some very old things were alive in my heart.

Outside the city, I passed the tall, white gates of Vergelegen, the estate that was once Dawid Malan's. His old Cape Dutch house was still standing, as was the stable in which he saddled those horses on the night of August 11, 1788. A few miles beyond, the four-lane highway banked into the mountainside and started climbing. This was Dawid Malan's pass, and that tumble of stones on the hillside marked the site of the cottage where he rendezvoused with Sara. It was all still there, the physical evidence, and the intangible legacy.

I crested the pass and pressed on across the Overberg beyond, following Dawid Malan's footsteps. I passed the town where he bought provisions, and the river he crossed on a ferry. And then I, too, was drawing away from the Cape, and entering Africa. The countryside grew rugged, and the roadside dust turned red. The very cast of the light seemed to change and grow harsh to the eye. I started seeing Africans, black Africans, walking along the verge of the road, sometimes hitching. I gave a ride to a black woman whose face was daubed with a reddish paste in the old Xhosa fashion. In Dawid Malan's day, she would have smeared red clay on her face; in 1986, the cosmetic was made from instant coffee. "Nescafé," she told me.

It was weird. I was traversing landscapes crisscrossed by highways and power lines. The hard-bitten white Boers of yore were now wearing dark glasses and driving Japanese pickups, and their Xhosa foe had become for the most part a downtrodden industrial proletariat, living on concrete under tin, going to work in coats and ties or hard hats. And yet, viewed in a certain way, nothing had really changed since Dawid Malan's day. On the outskirts of a town called Kirkwood, some fifty miles short of the Great Fish River and fifty miles south of the spot where Dawid Malan lay buried, I ran into an army roadblock. The soldiers were pulling blacks out of their cars and searching them, but they waved me straight through. I was white. As in Dawid Malan's day, you could tell the enemy by the color of his skin.

I checked into Kirkwood's only hotel and went for a walk in the twilight. The wind was blowing dust around, the streets were silent save for the scurrying of newspaper scraps and the creak of shop signs in the wind. One of those signs read Salters and rang some sort of bell. Jack Salters was Kirkwood's lone Just White Man, a British immigrant who married a colored woman. After that, many whites refused to set foot in his general store, claiming it to be permeated by a *vuil Hotnotstink*—"the foul reek of Hotten-tot." They turned their backs on Salters in the street and hung up "closed" signs when he tried to enter their shops. Then the town elders withdrew his business license. Now Jack Salters was gone, driven back to England, and the main street deserted save for me and the village idiot, a small mongoloid boy in a grown man's body.

As we talked, I noticed a mustached white man in a white safari suit watching us from across the street. When I walked on, the safari suit exchanged a few words with the idiot. I rounded a corner, and the safari suit came after me. I circled the block and found the idiot still standing on the same corner, still gaping into the wind. "Who is that man?" I asked him. "That uncle is a police," said the idiot. It made sense. In the prevailing climate of paranoia, I was a suspect figure. My hair was too long, my clothes were outlandish, and I was driving a car with Jo'burg plates. I decided to play a joke on my tail. I walked on until I saw the blue light of the police station. And then I walked right into the commander's office, flashing my press credentials, and introduced myself.

The commander was a slight, gray man, spick-and-span in his regulation blues. He had a kindly, rumpled face, indecisive blue eyes, and a golden cocker spaniel at his feet. The wall behind him was lined with plaques for border service, and the name on them rang another bell. Lieutenant John William Fouche. It slowly dawned on me that I was face to face with the notorious Butcher of Langa, the officer who ordered the police to open fire on an unarmed black crowd several months earlier in an incident that became known as the Langa massacre. Nineteen blacks had died, or twenty-three, or twenty-seven, depending on who was counting. In the judicial inquiry that followed, there was evidence that some of Fouche's men had taunted the crowd—dared the blacks to throw stones—then mowed them down once they did.

Fouche must have recognized the look on my face, because he started telling me he wasn't really the bad man the press had made him out to be. He spun his chair and drew my attention to a bravery citation on the wall behind him. He won it for rescuing 104 blacks from the flooded Gamtoos River, and now they were saying he was a racist butcher. He insisted it was not true. "I believe in change," he said. *"Ons kannie met n ossewa en perd voortgaan nie* [We can't go on as we are, in ox wagon and on horseback].

Things must change. I don't mind if a black comes to live next door to me. He must just behave himself."

Taken aback by Fouche's pathetic defense of unspoken charges, I asked him for his side of the story. He started talking about something terrible he'd seen in that very township, something that had shattered his nerve. At one point, he said, he and his detachment had been dispatched to rescue one of Langa's black "collaborators" from a riotous mob. They were too late. By the time they arrived on the scene, the collaborator's house was burning and his entire family was dead, one son shot by his own father to save him from being burned alive.

In the aftermath, Fouche told me, he saw a man carve a slice off one of the charred bodies and eat it. I shook my head in disbelief, but Fouche gave me his word. I checked it out later, and it was true in all save one respect—it had happened in the explosion of rage that followed the Langa massacre, not before it. Still, I seemed to have returned to a country in which anything could be true—even the most farfetched horror.

"It's easy to talk if you weren't there," Fouche continued. "They wanted to march through the white part of town. My orders were to turn them back, but they wouldn't listen, so what was I supposed to do? What would you have done?"

The subject clearly pained him, so I changed it. "How's the security situation?" I asked.

It was quiet these days, he said, quieter than before. A few months earlier, Kirkwood had been the site of an uprising, just one among thousands, barely reported in the press. The blacks burned the township's hated Bantu Administration office, along with a few buses and the homes of five black policemen. The police subdued them with tear gas and bird shot, and scores of protesters were injured.

A week or two later, an old Boer in an isolated farmhouse woke up to find a horde of Mandela comrades battering his kitchen door with axes. He fired through the door until he ran out of ammunition. Then the blacks broke in, and that was the end of the Boer and his wife. In the months since, all the whites whose farms abutted Kirkwood's black township had been driven off their land by arson and rustling. Once frontier, still frontier.

On the night before the rebellion started, a handwritten manifesto was nailed to the door of Kirkwood's Bantu Administration office. This is what it said:

Children of Africa, let us fight for our lives. We have lost our soldiers of Africa and they were killed by white pigs. Hollanders, Sea Dwellers, etc. Shoot us like birds, because we have no weapons. Those suckers of our bloods. I mean white pigs, Boers, white dogs, why does not emancipate our black nation from under this oppression? They must packed their bags and go to Holland their motherland. We are uprising against government. May God bless you. By Comrades Soldiers of Africa.

Soldiers of Africa versus sea dwellers. It remained an equation that Dawid Malan would have recognized instantly. Nothing had been forgotten, and nothing forgiven.

The following morning, I crossed the Great Fish River and pressed on across what was now Transkei, independent tribal homeland of the Xhosa people. Through the window of a speeding car, the Transkei looked like a giant billiard table, the green grass grazed to the nub, grazed flat as a bowling green by too many cattle. This, too, was part of Dawid Malan's legacy, the inevitable consequence of a policy that confined South Africa's black majority to only 13 percent of its land.

Here, too, there was political strife. A platoon of rifle-toting black soldiers was standing guard at the gates of the University of the Transkei. The road beyond was lined with black hitchhikers, earnest young men carrying bags and suitcases and cardboard signs stating their destination. I picked one up. He told me that the Transkei Defence Force had just moved onto the campus to quell an uprising against the homeland government.

The student's name was Mandla, and he was a nice kid, deeply religious and passionately idealistic. As soon as he saw I was sympathetic, he started ranting about the homeland's "stooge leaders" and his hatred for them. "Those bastards," he said, "they sell us out like Judas. They sell us out for the money. That's all they're interested in—the money that the Boers give them." He certainly had a point. According to a recently released report, at least R175 million ($85 million) of the Botha government's "foreign aid" to the tribal states had been diverted into the private bank accounts of its leaders. Even more staggering than the sum embezzled was the Botha government's reaction to it. In Africa, a government spokesman stated, such corruption was "natural." Mandla and I had a good laugh about that.

Indeed, the entire apartheid homeland setup was degenerating into a tragicomedy, especially in the Republic of Transkei. The country's founding prime minister, Kaiser Matanzima, had recently been banished by his brother George, the new head of state. George was an engaging fellow who kept untold millions of purloined rands in his bank accounts and a human skull in his office safe. He was shortly to be ousted by Stella Sigcau, "Africa's first female head of state," who would in turn be toppled by a military coup after only twelve weeks in office. Meanwhile, there were rumors of war between the Transkei and neighboring Ciskei, another apartheid banana republic, ruled by the brutal demagogue Lennox Sebe. Sebe was incensed by the Transkei's decision to grant asylum to his brother Charles, whom he accused of plotting against him.

"I *hate* these people!" Mandla cried. "I *hate* them!" It took him hours to vent his hatred of the system in all its many forms. Indeed, he was still ranting when we drew into the town of Elandsfontein, seven hundred miles to the north. I had to cut him off, with apologies, and drop him on the outskirts of town. I had business in Elandsfontein. I was on my way to visit the grave of one Dennis Mosheshwe, and to explore the meaning of his death.

Merle Beetge came from the white suburbs of Jo'burg, from a family that spoke English and supported the United Party, the party of choice among Englishmen who secretly approved of apartheid but couldn't quite bring themselves to side with the bloody Dutchmen. Merle might not have put it exactly that way herself, but then she wasn't really one to hold a strong political opinion. As a young woman, she had been much more interested in receiving flowers from her beaux, going out on dates, and weighing marriage proposals, of which she had many. She was very beautiful, a fine-featured, tiny woman with vivid blue eyes and Katharine Hepburn's sharp cheekbones. In 1967, she accepted a ring from Jurie Beetge, an advertising man who owned his own business in downtown Johannesburg. Her husband had grown up on a farm and yearned to return to one, so he and Merle made their first home out in Elandsfontein.

Elandsfontein isn't very far from Johannesburg, from civilization, but it is a different world. It is "the plots." All South African cities are surrounded by a belt of smallholdings known as the plots and populated variously by Portuguese market gardeners, recent British immigrants who put a pool and some ponies on their land and call it a country estate, and working-class Afrikaners. Out in the plots, a Boer too poor to afford a real farm can live out a fantasy of his tribe's rural past. He can own a cow and some sheep and grow himself some mealies. He can put his Chevy on blocks and gun the engine all night, tuning up the twin carbs. He can get pissed on brandy and Coca-Cola and shoot tin cans in the backyard. If you were white, Elandsfontein was a very pleasant place to live. If you were black, it could be hell.

One night, shortly after the Beetges moved into the area, there was a knock on the back door. A black man stood at the doorstep, begging for help. A second black man on the lawn behind him lay clutching his stomach and bleeding profusely. He had been stabbed in a fight. Mrs. Beetge ran to the telephone. First she called Baragwanath, Soweto's huge public hospital. Not our problem, said Baragwanath. Our ambulances don't go that far. Next she called the police. The duty officer at the nearest station umm'd and ah'd and said there was nothing he could do because both his vans were out on patrol. A man was bleeding to death on the lawn, but no one seemed concerned.

So Mrs. Beetge put the stab victim in her car and drove him to the hospital herself.

In Elandsfontein, this was a remarkable act of grace and mercy. There were no services of any sort for blacks in Elandsfontein, you see, and no other whites inclined to display such kindness. Word of Mrs. Beetge's good deed spread throughout the district, and she soon became black Elandsfontein's ambulance driver, ferrying an endless stream of maimed, ailing, burned, and beaten blacks to and from Baragwanath. She began to understand what it was to be a black farmworker or squatter in Elandsfontein. "If one died," she said, "that was just tough. Nobody cared. There was always another black to replace him."

Many of those potential replacements lived just over the horizon, in a squalid squatter encampment called Weiler's Farm. There were some five thousand black squatters there, 40 to 45 percent of them unemployed, and as many again bereft of passes entitling them to live in a white area. Once a week, usually on Friday night, the police raided the camp. Anyone caught without a pass was given a two-minute hearing in court, then sentenced to the traditional thirty rand or thirty days. Those blacks who could not pay the fine often spent their thirty days performing convict labor on white farms. When they returned, they would laugh ruefully and say, *"Ons is verkoop"*— "we were sold"—as if they were slaves. That squatter camp was a volcano of misery, and many of the miserable people it spewed forth made their way to Merle Beetge's door.

Sometimes, she would come home from work to find twenty desperate people waiting for her help or advice. The child had dysentery; the husband had tuberculosis. The child had kwashiorkor; the boyfriend was stabbed. The father had been "sold" as a convict; the children were starving. There were problems with the pass office or problems with the white *baas*. In Elandsfontein, it was not uncommon for economy-minded whites to fire a black laborer at the end of the month and refuse to pay him his wages. If the worker demanded justice, why, they just whipped the insolence out of him. "If you go to the police," one black man told me, "they just take you back to your *baas,* and they hit you some more." So blacks seldom went to the police. Instead, they went to Merle Beetge.

In 1983, Merle found herself driving yet another severely injured black man to the hospital. His name was Daniel Molefe, and this is his story. He was walking home on the footpath that ran past the land of the Viljoens, a crude clan of Afrikaners reputed to be trigger-happy. Local blacks called the Viljoens *Baas en Missies Skiethom*—"Master and Madam Shoot 'Em." Staying with the Viljoens at the time was their grandson Tony, a draft dodger hiding out from the military police. Tony couldn't hold a job, so he whiled away the days taking potshots with a BB gun at blacks passing on the footpath. In the plots, this passed for sport. Daniel Molefe knew all about the Viljoens, but he was in a hurry, so he decided to take a shortcut across their land. He was halfway through the danger zone when Tony came charging out of nowhere, knocked him down, and started kicking him. The black man was badly beaten and complained of an unbearable pain in his chest. As it turned out, Tony's boot had fractured his ribs, and one of the ribs had punctured a lung. By the time Mrs. Beetge got him to the hospital, his breathing was labored, and he kept losing consciousness. Five hours later, he was dead.

Mrs. Beetge was outraged. She was a demure, ladylike creature, but when her blood was up she could be fearfully determined. She put Molefe's widow in her car, drove to the police station, and threatened to raise a scandal unless something was done. The warrant officer on duty happened to be a decent sort. He went straight out to the Viljoen's place, put the cuffs on young Tony, and booked him on a charge of culpable homicide. Tony was tried, found guilty, and sentenced to four years in jail—a slap on the wrist anywhere else, but a triumph of justice in the plots. To the best of Merle Beetge's knowledge, it was the first time a white man from Elandsfontein had ever gone to jail for assaulting a black.

It would also be the last, as far as the white folk of the plots were concerned. After Tony's trial, they turned on Merle Beetge, thirsting for vengeance. There were anonymous calls in the dead of night, threats of death. White men in pickups shadowed her children on their way home from school. One night, a white man in a white car smashed through her front gate and careened across the lawn, trying to run down her manservant, John Mqaba. John hurdled a fence to save himself, and the car roared off into the night. Mrs. Beetge decided to give chase.

She was speeding along on the white car's tail when its driver caught sight of her in his rearview mirror. He braked, turned, and came charging at her head-on. She swerved to avoid a collision, and after that she became the hunted. The white car chased her through the plots at high speed for an hour, twice sideswiping her Renault in an attempt to run it off the road.

Mrs. Beetge eventually shook off her pursuer and returned home, shaken. She called the police. Just as they arrived, the white car came crashing through the gate again. The police pulled the driver out. He was one of the Viljoen clan, a cousin of the boy she had sent to jail. He was drunk and stoned. The police tut-tutted and took him home to sleep it off. "I got the impression," Merle Beetge said later, "that they thought it was all my fault."

A few nights later, unidentified white men driving a white car waylaid her manservant John Mqaba on a lonely road, fractured his skull, broke both his arms, and left him for dead at the roadside.

Such a place was Elandsfontein. Over the years, the conditions of black life had improved somewhat. White liberal organizations grew in strength and rallied to Mrs. Beetge's aid. White charities started working in the local black squatter camp. In the Botha era, the police grew a little more even-handed, but still—Elandsfontein remained Elandsfontein. When someone knocked on Merle Beetge's back door, it usually meant trouble.

One Sunday evening in the summer of 1985, Mrs. Beetge found two black women on her doorstep. Paulina Msimang was a slim, pretty girl, aged twenty-two. Her mother, Mavis, was middle-aged and already stolid in the way of African women. Mrs. Beetge sighed inwardly at the sight of the women and thought, Here we go again. But she smiled, and invited them in.

Merle Beetge knew Mavis Msimang quite well. She and her family were among the multitudinous clients of her private welfare service. Mavis was a rather pathetic character, small, quite pretty, maybe forty years old, and not unintelligent, but hopeless in many respects. She drank a lot, and was deeply fatalistic. She had babies one after the other, each by a different father. When she went into labor, she always came to Mrs. Beetge for help. If Mrs. Beetge wasn't there, Mavis would lie down on the lawn outside her house, waiting for "the madam" to come home and take her to the hospital. After the sixth such trip, Mrs. Beetge refused to fetch Mavis home unless she had her tubes tied.

Poor Mavis. She and her family were short of everything—food, clothes, education, pride, possessions, and even passes. It was hard to imagine black people surviving for decades inside white South Africa without passes, but the Msimang clan got away with it. They were so low as to be almost invisible. In 1985, most of the family was living on an aging grand-mother's old-age pension. It was seldom enough to get by on, so they often turned to Mrs. Beetge for help. When Paulina and Mavis showed up on her doorstep that Sunday night, she assumed they were once again in dire straits.

This time, however, they had come for help of another kind. They had come to report the disappearance of Dennis Mosheshwe, common-law husband of young Paulina. Paulina was convinced Dennis was dead. She said she could hear his voice inside her head, which led her to believe he must have entered the spirit world. She described the circumstances surrounding Dennis's disappearance, and the white woman's heart sank. Mrs. Beetge called the Black Sash, an anti-apartheid women's organization and asked for a lawyer to be placed on standby. On the basis of what she had heard, she had to agree with Paulina: Dennis might well be dead.

Dennis Mosheshwe came from Nancefield, Soweto, and he was a polished swell, at least in the eyes of a barefoot plots girl like Paulina. He was a slight, cocksure fellow who smoked Consulate cigarettes and dressed well. He read the newspapers, went to the cinema, and drank in the smarter shebeens. He had a good job of some sort, working in a white hotel, and dreamed of becoming a big-time bootlegger, a shebeen king. He was about twenty-two when Paulina met him, and he swept her right off her twenty-year-old feet. The attraction was mutual, so Dennis gave Paulina's mother a hundred rand as a down payment on her bride-price and took her away to live with him in Soweto.

Dennis was a grown man, but he still lived with his parents. He had no choice. His parents had no choice, either. There were no spare houses in Soweto. The mad scientists of apartheid didn't want more blacks in Soweto. They wanted blacks to leave for the tribal homelands, so they allowed a massive housing shortage to develop. Dennis's family had been waiting sixteen years for a house. Meanwhile, they were all living in a single rented room in someone's backyard. Ten people lived in that room, and Dennis's young bride made eleven. If he and Paulina wanted to make love, they had to ask everyone else to step outside. Or they had to wait. Mostly, they waited.

Paulina and Dennis's dreams were humble. They admired whites, and envied their wealth. They were afraid of the police, and of whites of a certain type. Beyond that, they had no politics. All they wanted was a room of their own and one day, a house, maybe even a car. When Dennis was off duty, they often went window-shopping in downtown Johannesburg, picking out goods they would buy if they ever became rich. One day, Dennis bought Paulina a fashionable pleated skirt, and it was the finest thing she had ever owned. And one night, he took her to see a movie—*Rocky III*, where the white boxer fights a black one. Paulina's eyes lit up as she described its plot and the dress and life-style of its characters. It was the first movie she had ever seen.

Then Dennis lost his job. Paulina didn't know why. In fact, she wasn't quite sure what the job was. She just knew that he had it, and then lost it. After that, he stayed at home with her, and started smoking *zol*. His person-

99

ality changed when he was stoned. He became jealous and paranoid, sometimes accusing Paulina of making eyes at other men behind his back. Once he beat her up really badly, and she lost the child she was carrying. She loved Dennis, though, and never thought of leaving him. She thought their life together would improve if they could just find a place to live on their own. When she heard that a white man named Matthew Homan was looking for a domestic servant, she leapt at the chance to get out of their crowded room.

Matthew Homan was twenty-seven years old, a fitter and turner by trade. He was a businesslike little man, four-foot eleven, with a neat mustache and a friendly smile. His wife, Rita, was all plump cheerfulness. They had met at church. Both were members of the Apostolic Church, happy-clappies in South African slang—into the laying on of hands, faith healing, and speaking in tongues. They had two small children, both girls, and lived in a working-class white area called Turffontein. Mr. and Mrs. Homan liked the look of Paulina Msimang and hired her to be their girl.

As the Homans' girl, Paulina was expected to cook, dust, wash dishes, make beds, polish shoes, clean windows, scrub floors, and mind the children while the *baas* and *missies* were at work. Her hours were seven to five, six days a week, and the pay was thirty dollars a month plus room and food. Mr. Homan sometimes shouted at Paulina, and she had to work quite hard. Overall, though, she considered herself lucky beyond her expectations. With the job came a room—a verminous, virtually windowless concrete cubicle in the Homans' backyard—but at last a place where she and Dennis could be alone. They exterminated the bugs, tore down the rotting wallpaper, and painted the room blue. They bought a transistor radio. At night, they lay in bed, arm in arm, listening to the Sotho-language service of Radio South Africa. They were very happy.

One weekend, they boarded a bus in downtown Johannesburg, carrying packages, and set off to visit Paulina's family in Elandsfontein. Paulina was very attached to her mother and, especially, to her grandmother, the widow Sina Msimang, who had more or less reared her.

Mrs. Sina Msimang had led a very hard life. Once she had lived in Soweto, in her own house, the proud mother of six children and married to a good provider. And then, around 1962, her husband died. This was an unimaginable catastrophe, with implications far beyond the loss of a loved one and his income. A husband's job entitled his family to residence rights in white South Africa. If the husband died, his family had to go "home"—to some barren tribal territory they had often never seen. One day, Bantu

Administration officials came to Sina's house with an eviction order and told her to get out. She piled her Primus stove, her pots and pans, her blankets, and six babies onto a donkey cart and trekked sadly out of Soweto.

She had no idea where she was going. Just over the horizon, however, she came to a place of open farmland where there was work to be had, doing stoop labor on white smallholdings. This was Elandsfontein. The widow Msimang stopped and reared her children there, moving from farm to farm, job to job, wretched hut to miserable hovel, earning two to four dollars a month plus food and lodging. By 1985, she was too old and ill to work any longer. She was living in a shack on the property of a senile Latvian named Max Weiler.

In his dotage, Max Weiler imagined that there were diamonds under his cow pasture, so he allowed blacks to squat on his land in return for a little digging. There were no diamonds, of course, but by the time Weiler discovered that, his barns and cattle pens had been converted into makeshift housing, and hundreds of tin shacks had sprung up around his house. There were almost five thousand illegal black squatters sharing water from a single outdoor pump and shitting in dongas—gulleys. It dawned on Weiler that there was money in this—more money than in dairy farming, certainly, maybe even more money than in diamonds. He started charging a rent of five dollars a month per shack. There were several hundred shacks, so it added up to a nice income.

Grandma Sina's shack was like a cave, an animal lair. Its walls and roof were blackened with smoke, and it reeked of unwashed bodies. Grandma herself was paralyzed by an ailment she could not name. She had lain for years on a wooden board balanced on some oil drums, covered with greasy blankets and tended by her sullen, drunken offspring. Into this squalid den one Saturday morning stepped her granddaughter Paulina and Paulina's man, Dennis. Poor as he was, Dennis was unnerved by Grandma Sina's gruesome poverty. He didn't have the stomach for it. He had no sooner arrived than he excused himself and took off for Soweto. He told Paulina he was going to see some friends and would be back by nightfall.

Toward evening, Paulina made a fire and prepared a meal of rice and meat—a special meal, and a rare treat for her crippled grandmother. Dennis didn't show up. After supper, in candlelight, Paulina sat at the foot of her grandmother's makeshift bed. They talked about Dennis, and about men in general. Grandma thought they were rotters, all of them. When she was middle-aged, her own late husband had taken a second wife, a young wife.

Whenever he wanted to make love to his new wife, he locked the old one outside, to sleep on the cold, hard ground. Sina advised her granddaughter to make the best of it—to put up with Dennis's philandering, and to pray.

Paulina prayed, slept, and woke, but there was still no sign of Dennis. She washed her grandmother's clothes in a bucket of cold water and hung them out to dry. At midday, Dennis was still missing. So Paulina decided to go watch a soccer match. Elandsfontein's home team was called AmaZion, or the Zionists. They played in the third or fourth league. Their stadium was a sloping stretch of veld, with wattle poles at either end to mark the goalposts. Paulina was walking back to her grandmother's after the game when she saw Dennis coming toward her on the footpath. She could see he was angry, and also that he had been smoking *zol* again, or maybe drinking all night. His eyes were flaming red. As Paulina came up to him, he shouted, "Where have you been? Who said you could go to the soccer?" And then he struck her in the face, opening an inch-long gash above her right eye.

Paulina fell down, bleeding and crying. Dennis hauled her to her feet. "I'm taking you home," he said, "and then I'm going to give you a good hiding." He grabbed her wrist and dragged her off down the footpath. She cried and resisted every inch of the way.

The path wound through the veld and past a house that belonged to whites. The house stood in a grove of acacia trees. A few old cars were rusting in the peach orchard, and there was a tractor in a tin shed alongside the house. A windmill marked it as one of the area's original farmhouses, but its edifice had been tarted up to look vaguely Moorish or Spanish. From the road, you saw a gravel parking area and beyond it, a Spanish archway leading into a garden. The archway was decorated with a frieze of burros, cactus trees, and Mexicans snoozing under sombreros.

Several cars sat in the parking area. One was a green VW, and Paulina thought she recognized it: She thought it was her boss Matthew Homan's car. She heard laughter and splashing coming from the garden, and the sound of familiar voices. She wasn't entirely sure, but she was willing to chance it rather than submit to further beating. So she broke away from Dennis and ran in under the archway, shrieking for help.

August de Koker was a plasterer by trade and what South Africans call a battler by nature. He was forty-two years old. He had a coarse, reddened face, a beard, and a murderous temper. Until recently, he'd lived in Roodepoort, a white working-class suburb of Johannesburg. He had two teenage sons and a wife whom he'd reputedly beaten into abject, quivering submission. He'd recently left her for Kathy Pelser, a peroxided blond half his age. Augie de Koker's interests in life were fast cars, big bikes, drinking, and fighting. If there is anything to be said in mitigation for Augie de Koker, it is that he was indiscriminately violent, especially when drunk. He hit his black "boys," and he hit strangers in bars. Once, in a drunken rage, he destroyed someone's car with a crowbar. More recently, he had beaten his own brother half to death. There was so much blood on the walls and floor that the African servants thought a cow had been slaughtered in the room where it happened.

After dispensing with his wife, Augie and his girlfriend moved into a cottage on the plots. Augie liked the plots. The air was fresh and the horizon was open, but Jo'burg was close enough for a jol. On drunken Saturday nights, he sometimes roamed the countryside in his *bakkie,* his pickup, poaching rabbits and steenbok. If the police saw his headlights and gave chase, he would tear through fences or ramp over streams, just like a stuntman in an American movie. Indeed, Augie's new life was altogether congenial. His cottage was quaint and rustic, and when the landlord was away, he had free run of the big house, the grounds, and the swimming pool.

That Sunday, the Sunday of Paulina's visit to her grandmother, Augie had invited a few of his chinas around for a *braaivleis,* a traditional open-air barbecue. The first arrivals were Matthew Homan and his family. They came straight from church. Homan's wife was the daughter of Augie's landlord. She had known Uncle Augie since she was this high. Next to come were Adriaan van Staden and his wife. It was a hot afternoon, so everyone jumped into the pool.

Ah, yes, the sweet life in white South Africa. Anywhere else in the world, save perhaps the United States, a blue-collar worker would consider himself terribly lucky to be floating face up in cool water under a hot blue sky in a country garden. In South Africa, however, such an experience was a white man's virtual birthright. Apartheid had failed in almost all else, but at least it had put Augie de Koker in a swimming pool on that Sunday afternoon.

One of apartheid's main aims, you see, was to help poor whites like de Koker attain the good life. For years, blacks were barred from entering Augie's humble trade. Such job reservation, or civilized-labor laws, shielded him from black competition and kept the price of his services artificially high. At the same time, the pass laws kept his black labor costs artificially low, and antisubversion laws prevented blacks from forming trade unions. Under these circumstances, only the dumbest white men failed to prosper.

A white man didn't even have to work very hard. Blacks did the heavy work, and those on Augie de Koker's construction crews worked very hard indeed. One of his "boys" told me that Augie was a cruel *mlungu*—a cruel white man. He worked his gang until their backbones ached, and if it started raining at midday he docked them a full day's wages. Augie's boys made forty or fifty rand a week, but Augie himself was quite rich—rich enough to buy his new girlfriend a brand-new Mazda 323; to stock up on beer, whiskey, and meat; to invite his friends for a *braai;* and to float on his back under the hot blue sky, savoring the good life, thanks to apartheid.

This idyll was rudely interrupted around two in the afternoon by the sound of screaming. Seconds later, a young black woman came running into the pool enclosure with blood streaming down her face. It was Paulina, Matthew Homan's "girl," and she was shrieking, *"Baas, baas, Dennis wil my doodmaak"*—"Boss, boss, Dennis is trying to kill me." And sure enough, Dennis was hard on her heels, livid with rage. Paulina ran into Mrs. Homan's arms, and Dennis bore down on them. Homan shot out of the water like a missile and punched Dennis in the face. Dennis staggered. "What would you do," he bawled, "if you caught your wife fucking around?"

"Hey!" shouted van Staden. "You don't talk like that in front of my wife!"

Van Staden threw a punch at the black man, and then Augie joined in, too, just for good measure. Dennis went down under a hail of blows and curled up like a baby, crying "No sir, please sir." After a while, Homan decided that the boy had had enough. He hauled Dennis to his feet, grabbed him by his shirtfront, and marched him off the property. At a safe distance, Dennis turned around and pointed a finger at Paulina. "You," he yelled. "When the boss is at work, I'm going to kill you."

Those words bothered Matthew Homan. They preyed on his mind a bit.

Dennis and Paulina lived in his backyard. During office hours, Paulina was alone at home with his two tiny daughters. Homan had visions of Dennis slitting Paulina's throat in the kitchen, and maybe slitting his daughters' throats while he was at it. The more he thought about it, the more it worried him.

He grew even more worried after taking Paulina up to her grandmother's shack to fetch her belongings. Dennis was lurking nearby. He was insolent and surly. He called Homan a *vokken Boer,* a "fucking Afrikaner." He even picked up stones and, as Homan put it, "throwed my car with it."

Back at the poolside, Homan gave voice to his concerns. Everyone agreed that he had a point. You never knew with these blacks; you never knew what they might do when they got hit up. And besides, Dennis Mosheshwe had been cheeky. He had called a white man a *vokken Boer.* Now that was going a bit too far. "You should have brought this boy back with you," said Augie de Koker. "I'd show you what I do with a kaffir like that." So Homan said he'd fetch him.

Overhearing this, a chill came over Paulina, because she knew what these white men were like. She was cross with Dennis but didn't want to see him hurt. So she set off running through the veld, trying to find Dennis and warn him to hide. The whites were in a car, though, and they beat her to him. She arrived at her grandmother's shack to see Homan and Dennis wrestling in the dust. Homan had the black man down, and he was yelling at his wife to bring a rope. "Bring the rope, angel," he called. In due course, Dennis was bound hand and foot and slung onto the backseat of the car. Homan said he was taking the boy to the police station, so Paulina jumped into the car, too. But Homan didn't go to the police. He turned off the tar and took the rutted dirt road that led across the veld toward Augie de Koker's plot.

About a year later, I went looking for Paulina in the company of a black man named Eugene. Eugene was an affable guy in his early forties, corpulent, with a hearty laugh. He drove a sporty Fiat and wore rings on several of his fingers. He was truly a Soweto swell, in with the big boys, the show-biz celebrities, the tycoons, and even the gangsters. He knew where to get a brand-new seven-series BMW with more or less clean papers for five grand cash, no questions allowed. He had a line on some brand-new VCRs that had fallen off a truck, and there was even talk of a few crates of fine Scotch going cheap. Eugene was no criminal, though. He was just from Soweto, from the adversary culture, where the great redistribution business was an honorable trade. His own trade was show biz. He played the piano, produced records, and sometimes worked on movies. He was between jobs that month, so he came along to Elandsfontein to be my translator.

We stopped off at Max Weiler's squatter farm to ask a few questions. Someone gave us directions to a nearby smallholding where several black families lived in a forlorn barracks in some white man's backyard. Paulina came out to greet us. She was a slender little slip of a girl, light skinned and very pretty. She was wearing a light summer dress, her feet were bare, and she was very shy. She brought out a wooden bench and set it down in the shade of a tree. She and Eugene sat on the bench, and I sat on the ground beside them. Then she started telling her story, with Eugene translating.

It was midafternoon by the time Matthew Homan returned to the party with his bound black captive. All the guests had arrived by now, and the pool was full of children. Their parents had made a fire and set out the vodka, whiskey, cold beer, and bread rolls on a picnic table. They were waiting for the flames to die down a bit so they could put their meat on the coals and start the *braai*. Augie de Koker was on the way to his seventh whiskey, and he was spoiling for a battle. So was his girlfriend, the one with peroxided hair. She had been boasting that Augie would show everyone how you dealt with an insolent Bantu. This aroused the partygoers' anticipation, and so when the green VW carrying Dennis came barreling back down the dirt road all the children got out of the pool and followed their parents down the garden path, under the Spanish archway, and into the gravel parking area, where Augie stood waiting.

Matthew Homan threw open the back door of his VW, and there on the seat lay Dennis, bound hand and foot. Homan grabbed the black man's ankles and hauled him out. Dennis found himself lying face down in the gravel and surrounded by, oh, maybe a dozen whites—men in shorts, women in halter tops, dripping children in bathing suits. Augie's girlfriend shrieked, "Show him, Augie! Show him!"

At that, Augie grabbed the black man by the ears and started grinding his face into the gravel. He ground so hard that Dennis's ears were partially torn from his head, his nostrils ripped off his face. Then Augie turned Dennis onto his back and leaned into the black man's bloody face.

"A mouth that talks like yours," hissed Augie, "is asking for a hiding."

With that, he clapped a hand over Dennis's nose and mouth so that he could not breathe. Dennis started writhing, and the white children squealed in anticipation.

And now you must steel yourself, for what is to come is hideous. Paulina was speaking through Eugene, telling her story sentence by sentence. At the end of her next sentence, Eugene got up and walked away into the veld. He buried his face in his hands, and kicked up sods of turf. He picked up a stone, and threw it angrily at a tree. He stared into the distance with tearful eyes. And then he finally collected himself and returned to tell me what the girl had said: "And then the white man started kicking Dennis in the side. The white women screamed, and the white children jumped up and down. I think they were happy."

Paulina spoke again. When she fell silent, Eugene walked off into the veld once more. He pulled himself together, came back, translated. This happened at the end of each of Paulina's sentences, so the story emerged slowly, like water torture, sentence by appalling sentence: "And then the white man laughed and said, 'These kaffirs have hard heads, you know.' He jumped high in the air and came down on Dennis's head with both feet.

"And then some of the whites said stop, but one woman shouted, 'It's good! Let him hit! Let him hit!'

"And then they picked Dennis up by his feet and neck and threw him like a sack of mealies onto the back of the pickup truck. He landed hard, with his neck hanging over the side.

"And then they held him there, and brought a heavy chain, and put it around his neck, and tied him to the truck with his face in the sun."

Augie grunted with satisfaction. *"Dis hoe jy 'n kaffer vasmaak,"* he said. That's the way to tie up a kaffir.

And then the whites went back to their *braaivleis,* for this was just the beginning, not the end. You must understand that a *braaivleis* is no mere barbecue. It is a profound cultural ritual, recalling the days when the Afrikaners rode the empty plains on horseback and brought down buck with a single shot. They built a fire and roasted the meat right there, in the open, beneath the sunlit blue heavens celebrated in the opening line of our national anthem. Even foreign admen understood the deep evocations of the word *braaivleis.* In my youth, Chevrolet South Africa mounted a hugely successful advertising campaign around the slogan *"Braaivleis,* Rugby, Sunny Skies and Chevrolet." It was a good slogan. It evoked all that was finest about the sweet white life in the land of apartheid. The slogan was plastered across huge billboards, across blown-up photographs of sunny outdoor scenes rather like the one we are looking at now.

Look carefully, for it is a uniquely South African image. The sky is blue and cloudless, and the veld is green from rain. The sun glints off distant church spires. We hear the somnolent drone of faraway traffic, the sizzle of meat on the grill, the good-humored banter of mustached white men. Their bellies are slumping over the belts of their short pants, and they are clutching cold beers in their fists. Their white wives and girlfriends are in bikinis and halter tops, their children in swimsuits. All these strong, suntanned white people are standing around a fire, stuffing meat into their mouths with their hands while a hog-tied black man squints at the sun through blood and moans for water in the background.

As the afternoon wore on, Augie got drunker and more belligerent. Matthew Homan wanted to let the boy go, but Augie snarled, "If you really want to make me cross, untie those ropes." Homan was suddenly frightened. He had seen the bloody room in which Augie had virtually butchered his own brother. He knew what Augie could do after a few drinks. So Homan backed down. He went off and sat alone, away from the rest of the party.

Paulina, meanwhile, was cowering in the tractor shed. The whites had ordered her to stay there until they decided what to do with her boyfriend. She was very frightened. She could hear the clink of ice in glasses and other sounds of white merrymaking. She could also hear Dennis moaning, "Water, water." She filled a soft-drink bottle at a garden tap and tried to sneak it to Dennis, but Augie saw her and yelled. "Hey! I told you to stay away from that *bakkie!*" If the kaffir wanted a drink, Augie would serve one himself. He drew a bucket of water, and walked over to the pickup.

"I hear you're thirsty," he said.

"Yes, *baas,*" croaked Dennis.

"Open your mouth," said Augie.

"Yes, *baas,*" said Dennis.

"Look up," said Augie.

The black man obeyed. The white man upended the bucket, poured the water over Dennis's face and walked away, laughing.

Matthew Homan thought himself a good Christian, and he suddenly was not sure that his daughters should see this. So he put his family and his girl, Paulina, in the green VW and went home, leaving Dennis Mosheshwe at the mercy of Augie de Koker.

* * *

Paulina couldn't sleep that night for worrying about Dennis. At breakfast the following morning, her *baas* and *missies* seemed oddly strained. They said nothing about Dennis. Eventually, she plucked up the courage to ask whether they had heard anything.

"Oh yes," said Mrs. Homan brightly, "I forgot to tell you. The other *baas* telephoned last night. He said he took Dennis to the police. He says we don't have to worry about Dennis anymore, ever again. The police have locked him up forever." Paulina was ignorant, but not that stupid. She knew how the law worked. She knew there had to be a trial, and evidence, and all that. She knew they were lying. She just didn't know why. She was too scared to ask.

The *baas* and *missies* went to work, leaving their daughters in Paulina's care. Monday was washing day, washing-and-ironing day. Paulina was laboring over the ironing board, weeping quietly, when the telephone rang. One of Homan's daughters answered it. "Mommy," she said, "Paulina's crying."

So Paulina was summoned to the phone and asked what the matter was. "It's Dennis," she said.

"What about Dennis?" asked Mrs. Homan.

"I hear his voice," she said. "He is telling me I must go to his mother and tell her."

"Tell her what?"

"That Dennis is dead."

There was a gasp on the other end of the line, and then a long silence. Finally, Mrs. Homan said, "Don't you leave my daughters alone. Don't go anywhere, you hear?" She slammed down the telephone.

Half an hour later, a car screeched to a halt in the driveway. Out got Mrs. Homan and a white man, a stranger to Paulina. They ordered Paulina to pack her things. They seemed panicky. They were in such a hurry that they even helped Paulina carry her belongings out to the car and stuff them in the trunk. Then they sat the black girl on the backseat, hit the M1 Highway, and sped south towards Elandsfontein. They dumped Paulina and her possessions on the roadside near her grandmother's shack and sped off without saying a word.

It was that evening that Paulina and her mother went to see Mrs.

Beetge, to ask her help. The white woman gave them a ten-rand note and sent them off to the nearest police station armed with a letter inquiring as to Dennis's whereabouts. The black women had no sooner left than there was another knock on Mrs. Beetge's back door. This time, some black youngsters were waiting outside. They had come to report the discovery of a body. She put them in her car, and they guided her to a coppice of Port Jackson trees a hundred or so yards off the main road that bisected the area.

Merle Beetge had seen a great deal of gore and agony in her eighteen years in Elandsfontein, but she had never seen anything like this. The corpse was ice-cold, stiffened in a fetal curl. It was covered with sand. There had been bleeding from the nose and ears. There was no skin on the soles of the feet. The ribs had caved in on one side. One hand was twisted like a claw. The ears were partially torn off the head. She rolled the body over gingerly. The face was a mask of coagulated blood. The lips were swollen; the nostrils ripped off the upper lip.

It was Dennis Mosheshwe.

At the trial, it emerged that Augie de Koker's *braai* had continued until sundown. When Augie had finally eaten and drunk his fill, he announced that it was time to take the prisoner to the police and have him charged with assaulting Paulina. The two brothers Borman, Johan, eighteen, and Morne, twenty-four, were asked to drive the pickup. Augie climbed onto the back, whip in hand. As they set off down the rutted country road, he steadied himself against the cab and started laying into his helpless black captive with the whip.

Halfway to the police station, he ordered the Bormans to pull off the tar. They parked in the coppice of Port Jackson trees. Augie hauled Dennis off the pickup and jumped up and down on his genitals. Then he took the spare tire and pounded it on Dennis's head. Then he tried to lynch him, but he was too drunk to get the rope over a bough, and besides, the black man was probably dead already. So Augie untied Dennis's bonds, because there was no point wasting a good piece of rope, and left him there, face down in the sand.

The Bormans claimed that they had done nothing but watch, so they were not charged. Matthew Homan was put in the dock, but he claimed it was all Augie's doing, and got off with three months or a three-hundred-rand fine. As for de Koker, he broke down and cried in the dock, claiming that he had not intended to kill the boy, only to teach him a lesson. This was necessary "for the sake of the children."

I guess the white judge might have taken that into consideration, because he somehow found that Dennis had "provoked" his own torture-murder. He also ruled that de Koker's seven whiskeys were a mitigating factor, and found him guilty only of aggravated assault.

As it happened, August de Koker and a black member of the outlawed African National Congress came up for sentencing on the same day. The ANC member had been caught in possession of pamphlets and literature advancing the aims of a banned organization. That was his crime. Augie de Koker tortured a black man to death. Augie de Koker got seven years; the ANC man got ten.

Eugene and I were talking about that as we headed home from Elandsfontein. We were talking about the judge and his lenient sentence, and about the fact that the barbarian de Koker was still free on bail—appealing his sentence because he considered it unjustly harsh. We were also talking about the ANC, and wishing it would abandon indiscriminate bombings and land-minings in favor of some pointed people's executions. I am not usually so bloodthirsty, but I was unhinged by the terrible image that lay at the heart of Paulina's story—that quintessentially South African tableau of *braaivleis,* rugby, sunny skies, and torture. It was all so fucking, heartbreakingly traditional. Dennis Mosheshwe died a completely traditional South African death. There is even a traditional word for it in the Afrikaans language: he died of a *kafferpak,* meaning a "kaffir hiding," a brutal beating of the sort whites have been administering to blacks since the day we set foot on this continent.

On the way back to Johannesburg I told Eugene a story I'd read in the archives, in the annals of Dawid Malan's time. The year is circa 1825, and a British administrator is riding across a lonely African plain. He comes across a lone Boer horseman, and they start discussing the Bushman scourge. The Boer tells the story of a Bushman hunt he once went on. He and his white neighbors tracked down a band of the stone-age hunters and slaughtered all of them, sparing only five women who seemed sufficiently sturdy to make useful slaves. The Boers set off for home, driving their captives before them. The little yellow creatures couldn't keep up with horses, though, so the white men decided to get rid of them. Some wanted to let them go; others had something else in mind. They dismounted and started priming their guns.

The Bushwomen sensed what was coming, so they threw themselves at the white men, begging for mercy, clinging desperately to their arms and legs. The Boers remained resolute. They peeled the women off their arms and legs and shot them one by one. The Boer shakes his head ruefully at the close of the tale and says, "May God forgive the land."

Hearing this, the enlightened British administrator imagines he's finally met a kindred spirit among the Boers. He starts talking of love and justice, only to have the Boer leap at his throat, challenging his right to criticize. The Bushmen are constantly killing our cattle, he says. Indeed, says he, they'd probably kill us too if they had the means and the power. The Boer seems to be arguing that his people have no choice, but he stops short and shakes his head again. "Rust, locusts, and drought we have had already," he says sadly, "and ten thousand plagues more may we yet expect, as punishments for the blood which lies upon this land."

That ancient Boer understood that there would be an accounting for his deeds, and yet he was unwilling or unable to stay his own hand. One hundred and sixty years later, his descendants were shedding as much blood as ever, and God's wrath had yet to descend. Eugene observed that the toll of plagues yet to come had probably risen somewhat since the 1820s. "I can't hate," he said, "but sometimes . . ." His voice trailed off, and when he spoke again, it was to pose a troubling question.

"Can you imagine," he asked, "how many people are going to die in this country?"

The South African Police are the guardians of law and order. In spite of the fierce and unfair criticism and the mistakes we have made—because we are not perfect, we also make mistakes—we shall continue to maintain law and order firmly but fairly, and with restraint. Chaos and anarchy will not be tolerated. Peace-loving and law-abiding people can rely on the protection of the South African Police.

—*A. J. VLOK, Deputy Minister of Law and Order, 1985*

The road to Samuel Mope's home is a six-lane highway that hurtles through Jo'burg's northern suburbs and out into the open countryside, racing toward Pretoria. On the way, it sweeps past a giant military base, affording travelers a glimpse of the *volk*'s military muscle—army trucks, jeeps, and armored cars by the square mile, neatly ranked in the blazing sun. A little farther on, a gray monolith rises out of the veld up ahead. As you draw nearer, it grows bigger and bigger, and by the time you come upon it, it has become a blunt, hulking chunk of gray concrete, virtually square and almost fifteen stories tall. This is the Voortrekker Monument, intended to symbolize the fundamental values and unshakable resolve of the Boer founding fathers. Beyond the monument lies the capital, Pretoria, a deeply conservative city in a deeply conservative country.

Samuel Mope happens to be black, and to live in a township just west of the city, but he is as conservative as any Boer in Pretoria proper. He was born in 1925 in a district called Skoolberg, an area of rural smallholdings not far from his present home. His father was a tenant farmer on land owned by a white man and as such, a member of a tiny and relatively prosperous caste. His father had no cash, but at least there was food to eat, and spare eggs and chickens that went toward paying the children's fees at the farm school. So young Samuel got a modicum of education, six years of it, and when he set out to seek his fortune in the white city he was able to land a reasonably good job with a construction firm. Within a few years, he had risen to foreman. He paid the bride-price for his first wife in 1948, but she died soon after. Subsequently, he married a niece of hers. In all, he fathered nine children.

Since 1955, Samuel Mope (say mo-PAY) and his family have lived in a house on Chilwane Street, in a township called Atteridgeville. It is a township like any other, dreary and dusty, and Mope's house, when he first moved in, was the standard government four-room concrete matchbox. Over the years, though, he has added on an extra bedroom and expanded the lounge and dining room. He has turned the outhouse into a shed, built a tiled bathroom, fenced his yard, and planted flower beds in the front garden. A carport alongside the house shelters a second-hand Renault. There is a big color TV in the lounge, and the furnishings are new and comfortable. The walls of the dining room, where he and I sit down to talk, are hung with sepia-toned photographs of his two wedding parties. The men and women in them are wearing tuxedos and ball gowns, and they have the prosperous, confident look of extras in Coppola's *Cotton Club*. Through an open door, I glimpse a bed covered with a plush, satiny spread and, mounted on the wall above it, a replica of the South African Defence Force's R1 automatic rifle. One of Mope's sons is a policeman. The rifle is a trophy, won at police training college.

Samuel Mope speaks fluent Afrikaans. He is tall and strong. There is plenty of flesh on his big bones, and his dark eyes seem to weigh and judge harshly all who pass before them. He sits at the table with his shoulders squared and his spine straight, his huge hands folded before him: a proud and stern black patriarch, and a translucently decent man.

On the day of our first meeting, he was hoarse and wheezing, wearing pajamas. He had been in bed with bronchitis. He got up to talk to me, though, because he wanted people to know how his son had died. But first, he had to talk about the church, because the church was central to the story.

"The child was killed because he was going to church," said Mr. Mope. "That was his only sin."

On the wall above Mope's head was a framed color photograph of a studious-looking, bespectacled black man wearing ceremonial robes. This was Bishop Lekhanyana, prophet of the Zionist Christian Church—the largest church in the country, with more than three million African adherents. Samuel Mope had been a member of the ZCC since 1951, and the life of everyone in his family revolved around the church. He and his wife attended prayer meetings on Mondays, Tuesdays, Thursdays, and Fridays. After the Friday night prayer meeting, there was choir practice for the children and teenagers, starting around ten and finishing at dawn the following morning. On Saturday, the faithful rested. Then they returned for a service that commenced around ten on Saturday night and continued, with breaks for meals and naps, until sunset on Sunday.

Such marathons of worship were designed to limit a Zionist's interaction with the sinful, mundane world: A strict Zionist went to work or school but otherwise spent almost all his time in church.

"I don't drink, and I don't smoke," said Mr. Mope. "I have never been arrested, and I have never been in jail." He pointed to a violet in a vase on the table between us. "I am clean as that flower," he declared. "That Bible, I like it."

Samuel Mope once had a son named Moses. "My last born," he said. Moses was thirteen years old when he died, and in the sixth year of his schooling. He was a very fine boy, Mr. Mope explained. He always did his homework, and teachers spoke optimistically of his prospects. "If he did well at school," said Mr. Mope, "I promised I would make him a lawyer." In fact, Moses was a fine boy in all respects. He swept the yard, tended the garden, and never disobeyed his father, or any of his elders. "My wife used to say she bore this child for other people," Mr. Mope went on; "he was always running errands for the neighbors." Moses liked to play soccer and watch Bible stories on the Sotho TV channel, but the highlight of his life, in his doting father's estimation, was the church choir.

The boy's voice was still high, said Mope, and he was a soloist in the choir, which performed "secret" Zionist music—a music unlike any other I had ever heard, remotely akin to New Orleans funeral marches, but faster paced and martial in flavor, with snare drums rattling and woodwinds braying and the choir singing African scales that were eerie and enchanting to Western ears. It was called secret because it was not supposed to be heard by outsiders, and was never played on the radio.

Anyway, come Saturday evening, Moses would don his church uniform—starched khaki pants and jacket and handmade white shoes known as *manyattas*—and set off to sing at the all-night church service. On that final Saturday, he left home at 7:30, walking through the dark streets of the township. Atteridgeville's streets were infested with *tsotsis*, unsafe after dark at the best of times. In these days of unrest, the danger was more acute than ever. The township had had its share of street fighting. Earlier that year, the Atteridgeville Youth Congress had taken its cause to the streets, and at least four protesters had been shot dead by the police. Dozens were injured.

After that, the comrades spray-painted a plea on the wall of the soccer stadium at the Atteridgeville entrance. It read, "Leave us in peace," but it had gone unheeded. The police were still out in force, patrolling in armored cars, and nobody was really safe. Just a few days before, a four-year-old had been killed by a tear-gas cannister. And before that, a thirteen-year-old schoolmate of Moses' was cut down by the proverbial stray bullet while on his way to buy bread for his mother. But Samuel Mope trusted in the Lord, and did not fear for his son. He simply bade the boy farewell and went to bed.

Shortly before midnight, one of his daughters tapped on his bedroom door.

"Father," she said, "they've brought Moses."

"What do you mean," he asked, "they've brought Moses?"

"No," she said. "Come and see."

Samuel Mope put on a dressing gown and went into the living room, where he found Moses lying on a couch, bleeding from the mouth and nose. Mope pulled up his son's T-shirt. Blood was welling from abrasions on the boy's rib cage and seeping from a wound on his head. Mope reached out and touched the wound, tenderly, but the child flinched. "Moses," he said, "where does it hurt?" The boy just grunted, and his eyes rolled back in his head.

So Samuel Mope picked up the limp body of his youngest son and rushed to Kalafong Hospital, a few kilometers down the road. It was a Saturday night, always a busy night in the ghetto, and the emergency room was full of people with stab wounds, bullet wounds, and burns. Like all black hospitals, Kalafong was understaffed and overcrowded. The attendants laid Moses on a stretcher and just left him there. After an hour, someone finally noticed the boy. "What about this one?" said an attendant to a nurse. "Have you forgotten about him?" After that, Moses was finally wheeled into the X-ray unit. A nurse came to say his condition was very serious: He had a fractured skull, and blood on the brain.

Mope and his wife sat in the waiting room, holding hands. An hour or so later, he saw the nurse coming down the corridor, her eyes full of professional concern. The nurse took his wife by the hand and struggled to find the right words. "There's no need," Mope told her. "I know my son is dead." Mr. and Mrs. Mope cried themselves to sleep in the waiting room. When Samuel woke up, it was already 5 A.M. He roused his wife, took her home, and then set off into the dark township to find out why his youngest son had died.

The people who brought Moses home had told a garbled story about the police, about how some white policemen had beaten Moses for no reason. Samuel Mope found that hard to believe. Why should the police beat his son to death? Moses was a Zionist, and Zionists had nothing to do with politics, street fighting, or stone throwing. "You may not take part in politics," the bishop told his flock. "You may not utter those strange words; you may not disobey authority."

Samuel Mope and his family had always heeded that command. "I didn't even want to hear about politics," Mr. Mope told me. Sometimes, as he rode the train to work, the people around him would be talking about the struggle, and he would put his fingers in his ears to save himself from subversion. A man once challenged him for doing this, and he'd had to "dodge" to avoid being branded a sellout.

"My ears are itching," he said. "I think I'll have to see a doctor."

It was dangerous to be branded a sellout. Indeed, there came a time when it was dangerous just to be a Zionist. In some townships, militant comrades took to stopping Zionists on the streets and forcing them to eat the silver star they wore on their chest.

As the struggle intensified, it became harder and harder for Zionists to maintain neutrality. At one point in 1985, Atteridgeville was virtually controlled by the young comrades. They set up "People's Courts" to try criminals and manned roadblocks at all the township's entrances, to ensure that the don't-buy-white campaign was observed. In their spare time, they launched a civic clean-up campaign, clearing empty lots of trash and garbage and transforming them into parks—revolutionary shrines, really, with names like Biko Park, Mandela Park, and Freedom Square. Each park boasted a symbolic cannon, its barrel trained on Pretoria.

Samuel Mope took a somewhat dim view of all this, but he understood how dashing and exciting it might seem to a thirteen-year-old. So he had taken Moses aside and given him a stern lecture. "Moses," he'd said, "I don't want you running around with these comrades. You go to school, and then you come straight home, and you sit in the house. If you see other children throwing stones at the police, don't you do it too. We are Zionists. If it is God's will that the government changes, it will happen. It is not for us to do. We are out of the things of this world."

Mope was convinced that his son had obeyed his edict. Moses was a good boy. And yet those people said the police had beaten him to death. It can't be, thought Samuel Mope. One of his own sons was a policeman, for God's sake; so was the pastor of his church. Mope himself had spent most of his working career building jails for the apartheid government. He didn't exactly admire the South African Police, but he found it impossible to believe they'd attack an innocent child without provocation. So he stalked into the Zionist church hall, just before dawn, disrupting the ongoing service. "I want the lighties [little ones] who sing with my son!" he bellowed.

There were four of them. Simon and Ntime Makgatholela were twins, aged twelve. They were tiny, deerlike creatures with big, round eyes and legs that twisted nervously around one another. Their elder brother, Joshua, was thirteen, and a head or so taller, and their cousin Surprise, also thirteen, was considerably fatter, but they were all small boys, shy little dirt-scufflers, too timid to meet a white stranger's eyes, let alone the Jehovistic gaze of a towering black man like Samuel Mope. He was glad they were frightened. He wanted them to be. He marched them outside for questioning.

"All right," he said. "You little buggers were causing trouble, weren't you? You were throwing stones at the police!"

"No, sir," cried the small boys. "It's not true, sir."

"Don't lie to me!" thundered Samuel Mope. "You were making jokes! You were calling the police names!"

"No, sir," cried the small boys. "You can hang us if that's true, sir."

"Very well then," said Samuel Mope. "Now I want the truth, and you'd better tell it, or there'll be big trouble."

This is what the boys had to say. They said Moses arrived at their house around eight the previous evening. The boys had sat down in front of the TV and shared a supper of tripe and porridge, eating with their fingers from a communal bowl, as was the African custom. After the meal, they washed their hands and set out for their friend Robert's house—five small boys, talking about girls and soccer. Robert lived a few blocks away, on Tshabangu Street. His father, Mr. Komane, owned a panel van. On Friday and Saturday nights, he loaded it full of uniformed Zionist choirboys and drove them up the hill to the church.

The streets were dark that night, because all the streetlights were out. In fact, streetlights went out in townships throughout the country at the height of the rebellion; the authorities claimed the power lines had been sabotaged, but blacks believed they were actually switched off so the police could do their dirty work unseen. The choirboys had heard stories about "the system," and how it could get you at night, so they walked quickly. They reached Robert's gate without mishap but didn't go in, because they were scared of Robert's dog. Instead, they stood at the gate, shouting and whistling for their friend to come outside.

Just then, a brown Toyota Corolla turned onto Tshabangu Street and cruised slowly toward them. They paid no attention. It was surely a civilian car. When the Toyota was abreast of them, however, it drew to a halt, and a voice yelled, *"Wat soek julle in die straat die tyd?"*—What the hell are you doing in the street at this time of night? Looking up, the boys saw white faces and blue police uniforms inside the car, and they panicked. "We knew they would think we were the comrades," said Joshua, the oldest of the boys. So the choirboys took to their heels, and cops exploded out of the car in pursuit.

Joshua hurdled a fence and made a clean getaway. Tiny Simon ran into the grounds of number 3 Tshabangu Street, ducked into the backyard privy, and huddled there, whimpering with terror. But Moses and the others were a little slower, and the police caught them. And then . . . well, they weren't really sure what had happened then. It was dark, they were scared, and they hadn't seen it clearly. It might be better if Mr. Mope heard the story from the lady at number 3.

The lady in question was a plump, forceful woman named Rebecca Mvalo. In township parlance, she was a shebeen queen, mistress of an illicit speakeasy. Samuel Mope had often passed her place and seen groups of men sitting on the incandescent yellow porch, sipping from quart bottles of Lion or Castle beer, but he had never been inside. Zionists did not frequent shebeens. Mrs. Mvalo took no offense. Indeed, she had respect for Samuel Mope and his stern, abstinent religion, so she told a white lie. She said she was entertaining "a few friends and relatives" over "cool drinks" when the incident occurred.

It was ten to ten, she said. She and her guests were watching TV3, the Tswana channel, when they heard a high-pitched scream right outside the window. Her first thought was for her daughters, who were out there somewhere, so she rushed to the back door, flung it open, and found herself face to face with a white *polies,* a policeman. He was holding two whimpering Zionist choirboys by the scruffs of their neck. The children twisted out of his grasp and ran into her arms, but the screaming continued. It was coming from the side of her house.

Mrs. Mvalo brushed past the cop, turned a corner, and entered the alley that separated her house from the one next door. It was dark, but the man in the alley was clearly a white policeman. He was steadying himself against the wall with one hand, holding onto the neighbor's fence with the other, and trampling something underfoot—a screaming child, by God. Mrs. Mvalo stormed down the alley shrieking, "Hey, what do you think you're doing?"

The white cop looked up, startled. Such boldness was rare in blacks. Mrs. Mvalo noticed that he was holding what she called a *skietyster* in one hand—a "shooting iron," or revolver—but she wasn't scared. She was *skelling* in Afrikaans—bawling at the top of her voice.

"How can you do this to a child?" she screamed. "Look at you, you great big bully, kicking a child! How would you feel if it was your baby? Hey? Would you feel nice?"

She planted her palms on the policeman's chest and shoved. He staggered backward, shattering a windowpane with the gun as he lost his footing, and finally fell flat on his back. The child got up and vanished into the darkness. The cop hauled himself to his feet and stood there, weaving drunkenly.

The little Zionist choirboys clutching Mrs. Mvalo's skirts were screaming something in the Tswana tongue. *"Kereke!"* they cried. *"Kereke! Kereke!"* The white cop wanted to know what it meant. "They're saying church, church," Mrs. Mvalo snapped. "They're not comrades! They're on their way to church!"

The policeman suddenly seemed unsure of himself. "Is it your children?" he asked.

Just then, someone parted a curtain and peered out to see what the commotion was about, and a shaft of light fell across the scene. Mrs. Mvalo got a good look at the policeman. He was very young, she said, with short hair and a neat mustache. He was wearing riot gear, a gray-blue bush jacket, baggy pants, and heavy boots. And he was so drunk, she said, that it seemed a struggle for him to focus his eyes on her. Just then, the second policeman, the one Mrs. Mvalo had encountered outside her kitchen door, came around the corner. He slapped his brother officer on the back and said, "Let's get out of here."

Mrs. Mvalo followed the policemen out into the street, still *skelling* for all she was worth. She screamed for someone to bring a pencil and paper and take down these bastards' plates. Her sister came out, planted herself in front of the Toyota's bumpers, and started jotting down the license number. The policemen were apparently too drunk to care. "So you're writing numbers?" they sneered. "Come stand in the headlights so you get it right! Write down the back one, too!"

Mrs. Mvalo's shrieks of outrage were attracting a crowd, and the policemen decided it might be prudent to leave before there was real trouble. There were four of them altogether—three young ones, barely out of their teens, and one a little older. Two climbed inside the Toyota and two stood in its open doorways. The car raced off to the end of the block, turned, and came charging toward the crowd at top speed, the outriders clinging precariously to the roof. The crowd scattered. The car screeched to a halt.

"Get inside!" the cops shouted. "Get off the street or we'll shoot!"

One of the policemen drew his revolver and fired two warning shots into the sky. Then the driver gunned the engine, and the car shot away in a spray of gravel. As it disappeared, an empty bottle came flying out of the car window and shattered against someone's garden wall.

Once the police were gone, Mrs. Mvalo looked around for the injured boy, but he was nowhere to be found. Moses had in fact staggered back to Robert Komane's house, clutching fences to keep himself upright. Mrs. Agnes Komane let him in. There were dusty treadmarks all over Moses' khaki uniform, she said, and his hair was matted with blood. He asked for a pencil and paper, which struck her as strange. She humored him, but once he had the pencil in his hand, he didn't seem to know what to do with it. Then he vomited blood. At that, Mrs. Komane grew alarmed, and rushed the boy back to his home.

The sun was up by the time Samuel Mope concluded his investigation into the death of his youngest son. He drove home with a heavy heart. He sat down at the kitchen table, and his wife brought him a cup of tea. "No," he said. "Don't bring me tea. Bring me a rope, and let me hang myself. Even today, when I look out that window and see the garden that my boy made for me, my heart comes up in my throat, and that is how I feel."

The following afternoon, a detachment of policemen led by two colonels, one white and one black, came out to open an investigation. The detectives took photographs of the scene and statements from the witnesses. The colonels promised Samuel Mope that justice would be done. It didn't quite work out that way, though. A twenty-year-old police constable was tried for culpable homicide, but there were glaring inconsistencies in the state's case. Such things were known to happen when policemen were investigating a fellow policeman and writing down statements in a language the black witness might not read or even speak. And besides, the little choirboys and the shebeen queen picked out different men in the lineup. So the constable in the dock was acquitted.

As if to rub salt into the wound, the police came around and broke up Moses' funeral. Moses was the apolitical son of an apolitical Zionist, and the brother of a policeman, but he was killed by police, and that made him a martyr to the struggle. The Atteridgeville comrades took over most of the funeral arrangements, draping Moses' coffin in the black, green, and gold flag of the ANC and singing freedom songs over his grave.

Samuel Mope asked the police to stay away. A senior officer gave his word, but it was broken. An armored Hippo showed up at the cemetery and followed the hymn-singing throng of mourners home to Samuel Mope's place. The policemen parked right across the street from the house and sat there, waiting. There were six white policemen in the armored vehicle, mostly young, some chewing gum and grinning insolently from behind dark glasses. Someone yelled an insult, and the cops started firing tear-gas grenades into the funeral party.

There were tears in Mope's eyes by the time he reached this part of his story. "I bought a cow for the funeral," he said. "It cost me 450 rand. There were tables full of food, and hundreds of people. I asked the police to stay away, but they came anyway, and then they fired that tear gas. I tell you, people were rolling around like pumpkins. All the tables were knocked over, and the food was ruined. I just stood there. What could I do?

"And then there was no case against that policeman. My son is dead, but nothing will happen. No white man has come here to say, 'I'm sorry your child is dead.' Not one. Nobody came and said, 'Here is my hand, I am sorry.' You are the first.

"The child was killed because he was going to church. That was his only sin. I still think that if I didn't let him go to church, he would still be alive. But how could I stop him? The church is our life. We pray to God, and we are out of the things of this world. And now there is no case against that policeman. When I think about that, my heart comes up into my throat, but I am black, and he is white. What can I do? I have no power, I have fuck-all. I can only pray. I can only say, 'Hallelujah, it is all over. The vessel has shattered, and the water has drained away.' "

And so, on October 15, 1985, Moses Mope entered the statistics, one of some 750 black civilians to die in political violence in the first thirteen months of the great uprising. The choirboy stands here to represent the untold slaughtered innocents, the black babies choked on tear gas, toddlers crushed by armored cars, little boys shot on the way to the shops, innocent bystanders clipped by "stray bullets," and yes, even the legions of martyred comrades, because there was something very innocent about a black kid confronting an armored car with only a rock in his hand and anger in his heart. Moses Mope stands also in representation of the thousands injured by rubber bullets and bird shot up to that point, the tens of thousands lashed with whips, and the hundreds of thousands teargassed because they were no longer content to have, as Samuel Mope phrased it, fuck-all.

He was such a decent man, that Samuel Mope, so stern, moral, law-abiding and God-fearing. An Uncle Tom, to speak plainly. He was the sort of black man the Botha government thanked God for in its nightly prayers, one of the moderate majority, patient as a donkey and endlessly respectful of white authority. I don't mean to belittle him. Samuel Mope was a man of immense dignity and great restraint. His story unfolded in a grave and impartial manner until the very end, when his face suddenly twisted and tears filled his eyes and he said, *Ek het vokol.* I am black, and I have no power; "I have fuck-all." In his mouth, that crude word was like a fist in my white face.

And so a question arises: With the killers of Moses Mope and Dennis Mosheshwe on one side, how could anyone but a monster not be on the other?

What then shall we do?

—LEO TOLSTOY

In October 1985, I was living in Cape Town, in a flat on a hill above the harbor. On the day of Moses Mope's death, like any other day, I got out of bed and walked down the hill to Mr. Ali's corner café, where I bought the morning's newspapers. I had been home a mere month or two, and even in that brief time the political situation seemed to have deteriorated drastically. Demonstrations, riots, and police shootings had become so common that the liberal *Cape Times* no longer had space to cover them all. Instead, it published a map on page 2, a political weather chart showing the movement across the country of a dark front of violence.

On the *Cape Times* map, each outbreak of political violence was represented by a numbered star, cross-referenced to a fine-print legend that gave sparse details of anonymous black casualties in obscure places, places most whites had never heard of. Some days, there was so much violence that the stars were bursting atop one another, their ink running together and giving the map the look of a Rorschach blot. Most of the rest of the news section was taken up with stories about the political crisis and its bloody consequences. It was harrowing, and yet if you wanted, if you were white and lived in a white suburb, you could just turn straight to the sports page, and see nothing at all. I often stood on the balcony of my apartment, peering in the direction of the townships where the blacks lived, expecting to see columns of smoke above the killing grounds. I saw nothing, though. It was too far away. It was all happening in another world.

One reason I'd left Los Angeles was that I could no longer bear to live in a place where my country's agony was something I read about in the newspapers. So I came back to South Africa, and in white South Africa, South Africa's agony was still something I read about in the newspapers. If anything, it was worse, because what you read about South Africa in its own newspapers sometimes bore no relation to what you saw and felt on the streets. The newspapers said that the racial crisis was intensifying, polariza-

124

tion deepening, and yet there were times when I would have sworn the opposite was true. On their deceptive surface, South Africa's big cities were integrated in proportions familiar to eyes grown accustomed to America. There were blacks in the bars, on the buses, and in the universities; token blacks in boardrooms and executive suites; black announcers on white television; little black cricketers on the playing fields of expensive private schools; and yes, blacks at the lunch counter in Woolworth's. There were even blacks in Cape Town's municipal swimming pools. What a hallucinatory sight that was: blacks splashing in the holy waters of Sea Point Pavilion.

I had arrived home during South Africa's Prague spring, or at least the tail end of it, and there was an astonishing freedom of speech and action. The *Cape Times* was utterly merciless in its attacks on the Botha government—much tougher than the *New York Times*. The *Cape Times* published politically explosive studies of torture in detention, ignored the ban on quoting the exiled liberation movements, and openly accused the police of the most flagrant lies and distortions. And yet it still appeared on the streets every morning, bearing news, among other things, of numerous antigovernment rallies and protest meetings. At that time, it was still possible to stage such events openly, and some of them were public councils of war.

At one township meeting shortly after my return, the proceedings opened with the singing of *"Nkosi Sikalel' iAfrika."* After that, a union organizer took the mike and started warming 'em up for the speakers.

"Viva socialism!" he shouted.

"Viva!" roared the crowd.

"Viva communism!" he yelled.

"Viva!" roared the crowd.

"Viva ANC!" the organizer concluded.

"Viva!" thundered the crowd. I looked over my shoulder, expecting to see the secret police closing in, but nothing happened. It was staggering. In the Vorster era, you scarcely dared whisper such sentiments to your most trusted friends; now they were being shouted from the podium at mass meetings. Works of leftist scholarship that would once have landed their owners and authors in jail were now hyped on display stands on the floors of chain bookstores. Cinemas were showing movies that would never have made it past the censor a decade earlier, and Cape Town's theaters were clogged with black people's-theater productions of the *Woza Albert* and *Asinamali* ilk.

I'd seen both plays in America, and been deeply moved by them. They were raw, powerful, and utterly revolutionary in content. They brought American audiences to their feet and made a vivid impression on American critics. I took the *Los Angeles Times* at its word when it reported that the creators of such plays were likely to be "jailed and tortured" if they dared make their statements on a South African sidewalk. That accorded with my memories of the country I grew up in. And then I came home, only to discover that black people's theater was actually performed in the glittering pantheons of white culture, before adoring audiences of tuxedoed and bejeweled white liberals who forked out ten bucks apiece to have abomination and calumny heaped upon their heads. When the curtain fell, the audience reacted just like its American counterpart; it rose to its feet and awarded its black tormentors a standing ovation. I didn't know whether to laugh or cry. I seemed to have come home from the far side of the planet only to find myself in a lost suburb of Los Angeles.

If I left my new home, which lay in a suburb called Greenpoint, and strolled south along the seafront, I came to a place that was uncannily evocative of my old home, of Los Angeles. Sea Point was vulgar and tacky and full of brazen, sunstruck hedonists sporting gold chains and golden suntans. The chamber of commerce put out promotional fliers infested with words like *international* and *cosmopolitan.* Sea Point wasn't content to be a white suburb at the foot of an awesome mountain on the tip of Africa. It tarted itself up as "the South African riviera," and even that was a misnomer, because there was almost nothing South African about it. Its restaurants were French, or Italian, or American, like the Seven Spurs Steak Ranch and The Drug Store, or Greek, or Indian, or just dumb hybrids, like American Croissants.

The jeans and paraphernalia store was called The Mafia, the local disco was Charlie Parker's, and the Israeli felafel joint at the far end of Main Street was Kazablan. At Kazablan, you could sit at an outdoor table, drink espresso, and read, say, *Style* magazine, a slick glossy virtually indistinguishable from the average American city magazine, or the *Weekly Mail,* voice of the aboveground white left. The *Mail* read rather like *The Village Voice.* It was apartheid atrocities from cover to cover, save for some columns in the back where the movie critic subjected Rambo to Marxian analysis and the art critic apologized for liking sculpture that lacked a specific anti-apartheid message. The *Mail*'s tone was sometimes blacker-than-thou, but its advertisers knew whom they were reaching. In one ad, a property developer invited white yuppies to purchase restored houses in a semiproletarian gentrification zone, dangling before them the enticing prospect of "rubbing shoulders with civil rights lawyers, alternative publishers, off-mainstream medics and subversive academics." For some whites, at any rate, this was what the anti-apartheid struggle had become—a device by which to sell real estate to trendy liberals.

Earlier I described the predominantly English-speaking and well-off white suburbs of my childhood as glass-bottomed boats adrift on a strange and violent sea. They remained just that, but the composition of the boats' companies seemed to have changed, to have grown much more sophisticated and cosmopolitan. The whites I passed on the streets looked just like whites in America—same hairstyles, same clothes, same gleaming white teeth, and similar cultural and political attitudes.

There were Boers aboard the dream boat, too—untold hundreds of thousands of them. They were called New Afrikaners, and they were people of the most civilized sort. They holidayed in Europe, collected art, drank fine Cape wines, and appreciated the best in books—especially the works of Breyten Breytenbach, the bad boy of Boer literature. The great Boer poet spent the sixties in exile in Paris and most of the seventies in a South African prison, paying for his role in a quixotic "terrorist" plot. In the eighties, however, he won Afrikanerdom's foremost literary award and returned from exile to receive it. Five hundred tuxedoed members of the High Afrikaner Establishment turned out to witness the ceremony. Breytenbach told them that they were disgusting. He said he could not breathe in South Africa for the stench of moral hypertrophy. The word *Afrikaner,* he added, had become synonymous with "spiritual backwardness, ethical decay, cruelty, dehumanization, armed baboon bandits, and the stigma of brutal violence." The Afrikaner establishment rewarded this tirade with another confounding standing ovation.

At a dinner party, I ran into an old school friend. In the decade since I'd last seen him, Anthony had become the quintessential Western ad exec. His ads for BMW, among other products, topped their American counterparts in subtlety and cunning. Anthony invited me to a party in a plush seafront condominium, where I met a generic *Cosmo* girl named Penny. Actually, Penny wasn't generic at all; she was beautiful and intelligent. She had a degree from a white university and a job on the local edition of *Cosmopolitan,* inserting quotes from South African experts or celebrities into articles from the American mother magazine. Her values were the values of *Cosmo,* which were also the values of the white suburb where she lived. Even her radical politics were expressed in terms appropriate to *Cosmo*'s ladylike pages. "Yes," she once told me, "a little revenge would be very sweet." She was interested in vengeance because she happened to be black—or colored, to split hairs.

Penny was black and I was white, but that scarcely seemed to matter in the place Cape Town had become, so I asked her for a date. After that, we went together for a while. In many ways, my friendship with Penny was just another glancing urban encounter with just another *Cosmo* girl in pumps and black stockings. In white Cape Town, apartheid often seemed a dim and distant menace. You could ignore it if you chose to. We ate in restaurants, drank in bars, saw plays and movies, and nobody ever hassled us. We might as well have been in New York. Sometimes we stayed home and watched TV, and most of that was American, too: *Hill Street Blues, Dallas, Dynasty, Mork & Mindy,* and even Bill Cosby, to one of whose TV daughters Penny bore a passing resemblance.

The lunatic white right hated Cosby. They called him *daardie lelike ding met die uitpeul oë*—"that ugly creature with popping-out eyes"—and claimed he was a propaganda tool in the hands of the traitor Botha. According to Eugene Terre'Blanche, leader of the fascist Afrikaner Resistance Movement, Botha was trying to brainwash whites into believing that most blacks were really suave, likable people like the Huxtables. The white right thought all this was deeply subversive, and they were right. Whatever else you might say about American sitcoms, the best of them were effective proselytizers for apple-pie American values—tolerance, fairness, sexual and racial justice. They seemed to have let a lot of light into the Afrikaner *volk*'s dark Calvinist heart.

One of the largest-selling magazines in the country, for instance, was the Afrikaans weekly *Die Huisgenoot.* In my childhood, it was a stultifying organ of Calvinist orthodoxy, standing for cleanliness, godliness, patriotism, and obedience, and against sex, adultery, pop music, and degenerate foreign culture. When I came home, it was running articles on Boy George. In my absence, there had been several seismic changes in Afrikanerdom: The Dutch Reformed Church had withdrawn its blessing of apartheid; the grand apartheid blueprint for a pure white South Africa had been scrapped; and the Afrikaner tribe itself had split into right-wing and ultraright factions. All this was astonishing, but it somehow paled alongside the change in that Boer magazine. If you'd told me when I was twenty-two that *Die Huisgenoot* would one day grant space in its pages to a long-haired, sexually ambiguous heroin-addicted British pop star, I would have howled at your idiocy.

So where was I? Ah, yes, talking about TV. There was something positive to be said for the entertainment fare on the state-run network, but news was another matter entirely. The South African Broadcasting Corporation dwelt lovingly on terrorist bombings in Paris, ethnic riots in Sri Lanka, and IRA knee-cappings in Belfast, as if to say, look, things are tough all over. It had very little to say about the ongoing mayhem in the townships, though. If it addressed the subject at all, it was to blame Communist agitators, who were said to be inciting children too young to understand what they were doing to sacrifice themselves in senseless acts of arson and violence.

After Bishop Desmond Tutu won the Nobel Prize for Peace, it became impossible to ignore him entirely, so the SABC tried to portray him as an agitator, too. That was rather hard, given the Bishop's generally moderate demeanor. The SABC did its best to catch him wearing shades, which gave him a cool and predatory look, and saying something that could be construed as incendiary. To get the quotes they wanted, they often had to cut him off in midsentence. The good Bishop would vanish from the screen in the midst of a subversive formulation, or the sound would die away, leaving him to mouth silently on the screen, a goldfish in a bowl.

SABC news was hopeless. The most insightful political coverage on the state network was an American science-fiction series called V, about a race of outerspace aliens that colonizes Los Angeles. The conquering aliens could take human form, but they were actually cold-blooded reptiles and oppressed the natives in cruel and devious ways. The parallels were not lost on black kids: It was not uncommon to see the letter V spray-painted on a township wall.

As in all things in the land of apartheid, there was white TV and black TV. In Cape Town, the Bantu channel spoke Xhosa, the tongue-defying click language that so perplexed travelers in Dawid Malan's time. I used to peer into Xhosa television for hours on end, hoping for revelations and insights, but the only show I could follow was *Spiderman*. Otherwise, I couldn't figure why people were laughing, or what the plot was. I couldn't even decipher the rules of the game show that came on at six on Saturday evenings. The set looked like a kindergarten playground for adults, full of brightly colored plastic ramps, funnels, and tunnels. Black contestants in bright orange overalls and crash helmets pushed one another around this indoor obstacle course in what looked like a golf cart. The host was a black Chuck Barris, a hugely cheerful and fun-loving fellow. He yelled encouragement into the mike in this incomprehensible language. The studio audience fell around laughing. Every now and then, the helmeted contestants climbed out of the golf cart and hung their heads in a wave of derisive laughter. Then they were dismissed, and more contestants brought on to perform the same antics.

I watched this show religiously for weeks, but I could never figure it out. Nor could Penny. In many ways, she was very much like me. She was black and I was white, but we had more in common with one another than with the indecipherable African world on TV2. Even the weather forecast was hard to follow because the map was completely devoid of familiar place names. There was no Johannesburg on TV2, no Durban, no Pretoria. Instead, all the cities had African names: *eGoli, Pitoli, Tegwini.* It was like looking at a different country, so we switched back to the white channel, and watched *Love Boat* or *Hill Street Blues* or something. Whenever I saw a familiar location, I whooped and yelled, "I've been there." Sometimes that seemed the most marked difference between us—that I had been there while she had stayed put.

One night, we went to see *Kiss of the Spider Woman,* a movie about two cellmates imprisoned in some South American despotism. One was a political prisoner, the other a transvestite. In some ways, it is a movie about political morality. The transvestite is apathetic and acquiescent; the political prisoner, an idealist. When the transvestite asks why he bothers, the idealist replies, "A real man doesn't allow anyone around him to be humiliated."

That line lodged in my memory, and later, when Penny and I were sitting side by side on a sofa, watching television, it brought on one of my periodic convulsions of conscience. I was suddenly struck by the improbability of our situation. She was black and I was white, and in spite of all that had changed the city blinking in the dark outside the windows was not New York or London. It was Cape Town, South Africa. There were still some whites-only signs out there. The government schools were still segregated; the suburbs, too, at least technically. Coloreds like Penny had to vote in coloreds-only elections for a sham, powerless coloreds-only House of Parliament. Penny was just like me, and yet she had been born a second-class citizen under apartheid, and remained one in terms of at least a dozen discriminatory laws still on the books. And Penny, let it be said, was lucky.

Somewhere out there, in some dark township, a black man was being beaten to death by white soldiers, or tied to a chair and shocked and tortured.

Somewhere out there, insanely brave black boys and men were ferrying guns from place to place, manufacturing petrol bombs, building barricades of tires in the streets or setting fire to government buildings. They were no longer willing to settle for *vokol,* for "fuck-all," and some of them would die as a consequence. Even as we sat there, someone, somewhere was dying, and in a day or two his anonymous death would be marked by yet another star on the *Cape Times* page-2 map.

So yes, in the end, the question stood: With the killers of Moses Mope on one side, how could there be any question as to which side Malan was on?

It might be a little early to spring this on you, my friend, but this is what white South African politics ultimately reduce to: a question of faith, preferably blind. Those who have it do fine, and those who don't . . . well, they sometimes find themselves in a state not so very different from the one Tolstoy described in "A Confession," his essay on religious torment. As Tolstoy saw it, members of his circle of the Russian aristocracy followed one of four paths in life. Some were too stupid to ponder the meaning of life. Some found the question bleak and depressing, and drowned it in debauchery and drink. Some gave careful consideration to the meaning of life, discovered that there was none, and committed suicide. And finally, there were those who reached the same conclusion, but were too cowardly to act consequentially. Among these, Tolstoy numbered himself. He felt that life was impossible without faith, and yet he believed in nothing. Logic called for him to kill himself, but he lacked the courage. "My position was terrible," he said.

Leo Tolstoy might have enjoyed South Africa. As a white man living in South Africa in the mid-eighties, he would have faced another choice of four paths. The first path, the most rightward path, was the road of eternal, absolute, and uncompromising white supremacy, leading into the arms of the neofascist far white right. There were two "respectable" political parties out there, plus a growing constellation of lunatic paramilitary sects. In the headquarters of one such sect, the mighty Afrikaner Resistance Movement, I saw a Hieronymus Bosch–like mural that eloquently summed up the white right's beliefs: In the center of a darkling plain stood a bound white Christian holding aloft the cross of knowledge. Like Gulliver in Lilliput, he was surrounded by swarms of antlike beings—in this case, blacks—all hauling on ropes, trying to pull him to his knees. Two puppets—Jimmy Carter and Andrew Young—were flying by on a magic carpet. The strings on their limbs led up through the clouds and attached themselves to the fingers of Leonid Brezhnev, depicted as a huge, leering puppet master. An ominous front of blue-black thunder clouds was rolling in across the landscape, transforming as it advanced into a battle formation of black warriors armed with hammers and sickles. A single shaft of sunlight fell from the darkening heavens and lighted up the face of the bound white Christian. His eyes were steely with resolution. They said, "Over my dead body."

The second path was the path of P. W. Botha's National Party, the path of gradual reform, leading to God knows what end. This was the path chosen by most whites, including my family, who tended to think of it in terms of sound government and conservative common sense. When I came back from the United States, my brother Neil slapped me on the back and asked, "How's my boy Ronnie?" My brother was a jocular fellow. He'd grown up to be a magistrate, a fervent Christian, and a great admirer of Ronald Reagan's. When he heard I'd passed through London on my way home, he slapped my back again and asked, "How's my girl Maggie?" In his judgment, Ronnie, Maggie, and P.W. were all of a similar ilk.

As for my father, his politics had evolved to the point where he would occasionally have colored colleagues over to dinner, shake his head ruefully over the stupidity of putting whites-only signs on entryways and elevators, and turn snarling on his own sister when her nose wrinkled at the thought of blacks coming into her church. He would sit in his armchair of an evening with a whiskey in hand and the day's newspapers spread out on his lap, drawing my attention to all that had changed or was about to change. President Botha had removed the ban on interracial love and marriage. President Botha had offered freedom to political prisoners who renounced violence. President Botha had promised "just and peaceful" solutions to the country's problems. "By the time Nelson Mandela gets out of jail," said my father, "there'll be nothing left for him to do."

It was a sweet sentiment, but rather naive. Like an American, my father thought that dismantling apartheid was mostly a question of allowing blacks to move to the front of the bus, use the drinking fountains, and sit alongside whites at lunch counters. He didn't grasp that the only issue was power. The Botha government was committed to sharing power with blacks under some nebulous new constitution, diagrams of which always looked like spiderwebs. Arrows of black influence crossed dotted lines of black advisory input, but the myriad strands always came together in the box labeled *State President*. The diagrams were accompanied by a torrent of indecipherable newspeak from Botha's constitutional theorists, but at least one thing emerged clearly: The Afrikaner National Party would compromise but never surrender. Power would have to be shared on white terms, with ultimate power remaining in white hands. In other words, Botha's policies were simply a new and slightly more compassionate variant of the ancient Boer doctrine of keeping blacks down.

The third path was the path of white liberalism, which led into the embrace of the Progressive Federal Party, party of choice in the glass-bottomed boat. The PFP stood for Western-style democracy, free markets, and negotiated solutions—ideas that struggled to find support outside the urban enclaves of upper-middle-class English-speakers. The broad mass of Afrikaners found the PFP unpalatable, and so did blacks. Since Dawid Malan's time, white English-speaking liberals had been standing in the wings, wringing their hands, manicuring their delicate humanist principles, and asking blacks to be patient just a little while longer. By 1985, white liberalism was a discredited, impotent force. I believed in everything the PFP stood for, and yet I found it hard to believe in the party itself. Indeed, the PFP no longer seemed to believe in itself. Soon after I came home, its leader resigned, saying that he had begun to take *himself* for granted. In an explanatory statement to the press, Frederik van Zyl Slabbert likened himself to "one of those mantelpiece music boxes that people dust off from time to time and listen to with a quaint nostalgia." Under the circumstances, the PFP appeared to have become less a choice than an evasion.

And that left the left, which forked into two paths. The first was the path of Steve Biko's Black Consciousness. Most of my black colleagues on *The Star* had long since disappeared down that path, but a white man could not follow. Black Consciousness organizations did not accept white members.

All that remained for a white man's salvation was the broad faith of Charterism. The charter in question was the Freedom Charter, credo of the exiled African National Congress and its internal wing, the United Democratic Front. The charter was an ambiguous, poetic document, open to almost any interpretation. Its opening line was "The people shall govern!" and it went on to state that the doors of learning would be thrown open, the land shared by those who worked it, and gold revenues by those who mined it. Liberals thought it a liberal tract, social democrats believed it reflected their agenda, and hard-line Marxist-Leninists saw nothing in it to contradict their point of view. To the extent that there was an agreed-upon canon, it consisted of this: Nelson Mandela is "our father," the ANC is our movement, and we stand for black rule in some sort of socialist state.

Those friends of my youth who had stayed in the country had for the most part evolved into Charterists. Susie was a doctor in a township clinic. She and her husband were founding members of the left-leaning National Medical and Dental Association, committed to "bringing the medical profession directly into the liberation struggle." In practice, this translated into digging bird shot out of the flesh of black teenagers without reporting the injuries to the police. Vasi had become a civil rights lawyer, suing the bastards when they ill-treated detainees. Most of the others had become journalists, dedicated to recording police atrocities with their notebooks and cameras, and at least one literally had abandoned the pen for the sword and joined the military wing of the exiled ANC. This was Faye, the radical feminist from my crime-reporter days. She was awaiting trial in a neighboring country for possession of Soviet ammunition.

Another figure from those times, the Belgian girl with whom I once shared my slum flat, had recently returned from Europe and thrown herself into "people's education," a critical front in the struggle. Joji had been away almost as long as I had. She'd spent seven years in Europe, earning a philosophy degree from the Free University of Brussels. In Europe, she'd become a Green, and if there was no Green on the ballot she voted for the Communist candidate. She was working for an organization called SACHED, the South African Council for Higher Education. Her boss, Neville Alexander, was a Trotskyite intellectual and a former political prisoner. If his faction of the left triumphed, Alexander hoped to become minister of education. He was readying himself for that day by drawing up alternative school syllabi, free of racist indoctrination and capitalist distortions of history. Joji was one of a team of researchers and writers working on the project.

She cast herself as a white radical, but her politics were a matter of emotion rather than science. She hated rockspiders, hated apartheid, and had "a good vibe with the Afs." She told me that she could see in their eyes, as they passed on the street, that they were friendly and kind. Earthy and pagan, too, and those were qualities she admired tremendously. She loved dancing and drinking, and cloaked herself in an aura of primal womanhood, which made her, at least in her own mind, a natural ally of Africans: They were also unfettered by the restraints of bourgeois white convention.

Joji lived in Tamboerskloof, an aging Cape Town suburb where rents were low and the atmosphere vaguely bohemian. She shared an apartment and had only one room to herself, but it was a pleasant room—full of flowers, sprigs of wild grass, and seashells—with a view of the gray slopes of Table Mountain. She slept on the floor, on a mattress covered by a colorful cloth called a *kikoi*, from East Africa. Another *kikoi* was draped across the ceiling. She had a huge collection of African music on tape, and danced in the African style, with bent knees, stiff torso, and much thrusting back and forth of the hips and derriere. With her African beads flying and African bracelets jingling, her skin burned dark by the sun, her green eyes closed, and her body moving to the hypnotic beat of the music, she looked almost African. In fact, she once told me that in some reach of her soul, she was African. She felt as though the African sun had touched her, and the rawness of it infiltrated her blood.

That was a pretty common sentiment in our circle of hell, which was the same circle as ever, the circle of bourgeois leftists, white-suburban division. It was hip to call yourself a white African and even to assume an African first name. East African *kikoi*s were in, as were car-tire sandals, African music, African jewelry, African political leaders, and the authentic pronunciation of the word itself, as in AAH-free-kah. All this struck me as a rite of sympathetic magic, performed in the hope that it would somehow make its practitioners less white, less complicit. It was silly, and yet it went much deeper than mere affectation. It was harder than ever to be white and conscious, now that things were coming to a head and blacks were being slaughtered in the townships. Many young whites genuinely yearned to shed their whiteness and the unbearable freight of bullshit and guilt that came with it.

There were so many white Africans that they had their own national magazine, a sort of bush-league *Rolling Stone* called *Vula*. *Vula*'s basic philosophy was fuck apartheid, let's dance, and it celebrated the jol, of which I have already spoken. The magazine was an odd mix of rock and politics, given to fanlike adulation of the new black heroes, and to covering political rallies as if they were rock and roll shows. In its pages, a young white writer once described the way he felt while watching the comrades dance at some rally, their black faces glistening with sweat, their feet thudding in unison, chanting the litany of the ANC's mightiest blows against the white system. I longed to be black, he said; I longed so bad that I trembled. But when the euphoria wore off and the music died away, he was still white, and doomed to play a supporting role in the revolution.

For many white Africans, that role was cultural intervention, arising from the idea that art should be subversive, and that artists played an important role in the struggle. To this, my friend Joji added amen. She was a member of Teenage Botha, an avant-garde rock band that was featured occasionally in the pages of *Vula*. Teenage Botha's songs bristled with cryptic references to the "violent riddle" of life in a country they described as "the penis of the West," whatever that meant. At some point in their show, they invited the audience on stage to talk dirty into the microphone. White kids in black leather would leap up and spit out the utterances or even just the names of Afrikaner cabinet ministers, and the winner would be awarded a funny hat. This was considered subversive, but the secret police were quite tolerant of white cultural intervention. Teenage Botha was silenced only once, when the guy next door to a party called the police to complain about the noise.

So yes, Joji had her frivolous side, but on Monday mornings she put her face on straight and returned to her chosen site of struggle. In fairness, her cause was a noble one. Some South African high-school history textbooks still referred to apartheid as a "final solution" based on "the Christian principles of right and justice." People who disagreed too strongly were still likely to find the secret police breathing down their neck, but Joji took it all in stride. She was a battle-hardened activist. In her student days in Brussels, her vanguard organization occupied a building on the campus of the Free University and turned it into a "people's" school of architecture. They managed to hold the building for months, and Joji was right there in the front line, clawing at the eyes of riot policemen or whatever. Her friends in Europe didn't understand why she wasn't at the barricades in South Africa, doing the same thing. She had always proclaimed her hatred for apartheid, and yet they never saw her among those black demonstrators and rioters on television, and her letters never mentioned taking part in "direct action" against the system. How come? Had she gone soft, or what?

It was difficult to explain to outsiders, especially if you were a socialist who endorsed liberatory violence and the historical inevitability of revolution. All the anti-apartheid resistance organizations were essentially socialist in orientation, but it was the whites who were the most dogmatic, the most prone to dotting *i*'s, crossing *t*'s, and enforcing doctrinal purity. You might find this puzzling, since whites had the most to lose in a socialist redistribution, but it made complete sense to a white South African. Whites who surrendered their claims to class privilege gained something infinitely more precious in return: relief from the guilt and complicity that preyed on their minds like a nightmare.

It was impossible to change race, you see, and almost completely pointless to be a liberal. As far as the black resistance was concerned, liberal democrats of Helen Suzman's ilk and racists like P. W. Botha were just different teeth in the same white mouth. "They help crush the food for the same throat," opined *Sechaba,* journal of the ANC. There was only one avenue of escape from this awful maw and it lay in the embrace of socialism.

First step on the road to redemption was to convince yourself that South Africa was being torn apart by class struggle, not race war. The second was to move into alignment with the black working class and its self-proclaimed vanguard, the nonracial, socialist ANC. Beyond that point, you were born again. South Africa became a country where enemies were determined by class alliance, not race, and since you were allied in theory to the black proletariat, your whiteness was theoretically irrelevant—an enormously comforting thought in an agony of racial polarization. In the eighties, socialism became the political religion of choice among younger and better-educated members of South Africa's white suburban aristocracy, a sort of opium of the elite. It numbed you pretty effectively so long as you stayed in your glass-bottomed boat.

As the center withered and white liberals became figures of ridicule, the boat took a sharp leftward turn. In a way, this was deeply heartening. In my youth, I prayed for a political realignment that would smash the racial monoliths and deposit substantial numbers of whites on the black side. This wouldn't have solved South Africa's problems, but it would at least have transformed the struggle into a political one. The alternative, as our late leader Vorster put it in a rare moment of lucidity, was too ghastly to contemplate: a war in which we slaughtered one another on the indiscriminate basis of race. In my first few months back home, it seemed to me that such a realignment was truly coming about. In my circle of hell, at any rate, everyone was jumping up and down and yelling hallelujah for the struggle. I should have been pleased, but I felt as if I were an atheist at a revival meeting; I longed to join in, but I was crippled with doubt. In order to be saved, it seemed to me that all I had to do was shout "I am saved! Hallelujah! Down with apartheid! Viva socialism!"

I tried it a few times, but it didn't work for me. I even joined the United Democratic Front's abortive march on Pollsmoor Prison, to deliver a message to Nelson Mandela. The black part of that march turned into a bloody street battle between police and protesters, but the white part was a sad affair. A few thousand scared and indecisive students gathered in the Great Hall of Cape Town's ivy-covered liberal university. There was a great deal of talk from the podium about "building socialism" and "demonstrating solidarity with the masses." Then we set off on the march, having agreed in advance that if the police insisted, we would turn back, so as to live to build socialism another day. There was some halfhearted singing of freedom songs, but they sounded a little silly in English, and lame in the throats of whites. Besides, hardly anyone knew the words.

And so, mumble-singing, we trooped half-heartedly down to the highway. A senior police officer and a handful of constables met us at the university's gates and warned us not to look for trouble, so we turned around and marched back up the hill again. After lunch, a small band of diehards decided to go it alone in a placard demonstration along the highway that skirted the campus. Such demonstrations were an old student tradition in white Cape Town, a ritualized pas de deux in which both sides could be counted upon to follow their assigned steps. Students lined up on one side of De Waal Drive, cops on the other. Sometimes, though not always, the police would disperse the demonstrators with a baton charge, but nobody was ever seriously hurt. The South African Police didn't kill white students, and white students never tried to kill them.

That afternoon's demonstration proceeded as choreographed. We waved signs in the air, cops glowered from the far side of the road. We refused to disperse, so they gratified us with a few rounds of teargas, and that was the end of that. The white left had fought apartheid, and now we were free to go home and crane our necks in the direction of the townships in search of smoke we could never see. We all hated apartheid, but when the chips were down, and it was high noon on the township streets, and the killing started, there were no whites on the black side of the barricades. None. Ever.

It was a Saturday in Cape Town, and we were "going in." That is how reporters put it: They always said, "We're going in today," and I always thought, That's a line from a John Wayne war movie, although I couldn't remember which one. Today, we were going in to cover the mass funeral of the Guguletu Seven, seven black men killed in a shoot-out ten days or so earlier. The South African Police had apparently got wind of an ANC hit squad in town, planning to ambush a van ferrying black cops home after their shift. The police laid an ambush for the ambushers. In the ensuing gun battle, seven black men were shot dead, and one white cop was cut up by flying fragments of a Soviet-made grenade.

In the aftermath, witnesses claimed to have seen white policemen walk over to two of the wounded and blow them away in cold blood. Worse yet, in the eyes of the *Cape Times,* at least two innocent bystanders appeared to have been caught in the cross fire. One of the dead black men was retarded, another a peace-loving Rasta who'd never evinced the slightest interest in the struggle. The police insisted that all seven dead men were trained terrorists, but then the South African Police constantly talked shit. So there was a hue and cry in the opposition press about the slaughter of innocents, and at least twenty-five thousand wrathful blacks were expected to turn out to bury their martyrs.

It was hard to predict how the day would turn out. A few months earlier, there would have been no question at all: The funeral would have ended in another bloodbath. The burial of martyrs was usually preceded by twenty-four hours of mourning, singing, and speech making. By the time the flag-draped coffin was lowered into the grave, the comrades were primed for battle, and the police could almost always be relied upon to provide a provocation. They would fire tear gas into the crowd, or order the group to disperse, and then the shit would hit the fan, with the unarmed crowd hurling itself at armored cars in a suicidal fury of grief, rage, and frustration. At such times, white skin became a grave liability in the townships.

The only white civilians who dared venture into riot situations were reporters and cameramen, and they went in on journalistic commando raids, driving fast cars, preferably rented ones. The model of choice was a BMW with a sunroof. In a sun-roofed BMW, a white reporter could shoot photographs and footage without setting foot in black South Africa, and make a quick getaway if necessary.

Some news crews plastered their cars with "foreign press" signs and wore T-shirts bearing the same message in English and two African languages. This was a brave gamble, because apartheid's riot police hated the foreign press, and clearly drooled at the prospect of a few foreign correspondents falling victim to stray bullets. Still, it was better to court danger from that quarter than abandon yourself to the mercy of the mob. Those foreign press signs were intended to say, We're on your side; we're here to amplify your cry of freedom, and document your terrible suffering, but sometimes the message failed to get through. At the height of the battle of Cape Town, in September 1985, a car seldom lasted longer than a day. At sunset, you returned it bent and dented, and in the morning you hired a replacement. It got so bad that some car-hire agencies stopped renting to news organizations. In those harrowing times, going in was like jumping from a plane, or clambering out of a Flanders trench into the teeth of a machine-gun gale.

In the months since, the tension had ebbed somewhat, but still, you never knew; you never knew. That very week, a BBC TV crew had driven into a roadblock of boulders and oil drums in a township called Duncan Village. Some five hundred black children sealed off the road behind them and closed in on the trapped BBC car. And then the stoning started. Every window in the car was shattered, but the newsmen couldn't move. Panic-stricken, they rammed the car up the pavement, across a gutter, and limped away on flat tires, nursing cuts and bruises. Yet another rental car wrecked.

My companion on this trip to the front line was Victor Mallet, Reuters' Cape Town correspondent. He was a rosy-cheeked, dark-haired English lad, twenty-five years old, the scion of a foreign service family and a graduate of Oxford. On our way in, we were ruminating on South Africa's unique occupational hazards and worrying about the day ahead. I had been stoned a few times, but Victor was a veteran. He'd been in the thick of it since the uprising started and had had several close shaves. In the aftermath of the Langa massacre, for instance, he had himself smuggled through a police roadblock in the trunk of a Reuters car. Just inside the seething township, the car ran into a mob. Victor's black driver fled, and the crowd started rocking the car as a prelude to burning it. At this, Victor popped out of the trunk, grinning nervously and waving his foreign press credentials. The blacks weren't much impressed. They were holding Victor by the scruff of his neck and pondering what to do with him when a passing black reporter came to his rescue. "These days," Victor concluded, "I avoid going in unless it's absolutely necessary."

By now, we were crossing the buffer zone, the stretch of industrial wasteland that isolates black Guguletu from white Cape Town, and I found myself wishing that Victor hadn't told that story. This modern no-man's-land was strewn with garbage and the hulks of rusting cars, but it fulfilled exactly the same function as the buffer zone that separated the Boers and Xhosa in Dawid Malan's day. As we neared the township, the old psychic toxins started flooding my brain, and my viscera began to churn uneasily. By the time we entered the township itself, I was lighting my next cigarette on the butt of the one I'd just finished.

The auspices seemed favorable, however. The streets of Guguletu were calm this morning: no angry crowds, no smoke in the sky, no barricades of burning tires. We wove our way through the maze of boxlike houses to the football stadium, where the funeral would take place. The ceremony wasn't due to start for another hour or two, so Victor and I joined the knot of white reporters and cameramen loitering outside the stadium gates. The *Washington Post* was there, and the BBC, *Libération,* the *Miami Herald,* Reuters, some German news agency, *ITN,* the *Cape Times,* the *Cape Argus,* and a dozen or so scribes I didn't recognize.

CBS News was represented by Allen Pizzey, an amiable Canadian who had been in South Africa for fifteen years. In my days as a lowly crime reporter, he held a glamorous job on *The Star*'s Africa News Service. I had not forgotten Allen Pizzey. In the final year of my American exile, I saw his face on Dan Rather's newscast almost every night, talking about the latest apartheid atrocity, about the hideous injustice and unfairness of it all. Pizzey and I stood together for a while, talking about the old days and watching the passing show.

Blacks were streaming into the stadium. One of them, an old man, detached himself from the passing throng and approached the knot of white pressmen. He halted five yards from us and started railing like an Old Testament prophet. "We are not fooled!" he shouted. "We know how you live, with your cars, your big houses, your swimming pools!" The passing stream slowed to a halt, and several hundred black faces turned toward us. The white press fell silent. "I am sorry for you," the old man yelled. "You will die! I am sorry for you!" He was unsteady on his feet, drunk on liquor and hatred. The white press stared variously at the dust, at the scudding clouds, at their shoes and watches. It was one of those exquisite South African moments. It seemed unwise to meet the old man's fiery eyes, or to say anything at all. Eventually, a marshal came to the rescue and led our tormentor away.

The day was warming up, and the crowd was growing. The forbidden black, green, and gold colors of the outlawed African National Congress were everywhere: on streaming flags, on banners, in scarves, on lapel pins, and on the epaulets of the black marshals, who looked like so many Che Guevaras in their black berets and khaki fatigues. Inside, an army of young comrades was raising dust on the floor of the stadium. They were dancing the *toi,* the township war dance, running on the spot, their feet thundering in unison. They were cradling imaginary mortars, bazookas, and AK-47s in their arms and singing war songs about soldiers coming to free them. A tiny black tyke led them through a call-and-response routine. In America, such a boy would have been playing video games, but here he was already a soldier, smiting the sky with his tiny fists, puffing out his child's cheeks and howling, "Harrrrrrrrrrrrrrr," in electrifying imitation of a machine gun.

You'd have had to be dead of heart to remain unmoved by such a crowd, by its passion and its sense of invincible righteousness. I was moved, all right—toward confusion. Part of my heart was with them, but my own surname kept cropping up in the chanted litany of those who would one day die. The reference was to General Magnus Malan, minister of defense, but another song broadened to include me. Its refrain ran, *"Gibela pezul qwenthlu abatchela, Jabula maní shaya amaBunu"*—"I climb up on the roof and shout it out, my mother is happy when I hit a Boer." My heart always sank when I heard that song.

I was still chatting with Pizzey when a column of black women rounded a corner and bore down on us, dancing and singing their way toward the funeral. This was the contingent of the United Woman's Congress. The sisters were wearing uniforms and berets, jogging along in tight formation. Running abreast of them was a gawky white girl, a student by the look of her, wearing jeans and thick glasses, hair tied back in a sensible bun. She was trying to insinuate herself into the packed black ranks. She was smiling nervously, waving her fist in the sky, and copying the black sisters' steps, but there was no room for her in the formation. Pizzey and I turned to stare at her. "Oh, baby," chuckled the CBS News correspondent, "when the day comes, you'll still be whitey."

When the day comes, you'll still be whitey. Here was a fine how do you do. I was gifted by a vision of Dan Rather saying, "In South Africa, some whites are stupid enough to believe in civil rights and democracy, and think they can change sides in a race war. Allen Pizzey has the story." The image was so absurd that I found myself chuckling along with the Canadian newsman. In truth, I tended to agree: Baby was a little ridiculous. Whatever her politics, Baby remained whitey when the chips were down, which is why there were never any whites at the burning barricades. If you were white in the wrong place at the wrong time, you were a target.

It seemed entirely fitting that the comrades should stone me, given my advanced degree of genetic complicity and my secret racist heresies, but most victims seemed to deserve better. It was never the bad guys, the Augie de Kokers, who got into trouble in the townships. It was almost always one of the tiny, tiny minority of whites who were willing to break the unwritten rules that governed everyone else. An idealistic foreign doctor who came to South Africa to work in a black hospital was knocked off his motorcycle in Soweto and set upon by a mob armed with steel fence poles. A kindly white woman taking her servant home to the township of Sebokeng ran into a mob that put a brick through her window, killing her baby. In Cape Town, a building contractor's willingness to spare his black laborers a long walk home cost him his life—his pickup crashed in a hailstorm of stones, and a mob beat him to death. And in a small Free State town called Parys, going into the township cost my Uncle John his certainties.

Uncle John was certain that blacks loved him. As you may recall, he was one of the few adults in my childhood who actually *saw* blacks, who shook their hands and treated them like men. My uncle was an old man now, but he still had his shop on Dolf Street, his "boys," and his black friends. All that had really changed was the nature of his handshake. When blacks bounded into his shop to buy something or just to say hello, Uncle John greeted them with the elaborate handclasp of black power and solidarity. He still voted for Botha, and I doubt he knew that the handshake had vaguely subversive connotations. He wasn't a leftist or anything, just a thoroughly decent old man whose view was not obscured by fear, not even when the uprising started and unrest broke out in the township on the far side of the railway tracks. He still crossed the bridge to deliver gas to black customers or to confer with black men who'd served alongside him in South Africa's forces during World War II. They had become old men, too, but the government was sometimes sticky about granting them their veterans' pensions. So my uncle often went into the township to help some struggling old comrade-in-arms draft his proof-of-service petition.

On one such excursion, he saw a crowd of uniformed black schoolchildren on the road ahead. They seemed to be waving at him. He was accustomed to being waved down for a friendly chat, so he slowed as he neared them, rolled down his window, and leaned out to greet them. And that is why their stones caught him full in the face.

My uncle was lucky. His face and forehead were badly cut, and every window of his pickup was shattered, but he survived. At dawn the next morning, Africans started knocking on the door of his home to say how sorry they were. By sunset, my uncle's spirits had revived somewhat, but the incident left *me* deeply dismayed.

I mean, *nobody* was exempt from the law of genetic complicity, not even foreign dignitaries. Around that time, the recently deposed socialist prime minister of France, Laurent Fabius, and his former minister of culture, Jack Lang, visited South Africa at Bishop Tutu's invitation. They had come, as Fabius put it, "to support the fight against apartheid," but that was more easily said than done. In Johannesburg, Alexandra township had become so dangerous for whites that the Frenchmen couldn't set foot in it. In Cape Town, they were bold enough to actually go in. Unfortunately, the comrades of Old Crossroads didn't recognize eminent socialists on sight. They saw whites in a van, so they stoned it. Later, standing beside their shattered vehicle and looking somewhat shaken, Fabius and Lang said thank you. "I'm pleased I had this experience," Fabius told the press, "because I can now understand the level of frustration and anger in this country." At that, the Frenchmen boarded an airliner and flew away, trailing the usual high-sounding denunciations of apartheid.

It seemed to me that they'd left a rather haunting question unanswered: How did you fight apartheid and build a just society if the people you were doing it for stoned you because your skin was white? White Charterists looked at me as though I were insane for even asking, let alone harping on the question the way I did. I couldn't help myself, though. It seemed a central fact of political life. Whites were clinging to power because they were apprehensive about blacks' intentions toward them, and events like Fabius's stoning reinforced and intensified those fears. Most whites were so afraid of Africans that they never went anywhere near the townships, not even in peacetime. They crossed the road when they saw Africans coming, or locked the doors of their cars. They were so scared that they wouldn't even attend professional soccer matches in the secure heart of white Johannesburg because they knew blacks would be present in large numbers. White Charterists mocked and scorned such backward people, but when it came down to it they weren't that different themselves. They stayed away from the burning barricades because they were frightened, too.

That line of argument lost me several friends, including another former lover. Her name was Jill, and she was a fairly devout white radical. When the resistance called a stay-away, she stayed away from work, and when it called a boycott of white business, she drove miles to shop at stores owned by Indians. My talk of genetic complicity enraged her. "You don't argue," she said. "You just trample on our flowers." She was right, of course. I thought her flowers were weeds. I thought that random stonings of whites because they were white undermined the Charterists' nonracial doctrine, and I had lost faith in socialism besides. "You have become one of them," she once told me, meaning that I had become an American. In South African resistance circles, this was the most cutting insult imaginable.

The endless bickering was poisoning our relationship, so we went camping one weekend, to see if there was anything to be salvaged. Not much, it turned out. We bickered all weekend, and we were still bickering on the way home. What did our whiteness mean in the context of the South African struggle? Nothing, she said. Everything, said I. It was a Sunday night, and we were crossing the dark Cape flats in a speeding car. In the distance, we could see the floodlit face of Table Mountain, and the lights of the white city at its feet. The night around us was dark, however, and full of the winking campfires of squatters—Africans who had come to the city in defiance of apartheid's influx-control laws and built shacks in the dense bush on the flats. It was no way to live, but such people had no choice. For that reason, among others, the road was no longer safe at night. There had been stories in the newspapers about blacks coming out of the bush to stone passing cars, or to drop bricks from bridges. A brick in the windshield at seventy miles an hour can kill you, so Jill and I were tense.

Halfway across the flats, the headlights picked out a strange apparition at the roadside. From the corner of my eye, it looked like a giant water boatman, skating down the shoulder of the freeway in the dark. I twisted around for a second look and saw a crippled black man flying along on a single roller skate, his thin, useless legs drifting beneath a wasplike torso. His elongated crutches were sweeping back and forth like oars, and he was literally rowing toward Cape Town.

The instant we passed him, Jill spoke sharply. "You're not going to stop," she said. I didn't really want to. In fact, I'd have preferred to pretend we hadn't seen him at all, but now that she'd mentioned him, I felt obliged to act. So I braked and pulled off the freeway.

Jill said nothing. We sat there in silence, peering into the surrounding darkness for signs of ambush. I shuddered and thanked God the car hadn't broken down out here. After what seemed an eternity, the cripple drew abreast of us and gratefully accepted a ride. He tossed his oars in the backseat and started tugging at the system of buckles and belts that crisscrossed his chest. For an instant, I thought he was going to unbuckle his legs, and that I was fated to drive back to Cape Town with a talking torso on the seat beside me. It turned out, however, that he carried the tools of his trade in bags slung around his chest, bandolier-fashion. The tools followed the crutches into the back. The crippled man slid onto the front seat between Jill and me, and we pulled back into the traffic.

The cripple turned out to be a most congenial fellow. He smiled and laughed and chattered away at the top of his voice in Xhosa. I gathered that he fixed Primus stoves for a living, and that he was going to Guguletu, some miles down the road. Beyond that, everything he said was Greek to me; I laughed when he laughed, but I had no idea what he was saying.

And then Jill broke in. She spoke over the cripple's head, as though he were not there at all, and I guess he might as well not have been, for all the English he understood. "Tell him you can't take him home," she said. She meant, tell him we're not going into any township for his sake, even if he is a cripple. But she couldn't say that, of course, so she said, "Tell him you're running out of petrol." I glanced down at my fuel gauge. The tank was more than half full. Jesus, I thought, what if he knows how to read a fuel gauge and catches me lying? There had to be another way out of this. I was trying to dream one up when Jill tapped the cripple on his shoulder. "Petrol finish!" she shouted. "We not take you home! Petrol finish! Understand?"

It was by no means clear that he did. He laughed and nodded his head and chattered on in Xhosa. I ransacked my memory and tried to tell him the bad news in Fangalo, the African Esperanto spoken in the gold mines. *"iPetroli pelile,"* I ventured—"the petrol's finished." At this, he laughed louder than ever, tapped the fuel gauge, and nodded his head vigorously. Oh, shit, I thought, I'm going to have to do better than this.

I was trying to figure out a solution when a fluorescent blue sign reading Guguletu flashed by in the windshield. I snapped on the indicator and started cutting across the lanes toward the slipway leading off into the heart of darkness. I was halfway there when Jill lunged across the dashboard and grabbed the steering wheel. "We're not going in there!" she hissed. The car swerved back and forth as we wrestled over the wheel. By the time I'd regained control and pulled onto the verge, we were a hundred yards beyond the Guguletu offramp, and I had still more to apologize for.

So I got out, helped the cripple into his harness, shook his hand, and tried to explain. "We would like to take you home," I said, "but we are scared we will get killed if we go in there." I don't know if any of it got through, or if it mattered anyway, because he was still smiling as we drove away.

And that's how it was in white South Africa at the height of the great black uprising. Some of us supported apartheid and some of us didn't, but we all had something in common with Dawid Malan: We approached Africa in fear and trepidation, or better yet, we didn't approach Africa at all. It seemed to me that this was surely our central problem. We had yet to come to terms with Africa, and doing so was not going to be easy. I mean, how do you come to terms with something you don't really understand?

Friday has no command of words and therefore no defence against being reshaped day by day in conformity with the desires of others. I say he is a cannibal, and he becomes a cannibal: I say he is a laundryman, and he becomes a laundryman. What is the truth of Friday?

—J. M. COETZEE, from the novel Foe

Now comes another tale of ordinary life and extraordinary death in my country. Take my hand, and let's fly like gods to where it happened. Let's swoop down on the Indian Ocean port of Durban and race north along the torrid coastal lowlands, over gleaming seaside mansions and palm-fringed resorts, over the Tugela River, and into Zululand.

A little more than a century ago, a British army crossed that muddy river and conquered the mighty Zulu nation. The land we're passing over is the land those redcoats opened up for white settlement. From the air, the whites' land is a broad river of lush green sugarcane flowing north into the heart of Zululand. Here and there, on a hillock, stands a big white house with cool slate floors and French windows open to catch the breeze that comes up off the Indian Ocean in the late afternoon. The life of a Zululand sugar baron is very sweet. In Zululand, the sun always shines, the rains seldom fail, the flowers bloom all year, and there are always enough Zulus to cut your cane and serve your gin and tonic at sunset.

Every few miles, a tributary of sugarcane flows out of the hills to join the main channel of this river of white man's land. If we bank and follow one of these tributaries inland, into the hills, we soon find ourselves in another world. As we advance up the fertile river valley, the land grows drier and the slopes grow steeper, and eventually the sugarcane peters out altogether. The land beyond is too dry or mountainous to be farmed profitably, so it has been left to the Zulus. It is a sad landscape of weedy corn patches and dusty roads, mud huts, tin shanties, dilapidated schools, and crumbling mission churches. It wounds our eyes, so we turn back to the great green river of white-owned land and follow it northward.

Some ninety miles north of Durban, in the headwaters of the white land-river, lies a town called Empangeni—a fitting name in South Africa, for its roots lie in the Zulu word for *loot* or *plunder*. Empangeni is built on plunder, on rich black soil that belonged to the Zulus a century ago. The town rises like an island from a sea of green cane, and the sky above it is often stained by the smoke from a fuming sugar mill.

It is sugar that creates the wealth that gives white Empangeni its prosperous gloss, its look of a boomtown in the American Sunbelt. There's a brand-new mall downtown, vaguely Moorish in architecture, and one or two multistory office blocks on the main street. The parks are clean, the schools spacious, the streets and driveways full of shining new Toyotas, Hondas, and BMWs. A blight of split-level ranch homes is spreading out across the surrounding countryside. In white backyards, uniformed black maids are hanging out the washing, bare-chested black garden boys trimming the hedges, and the white madams are . . .

Well, Debbie Good is seated on a comfortable sofa in her living room, sipping tea. Her ginger hair is permed just so, her fingernails are long and red, and she favors polyester slacks. She has three young children and a husband named Bennie, who is puttering around the garden in short pants and rubber slip-slop sandals. Bennie is a good-natured bloke with blue eyes and a blond shock of Shirley Temple curls. The skin exposed by the V of his shirt has been burned bloodred by the sun.

Debbie and Bennie own a farm on the very edge of Empangeni, just beyond the last row of brand-new American-dream suburban tract homes. This land was settled by Debbie's grandparents in the early twenties, when it was still quite wild. Debbie's grandfather died young, and it was her grandmother who plowed the swamps with mule teams and planted cane. Grandma also built a spacious house with a cool veranda, and lined the dirt road leading up to it with fir trees, to make it feel a little more like home. Home, of course, was England. Most of the original settlers in these parts were British, empire loyalists and cricketers to a man. They named their farms Brandon Hill and Briarley Grange and sent their sons to a "public" school, Michaelhouse, where they were taught to keep a straight bat and a stiff upper lip.

The Goods' farm is called Carsdale, and it is but one of three they own. They have a second sugar farm south of here, and a sheep ranch in a place called Mooi River. At first glance, their life seems very sweet, but it is less so than it appears. Debbie is only thirty-something, but she is already talking about the good old days, when the Zulus were childlike in their simplicity, too innocent to harbor a capacity for guile, cunning, or envy. She remembers walking home from high-school parties carrying a lantern and being not at all afraid. She remembers hot summer nights when you could sleep with your doors and windows open and be bothered by nothing but mosquitoes. In those days, the Zulus were loyal and faithful and obedient, and whites honored and loved them in the way they might have loved a good dog. They were "our Zulus." They didn't steal or drink white liquor; they didn't demand higher wages, and they didn't go out on strike.

In those days, the Zulus knew their place and kept to it, scurrying around on the periphery of white lives, bearing gin and tonics, responding to bells, cutting cane, and minding children. You could walk across the farm or around town, and all the Zulus you passed would smile and greet you respectfully. But now . . . Debbie can't put her finger on it, but she knows something has changed. As a child, she used to hang around the black cane-cutters' shacks, sharing the wild spinach and *putu* they cooked in iron pots on open fires. She'd never allow her six-year-old daughter to do that today. She just doesn't trust the Zulus anymore. "You never know with them," she says.

They haven't harmed her in any way, apart from pilfering the odd stick of cane. They've just grown "cheeky." They talk back. They don't greet whites any more. And there are so many of them. On shopping trips, white madams have to jostle their way to the counter through throngs of noisy blacks. At the bank of pay phones outside the post office, the queue is always ten blacks deep. In the chemist shops across the street, row upon row of shelves are given over to black cosmetics and skin-lightening creams with brand names like Hollywood, Kool Look, and Jet Set Four-in-One Lite Lotion. In the old days, such merchandise was available only in "coolie" trading stores near the railway station, but now it's everywhere—even the big department stores and supermarkets carry it.

Of course, Debbie doesn't mind the Zulus getting ahead, growing worldly and sophisticated, wearing makeup and high-heeled shoes, and driving cars and all that. She's not a racist. In fact, she is genuinely "nice" to the "girls" and "boys" who work for her and Bennie. She wishes them all the best in the world, but she doesn't want them forced on her. She likes them, but not enough to have them in her home. After all, what would she and a Zulu matron talk about? They have nothing in common. She knows it's not much fun to be black in South Africa, but she bristles at the notion that it's all the whites' fault. As she sees it, the blacks want everything whites have, but they're not willing to improve themselves or work for it. "They want it all on a plate," she says. "It's because of that that they're so bitter."

She says such things without having any real familiarity with conditions in Ngwelezane, the local township. She can see it creeping over the lip of a hill on the eastern boundary of the family farm, but she seldom sets foot there. The government has built no new houses in Ngwelezane for twenty-six years, because Pretoria's mad scientists don't want more blacks in "white" South Africa. They want them to stay in the hills, in the reserve, and remain wards of KwaZulu, the Zulu state. It is the same old dilemma. Blacks can't get jobs in white South Africa unless they have residence rights in the townships, and they can't get residence rights unless they have jobs. Those cunning enough to solve this conundrum are crammed in ten to the tiny house. The schools are overcrowded, the teachers incompetent, the hospital understaffed and inefficient. Unemployment has virtually doubled in recent months. In Ngwelezane, life is a grim struggle for survival.

In the hills outside town, in the Zulu homeland, times are even harder. Almost four million black peasants live out there in mud huts and tin-roofed hovels, paying obeisance to traditional chiefs. A bus service called Washesha plies the rutted roads leading into and out of the reserve. Each year it brings a million black passengers to town, to shop or look for jobs. There are no jobs in town, but out on the reserve there is nothing at all, not even hope. It hasn't really rained in almost four years. Cattle are dying; crops are shriveling. Some people think the drought is God's punishment for apartheid. Others think the end of the world is approaching.

In fact, things are building to a thunderhead throughout the country in this late winter of 1983. The rumble of black discontent is growing. The Afrikaner government, running short of options, is suddenly talking about reform and negotiation, about peaceful change and power sharing. Prime Minister P. W. Botha has just unveiled his proposed new constitution, which extends a vote of sorts to Indians and colored people but leaves blacks out in the cold. As far as many Africans are concerned, this is the final insult. Even moderates are outraged. Chief Gatsha Buthelezi, ruler of KwaZulu, the self-governing Zulu homeland that borders on Empangeni, has denounced Botha's constitutional proposals as a "blueprint for violence." The insult embedded in the new constitution, he warns presciently, will trigger a devastating explosion of black rage. "It draws us nearer," he says, "to the night of the long knives."

Debbie shudders to hear such talk. So many whites have already left the country because of it. They've taken their families to Australia, or "home" to England, because they were afraid of being butchered in bed. She sometimes wonders whether they'd done the right thing, because she, too, is scared of being butchered in bed. Almost all white South Africans are. It's a given. They're all waiting for the night of the long knives. You never know when, but you know it's coming.

And then one night you go to bed around ten. You hear the old red setter barking outside, but you don't bother to get up; you doze off again, so you don't hear the mosquito screen on the kitchen window being peeled back, and you don't hear someone climbing quietly into your house. You don't hear him coming down the passage on his bare feet, and you don't hear him easing open the bedroom door. All you remember, really, is the split second of terror when you wake up. Bennie is thrashing around at your side, and there's a dark figure looming over the bed. And then the hammer smashes into your temple, and the next thing you know you've woken up in a surreal horror movie. Blood is dripping all over the telephone, the children are screaming, and your husband is tottering around in circles, drenched in blood, looking for his guns. You're trying to phone the doctor, but you can't remember how to dial.

Major Reginald Reynolds of the South African Police, detective branch, is a darkly handsome man in his forties. A sportsman. A visitor is likely to find Major Reg Reynolds hunched over a table, lovingly cleaning and oiling his small arms and hunting rifles. "Eleven months I hunt men," he says, straight-faced, "and in the twelfth I hunt animals." Major Reynolds usually enjoys both his blood sports, but Debbie and Bennie are friends of his, so he's upset when he's called out to their farm in the dead of night. He's even more upset when he gets there, because he's seen all this before. Same modus operandi, same means of entry, same circular lesions on the skulls and faces of the victims.

The first victim was Peter Trollip, a young fellow who works for one of the local hotels. Peter and his wife, Wendy, live in the blight of split levels that has crept up to the border of the Goods' farm. Three weeks ago, a black man stole into the Trollips' home and bludgeoned Peter unconscious as he lay sleeping. Wendy woke up to find herself face-to-face with a demon from her darkest subconscious: a huge black man with bulging muscles, standing at the foot of the bed with a bloody claw hammer in his fist. He advanced on her, whispering "Sssh, sssh." She screamed, "Bring the gun! Bring the gun!" There was no gun, but the ruse worked. The black man climbed out the window and disappeared into the darkness.

Who is this guy? All Reg Reynolds knows is that he's black. He takes off his shoes and wears his socks as gloves, so he leaves no prints. His weapon is an ordinary claw hammer of the sort you can buy in any hardware shop. He doesn't rape women, and he doesn't harm children. Debbie Good's six-year-old daughter woke up during the attack and came wandering down the passage toward her parents' bedroom, crying for Mummy. The intruder heard her coming, intercepted her in the doorway, took her by the hand, and gently led her away from the carnage. And then he disappeared. Major Reynolds thinks that's a little weird. I mean, an ordinary criminal would surely have smashed the child's head in, too, and thoroughly ransacked the house.

The ambulances come and take the injured to the hospital. Bennie winds up in intensive care, and Debbie undergoes surgery for brain damage. They were lucky. The Magaskills weren't.

Graham and Anna Magaskill are warders at Empangeni's jail. They and their young son live in a house on the grounds of the prison. One stiflingly hot night, three months after the Good attack, they leave the French windows in their dining room open. The Hammerman steals into their house after midnight. He kneels on the bed between the sleeping couple and rains alternate blows on their heads and faces. He has perfected his technique, and this time he drives the hammer right into Graham Magaskill's brain. He beats Mrs. Magaskill's head and face to a bloody pulp. He keeps hitting until both of them are dead. Then he takes some loose cash and slips out of the house without waking their sleeping son. Once again, there are no clues, no fingerprints, nothing.

Empangeni is a small town. Almost everyone in white Empangeni knows everyone else. If you didn't know the Magaskills, you knew the Goods or the Trollips, and you had to wonder, Why them? Who's next? It could be you. The terror begins in earnest.

Who is the Hammerman? Is he a psychopath? Whenever he strikes, he helps himself to whatever's lying around, but robbery seems a barely adequate motive. He never bothers to loot systematically. Is he killing because he hates whites? Some blacks think so. His weapon is Africa's traditional pig-killing instrument; a black magazine called *Pace* thinks this may be a point to consider. *Pace* speculates that the Hammerman might be "a maniac insurgent from the ANC or PAC camps." The police doubt it, because the modus is too crude. But they remember the Mau Mau, who butchered Kenyan settlers with pangas, and they remember Poqo, a local terrorist band that hacked a few isolated white farm families to death in the early sixties. So they're taking no chances.

They cast the largest dragnet in the history of the province and tell the press they're closing in on the Hammerman, but they're lying. They have no leads, no fingerprints, and there's nothing coming in on the informer network. Major Reynolds and his men are spending their nights lurking under bushes in suburban gardens, watching everything that moves. The Hammerman doesn't show himself. So Pretoria sends in a posse of reinforcements from the big-city Murder and Robbery squads, cannibal cops who stop at nothing to get their man. Any African on the street after dark is liable to be collared, questioned, told to produce his pass, maybe knocked around a little if he doesn't give straight answers. This sort of thing hasn't really happened in Empangeni in years. Whites know it's souring race relations, but that's too bad. They're scared. Gun sales double; sales of burglar bars triple. Some white hard-liners demand a racial curfew; they want all blacks off the streets at night. Whites start going to bed in crash helmets, with guns under their pillows.

And so the fear mounts toward hysteria, fed by increasing turbulence in the political sphere. One day, the tabloid *Zululand Observer* appears on Empangeni's streets with the headline "Bloodbath!" emblazoned across its front page. War has broken out at the nearby University of Zululand. Six black students have been killed in a clash between moderates and radicals. The night of the long knives is apparently starting, and the Hammerman is still at large. Rumor has it that he has struck repeatedly, and that news of his depredations is being suppressed to prevent panic. The *Observer* publishes an editorial headlined "Attack Rumors and Paranoia." It cautions its white readers against panic, and dispels rumors of "an imaginary monster . . . battering children and raping young girls."

To understand such things, you must see them in the context of the state of elemental guilt and fear in which white South Africans live. The Hammerman's killings raise the specter of indiscriminate black retribution; they force whites to examine their lives, and the structure of their society, and when whites do so, they see that they cannot escape complicity. That quickens the fear into a fever. They hear the Hammerman rustling in the garden; they see him lurking in the bushes; they hear his footsteps on the path; his shadow falls across the curtain. The police are inundated with false alarms.

"Perhaps he watched our house today," says a columnist in the *Observer*.

> Perhaps he's already decided where he will strike next. It's as if the darkness and insecurity is filtering in through our very windows. . . . The fear has become an infectious disease . . . it grows and intensifies in the hours of the night, and yet it gets us nowhere. When fear of the Hammerman recedes, a new fear will take its place. Every new day will bring new fears, because we don't know, and not to know is almost always to fear.

Ah, yes, now we're hearing the heart of the matter. Whites don't know blacks, or what their rise portends. To most whites, blacks are inscrutable; they can't talk to them, don't understand them, and struggle to see them in three dimensions. Blacks are merely black; they are blank screens onto which whites project their own fears and preconceptions.

Empangeni's district surgeon, for instance, is a kindly man named Louis Fourie. Dr. Fourie is a cosmopole, a so-called new Afrikaner. He lives in a magnificent house and drives around his district in a white Land Cruiser, wearing an immaculate white safari suit. He owns a fine collection of African crafts and a cellar full of vintage Cape wines. His elegant, blond wife, Ronelle, was reared to be a concert pianist, and Louis is a passionate ecologist. On his study wall hangs a framed copy of Chief Seathl's moving plea to white men, to cease their rape of the earth. In South African terms, Louis and Ronelle Fourie are a most enlightened couple.

The Fouries have two blond daughters, both still in primary school. Their father is worried about them, so he takes precautions. He has the burglar bars checked, then opens his diary and writes down a plan to thwart the Hammerman. He will drape a fishnet over his marital bed, to catch the hammer as it descends. He and his wife will henceforth sleep with their heads at opposite ends of the bed, each with a pistol within reach. In Dr. Fourie's view, such precautions are merely sensible.

The Fouries' houseboy is a luminously gentle and loving young Zulu named Emmanuel. Emmanuel is an old-fashioned Zulu, a mission boy. He is a figure from a romantic African novel of an earlier age, the loyal gun bearer who sacrifices himself to save the *bwana* from the lion. He cares so deeply for his white master's family that whenever the doctor is called out after dark, the houseboy stands guard in the garden. He does this of his own volition, without telling the madam. One night, the madam peers out into the menacing darkness and sees the faithful black retainer standing in the shadows, watching the house, and a shiver runs down her spine. She thinks, Oh, God, it's Emmanuel; he is the Hammerman. So she suffers frightful terror until her husband comes home and sorts it all out.

"You never really know what they're thinking," she explains later, somewhat shamefacedly.

Justin Smith and Dave Brauteseth are also wary of "the black." They're easygoing, beer-swilling white guys, Jo'burg boys, brand-new in town. They've just taken over the lease on the African eating house down at the bus terminal, and they're doing very nicely, thanks. The buses carry eighteen thousand potential customers to their doorstep every week, and their joint is so busy it's anarchic. They're selling tankersful of iJuba Special, African sorghum beer, and truckloads of *palishi*, or corn porridge. An Indian does the books; blacks do the heavy work; and Dave and Justin—Jay—take alternate weeks off to relax or go fishing.

Dave and Jay used to smoke *zol* and jol, but they've outgrown all that. They're both turning thirty, both newly "turned on to free enterprise." Jay has a wife and two kids already, and Dave has just acquired a "steady bird." They're sharing a house on the edge of town, one of those big white farmhouses with a swimming pool and big windows to catch the breeze off the distant sea. They're somehow Australian, in their short pants, slip-slops and suntans. They like the "Afs," but they're a little wary of them, because, well—because of those troublesome hawkers, for one thing.

Dave and Jay paid 150 grand for their lease, and then these black hawkers set up tables on the very doorstep of their eating house, selling flyblown tripe and grilled chicken innards. The police chase them away, but there is no work out in the reserve, no food, no rain, and no hope, so they're always back the next day. Dave figures they're costing him five hundred a day in lost business, so he takes the traditional approach. "I used to go beat the shit out of them," he says.

According to tradition, blacks are supposed to cower and run away when the white man cracks his whip. Times are changing, though. One day, the hawkers stand their ground, and Dave finds himself surrounded by a menacing black crowd. It is a very ugly scene. So Dave gets his mate Roger, and they both get their guns, and then they go out on the plaza and threaten to blow some cheeky black heads off. "It's the only way," says Dave.

Since that is Dave's way, perhaps he and Jay have cause to be wary. Jay sleeps with the .32 within reach, and Dave keeps an ax under his bed. The Hammerman is seldom far from their minds. Every day, a "big coon" comes into their joint and sits in a corner, nursing a beer. He's an undercover cop, working on the Hammerman case; he's waiting for some drunkard to loosen up and say too much. And then one day, yet another demon from the depths of a disturbed white subconscious materializes on the other side of the counter: "A man with eyes like fire," Dave tells the *Zululand Observer*. The Hammerman. At least Dave thinks it's him. He looks something like the IdentiKit picture in the newspapers. Dave calls the police, but by the time they come the suspect has vanished.

This visitation leaves Dave and Jay feeling a little uneasy. Is the Hammerman after them? Has someone told him about the rough way they deal with the hawkers? They take no chances. That night, Jay and his young wife bed down with the .32 on the bedside table. Dave, being single, goes out. He gets smashed on beer at the Rugby Club, gets home around 1:30, and passes out in the car. He wakes to find the sun rising. It's already 5:30; they should have opened the eating house thirty minutes ago. Where the fuck is Justin?

Dave staggers into the house and barges into his buddy's bedroom. Jay is slumped against the wall, dead, with a dozen hammer holes in his skull. His half-naked wife is lying on the floor. She'd spent hours spinning around in a pool of her own blood, trying in vain to get up. Her underpants are full of stool, passed reflexively. Her face is a bloody pulp, and now she's dead, too.

Dave hears whimpering and, turning, sees Jay's tiny daughter, Leanne, standing up in her cot and calling for her mother. Dave picks her up, covers her eyes, and walks away to call the police.

Once again, there are no clues, no prints—nothing but a single drop of blood on the pajamas of one of the Smith children. In his mind's eye, Major Reg Reynolds sees a muscular black man standing in a moonlit bedroom, listening to the soft breathing of a sleeping white child while blood drips from his bloody claw hammer. Weird. Who is this man? Reynolds is gaunt and gray from exhaustion. He's working this case night and day, because he's worried that his career might be blighted if the big-city Murder and Robbery cops solve it before he does. He's working so hard that his marriage is disintegrating, but he's no closer to an arrest than he was six months earlier, when Peter Trollip was attacked. The only good news, as far as Major Reynolds is concerned, is that Jay's .32 has disappeared. Reg Reynolds knows in his bones that the Hammerman's going to use it, and when he does, he might break cover.

A mere ten days later, Sergeant J. J. Myburgh of the dog squad is out on patrol with his faithful Alsatian and his faithful Bantu constable. The radio reports a shooting in the Zulu reserve on the edge of town, so they leave the tar and head up into the hills on a dirt road. In a shack three miles from town, they find a black man hiding under a bed, bleeding from several bullet wounds. His woman, Mavis, is yelling indignantly. She tells the police that her Moses had a fight with his step-brother, Simon, and that Simon pulled a gun and shot him. The gunman has apparently fled to the white suburbs, where his girlfriend works as a domestic.

As the sergeant and his entourage roll up at the given address, a disheveled black man appears in the doorway of the servants' quarters. He smiles wanly when he sees the police, and offers his wrists. "Well," he says in Afrikaans, "you may as well put the cuffs on." Sergeant Myburgh is a dull cop, and not at all given to poetry. He is moved to observe, however, that to his way of thinking, the suspect seemed "spiritually weary."

The suspect's name is Simon Mpungose; pronounced mm-pon-go-say. He is thirty-five years old. At the police station, he says, "I am the Hammerman." Within three hours, Major Reynolds has him up before a magistrate, formally confessing to four murders, four assaults with intent, and one armed robbery, committed with Justin Smith's .32. He describes his killings in graphic detail and concludes, somewhat enigmatically, that he has committed these crimes because he wants to die. "All I want," he says, "is to go to the gallows."

* * *

August 27, 1984. We're in Empangeni's courthouse, a single-story brick building next door to the post office. Mr. Justice John Broome, presiding, is a dignified eminence. His manner is ascetic, his language grave and precise. Glenda Sanders, counsel for the defense, is young, blond, and brilliant. She has a Cambridge degree behind her and a job with a major American law firm in her near future. The prosecutor, Dorian Paver, is a graduate of the liberal University of Cape Town. Save for the interpreter, the officers of the court are all white.

It's not just their skin that's white; their minds are white, too. They are generic white people with generic Western values. The ritual of justice they are about to act out is white, Western, ancient, and alien. It has nothing to do with Africa.

Africa is outside. You can hear it through the window—a clamoring throng of several hundred Zulus held at bay by cops with dogs. They're climbing trees and standing on one another's shoulders to get a glimpse of their hero of the moment, the captured Hammerman.

Simon Mpungose is solid, chunky, muscular. His skin is smooth, brown, and shining. He has a mustache and a goatee. He's wearing a short-sleeved sports shirt, white slacks, and ankle shackles that rattle as he moves in the dock. His dark eyes are full of humor and intelligence, and when he smiles there is something truly charismatic about him.

Simon smiles a great deal. In fact, he's done little but smile and laugh since the trial opened this morning. Simon is on trial for his life, but he seems very happy. His fellow Zulus reach for words meaning "full," "high," or even "transfigured" to describe the state he is in. He has fulfilled his destiny: He is ready to die.

He has refused to mount a defense. The moment Judge Broome gaveled the court to order, Simon demanded that the trial be aborted. He had committed the murders, he said, and that was that. He wanted to be taken away and hanged. The ritual of white justice had to take its course, however, so Judge Broome ordered him to sit down and shut up. Simon responded by instructing his counsel not to challenge the state's case in any way. And then he sat back, smiling sympathetically while a parade of state witnesses told their stories.

The gist of the state case is that the accused is a common criminal.

Dorian Paver contends that Simon broke into white homes because he wanted a gun and murdered their white inhabitants for fear they'd wake up and catch him. It isn't really necessary for the prosecution to establish a clear motive, however, because the accused has admitted everything. Indeed, Dorian Paver's most serious problem is making himself heard above the din of Africa, above the constant hubbub coming in through the windows.

Even Judge Broome finds it trying. "I don't like people peering through the windows," he says at one point. "It is unsettling and objectionable."

Paver plods on, laying out his case. There is the story of Wendy Trollip, who woke up in a bed drenched with blood. There is the story of Debbie and Bennie Good, who woke up in intensive care. There is the story of the Magaskills, who didn't wake up at all. And finally, there is the testimony of Dave Brauteseth, who tells of the morning he discovered Justin and Terri Smith dead in their bedroom. On that note, the state closes its case, and it is Simon's turn.

He shuffles out of the dock and into the witness box, leg-irons clattering. He lays his hand on the Bible and swears to tell the truth. The Zulu interpreter, a dapper man in a dark suit, stands beside him, and Simon starts speaking. His voice is pitched oddly high for a man of his bulk. He speaks in Zulu, but his words emerge in the curiously Victorian English of the interpreter.

At the outset, Glenda Sanders asks him a few questions, but Simon doesn't want to be led. He knows that he is doomed and that these are his last public words. He wants to talk to his judge, man to man. He wants to tell him what it is to be black in South Africa.

"Everything that is happening today," he says, "I have seen it before. I have seen it in my dream, in the prison at Barberton."

In many ways, the story Simon told his judge was the tale of a black Everyman. Simon was a Zulu. His tribe was broken by whites in 1879 and stripped of its best land. The Zulus were ground down by the British and ground down still further by D. F. Malan, who came to power in the year of Simon's birth. Subjugation was his birthright, and further oppression awaited his people.

During the years in which Simon should have been in school, South

Africa was ruled by Dr. Hendrik Verwoerd, a blatant racist who openly opposed education for blacks. They were destined to wield shovels, Verwoerd argued, so why teach them to read and encourage them to imagine that they might be allowed to enter "the green pastures of European society"? So Simon never set foot inside a school. His mother died when he was young, and he was farmed out to relatives who didn't want him and treated him cruelly. By the age of twelve, he was laboring in the cane fields on nearby white farms, or washing dishes in farmers' kitchens. The money he earned was never enough to live on, so he got into trouble for pilfering. He ran away with a friend and lived in the bush outside a big city. The South African state made little provision for such children, so Simon begged and stole to stay alive. His juvenile criminal record was pathetic, and left no doubt as to his desperation. On one occasion, he was flogged for stealing ten cents; on several others, for stealing food.

In his late teens, Simon came up before a white magistrate who took a look at his lengthening record and decided to put an end to his nonsense. Simon had no lawyer: The state provided a defense for blacks only in capital cases. He was illiterate and could barely speak English. He wanted to tell the court that he stole only because he was hungry. He wanted to say that he had never harmed anyone or used violence, but he was not asked to explain himself. Simon was just another larcenous black, so the magistrate sent him to prison for seven years. "I felt," he said later, "that they slammed the door on me, and wrote 'closed' upon it." Simon was so despondent that he tried to hang himself, but the rope snapped, and he found himself sitting on the floor of his isolation cell feeling more desolate than ever. It was the first of several suicide attempts.

Next, he launched a suicidal escape attempt, hoping to be shot in the course of it. He escaped unharmed, however, and returned to his life of theft and pilfery. In due course, he fell afoul of the law again. This time, the charge was burglary. Simon's original sentence was lengthened, and he was sent to Barberton.

Barberton is a country town in the eastern Transvaal. A few miles outside town lies a blacks-only prison farm, a complex of low-slung buildings, tilled fields, and rock quarries, surrounded by barbed wire and guard towers. None of South Africa's segregated black prisons was a pleasant place to do time, but Barberton Prison was hell. It was the most notorious prison in the entire country. On the day of their arrival, Simon and the rest of the men in his intake were stripped naked and given the traditional welcome. A white lieutenant explained the brutal verities of life. "You are in Barberton now," he said. "The train does not go past Barberton. There is no turning back. Here, even the human brain changes. There are only two ways here. It is death, or living. Don't think of anything; just crack the stones. There must be no other thoughts for you if you want to live."

And then the initiation rite began, a ghastly game of ring-o-roses. Some fifty warders and trustees stood in a circle, and the naked convicts ran around its inner circumference. The warders and trustees were armed with lengths of hosepipe, and lashed the convicts as they passed. Round and round the convicts ran, until they all fell down. Simon was so badly injured that he could not walk for a month.

Once he recovered, Simon was returned to the general prison population and sent to work on the farm. Discipline was ruthless. Simon once saw white warders ironing the body of a black prisoner they had beaten to death. They were trying to erase the welts on the corpse, to avoid troublesome questions. On another occasion, he witnessed an atrocity worse than any dreamed of in movies of the chain-gang genre.

It was December 29, 1982, and the prison's white commandant had a minor disciplinary problem on his hands. Some prisoners had talked back to the warders and had to be taught a lesson. So they were shackled hand and foot, marched into the fields, and ordered to push heavily laden wheelbarrows up and down a slope. It was a brutally hot day. Some of the black men were old, one was crippled, and one was recovering from surgery, but the warders showed no mercy. They whipped the shackled convicts up and down that hill until they started collapsing, then whipped them to their feet again.

When the commandant arrived on the scene, a hellish vision greeted his eyes: some twenty convicts lay half-conscious in a bloody heap, while the rest reeled around like drunkards, too exhausted even to scream. The commandant hadn't come to stop it, though; he'd brought more blacks to be dealt with. *"Slat die drie dood,"* he ordered—beat these three to death. Then he walked away. By sunset, thirty-four convicts were in hospital with heat exhaustion and trauma, and three black men were dead.

Beat them to death, the white man said. Simon worked in the prison quarry, under white warders' whips and guns. All day long, he broke the rocks with his hammer, and thought about things he had seen. "I liked the white man," Simon said later, "but there came a time when it ceased in me that I fear a white person. And I also lost love of him." The rocks that Simon smashed with a hammer were whitish in color. "You hold them in one hand," Simon said, "and break them easily. It is not long before the rocks are the white man's head."

In Barberton, Simon was visited by a dream, a prophetic dream. In it, he saw himself swelling and bloating, growing taller and taller. He flexed his muscles, and the prison walls crumbled around him. The white warders opened fire, but their bullets passed through without harming him. Simon crushed the warders like insects, and then rolled away across the landscape like a thunderstorm, obliterating all the whites in his path.

In that state, he encountered a figure of overwhelming power. "This man," he said, "this person, my persecutor, did not have a face, but his head looked just like the rocks that I broke with my hammer. It is easy for those round white rocks to take the shape of a head. So I killed him. And when I had killed him, they took me away and I was small again, and they put me to death and I had freedom from torment."

A Zulu cannot ignore such a dream, for it is a message from his sacred ancestors and reveals his *isipiwo,* his destiny. As Simon put it, "The dream was like a voice from the gods, a messenger I should not deny." Like Moses in the Old Testament, Simon trembled at his gods' command, and sought to escape their fearful dictates. He converted to Christianity and prayed to his new God to free him from the destiny revealed, but the God of whites did not heed him. Many years passed, but the dream remained strong in his heart.

In 1983, the prison authorities informed Simon that he was about to be paroled. Upon hearing the news, Simon asked for an interview with Barberton's white commandant. He could not very well tell a white man what was really on his mind, so he asked instead to be deported from South Africa. Failing in that, he asked the major to get him a job on Johannesburg's gold mines, where he would live in an all-black compound and be spared contact with whites. He was even willing to stay in prison, if that was the only way to avoid being sent home. The white man just laughed at him. "Go away from here," he said. "You are mad."

And so, in July 1983, Simon Mpungose was given fifteen rand ($7.50), an ill-fitting suit, and a cardboard suitcase containing two shirts and two pairs of underpants. Then the warders took him to the station and put him aboard a train bound for Empangeni.

* * *

In Simon's memory, Empangeni was a small town with hand-cranked telephones, swooning in a malarial trance. The Mhlatuze River skirted the village and emptied sixteen miles downstream into the estuary of Richard's Bay, a crocodile-infested swamp in Simon's day. Sixteen years later, the crocodiles were still there, but now the waters in which they lurked were tinted orange at night by the flames of industrial smokestacks. The Empangeni–Richard's Bay region had been declared a growth point by the state. The bay had been transformed into a huge concrete-lined harbor. A railhead had been pushed through the swamp, to carry coal to the wharves, where it was loaded aboard Japanese freighters and carried off to the far side of the planet. Giant factories had risen on the marshes. There was now a white town called Richard's Bay where there had been no town before, and Empangeni had become a small city, with bright neon lights and city vices. When night fell, Zulu girls put on high heels and makeup and trawled the streets for white johns. Simon hardly recognized the place. Everything was different: everything was strange. "I felt like a just-born baby," he said.

A free man at last, he trudged into the hills, to the village where he was born. There was nothing left of it, or so he said, but a cluster of ruins and tombstones. His entire family was dead, or so Simon said. So he walked back to the township of Ngwelezane, where people had little to spare for him save sympathy. Simon was alone in the world. He had almost no money, no food, and nowhere to stay. He didn't even have a pass, so he had no legal right to work—or even to be—in Ngwelezane.

To South African blacks, the pass was the single most loathsome aspect of a loathsome control system. A black man had to carry his pass with him at all times, and produce it on demand. Unless it bore the name of his employer, and the signature of his white boss, he was not allowed to be in white South Africa. Blacks hated the pass and the state of virtual serfdom it symbolized.

Even so, a pass could be hard to come by. To get one, you had to step onto an infuriating bureaucratic treadmill manned by scornful and obstructive clerks. You had to stand in the sun all day outside the Bantu Administration Bureau, waiting your turn at the counter. When Simon finally reached the head of the line, the clerk said, "Where's your photograph? You must have a photograph." But a photo cost three rand, and Simon had less than half that in his pocket. So he begged the balance, had his snap taken, and returned to the endless queue.

This time, the clerk behind the counter wanted to see the signature of Simon's tribal chief, granting him permission to leave his home district. Simon's chief had three kraals, three far-flung homesteads out in the reserve. It would have taken days of walking to visit them all. So Simon begged for an exemption, and the clerk grudgingly granted him a "duplicate," a temporary pass, good for three months.

Pass in hand, he trudged the streets until he landed a job as a laborer on a construction site in white Empangeni. The work was very hard, and the wages too low to live on. "Yes, I wanted money," Simon said later. "No, not to be rich. All I wanted was enough to live on, like the other people of means." Many black workers felt that way, but few had the temerity to complain about it. "I told the white man how much my traveling expenses were, how much the food cost me. It was too little to live on. When I told the white man so, I noticed his face, how it changed. He told me in Afrikaans that he was not happy with what I had stated to him. His face also told me this." The white man snatched Simon's hard-won pass and tore it to pieces before his eyes. "Now try and find work," he snapped.

"I looked at him," Simon recalled, "and a thought came into my mind, saying, well, this white man is in the dark. He does not know what is going on in my mind. He doesn't think that black people have also got brains in their heads and they can think." Simon Mpungose could think. He thought the matter over and decided to go to the police. After all, it was a criminal offense to deface a passbook. This was a lesson many black South Africans had learned the hard way, when they were jailed for burning the loathsome document in protest. When Simon told his story at the police charge office, though, the white constables on duty just shrugged. So he trudged into Empangeni to report the matter to the white municipality, which referred him to the Bantu Administration authorities, who referred him back to the police, who just laughed at him.

And so Simon found himself back on square one. He was thirty-four years old then, and he still had nothing—no pass, no job, and no money in his pocket. He couldn't face the thought of returning to the lines outside the pass office, and then pounding the streets in search of a job he might never find. "There were lots of people looking for work," he said. "So I laughed with myself. I have been trying to live a decent life and be a good citizen, but from what I have discovered, it means I am an outcast." He thought deeply about his plight, and decided he had had enough. "I saw there was no point in running away from it," he told his judge. "I saw there was no other way but to follow the swallows and disappear into the mountains."

To follow the swallows is a Zulu proverb that means to die, but what do white judges and lawyers know of such things? That would only have confused them. So the interpreter declared that Simon decided "to start another type of life," and left it at that.

Simon's next statement was rooted in an even more obscure rural Zulu metaphor—the metaphor of the furrow that carries the waters of life. Simon spoke of laboring to open the furrow, so that the water might flow in behind him and carry him away, but white men knew nothing of these things either, and even less about the confounding allusions to doom and destiny that followed. The prisoner's words defeated the interpreter. He tried, but all that really came through was the image of a man digging "a deep furrow or a trench." It sounded, to white ears, as if Simon had merely garbled the old English saying about digging one's own grave.

As Simon listened to the translation, a change came over him. His smile vanished. He turned his face away from the court, sat down on the rim of the witness box, and lowered his head between his knees. A great sob racked his body. And then he was suddenly bellowing and howling, like a man in unendurable pain. It was a harrowing sound, the sound of a bull with a sword in its heart, an animal with its leg in a trap. The judge paled, the courtroom fell silent, and the noise outside subsided. All who heard that sound were stricken, for it was surely the scream of a black man tormented beyond endurance by apartheid. At last, the scream subsided and the judge said, "Please stand up. Please stand up."

Simon accepted a tissue from the interpreter and dried his eyes. The judge asked whether he required a short adjournment to recompose himself, but Simon pulled himself together, took a deep breath, and continued. In the next few minutes, he delivered as moving and powerful an indictment of white South Africa as had ever been spoken.

"I know," said Simon, "that a white person on this earth, whether he claims to be a Christian or not, all what he prays for is that he lives for a long time and that he enjoys life. A white person does not pray to God that God causes us, irrespective of color, to live peacefully and in harmony. The whites always talk of peace when they in fact do not exercise peace.

"I once feared a white person, m'lord. I also respected a white person and liked a white person, m'lord. In fact, in the whole of my life before, I had never resorted to violence on another person. Even if I met a white person, a brown person, or a black person, I used not to lift my hand at that person. What I used to do—I used to break into places and steal, that is what I was doing. I never resorted to violence. But when I got to the stage where I developed the disliking of the white person, it was then that I decided that I should shed blood—that is, the blood of the white people. So I started last August. I went and attacked the white people at their houses at night whilst they were asleep. I did so here in town.

"Another thought came into my mind and that was the thought in regard to the children, as to what I would do if the children happened to see what was happening to their parents and they started crying out. M'lord, I wish to state this in court that I am a Christian. I belong to a certain religion. In fact, if I may mention this, m'lord, on each occasion, before I set out to attack these people, I used to go down onto my knees and start praying. So I decided, well, I should not touch the children. No matter what they were doing. I should not touch them, seeing that the children really do not know what is happening on this earth. The children will be left untouched.

"M'lord, I am not going to go into the details of what I did. The court is fully aware of what happened. Everything is recorded down in the documents which have been produced in this trial. In fact, m'lord, I might state quite bluntly that I am not sorry for all what I did. In fact, my heart is free, and I feel relieved.

"White people like to kill black people in various ways. Once that white person is brought to court for trial, you will find that he has instructed an advocate to defend him or her, so that his life, his or her life, is saved. I disagree with such a thing. If one has killed another, he must come forward and tell the court, 'Look here, I did this, so I must be executed as well.' In what I am saying here, m'lord, it is not that I am trying to defend myself or trying to put excuses of some sort as to why I did this. In fact, I am not to live, because of what I did.

"I have given the reasons that caused me to act in this manner. It is because of what I had witnessed happening to my fellow black men and also to me, because of all that was done to us by the white people. There is no fairness on this earth. One must know that as a fact—that in my life, I have noticed there is no fairness in this earth. So, I must die, so that what I dreamed in 1972 be fulfilled.

"That is all I wish to say."

* * *

Ah, Simon, Simon, in spite of all I know about you, your words still break my heart. Simon was a killer, and yet, as a friend of mine pointed out, his story seemed to unfold like the story of a saint, deeply disturbing in its biblical parallels. A dream sets his task before him, but he does not accept its inevitability. He tries again and again to sidestep his destiny. "And he went forward and fell on the ground and prayed that if it were possible, the hour might pass from him."

But Simon was black in white-ruled South Africa, and his life proceeded along its inexorable course. Fate threw him up against a white man who tore his pass to pieces. "In this world," Simon said, "sometimes the little things change to a big thing." That white man's act, such an ordinary act of white cruelty and contempt, set off a chain of events that grew very big indeed. Four whites died beneath Simon's hammer, three others were seriously injured, and finally, Simon himself was taken to the Central Prison in distant Pretoria, where he was given a cell on death row, and a scribe to take down his last letters. And finally the moment came. He was borne through the night by the hymns of doomed brothers, and when the sun rose he was taken to the gallows and hanged from the neck until dead.

The date was November 20, 1985, and Simon's death was just one among many. It coincided with a massive upsurge in political carnage and merited only a few paragraphs on the inside pages of the newspapers. Still, it struck me as a remarkable parable of life in a country where blacks were being kept down lest they leap up and slit white throats. This was Dawid Malan's law, and it fulfilled its own grim prophecy: If you treat a black man that way, he will indeed leap up and drive a hammer into your brain. That seemed to be Simon's message. I heard no hatred or despair in his last words, just clarity, which he seemed to be offering as a man offers a gift—a gift of understanding, I thought, and a warning. It seemed a rare offering, and so, some months after Simon's execution, I went to Empangeni to receive it.

The first sight that greeted my eyes as I drove into town was a giant black fist, huge as a train, smashing through the price barrier on a billboard. It was just an ad for Power Stores, but in that time, in that place, it was easy to see it as a symbol for rising black rage. Indeed, it was very easy for me to see Simon himself. He was right there in my mind's eye, a black man barely six years older than me. His life had surely been shaped by forces I knew and understood—by D. F. Malan's apartheid, by Verwoerd's Bantu Education policies, and by Vorster's barbaric prisons, I presumed to know exactly what Simon meant when he spoke of a world without fairness. I presumed to know exactly what that billboard symbolized. As it turned out, I presumed a great deal.

A man who is isolated and alone can be regarded as a sort of discarded person. He is a man cast out of society, and that type of man, in the old days, would have been killed. Let me say this—and I say it very seriously: there is nothing worse than being isolated.

—*DINIZULU, king of the Zulus, c. 1910*

The teenager at the wheel was a white Zulu. His name was Rauri Alcock, and he grew up in a mud hut on the banks of a river in northern Zululand, but that is another story. He spoke Zulu like a Zulu, and his role on this expedition was to act as an intermediary between me and the grave black dignitary in the backseat. Majozi Nxongo (pronounced nongo) wore ragged khaki overalls and had huge holes in his earlobes, into which brightly colored disks might be inserted on ceremonial occasions. In the white cities, where he had worked most of his life, he had been some white man's "boy." In his own world, however, he was a figure of great power and influence. He was the chief *induna,* or prime minister, if you will, of the Thembu tribe, a subtribe of the Zulu nation, and a guardian and interpreter of the Zulu *mthetwa,* or laws.

I turned to Nxongo for guidance because my inquiries about Simon had dead-ended in a wall of silence. I was unable to find the cold-hearted Afrikaner who had supposedly torn up Simon's pass, but that was the least of my journalistic problems. I had been unable to find Simon himself. The Hammerman's tale had turned out to be something of a fable. It contained many half-truths and at least one outright lie. Simon was no orphan. He had a family. At the time of Simon's release from jail, his father was living in Ngwelezane, undergoing a witch doctor's treatment for tuberculosis. Simon, for some unfathomable reason, chose to deny him, even to his face. On the day they were reunited, Simon said, "I don't know you, old man. Go away!"

Why? The black lawyers and tradesmen of Empangeni were eager to air their sympathetic views of Simon, but few of them had ever met him. Those who had—his family especially—would not answer questions. Some wouldn't even talk to me. Simon's cousin Sipho Mpungose, for instance, told me, "Simon had a secret problem," and walked away. A man who had grown up in the same household as Simon said he knew nothing about the Hammerman's childhood. When I asked why, he said, "Our eyes did not meet. He never became human." He refused to elaborate further.

It was really eerie. It was as though they were talking about an unperson, about the living dead, and when I stopped to think about it, I realized Simon had sometimes spoken of himself in similar terms. In court documents, psychiatric reports, and police interrogations, he had occasionally referred to himself as a dog, an outcast, a man who "didn't fit in anywhere" and "could never be like the others." He told a psychiatrist that he had had only one friend and only one lover in his entire life.

Why? Nobody would tell me. I wandered around Empangeni and the surrounding hills for weeks, filling notebook after notebook with cryptic evasions. I seemed incapable of even formulating the questions that might have elicited the truth about Simon. One day, however, a Zulu woman took pity on my floundering and whispered a secret in my ear. Her name was Mavis Khumalo, and she said, "Simon was born wrong." Her explanation was so confounding that I had to turn to anthropology texts for understanding, and finally to Nxongo in his capacity as guardian of beliefs I thought long dead. "Something is hiding in this story," he said, and agreed to come into the hills with me to ask those questions that lay beyond my imagination.

And so there we were, tooling through the lush green cane fields of Zululand in a borrowed Mercedes. Five miles outside Empangeni, we peeled off the tar and entered the Zulu reserve. We passed a memorial to the great king Shaka and an old Lutheran mission. Some miles farther, we coasted to a halt alongside a whitewashed stone. This was Bus Stop Four, in the vicinity where Simon Mpungose was born.

As far as the eye could see, green hills rose and fell like the steep breasts of young girls. The nipple of each hill was topped by a kraal, a circular cluster of mud huts, and gurgling streams flowed through each of the valleys between. There was nobody in sight save an old man sitting alone on the crest of a ridge above us, watching his cattle. Nxongo hailed him, and he came tottering down toward us. He was wearing a tattered tweed jacket and a jaunty feather in his homburg. He hobbled across the road, bent double over his cane, and stuck his head through the car window. His toothless gums clattered, and his black eyes darted hither and thither, full of curiosity.

"We are looking for the kraal of Simon Mpungose," said Nxongo. The instant Simon's name was spoken, the old fellow started yelping and howling with outrage. *"Mtagaat!"* he shrieked. "Sorcerer! That boy was a sorcerer! He killed the white men, who are my gods! I am getting an old-age pension, and he is killing the people who are giving me my old-age pension!" He was flailing the air with his stick and hopping around in the road, cursing and laughing simultaneously.

"So you knew this man," Nxongo observed drily.

"Myself, I am Mpungose," said the old man. "I was cousin to his father."

When Nxongo suggested he tell us about Simon, however, the old man lapsed into a muttering silence. His face clouded, and he stared off into the distance. "I don't know," he said. "No, I cannot say anything about this matter. I am not the head of the family. If you want to know about this matter, you must ask my older brother."

It seemed inconceivable that such an ancient man could have an older brother. "Where is your brother?" asked Nxongo.

"There," said the old man, pointing.

Several hundred yards away, we spotted a man lying on his back in tall grass at the roadside. I asked Rauri to fetch him, but the old man declined to ride in the car, so we had to wait while he made his way toward us on tottering legs. When he finally arrived, panting, Nxongo asked why he was afraid of automobiles. "I am from the time before cars," he replied. He and Nxongo started exchanging the elaborate courtesies demanded by rural Zulu etiquette. What is your clan? Where do you come from? Has it rained there? *Eh-heh.* I lay on my back in the grass, listening. I couldn't keep my eyes off the old man's bare feet, and the geological accumulation of callus on his soles and heels. His feet looked like weathered rock, or the hooves of a wild animal.

Meanwhile, we had attracted an audience. At first glance, this landscape had seemed empty, but now people were rising up from the earth and converging on us from all directions, drawn by the unusual presence of whites. Older men sat down alongside Nxongo, younger men formed a row behind us, and women parked themselves at the very limit of earshot, where they sat in respectful silence. I smoked two cigarettes before Nxongo deemed it time to get down to business. "We are here," he said finally, "to find out the whole story of Simon Mpungose."

Anger flashed in the elder brother's eyes. "We do not speak of those people," he snapped. "They are the abomination of the Mpungose clan." In Zulu, he used the word *nyala,* which connotes "disgust," "filth," "disgrace."

The audience fell silent and waited to see how we would deal with this rebuff. Nxongo was a statesman, however. "We already know the secret," he said. "We have merely come to find out if it is true." The old man demanded to know how we had found out. I said it was in the court papers—a white lie, so to speak, but it freed the old man from the stigma of being an *impimpi,* one who betrays secrets to whites.

"Yes," he said sternly, "what you heard is true. It is a horrible thing. I will answer, but ask only the questions you need."

We heard it first from his lips, and heard it again and again in those hills. It was always the same story, told in the same manner, from the very beginning, as all stories must be told. It always began "in the years of the Great War"—the war of 1914–18—in the kraal of Bhaleni, a Zulu man of noble blood. In formal terms, his name was Bhaleni ka Gawozi ka Silwane, marking him the son of the great warrior chieftain Gawozi, and grandson of Silwane, a legendary figure in Zulu history. Silwane was one of the first subchieftains to ally himself with Shaka, the great king who forged a scattering of Zulu-speaking clans into a mighty nation in the early nineteenth century. With Silwane at his side, Shaka launched a blitzkrieg on his neighbors, eventually laying waste to half the subcontinent and inspiring such terror that some refugees fled almost to the equator to escape his fury. In Zululand, the names Shaka and Silwane are still spoken with awe.

Bhaleni Mpungose's kraal stood on a hilltop not far from Bus Stop Four. Bhaleni was very old, so old he could no longer move. In the morning, his wives dragged him into the sun on an oxhide. In the evening, they dragged him back into his hut. He had many wives, many cattle, and hordes of children. The exact numbers are lost to memory, but it is remembered that Bhaleni's favorite daughter was a girl named Musa. She was about sixteen years old when the story opened, and very beautiful.

Musa was the daughter of Bhaleni's old age, and he was very old indeed. His memory stretched all the way back to King Dingaan, who ruled from 1828 to 1840. In his time, Bhaleni had been a fearsome warrior. He had fought at Isandlwana, the bloody battle recreated a century later in the movie *Zulu Dawn.* At Isandlwana, in 1879, the Zulus slew 858 British soldiers—the worst defeat ever inflicted by "savages" on white men armed with guns. It was the Zulu's last great feat of arms, or spears, if you will, for their lack of guns doomed them to ultimate defeat. In the end, the redcoats rolled across the Tugela River and smashed the mighty Zulu nation.

His tribe was broken, but Bhaleni himself was not reconciled to defeat. He refused to learn the white man's language or don the conqueror's clothes. To the very end—and he died long after Zulu glory had faded—Bhaleni wore the *beshu,* the skirt of civet tails, and remained a fierce traditionalist. He even resorted to murder in a futile attempt to halt the spread of Christianity among his people. One of the first Zulu converts in the district vanished without trace. This was held to be a miracle, and a monument was erected to mark the spot where Thomas Khanyile was supposedly lifted up to heaven. The police were a little skeptical about miracles, though. They believed Khanyile had actually been murdered. So did the Zulus. They even knew who had done it: Bhaleni.

It was during the Great War that the greatest misfortune came to Bhaleni's kraal. It began when his favorite daughter was stricken by *ufufunyane,* an affliction that became endemic among the Zulus after the white conquest. It was a disease that struck only young girls. They would lose control and run amok, howling and hyperventilating and jabbering in strange tongues. Today, white scholars will tell you that they were suffering from sexual hysteria, but the Zulus themselves believed that the girls were possessed by demons—by the spirits of whites or Indians, hundreds of them simultaneously, in a truly serious case. In this weak-minded condition, someone took advantage of Musa, and she became pregnant.

This was scandalous. The Zulus were a highly moral people. Premarital sex was forbidden. Girls were regularly inspected by older women to ensure that their hymens were intact. Bhaleni demanded to know who had defiled his favorite daughter, but Musa would not name the culprit. In due course, she gave birth to a son. When the son was weaned, she became pregnant again, yet she still refused to name the father. This time, however, the older women bore down hard on her. "Where did you get this stomach?" they shouted. "Where?"

Musa hung her head. And then she pointed to her own "brother," Sonamuzi, and said, "It was he; he is the father of my son, and of the baby I am carrying."

There is little to tell about Sonamuzi. I cannot even tell you his real name, for he was born under another name, a name that is no longer spoken. All people would say of him is that he was black, and "lower than a dog," because only dogs and animals have intercourse with their own mothers and sisters. Actually, Musa wasn't even his sister. They called one another brother and sister, as was the custom, but they were actually first cousins. In Zulu eyes, the distinction is insignificant. Incest is forbidden not because of the danger of deformed children. It is forbidden because it outrages the ancestors.

And now we must talk of the ancestors, the *amaDlozi*, the forebears worshiped by living Zulus. Almost all Zulus venerate their ancestors, even today. If you are a Zulu Christian, your dead father becomes an intermediary between you and Christ. You pray to him as if he were a saint or an angel. And if you are pagan, you worship him in the old-fashioned manner. Either way, the ancestors are with you. They are entities that live in your house, and hover over you at all times—helping, advising, punishing. Some anthropologists call them shades rather than gods, because every man casts a shadow; it falls on his heels, and follows him everywhere. The ancestors are that close, that omnipresent.

The shades command obedience to the traditions and laws of the nation, one of which holds that you may not take as a wife anyone within your own clan, even if this clan is tens of thousands strong. You may not marry a woman from your father's bloodline, or your mother's. You may not marry anyone from a family that has married into your bloodline, and of course, you may not marry within your own family. Of all the degrees of kinship off-limits to a lustful man, a sister or a first cousin is the most profoundly forbidden of all. The thought of sexual congress between a man and woman so related evokes "horror" in a Zulu, because it causes harrowing turbulence in the spirit world.

The instant a man deposits his sperm in a woman, the shades converge in anticipation of a new birth. They come expecting to meet honorable shades from other clans and exchange mutual respect. If the seed has been deposited in a forbidden womb, however, the shades come face-to-face with their own kin, with the spirits of their own brothers, fathers, and grandfathers. This cannot be. Such a meeting drives the shades mad with rage; they wrestle among themselves, and also turn their terrible wrath on their living descendants, on those who have subjected them to this ghastly indignity. There is little hope of forgiveness. It is said that the shades will hound the guilty until they and their entire bloodline are extinguished, or until the world itself ends. "This sin," Nxongo told me, "is the last sin. You cannot disown your own blood. You cannot cast off your shadow. Even if you try to hide from the shades, they will finish you. If you have this sin in your family, there is nothing you can do. It is better you die."

A decade or two earlier, Musa and Sonamuzi and the child of their union would have been put to death on the spot, to placate the shades. But now Zululand was ruled by white men, and they would not understand why such killings were necessary. They would arrest the killers and hang them. It is said that Bhaleni was willing to die in order to efface this disgrace from his bloodline, but he was too old to stand up, let alone kill anyone.

And yet something had to be done. "This matter could not lie down," I was told. The case was brought before the chief and debated in tribal council. Meanwhile, Bhaleni and his entire household were placed under quarantine. "We were not allowed to eat food prepared at the kraal of Bhaleni," I was told, "or even approach it. It was as though his kraal was the lair of wild beasts." The trial dragged on for months, but Chief Mbango and his elders remained confounded. There was no guiding precedent in the law. It had never come to this before, because in the past the offenders would simply have vanished from the face of the earth. In the end, the chief concluded that the crime lay beyond his powers of punishment—beyond any man's power of punishment, now that the whites were in charge. He washed his hands of the matter, and left the final decision to Bhaleni.

Bhaleni summoned the father and gave him his new name, Sonamuzi, meaning "sin of the family." And then Bhaleni renamed his infant grandson, whose continuing existence was a hideous affront to the shades. Henceforth, he decreed, the child would be called Mkhonyoza, which means "to wrestle," or "to press with muscular force." The purpose of that name, it is said, was to remind all who met him that he should have been throttled at birth.

And finally, Bhaleni banished them all from his sight forever. Sonamuzi hung his head, took his pregnant sister and his abominable son, and led them away into purgatory.

After their expulsion, Sonamuzi and Musa wandered the hills of Zululand, homeless and unwanted. It is said that they settled briefly in the Zulu capital of Mlhabatini, but their secret was discovered and they were driven out. The same thing happened in Nkandla, in Mtunzini, and in Umfolozi, according to various accounts. Musa gave birth to a second son, who was named Amon, and a third, who was named Jonas. She and Sonamuzi became Christians and took Christian names, perhaps hoping that the white man's God would be sufficiently powerful to protect them from the shades. That He may have been, but the God of the Christians could not protect them from living Zulus. They were still unwelcome everywhere. "Until the day he died," I was told, "Sonamuzi never built a house. Till he died, he wandered."

Bhaleni, meanwhile, had become deranged by the knowledge of his daughter's sin, and the terrible fury it was surely causing in the spirit world. He must have been mad, I was told, or he would never have done what he did. In his agony, Bhaleni somehow convinced himself that his beloved Musa had been married according to the law. Under Zulu law, the father of the bride receives a bride-price in cattle from the father of the groom. So Bhaleni summoned his brother, his own brother, father of Sonamuzi, and insisted that he pay sixteen cattle for Musa's hand in marriage. To the Zulus, this was not merely wrong, it was insane. A man could not buy his brother's daughter as a bride for his son. It violated every law, every tenet of Zulu religion. It was yet another terrible affront to the shades.

And yet the transaction took place, and Bhaleni got his sixteen cattle. Nobody else would touch the beasts, for they were said to be tainted, so he ate them all himself. It is said that Bhaleni realized as he lay dying that he, too, had committed a terrible sin, a sin that doomed his entire house. On his deathbed, the man who once murdered a Zulu convert gave his own soul to Jesus in the hope of passing on to the Christian heaven rather than to the Zulu spirit realm. It is said that Bhaleni was afraid to face the shades of his noble forebears—of brave Gawozi and ferocious Silwane. In the spirit world, a man who had sold his daughter to his own brother would endure unimaginable torments.

Many years after Bhaleni's death, Sonamuzi, Musa, and their sons returned to the hills near Bus Stop Four. By then, all the tribe's elders were dead, and Sonamuzi hoped his sin had been forgotten. It hadn't. "That man was an abomination all his life," I was told. "The people would just look at him and not know what to do. If they'd had the power and strength, they would have chased him away, or killed him, but they could not do that anymore. A brother and sister living together? Nobody accepted it. But what could we do?"

They could only wait for the shades. Everyone knew that the shades would act in due course. Tradition said that a man guilty of incest would rot alive. Nobody was surprised, therefore, to hear that Sonamuzi was holed up in a hut, his flesh decaying, his breath reeking of putrefaction. In due course he died. "Nobody really felt it," I was told. "Nobody was sorry." There was no ceremony to bring home his spirit, because nobody wanted Sonamuzi's spirit anywhere near them. Even the Lutherans, among whom Sonamuzi numbered himself, did not want him in their graveyard, so he was buried on a faraway hillside. A few years later, Musa was also obliterated by the shades. She walked behind a horse that lashed out with both hooves, striking her in the forehead. She died instantly.

So Sonamuzi and Musa were gone, but their three sons lived on. The youngest, Jonas, vanished as soon as he was old enough to fend for himself. The second son, Amon, mysteriously lost his voice as a teenager. This was a sure sign that the shades wished to efface him from this earth. Amon was said to be infected with the "sickness" of his family, and to yearn only for the flesh of women of his own bloodline. Since they were untouchable, he spurned all contact with women, becoming "a mule."

In the fifties, Amon also disappeared, and the last son left was Mkhonyoza, the boy who should have been strangled. Stigmatized by his very name, he was taunted and scorned wherever he went. The people of Bus Stop Four called him Mpungose *impela,* meaning "pure" Mpungose, or Mpungose "both sides." It was so bad for him that he eventually made a jester of himself, introducing himself to strangers as "the pure Mpungose" and cracking black jokes at his own expense. He was continually drunk, had no fixed abode, and worked only to earn enough money to get drunk again. "That man was not well in his head," I was told. "Even if you looked at him, you could see he was not really human."

For such a man, marriage was out of the question. "When Zulus meet each other," one Zulu explained, "we want to know, Where your mother come from? Where your father come from? Where your grandmother and grandfather come from? For courting, you must know these things. You must know the whole background." Mkhonyoza was once betrothed, but his intended discovered "the whole background" and broke the engagement. In the late forties, however, he met a widow named Colinda Ngobeshe. She had a son to support and a thirst for liquor, so she allowed Mkhonyoza to move in with her. In 1948, she gave birth to a son, and called him Simon. Simon was his Christian name, but in Zulu he was Mnotho, which means "plenty." He was given this name, I was told, because life was good in the first year of apartheid. "The water never dried up in streams, the cattle always had milk, and the sweet potatoes never ran out."

Simon's name meant "plenty," but his parents had next to nothing. Simon and his half-brother, Moses, were brought up "like animals," according to one of my informants. Their parents were usually drunk, and little Simon was taunted by other children and even by adults. "People would use him for an amusement," I was told. "Truly, truly, truly, that boy suffered!"

Simon's mother died when he was ten or so, and he was dumped on the Khumalo clan, distant relatives of his deceased mother. Simon's father seldom visited, and contributed nothing to his upkeep. Simon was never really welcome in the kraal. His peers, the boys who grew up with him, never invited him to participate in the rituals of their Zulu boyhood—never invited him to herd cattle or to fight with sticks. They called him *umqola,* a term of scathing derogation meaning "old woman" or "hag." In the stories they told, there was a recurring image of the boy Simon sitting alone in a corner of the hut, not speaking and not spoken to. It was a Khumalo man who had told me that he grew up with Simon but knew nothing about him, because "our eyes did not meet." It was dangerous to have too much truck with someone of Simon's background, because his "bad luck" might contaminate you, too.

Simon was expected to turn out badly, and he did. When he was still tiny, the neighbors would come home to find him stealing food from their pots. They whipped him, but he was incorrigible. They sent the brightest of their own sons to the mission school down the road, but nobody seemed to care what Simon did. He was doomed anyway. In his early teens, he started pilfering from neighboring white farms. The patriarch of the Khumalo clan sent him away, saying, "I don't want to see you here, because you are going to influence and spoil my children."

The patriarch had acted too late, however, because when Simon left, he took one of the patriarch's sons with him. This was Mdadune, whom Simon would later describe as the only friend he ever had. Simon and Mdadune lived together in the bush, thieved to stay alive, and were always in trouble with the law. When Mdadune was sixteen or so, he was shot dead while fleeing from the police. The Khumalos held Simon responsible. "We swore," they said, "that if we ever see him again we will kill him, because our son is dead through his influence."

The people of Bus Stop Four had not seen Simon since, but they had kept track of his progress. They knew he'd gone to jail and had tried to kill himself there. "If you have this thing in your family," they said, "it is better you hang yourself." They were not surprised to hear that Simon had asked to be kept in Barberton. "When you have this thing in your family," they said, "you stay nicely in jail, because nobody knows the background." They knew Simon had invented a fictitious past for himself, and denied his father to his own face. They knew he had killed white people, and that his first words to his captors were, "All I want is to go to the gallows." None of this surprised them. Of course, Simon wanted to die. It was the only way to escape the wrathful shades.

All Bhaleni's descendants were being hounded by the shades, they said, reciting the woes that had befallen Simon's kin since the terrible deed was done. Some had lost all their money, others had gone mad. Several were homosexual, a condition abhorrent to most Zulus, and one—horror of horrors—was a hermaphrodite. "These things are all linked," I was told. "They are definitely linked. The shades will never be at peace because of this matter."

Those old men on the hillside above Bus Stop Four did not know that Simon had been hanged, but they were glad to hear it. "About time," they said.

Everyone laughed.

So what was the truth of Simon? I was so certain in the beginning. As I read the Hammerman's moving courtroom testimony, Simon sprang to life in my imagination, fully fleshed and three-dimensional, a victim and martyr, a potentially good man made monster by apartheid. And then I went into the hills, and ducked into the huts of Simon's kin, and found myself in a parallel world, a kingdom of unconquered consciousness that had somehow proved invulnerable to the white man's guns, his corruptive culture, and his truculent missionary faith. In that world, there was no Simon. There was only Mnotho, the boy who could not become human. Who was the Hammerman? In the end, I couldn't say.

In Johannesburg, however, I met a white man who had come face-to-face with the Hammerman and had formulated some strong conclusions about him. Bruce Gillmer was a practitioner of "political forensic psychology," a left-leaning discipline whose adherents hold that apartheid has brutalized black psyches to such an extent that apartheid itself constitutes a mitigating circumstance for any crimes they might commit. Toward the end of the Hammerman trial, Simon's lawyer realized that the only way to save her client from the gallows was to convince the judge that he was insane. So she had called Bruce Gillmer in to conduct a psychological evaluation.

Like most whites who met the Hammerman, Gillmer was profoundly affected by the encounter. Simon was no ordinary man, you see. He had the power of a great novelist, the power to draw whites into his black nightmare, to take them into punishment cells awash with blood, to show them the broken corpse on which the warders were erasing whip welts with hot irons. When Simon described his days in Barberton, you felt the sun burning down on the back of your own neck, the sweat pouring off your brow; your own eyes saw rocks transformed into the heads of white oppressors and explode under the blows of a sledgehammer. Listening to Simon, Bruce Gillmer felt as though he was looking into the man's soul, and as though he was finally understanding what it was to be black under apartheid. "I know it sounds absurd," he told me later, "but I never *felt* it before."

Gillmer swiftly concluded that he was dealing with a man of superior intelligence. Simon had a logical, observant mind and a vivid way with words. His explanation of why he hated whites was entirely lucid. "I spent my whole life in prison," Simon said, "for things for which I should have spent a few months." He talked of lurking in the dark sugarcane, peering through windows into the well-lit white world from which he was excluded. He described the rage that overwhelmed him then, and the pity he felt later for his victims. Tears welled in his eyes. "I am not crying because I am scared of dying," said the Hammerman. "Dying is what I want. But when I recall all what happened, I feel very sorry. As you see me, I am not a man with a bad heart."

In the end, Bruce Gillmer could not contest that assessment. The following day, he called Simon's lawyer and told her that, in his opinion, Simon was sane. As a political strategy, beating white civilians to death made little sense, but given Simon's life experience, given what Gillmer *felt* in that prison cell, it seemed entirely understandable.

Toward the end of his interview with the Hammerman, Gillmer said, "You are a Christian. Aren't you afraid you'll go to hell for what you did?" Simon looked him in the eye and smiled. "Nothing could be worse than this," he replied. Gillmer was left with absolutely no doubt as to what Simon meant. He was talking about the hell of being black in South Africa.

Or was he?

Bruce Gillmer is a white man who has lived at the farthest conceivable remove from the mud huts of Simon's childhood. He is sensitive, compassionate, politically progressive, and rational, and for that very reason, he assumed that the old gods of Africa were dead. In all the massive literature on apartheid, there is scarcely a word that casts light on Simon's secret. If the old gods are mentioned at all, it is in the context of lost cultural values, or some such. This is the civilized, progressive position, and Bruce Gillmer is a civilized man. It would never have occurred to him to ask how matters stood between Simon and his shades, or exactly what he meant when he said he could never be like the others. Consequently, Gillmer knew nothing of Simon's background, or his secret, and when I brought it up he said it sounded "mythical."

That is exactly what I would have said once, but it wasn't mythical at all. Whatever else was true of Simon, he remained an abomination in the eyes of his own people: the son of a man who should have been strangled at birth, and the grandson of a Zulu warrior who committed murder to save his people from the rot of Christianity. These were facts, not myths, although what freight they carried I could not say. I was deaf in Simon's language, and blind in his culture.

In the end, all I really understood of Simon was that terrible scream, the scream torn from him when he broke down in the dock. I understood because it was couched in a universal human language, the language of pain. But what did it mean? The transcript gave no clear indication as to why he was stricken with sorrow at that particular point. So I obtained a copy of the official tape recording and had it translated authentically.

The tape made for intriguing listening. After all I had learned about Simon and the world he came from, his trial seemed truly farcical—less a miscarriage of justice than theater of the absurd. The court was so white, so Western, and Simon so black—or more truly, so African. The psychiatrist who ultimately testified in the Hammerman's defense was also "black," also a victim of apartheid—but he was Indian, not African, and as culturally alien from Simon as I was. He, too, had failed to ask the telling questions. He reduced Simon's resonant dreams to pathological hallucinations and saw his lifelong loneliness as evidence of a psychopathic disorder. What on earth would the word *amaPsychopath* have meant to an illiterate Zulu? As little, I daresay, as Simon's real words would have meant to his white judge.

Simon was sitting right before him in the dock, laughing in the face of death, but in many respects he wasn't there at all. He could not speak for himself and was not expected to. He spoke through an interpreter, in images, poetry, and metaphors that did not translate easily, and would have meant nothing to whites, nothing at all. The interpreter simply rendered them into serviceable English, into words and ideas white men could understand. In that way, Simon had his tongue cut out, too, just like the black man Friday in Coetzee's novel.

But I am straying from the point. I obtained the tape to find out exactly what was on Simon's mind when he broke down. These were his true words. He had just told the judge that he had decided to "follow the swallows," to commit crimes that would precipitate his death in the manner so long foreseen. He continued thus: "And I saw that *ay!* No! It is necessary that I start now because everything is coming to an end ... the in-laws, and the order of things, and their children, and the few pennies I had. I must set my heart and mind on the one thing only. I saw there was nothing I could do to prevent it. I would start a life of damaging things and others, knowing it was a path of no return. Where I am going I must open a furrow,* so that when I look backward I find I do not know how to come out again.

"All the time my heart was sore, because when I look at my forebears . . ."

And there the Hammerman broke down. His heart was rent open, and that is what was in it.

---

*The metaphor of the furrow refers to an inherited weakness, predisposition, or destiny. If a son dies in the same manner as his father, Zulus say, "the furrow has opened."

After all, we are all blood brothers and sisters.

—*BREYTEN BREYTENBACH, The True
Confessions of an Albino Terrorist*

I must add something to Simon's story. Perhaps I should begin by showing you a photograph, a black-and-white snap taken toward the end of the fifties with a Brownie camera on an ordinary Sunday afternoon in an ordinary suburb of white Johannesburg. It shows two gap-toothed white boys enfolded in the arms of a handsome African woman. The black woman's face is partially obscured by a curtain of beaded hair. She is wearing goatskin thongs and a skirt of stiff, uncured leather. There are dozens of strands of beads and totems around her neck, and she is holding a ceremonial fly whisk in one hand. One of the little white boys is me. The other is my brother, Neil Stephanus. The black woman is Lena Sithole, our resident *sangoma,* or witch doctor.

Lena lived in our house, in a room next to the garage. During the day, she washed dishes and made beds. After hours and on weekends, she donned her beads, braided her hair, and received clients in the servants' quarters. I have no idea what passed between them. I never asked. Once, I beat a small snake to death with my pogo stick in the garden, and Lena took the corpse away to make a *muti*—a magic potion. I didn't ask what the *muti* was, exactly or what it was used for. Nor did my parents. Lena's other calling did not seem sinister or even particularly mysterious to us. It was just something the natives did, like donning robes and dancing around fires, or sleeping with their beds on bricks for fear of the night-stalking *tokoloshe.*

We seldom saw Lena in her *sangoma* regalia. One Sunday afternoon, however, my mother caught her sitting in the sun outside her room, swathed in beads and totems, with the fly whisk in her lap. My mother thought, how quaint, how colorful. She brought out the Brownie, sat my brother and me down on Lena's lap, and told us to say "cheese." When the shutter clicked, we were all laughing.

Looking at this photograph, I cannot believe how blind I was, how blind we all were, we white people. I was reared until the age of five by a witch doctor, by a woman whose shades must have come to her in dreams and told her that she was chosen, that she had been given powers denied to most others and must now learn to use them—the power to heal or divine, to bewitch or protect. Behind Lena's dark eyes lay a world of profound mystery and deep religious mysticism, but none of us could see it. This is the trouble with white people in my country. Our eyes are sealed by cataracts against which our white brains project their chosen preconceptions of Africa and Africans. Some whites see danger, some see savagery, some see victims, and some see revolutionary heroes. Very few of us see clearly.

Consider the eyes of Joseph Lelyveld, a *New York Times* correspondent and author of *Move Your Shadow,* one of the most penetrating accounts of apartheid ever written. In his book, Lelyveld recounts a meeting with Credo Mutwa, a renowned *sangoma* and author who once ran a state-supported witchcraft museum in Soweto. In Lelyveld's eyes, Mutwa seems a charlatan, and his museum a bizarre Potemkin village, set up by the ruling white racists to fool foreign tourists into believing that "these people really are different, in more ways than you can imagine." Lelyveld quotes a few of the witch doctor's weird utterances, then mocks him as a salesman who knows his market. "I don't mean to imply," Lelyveld writes, "that Mutwa occasionally pandered to white prejudice. I mean to say that had become his essential business, so that finally the Africa he portrayed was an almost perfect reflection of the Africa whites want to see." Lelyveld walks away from the encounter muttering about "cultural wounds" and "lost values," as if Mutwa was a pathetic relic of an era long gone.

In 1985, the year in which Lelyveld's book won a Pulitzer Prize, some 10,000 *sangoma*s and *inyanga*s were practicing in greater Johannesburg, consulted by 85 percent of all black households and supported by a network of approximately 40,000 traders in healing and magical herbs. The African "Traditional Healers Association" claimed a nationwide membership of 179,000, outnumbering Western doctors by a crushing factor of ten to one. Most of Soweto's dashing professional soccer teams had a witch doctor on staff, throwing the bones to ensure victory, and its business tycoons hired diviners to advise them on deals. The classified sections of Soweto's newspapers carried ads in which "traditional healers" or "herbalists" offered to restore love to the lovelorn, seal homes against evil spirits, thwart the designs of enemies, and cure disease. On weekends, makeshift corrals appeared on Soweto's roadsides, full of goats destined to become "beasts for talking"—to be sacrificed to awaken the shades.

Soweto's newspapers and magazines frequently offered accounts of zombies raised, sorcerers sniffed out, ritual murders, and, once, a high school closed down when the entire student body started experiencing supernaturally induced hallucinations. The subject cropped up from time to time in political coverage, too. Some of Soweto's militant black trade unions were demanding that white employers grant black workers the right to take paid sick leave if a *sangoma* or *inyanga* advised it. Some of Soweto's militant young comrades were using witchcraft to strengthen themselves in their struggle against apartheid's police.

This did not necessarily mean they weren't Christians, though. In fact, they probably were. A majority of African South Africans are Christians, but the faith means different things to different people. For whites, it means traditional Western theology. For almost ten million Africans, it means membership in one of the myriad "Zionist" or "Ethiopian" churches—sects that preserve the "lost values" of African ancestral religion in a shallow amber of European Christianity. These "free" African churches—as in free of European religious imperialism—worship the Holy Trinity but also believe in divination and magic, and in dreams as communications from the shades.

Beyond that, untold millions of Africans are simply and proudly pagan, for lack of a less judgmental word. They honor their ancestors and cleave to the central tenet of African religion: Illness or misfortune results from "loss or damage to the soul," inflicted either by witchcraft or wrathful shades. In the cities, 45 percent of Africans hold this to be true; in the rural areas, around 80 percent. Angry shades may be appeased by sacrifice, but evil witches are sometimes killed. In 1985, eighty-four evil witches or sorcerers were burned or stoned to death in the Northern Transvaal alone. They were victims, one assumes, of "lost cultural values."

In my circle of hell, the circle of white left liberals, discussions of such matters are fraught with curious peril. Elsewhere in the world, veneration and respect for non-Western cultures is the hallmark of the humane and open-minded white man. In South Africa, it is quite the opposite. One of apartheid's underlying tenets is that there are distinct and immutable cultural differences between races, and that it is God's will that they be maintained. Under the circumstances, any acknowledgment of differing cultural values threatens to sound like an oblique argument in apartheid's favor, and an insult to Africans besides. That is why I, as a Just White Youth, never asked blacks what the night-stalking *tokoloshe* looked like, or who they worshiped when they danced in robes around fires. Such questions seemed impolite, even racist. It was much easier, and more fashionable, to talk of lost cultural values.

By the time I returned from exile, it was easier than ever. Millions of black South Africans had moved decisively into the First World. There were black physicists, MBAs, doctors, systems analysts, novelists, engineers, and newspaper editors. A sector of Soweto had been dubbed Beverly Hills and boasted mansions worthy of the name. There was a glossy black magazine called *Tribute,* full of ads for Chanel, Chivas, and BMW. On TV, advertising was pitched at the emerging black middle class's fondest image of itself—an American image, usually; sleek black Americans in black American settings, listening to soul or jazz and consuming products with names like "Manhattan Lemon Sting." At my old private school, black parents had vaulted right over white South Africa in their westward hurtle. When Zulu was introduced into the school's progressive curriculum, black parents demanded that it be dropped: They didn't want their children learning an African language.

One of the best-known denizens of this brave new South Africa was Soweto's redoubtable Nthatho Motlana, M.D. Like many members of South Africa's black elite, Motlana was born on a Christian mission and blessed with the sound education denied to most other blacks. He earned a medical degree in the fifties, when black doctors were still something of a rarity, and had practiced in Soweto ever since. Over the years, he'd become a figure of great renown—physician, community leader, outspoken foe of apartheid, and a familiar face on the world's TV screens. His Soweto surgery was a low-slung, modern affair, his receptionist exquisitely polite and lovely to the eye. The magazine rack in his waiting room featured the *New Statesman* and the *Manchester Guardian Weekly*—unusual reading materials, in a country such as mine. There was a message from the BBC in London on the doctor's desk as I walked into his office, and the doctor himself was on the phone. He nodded and motioned me into a chair.

In the flesh, Dr. Motlana was a handsome sexagenarian, spry and impish, with lively eyes and a full beard streaked with gray. His tongue was lashing the person on the other end of the line. "Let me speak to Joe," Motlana snapped. When Joe came on the line, the doctor greeted him in the half-Afrikaans patois of the streets—*"Hoe's my 'bra?"* he said—and then switched into Tswana. After that, the conversation kept leaping from language to language, but I was able to glean its gist. It revolved around a bright and talented black executive who managed a medical clinic or hospital somewhere in South Africa. The institution's white funders were so impressed by this man's performance that they wanted to take out a ten-million-rand "key man" insurance policy on his life.

As a director of the medical facility, Dr. Motlana was strongly opposed. The white donors seemed to be implying that the black man in question was uniquely intelligent and irreplaceable, and Motlana was insulted by the idea. He was whooping with indignation, virtually dancing in his chair, clearly relishing his own anger. Whenever he got in a real zinger, he'd chuckle wickedly and wink conspiratorially across the desk.

After fifteen minutes or so, Motlana put down the phone, turned his charismatic smile on me and said, "Well, Mr. Malan, what can I do for you?" I launched into a rambling, half-apologetic preamble about differing cultural values and their significance in South African life. I tried my best, but it still came out sounding like an oblique justification for apartheid, and an insult to Africans besides. The doctor caught the drift, and cut me off before I was through. He spun in his chair and drew my attention to a volume on the bookshelf behind him: William L. Shirer's *Rise and Fall of the Third Reich.*

"Culture," said Dr. Motlana, "is a word that became disreputable because of Hitler, who made culture synonymous with race. I worry about the misuse of that word. We use it to divide mankind." As far as he was concerned, there was no such thing as "Western culture, per se." He made some pithy remarks about "white bastards" who refused to acknowledge that their "so-called Western heritage" owed a huge debt to the Chinese and Arabs, among others, and wound up talking about the global village. "I've been to Japan," he said. "I've been to Israel. I've been to Europe. I've been to Canada, I've been to Nigeria—I've been all over the world, and what I've seen is that the influence of American television, music, and film is driving people together."

This implied that a similar process was underway in South Africa, and yet, on the basis of Motlana's own evidence, the reverse could well be true. Dr. Motlana was engaged in something of a crusade against what he called "the tyranny of superstition"—the influence of the witch doctors and their allies, Africa's traditional medicine men. When neighboring Mozambique started throwing witch doctors into reeducation camps, Motlana expressed approval, and he was constantly demanding that the South African authorities enforce their own anti-witchcraft laws. It was a curious campaign, and the most curious aspect of it was that Dr. Motlana appeared to be losing.

In a recent speech, he had noted that there were "several hundred" witch doctors practicing in his Soweto neighborhood, where thirty years earlier there had been hardly any at all. On a recent visit to the mission village of his birth he had been astonished to hear the drums of Africa pounding in the night. In his childhood, the German missionaries had strictly forbidden all "pagan" rites. I drew Dr. Motlana's attention to these anomalies and asked how they might be accounted for.

He leaned forward in his chair, slapped a palm on the desk, and gave me a piece of his mind. "As if in anticipation of this discussion," he began, "I spent the evening last night with two men from my civic association and we talked about something similar. One of these young men was a Pedi-speaking fellow from the north, where you have this rampant belief in lightning-control and many cases of people being burned as witches. This Pedi boy seemed to be suggesting that there might be something to all this, and I got very agitated. So he turns to me and says, very innocently, 'But isn't it our culture?' He sent me up the wall! I mean, I just crawled up the ceiling in anger! I said, 'My culture is not synonymous with superstition and ignorance and denial of everything scientific!' " Dr. Motlana was dancing with indignation again, his voice leaping into a higher register as he warmed to the theme. "My reaction is *fuck* this old *shit*," he said. "That is my reaction!

"Don't confuse culture with belief in the supernatural," he warned me. "African culture is such things as respect for your elders, knowing your place in society, avoiding vulgar language, love of your neighbors, the care of orphans and widows. That's my culture. Not shit about lightning, man, or scarification, or some charlatan who gives you herbs that make you shit the whole night until you die! I get really agitated when whites start romanticizing this stuff. It's as if there is a bloody conspiracy to lock us into ignorance and superstition. *Do you get my point?*"

I did indeed, but I had just enough spunk to pose a final question. "When you speak this way," I asked, "do many Africans agree?"

"Do I get support from the black community?" said Dr. Motlana. The question seemed to stop him in his tracks. His agitation subsided and a rueful smile creased his face. "Oh, no. Oh, no. On the contrary, a chorus of attacks. Phew!" He wiped imaginary beads of sweat off his forehead, illustrating the heat he had taken.

"They say, 'This is our culture'?"

"*Exactly!*" the doctor replied. "Which is absolute shit, man! It's all a lot of nonsense!"

Was it all nonsense? My friend Eugene would disagree. He was the show-biz promoter, musician, and aspirant movie director who, as you recall, occasionally worked with me as an interpreter, more as a lark than for the money. Eugene wore trendy clothes and rings on several fingers and had lived, until very recently, in the part of Jo'burg we called the Bronx—a region of high-rise apartments colonized by forty thousand blacks in defiance of whites-only laws. He had an amazing range of friends and contacts—white lawyers, gay activists, black revolutionaries, criminal aristocrats, pop and movie stars. He was cinema-literate, witty, and sophisticated. His taste in music made me feel decidedly square. At the time I met him, he was planning to cut a record album inspired by Brian Eno and David Byrne's arcane experiments with found sound. The idea was to collect snippets of Botha's and Tutu's speeches and lay them down atop some funky dance tracks, creating an aural pastiche of South Africa's warped political reality.

One night, on the way home from one of our forays into the townships, this African renaissance man started talking about witchcraft and its role in the entertainment industry. It was like listening to a Hollywood hustler gossiping about agents, save that Eugene was talking about *sangoma*s and *inyanga*s—wizards and witch doctors. Sipho "Hotstix" Mabuse consults this one, he said. The Soul Brothers use that one. Brenda Fasi of Brenda and the Big Dudes had no *sangoma* at all, and she was looking for trouble. In Eugene's estimation, it was virtually impossible to stay on top in a field like show business unless you had a crack witch doctor on your side. He illustrated the point by recounting the inside story of the rise and fall of a famous black playwright called . . . ah, let's just call him Phil.

Phil's mother was a sorceress, Eugene explained, a mistress of dark forces. She gave her son a "thing" to watch over him and advance his career. This "thing" was a white woman, and she propelled him to great fame and fortune in the seventies. In return, Phil had to follow certain rules. He had to make frequent sacrifices and never allow anyone to see his "thing." One night, however, his wife caught a glimpse of it, sitting naked at a dressing table, combing its hair, and that was the start of Phil's downfall. Soon after, he stopped making the requisite animal sacrifices, and now he was a complete nonentity. He hadn't had a play produced in years. Eugene shook his head sadly. "That's typical," he said. "His ship comes in, and suddenly he's too good to sacrifice, because you get blood all over your house, and it smells like an abattoir."

"How do you know?" I asked, too taken aback to think of anything else to say.

"Oh," he said, "I sacrifice. It's our religion."

All this was a prelude to a pitch. Eugene felt that his own rise toward the top had slowed a little of late, so he wanted to make a pilgrimage to Maputo, Mozambique, to see a legendary witch doctor. His own car was unreliable, so he wanted me to take him in mine.

I was honored to be asked to accompany him, greatly honored. Black men seldom took whites into their confidence on such matters. It was the last thing I expected to hear from Eugene, though, not that it affected my judgment of him either way. After eight years in Los Angeles, a city infested with chanters, channelers, crystal gazers, tarot readers, televangelists, and flotation tankers, all superstitions and religions seemed pretty equal to me. In South Africa, however, they tended to differ according to which side of the racial divide you stood on.

I was always aware of that, I suppose. I saw the signs of Africa, but they were like stars in the sky; they were just there. Lena was a witch doctor, Zionists danced on Thursday, and witches were sometimes burned alive in the *bundu*. After Simon, I looked at these things again and felt like Galileo, because the heavens had reordered themselves before my very eyes. In Galileo's time, man in his arrogance assumed that the heavens revolved around him. In my time, in my country, white men assumed that they were the center of the black universe—that they had subjugated the dreams and psyches of Africans, along with their bodies. It simply wasn't true. That is what Simon taught me.

I cannot say what all this means, but I do know that religion and culture are forces of awesome power, and that nations are to some extent welded together by shared languages, shared religious and cultural mythology. After a year of pursuing the truth of Simon, I was no longer sure that such commonality existed in South Africa. I prayed it did, though, and that we would all find it in time. Without it, I feared we were doomed.

There is nothing in man that was not put into him when he sprang from the reeds in the beginning.

—African saying on the origins of rage

This is the story of a man who died on the boundary between rival kingdoms of consciousness, under circumstances embarrassing to both sides. Whites were embarrassed by the cold-blooded manner of his killing, Africans by events that led up to it, and hardly anybody would talk about him in the aftermath. This account is thus constructed from leaks, off-hand remarks and fragments, and its central figure remains something of a mystery to me. All I can really tell you about Themba Ngwazi is that he was short, stocky and twenty-nine years old, and that he wasn't afraid to die.

Themba was a Xhosa from the Flagstaff district in the nominally independent Transkei. I once drove there in search of his family—the wife, the two children, the heartbroken father, who was said to have a hunchback and to be of royal blood—but I couldn't find them. All I found was a homeland whose deceptively green and pleasant face concealed desperate unhappiness. In Flagstaff, the cattle were scrawny, the fields barren, the people bitterly poor. Whenever I stopped to ask the way, little children surrounded the car, rubbing their stomachs and saying, "Hunger! Hunger!" or "Ten cents! Ten cents!"

There were few grown-up men in Flagstaff, because there was no work there. If you were a man born in Flagstaff, you went to work in the distant white cities. Or, as in Themba's case, you left your wife and children, walked to the nearest depot of TEBA, and signed your life away to the mines. TEBA was The Employment Bureau of Africa, recruiting arm of the Johannesburg Chamber of Mines. The officials at TEBA gave you a number and a contract and put you on a train bound for eGoli, the city of gold.

In eGoli, you were taken to the Chamber of Mines hospital, ordered to strip, and sent into an acclimatization chamber—a giant Turkish bath, really, unbearably hot and humid in emulation of underground conditions. You and your fellow recruits, hundreds of you, were placed in front of small steplad-

192

ders and told to climb up and down, up and down, for hours on end while
the sweat cascaded off your naked bodies and white men in lab coats listened
to your heart with stethoscopes or fondled your testicles in their hands,
checking for a hernia. This rite of mass humiliation was designed to make
sure that new recruits wouldn't drop dead on the job, down in the bowels
of the earth. It went on for days and days. If you were judged tough
enough—and Themba was—you were sent to miners' school and then sent
underground.

This is how Joel Matlou described his first day down there:

At 7:15 A.M. the bossboy took us to the lift. As it went down my
ears went dead and I saw dark and light as we passed other
levels. The lift stopped at 28 level. We gave our tickets to the
bossboy and walked for one hour to the end of the shaft. The
mine shaft was very hot. The sweat ran off me like water. There
were three tunnels. The small trains had red lights on the back
and front indicating danger. Before the blasting, small holes were
drilled in the walls and a man referred to as a chessa-boy put
explosives into them. After the blasting we found broken pipes,
bent rails, a cracked wall and other damage. The blast gave us
heavy work. The small trains and their trucks were called to
collect all stones. You can find a stone weighing 450 pounds far
from the blast. Water leaked from the top of the walls. Sometimes small stones fell on us. My boots were full of water. A Zulu
from King Williamstown was digging water concrete when part
of the ventilator fell on him and his left leg was trapped under
it. The boss called us and we lifted the ventilator to take out the
trapped man. His leg was broken and bloody. . . .

And so on. What is true on one mine is not necessarily true on another,
and the gold mine where Themba worked was cooler and safer than most,
or so its white officials told me. The mine was called Randfontein Estates,
and it lay twenty-five miles southwest of Johannesburg, on the western arm
of the gold reef that made white South Africa rich. It was a vast complex,
with a perimeter at least ten miles long. There were at least three shafts,
judging from the headgear I saw rising from the veld, and possibly four
separate compounds, or hostels, for the black workers, who numbered
fourteen thousand. Security on the mine was very tight. You couldn't just
walk in, and you certainly couldn't go down underground unless you were
invited, which I wasn't.

So I hung around the mine gates and buttonholed a white guy in a hard hat. I told him that management said his mine was cooler and safer than most, and he seemed a bit taken aback. "All I can say," he said, "is that it's bloody hot down there anyway." He said Randfontein Estates was so deep that it took half an hour to descend to its deeper levels, and another half hour to travel to the working face. It was like a city down there, he said, or a giant underground factory, so noisy that your brain seemed to rattle inside your skull. Trains thundered, machines clattered, drills yammered, and the shock waves of muffled explosions came rumbling out of the mouths of dark, claustrophobic tunnels. It was a frightening place to work, he said, what with a mile of rock between you and the sun and cave-ins an ever-present danger. Beyond that, he had no real complaints. He was white, and white miners made very good money.

The same was not true of Themba and other black men who labored in South Africa's mines, digging the gold, diamonds, coal, and platinum that made white South Africa wealthy. I once asked a trade union organizer how he went about "conscientizing" black miners, and he said, "I begin at the beginning. I say, 'The whites came here in 1652, and ever since it has been bad for us. They stole our fathers' cattle, and they stole our fathers' land. Then they found the gold, and started stealing our fathers' labor.' " He went on to talk about the "hut taxes" and "livestock taxes" imposed on rural Africans around the turn of the century at the behest of Johannesburg's mining capitalists. The aim was to force black tribesmen off the land and into the mine compounds, where cheap labor was desperately needed.

South Africa's mines were the deepest in the world—a mile and a half deep, in some cases—and so close to hell that the walls and roofs of the shafts were sometimes too hot to touch with bare hands. The work was exquisitely uncomfortable, and for decades it earned black miners a mere pittance in pay—R10.70 a month as late as 1970. That is why South Africa's gold mines were so obscenely profitable, why their shares were among the bluest chips on the world's stock exchanges for more than a century. As recently as 1985, I heard an American congressman on network television refer to black miners as "slave labor."

He had a point, I suppose, but he'd missed the moment to make it. By 1985, the slaves who dug the gold were doing relatively well. Themba Ngwazi, for instance, was pulling down around five hundred rand a month, plus free board and lodging. In South Africa, this was a living wage. On the other hand, it was barely a quarter of what a white miner made, and it was very hard for Themba to make more, no matter how intelligent or capable he was, or how hard he tried. He was black, you see, and all the highly skilled and best-paid jobs on South African mines were reserved by law for whites only.

Themba could never become a blaster, for instance. Only a white man was allowed to hold a blasting certificate. This was insulting and hurtful in itself, but it had an even more invidious consequence underground: It encouraged white bosses to sacrifice black miners' lives. White blasters were paid according to how much rock they broke, so they took risks—or rather, they ordered black men like Themba to take risks. If black miners were killed, that was just too bad. "They're just baboons anyway." So said Arrie Pollas, leader of the reactionary white Mine Workers' Union.

And so black "baboons" died by the thousand in mining accidents—fifty thousand deaths since the turn of the century. Mine safety conditions started improving in the seventies, but blacks were still dying in disproportionate numbers, partly because they had no right to refuse to work in dangerous areas. If the white boss gave Themba an order, Themba had to obey. If he balked, he risked being fired, and if he was fired, there was no union to fight for him—not prior to 1982, at any rate.

Prior to the Botha reforms, black trade unions were denied legal recognition in South Africa, and black mine workers made their arguments in other ways, sometimes with acts of sabotage. They threw spanners into engines, started fires underground. Now and then they'd explode with rage and frustration, and wild rioting would break out in the compounds, at which point the police were called in to subdue them, often with loss of life. After that, the troublemakers were usually fired and replaced. It was so easy to replace a black mine worker. Out in the bush, in the homelands and surrounding countries, almost half a million men were on the waiting list for jobs on South African mines.

This is how the writer Joel Matlou felt at the end of his first shift:

> The time for clocking out started to roll round, so we followed our bossboy back to the station. We switched off our lamps while we waited in the queue because at the station there were electric lights. We were wet like fishes and ugly like hippos. Some were sitting and resting with empty stomachs. After twenty minutes, the lift arrived. The guard opened the door and we flowed in. The notice on the door said the lift took only 20 people, but we were packed like fishes in a small can.

Back up in the sunlight, black miners lived in bleak all-male compounds, far from their homes and families. Themba's compound looked rather like a prison to me—a model prison, to be sure, with sports fields and recreation facilities, but still: not the nicest place to live. It consisted of nine single-story face-brick buildings, strewn in a crescent across several acres of lawn. In the center stood a giant mess hall, and off to one side was an open-air amphitheater, where movies were sometimes shown. The whole was surrounded by tall fences, and accessible only through an elaborate gate flanked by guardhouses teeming with security men.

The security barracks lay a mile or two away. All I could see from the outside were a few "riot vehicles"—armored Toyota Land Cruisers—parked on the tarmac, but I gathered that they had some serious weapons in there: razor-wire trailers, water cannon, armories of semiautomatic rifles, shotguns, and "stoppers," devices for firing tear gas or rubber bullets. There was also a guard-dog school somewhere on the premises, and even a secret service of sorts, controlling a network of management spies.

White mine managers bristled at the suggestion that there was anything sinister about all this. They insisted that the guns and war toys were necessary to guard the gold and keep the peace among men from mutually hostile tribes. They had a point, I suppose, but then they would also say their workers were quite contented, and I'm not sure that was entirely true. To hear Joel Matlou tell it, black mine workers were miserable.

"There was no time or chance to prove yourself," he wrote, "who you are and what you want."

I did not wash my clothes or bathe because I did not have soap or other clothes to put on. All I did was eat and sleep on the grass. . . . The mine injection makes you forget about your parents, relatives and friends, even your girlfriend. The injection makes you think only about work underground. After three weeks underground, I was part of that world. Washing, bathing, cutting nails, dressing in clean clothes and reading newspapers was far from me. It could be about 640,000 miles far from me. Life was so bad; for me life was a little piece of stone.

Themba Ngwazi had lived the life of a stone for most of his adult life, and he was very, very tired of it. That is one thing I can say with certainty: Themba was an angry man.

* * *

This is a parable about industrial relations, about the struggle of workers against bosses. We have met Themba, and now we must meet his antagonists. Once again, I know less than I'd like to about them, because they decided not to talk to me after an exploratory interview or two. I visited their headquarters, though. It was a windowless monolith in Johannesburg's financial district, vast planes of reflective glass on the outside, and strikingly sumptuous within. The lobby was full of expensive art. In the elevators, a disembodied voice reminded travelers which way they were going and when they'd arrived at their floor. The corridors were deep and plushly carpeted. The desks were broad and imposing, the white executives behind them well tailored and fed. There was a smell about the place that reminded me of America. It was the smell of money and power, the smell of a big oil company, or an insurance conglomerate, maybe.

This was the headquarters of JCI, or Johannesburg Consolidated Investments, a mining house with assets of three and a half billion rand and net annual revenues of R322 million. JCI owned Randfontein Estates, and was a subsidiary of Anglo American, the giant gold- and diamond-mining conglomerate that owned many of South Africa's richest mines and almost everything else besides—including a controlling interest in around 60 percent of the companies listed on the Johannesburg Stock Exchange. The Anglo American Corporation was South African capitalism personified.

In my leftist youth, I thought institutions like Anglo American and JCI were evil, but I was no longer so sure about that. The white men who ran the Anglo empire were businessmen, no more or less moral than their counterparts elsewhere. Most were liberals, in the English-speaking South African sense, and most collaborated with apartheid in the decades when it was good for business. By 1985, however, apartheid had become a liability, and the liberal capitalists were turning against it—not for moral reasons, but because it was causing turbulence and instability, threatening the flow of profits and fostering the growth of bolshevism among increasingly antagonistic black workers. The capitalists saw which way the wind was blowing, and started repositioning themselves.

By 1985, they were doing their best to endear themselves to the angry black masses. This entailed, among other things, the granting of exponential wage increases to black workers and some sly encouragement of trade unionism on the mines. Some of South Africa's capitalists were very sophisticated, and saw that it was in their own best interests to help the emerging black trade unions to their feet. That way, they might be molded, tempered, and turned into organizations with whom the capitalists could work in the long run. And so, when a militant black union informed JCI that it wanted to conduct a recruitment campaign on Randfontein Estates, JCI smiled graciously and invited the union in.

The union in question was NUM, the mighty black National Union of Mineworkers, headed by a charismatic young lawyer named Cyril Ramaphosa. NUM was only three and a half years old in 1985, but it was already the country's largest black union, with 230,000 paid-up members and a solid foothold in the mines. In some respects, NUM was a wages-and-working-conditions trade union; in others, a revolutionary force, clearly bent on a far-reaching restructuring of South African society. It elected Nelson Mandela its honorary president, spoke warmly of socialism, and established ties with the exiled ANC. All this was no doubt alarming to JCI's urbane capitalists, but it was the shape of things to come. NUM was a force to be reckoned with, even appeased, maybe.

The union's "access agreement" at Randfontein Estates was thus quite generous in its terms. NUM was given leave to hold meetings and distribute literature on mine property. It was even given an office at the mine. The agreement was valid for a year, and stipulated that JCI would recognize NUM once it recruited a majority of workers as members. Given the size of Randfontein Estates workforce, it was an important campaign, so NUM sent one of its best men in to run it.

His name was Blackie Mshotshiza, and he was barely twenty-seven years old. He wore his hair in an Afro, had a fondness for fancy fitted shirts, and lived in an apartment in a once whites-only part of Johannesburg. A former student activist from one of the independent homelands, he'd come to Johannesburg in 1982, matriculated at a private high school, and gone straight to work for NUM. In the three years since, he'd risen to be a regional organizer, in charge of NUM activities on nine huge mines west of Johannesburg.

Themba showed up at the very first NUM meeting on Randfontein Estates and immediately caught the union organizer's eye. "He was singing, you know, these songs of Africa," Blackie told me. "He was leading the singing and dancing. I was hearing that he came from a blood family, that his father was a chief or something—that is why he was so much strong, because he was coming from a blood family." Themba couldn't read or write very well, but this did not mean he was dumb. "He could understand what you were talking," said Blackie. "As for his politics, I will just say he was hating the whites. That's all."

"I started liking him straight away," the union organizer added. Indeed, Blackie liked Themba so much that Themba became a NUM shaft steward, and a spearhead of the recruitment drive.

In spite of the spectacular grievances among Randfontein Estates' black miners, the drive got off to a disappointing start. Many black miners were simply scared of joining the union, scared of losing their jobs. Others were ill-educated men from isolated areas, unfamiliar with the concepts of trade unionism and resistant to the idea of paying dues. To complicate matters still further, a significant percentage of Randfontein Estates' workers were Shangaan tribesmen from Mozambique, and they were utterly terrified of getting into trouble and being sent home. Their country was racked by war and famine, and they were liable to starve if that happened.

On top of all this, NUM accused management of hampering it at every turn. The white bosses expected Blackie to hold meetings only in his office—not in the compounds. If he wanted to distribute pamphlets, he had to get the bosses' approval, and if he failed to do so, his literature was confiscated. As far as management was concerned, all this was in keeping with the small print in the access agreement. They took the drive's halting progress as proof of their own most cherished contention—Randfontein Estates' black workers were actually quite happy.

Whatever the truth, Blackie and Themba made little headway. By November 1985, NUM was still drawing barely a hundred supporters to meetings, and the access agreement was soon to expire. JCI was willing to renew it, but the union was in a hurry. It wanted to sign up all 600,000 of South Africa's black mine workers and weld them into a weapon with which to cudgel the apartheid state. There was no time to waste. The townships were on fire; the children were fighting and dying; the time for the conclusive uprising had come. NUM's president, James Mahlatsi, was saying that South Africa would be a socialist country within the year, but even this prospect failed to ignite the workers of Randfontein Estates. The mine remained quiet. Some union militants seemed to find that disappointing.

On November 13, Blackie Mshotshiza called a meeting and took the mine's apathetic majority to task. His speech focused on a change in labor-contracting procedures known among miners as the *waya-waya*, or "why-

why." Once upon a time, migrant mine workers had enjoyed something approaching job security. At the end of any given contract, they went home to their wives and cattle armed with a "record of service" containing a "coming-back date." On the coming-back date, a man reported to the nearest TEBA depot, and was put aboard a Jo'burg-bound train. These days, however, the mines were mechanizing, cutting down on unskilled labor, employing fewer men. These days, many workers received a record of service containing no coming-back date. The bosses promised that they'd be recalled when they were needed, but sometimes, the call never came. The workers asked, "Why? Why?" Why must it be this way? Workers at nearby Kloof mine were fighting the why-why. So were the workers at Vaal Reefs and Western Areas. But the men of Randfontein were just sitting on their hands. Blackie accused them of being "old women," too frightened to join the union.

"Wake up and fight!" he said.

In due course, Blackie's "emotional and aggressive" remarks reached the white mine managers' ears. Randfontein Estates ran an intelligence system almost as sophisticated as the state's—black men with code names such as Foxtrot-Foxtrot, Delta-Delta, or Golf-Whiskey planted in the compounds to keep an ear open for subversive undercurrents. In the days following Blackie's speech, the spies' reports took on an increasingly unsettling tenor. One spy caught wind of a plan to attack the mine's security force and "kill the white dogs." Another overheard someone say, "Black Africa belongs to the blacks. The whites must be driven away." A third reported a plan to chase "dogs like security staff, hostel representatives, *induna*s and personnel" off the mine. The dogs in question were "management lackeys"—blacks of the supervisor caste.

By December 7, the tide seemed to be turning in the union's favor. A big union rally was scheduled for that day. NUM hired a fleet of buses to pick up its supporters, but Randfontein Estates refused to let them in. Management was clearly growing uneasy. Undaunted, several hundred miners jumped the fences, hoisted Blackie onto their shoulders, and then piled onto the buses, singing freedom songs.

The rally must have been quite an event. When the miners came home, thirty-six hours later, they were utterly intoxicated by the freedom spirit and in the mood for action. Their demand was, "No more why-why," and to back it up, they imposed a boycott on the canteens—management-run beer halls where workers relaxed over mugs of the African brew called *tshwala*. Once the beer halls were shut down, the militants turned on the so-called Jew shops, concession stores that traded in soap, shoe polish, tobacco, and other small necessities. On its way to close one such store, a throng of singing miners had to cross a public road. They ran into the police at the intersection. Stones were thrown, and the cops opened fire, killing one miner, injuring thirteen, and arresting thirty-seven.

At that, the real troubles began. As word of the shootings spread, workers started downing tools. By nightfall, at least a thousand were on strike. The Shangaans wanted no part of this and set off for work as usual. The militants waylaid them on their way to the shaft head, and several were beaten up as scabs. Next morning, the Mozambicans decided it might be prudent to stay in their rooms, but the militants were having none of that. They surged through the Shangaans' quarters, smashing furniture and driving the cowards out before them. Soon, almost three thousand workers were out in the quadrangle, dancing, singing, and roaring, *"Amandla! Amandla!"*—"Power! Power!" The bosses were shaken by their fury. "I shat myself," one said.

The mine's white supervisors retreated into their offices and watched the revolution through the windows. The dancing went on day and night and the whites grew delirious with exhaustion. Indeed, there came a point, forty-eight hours into the strike, when they were dancing and shouting *amandla,* too. Every now and then, a delegation came in to confront Piet Rademeyer, the mine's manpower manager. Rademeyer was a painfully earnest Afrikaner, and an old-fashioned compound manager by repute. Until the struggle came to Randfontein, being manpower manager was a little like being a colonial magistrate. You could walk without fear through the teeming compounds. The tribesmen would call you *nkosi,* or lord, and pass the time of day with you in Fanagalo, the half-Zulu lingua franca of South African mines. Piet Rademeyer had always assumed that the blacks were quite fond of him. Now he was learning otherwise.

One afternoon, Themba led a delegation into Rademeyer's office to present some new demands. Rademeyer listened politely, then tried to put across management's point of view. "We're not concerned—" he began, but Themba cut him off. "You're not concerned about what?" he snapped. The rest of the delegation took up the chant in Fanagalo: "You're not concerned about what! You're not concerned about what!" Then Themba stood up and waved a finger in Rademeyer's face. "You, Piet!" he shouted. "You too clever! You shut up!" Themba was a very angry man. As far as he was concerned, the boss was going nowhere until the workers' demands were met.

What were their demands? They wanted their thirty-seven comrades released from police custody. They wanted the mine security force abolished. They wanted the *indunas*—bossboys—fired and replaced with "worker representatives." And finally, they wanted no more why-whys. They wanted coming-back dates. They wanted job security.

According to Rademeyer, management was willing to make concessions but didn't know whom to talk to. They couldn't exactly talk to Themba. He was illiterate and hardly spoke English. And yet they had to talk to someone, because the situation was getting out of hand. In the end, they called Cyril Ramaphosa at NUM headquarters and pleaded for his help. A deal was duly cut, and NUM sent Blackie Mshotshiza out to the mine.

It was almost midnight by the time Blackie got there. There was thunder and lightning in the sky, and the strikers were waiting in pouring rain. According to the reports of management spies, Blackie pointed to the silent headgear of the nearest mine shaft. "You see those wheels?" he asked. "They are not moving. Through your power and unity, this mine has come to a standstill. Now you see, this mine belongs to the blacks. We have the managers where we want them." The miners cheered.

The time would come, Blackie continued, when the union would tell Piet Rademeyer to "take his jacket and fuck off," but the time was not yet ripe. For now, they should go back to work. The miners cheered again, donned their helmets, and went back underground.

A day or two later—on December 12—a delegation of NUM higher-ups and Randfontein miners trooped into JCI House and sat down to talk with the bosses. They came out with at least one major concession—an end to the why-why system—and the promise of more to come. It was something of a triumph for the union. NUM had humbled the mighty mining house, and brought the capitalists to their knees.

The peace lasted only twenty-four hours. On December 13, trouble broke out again. The issue, this time, was a gate—a massive red gate that separated the mine from the township of Bekkersdal. Themba wanted the gate open, but management insisted it stay closed, citing security reasons. Themba refused to swallow that. As far as he was concerned, Rademeyer was trying to break the beerhall boycott by denying workers the right to go drinking off the mine. When management declined to yield to his demands, Themba drummed up a crowd and staged an unruly demonstration. Blackie showed up just in time to negotiate a truce. The bosses backed down, the gate was opened, and Themba's followers dispersed.

Four days later, Themba came up from underground to find the red gate locked again. The bosses claimed that black supervisors and personnel officers had asked for it to be closed, on the grounds that *tsotsis* from the township were coming in to rifle their cars. Themba wasn't buying that, though. He and his followers were outraged. They uprooted the giant gate with their bare hands and dumped it outside the compound manager's door. Looking around, they spotted two bosses standing a hundred or so yards away. "They came charging at us like a rugby team," one of the white men told me. "It was a bloody frightening sight." The whites ducked into an office and closed the door. Hundreds of workers gathered on the lawn outside, dancing and singing again. NUM shaft stewards rushed to the scene, but Themba's band apparently brushed them aside. Darkness fell, tension mounted, and the situation degenerated into confusion.

I think it only fair to mention that this narrative is drawn in part from a confidential document leaked to me by the proverbial disgruntled employee. It was JCI's internal report on Themba's uprising, and it mentioned several people I had never met—among them Cyril Ramaphosa, founder and leader of NUM. When it was all over, Ramaphosa's union would proclaim Themba a loyal shaft steward, and a martyr to the cause. JCI's report told a somewhat different story. According to the report, a worried white mine official named H. Fischer called union headquarters around eight that night and found himself speaking to Ramaphosa himself. Listen, said Fischer, the situation here is getting out of control, and your men don't seem able to contain it. Ramaphosa is said to have groaned, "Oh, no," and promised to see what he could do.

Not much, apparently. Over the next ten days the mine started sliding into anarchy. There was a rash of wildcat work stoppages, called by God knows who. The work force seemed to split into factions, each claiming to be the union, each putting forth its own demands. All issues seemed to become one issue—the issue of white bosses, white power, white privilege, white rule. It got to a stage where nobody knew what was happening, not even the person who compiled JCI's secret report. There were scattered outbreaks of tribal fighting, and several violent clashes between militants and mine security. More scabs were beaten up, and then it was the *indunas'* turn. The militants insisted that they all be fired. Immediately. The *indunas'* lives were in danger, so management evacuated them from the compounds.

As far as the militants were concerned, this wasn't good enough. One afternoon, a leaderless mob of three hundred miners marched on the bosses' office and demanded to know why they still saw *induna*s on the premises. They called another strike. That evening, there was renewed fighting between the militants and the reluctant Shangaans. This had been going on for almost a month now, and management decided to step in and stop it.

The capitalists were reluctant to use force, because they saw far, and carefully calculated the consequences of their action, but once they'd decided to use muscle they proceeded with deliberation and determination. The mine's own forces were mobilized. A command-control helicopter was borrowed from Anglo American, two riot teams from a neighboring mine. The South African Police were invited to send a detachment too, just in case. Two days before Christmas, this ad hoc army moved in to crush the militants, who numbered around a thousand, according to the mine's intelligence estimates. The orders were rubber bullets only, no lethal force, but someone loaded his rifle with live ammunition, and one miner was shot dead. Another, hit in the head by a rubber bullet, died of his injuries. In all, twenty-two men were hospitalized. In the aftermath, management tightened security and banned meetings of more than ten men on mine property. The unrest was finally over, or so it seemed.

And then, early one Sunday morning, an alert security guard noticed something odd happening in a marsh just off mine property, and it started all over again.

It is Sunday, January 19, 1986, 8:30 A.M. on a southern summer morning. The rains have been good this season. The grass is lush and dewy, and there is a blush of intense green in the boughs of the willows and poplars on the banks of the marsh that Eric Magnus is studying through his binoculars. Eric Magnus is white, in his late thirties, and wearing jeans, a light summer shirt, and the ubiquitous white South African mustache. Magnus and a black man in combat uniform are standing beside a car on a dirt road, looking out over a semirural landscape. Behind them, we see the towering headgear of a mine shaft, and mine dumps yellow as beaches and high as hills, partially obscured by groves of blue-gum trees. A line of split-level houses along the horizon marks the outskirts of the gold-mining town of Randfontein.

Eric Magnus is a cop; one look at his blunt face, and you know he's a cop. He was once a lieutenant in the South African Police, but these days, he's chief of security at Randfontein Estates Gold Mine, commander of the mine's 460-man private army. This is supposed to be Eric Magnus's day off, but he's been called in to take a look at what's happening down in the marsh. The reeds are eight feet tall in some spots and so dense that an army could be hiding in them. Magnus has been watching for fifteen minutes already, but he's still not quite sure what he's seeing.

At first, he thought they were Zionists, African Zionists, conducting baptisms in the muddy rivulet that trickles between the beds of reeds. There is no "prophet" to be seen, however, no be-robed pastor dunking the faithful in the drink, and there's none of the clapping or singing that usually accompanies such ceremonies. Just forty or fifty black men, some wearing underpants, some completely naked. They're just standing around in a marsh without any clothes on, as if this is a perfectly ordinary thing to be doing at dawn on a Sunday morning. They seem to be aware that Magnus is watching, and waiting for him to go away. Why on earth are they naked? They certainly aren't swimming. Eric Magnus can't figure it out, but it makes him feel uneasy.

He recognizes several faces among the crowd. One is a yellow-faced, fattish fellow with tribal scars on his cheeks. What's his name again? Ah, yes, Themba. And there's Comrade Bala, too. Comrade Bala is a real hard case, a hard man with a strong body and intense, coal-black eyes. A holy warrior. What's he doing down there? It worries Eric Magnus. Another thing that worries him is the way some of those men are tearing branches off trees and snapping them into sturdy three-foot lengths, the length of a traditional fighting stick. Magnus doesn't like that at all.

He swings his glasses toward the house of the white man on whose property this gathering is taking place. The farmer is out in his backyard, also observing the situation through field glasses. Traversing back across the dewy green landscape, Magnus discovers a new element in the tableau—a yellow South African Police pickup, pulling off the tar and heading down the dirt road toward him. The cops pull up and say howzit. One of the policemen jerks a thumb at the blacks in the marsh. "What are those guys doing down there?" he asks. Magnus shrugs. "You tell me," he says.

It turns out that the cops are here on business. The white farmer on the far side of the marsh has asked them to clear the trespassers off his land. Neither of the cops speaks an African language, so Magnus offers the services of his black sidekick, and the loan of his PA system, too. The cops tell the black man what to say. He clicks on the microphone, clears his throat, and makes the announcement in Xhosa. "Attention!" he says. "Attention! You are on private property! Please leave now!"

In response, there is an astonishing stirring at the waterside, and several hundred hitherto invisible black men rise from the reeds. Some are naked, others armed with staves cut from surrounding trees. They turn toward the white men and stare at them, silently. Eric Magnus is suddenly very uneasy indeed.

"Uh-oh," he thinks. "Here's trouble."

In his days as a South African Police detective, Eric Magnus was assigned to track down the right-wing terrorists who sent acid-impregnated T-shirts to the children of liberal newspaper editor Donald Woods—an incident immortalized in the movie *Cry Freedom*. Just as he was closing in on the culprits, the police brass pulled him off the case. Magnus quit in disgust because of that, and he seldom misses the force save in moments like these. If this were a South African Police operation, he could step in right now, throw his weight around, and nip the trouble nicely in the bud. But that's out of the question today. Eric Magnus is a civilian now, answering to a civilian boss. JCI's vice-chairman has laid down a policy: "Mine management must endeavor to maintain a low-key security profile, and at the same time retain complete control."

Maintain a low-key profile, but retain complete control. What on earth does that mean in a situation like today's? Magnus thinks it over and decides that JCI's vice-chairman would probably want him to walk out into the marsh and have a friendly chat with the workers. So he does that. He goes strolling among them, nodding hello on this side, good morning on that. "Aren't you cold?" he asks those who are naked. The mine workers seem a little surly and resentful, but they aren't at all hostile at this stage. With a little encouragement from the white man, they put their clothes on and start walking back to the mine.

Magnus heaves a sigh of relief, climbs into his car, and follows. He's crawling along behind the marching column when he hears a sound that makes his heart sink. The mine workers are singing. Their song is hauntingly beautiful—"the most beautiful song I've ever heard," Magnus says—but he'd rather not be hearing it right now. It's the song Xhosa warriors sing as they go into battle. The mine workers start waving sticks and fence-droppers in the air. Some stoop to pick up stones from the road. A disembodied arm rises from the center of the throng, holding a knife in its hand.

At this point, Piet Rademeyer shows up. He takes a look at the crowd, turns to Magnus, and says, "We can't let them in with those weapons." So Magnus gets on the radio and calls out a riot team or two—forty or fifty black men in combat boots and visored riot helmets, armed with truncheons, shotguns, and stoppers. Reaching the gate of their compound, the miners discover themselves outgunned. Piet Rademeyer steps out to talk to them. We don't want another fight, he says. You guys just put down your weapons and come inside, and we'll forget this ever happened. The miners find this acceptable. One by one, they start passing through the gate.

As they come in, a mine official named Jan Oosthuizen notices something curious. Most of these men have tiny cuts on their bodies, two tiny parallel incisions on their cheeks, between their eyes or behind their shoulder blades, in the case of those still shirtless. At first sight, this doesn't strike him as unusual. You often see ceremonial tribal scars on the faces of black South Africans. Even ANC leader Oliver Thambo has them. The only odd thing about these scars is that they aren't relics of adolescent initiation rites. They're fresh. A dark, gooey substance seems to have been rubbed into them. Oosthuizen has no idea what to make of this, so he just puts it out of his mind.

As he passes through the gate, each miner is patted down by a security guard. Then he joins a knot of comrades seated on the lawn fifty yards away. They are waiting to make sure everyone makes it safely through the security cordon. They do. As soon as they're all disarmed, though, the South African Police step in and collar two apparent ringleaders for questioning. This is treachery. Rademeyer gave his word. The mine workers start shouting angrily. The cops swiftly release their two suspects, but it's too late.

The miners start breaking down trees, tearing down washing lines, and breaking them up for weapons. Some run into the nearby compound to round up reinforcements. Rademeyer hears an incredible racket as the militants move through the building, smashing the walls and ceilings with sticks, driving the timid out before them. Men start boiling out of the doors and windows, leaping fences, fleeing the militants. The crowd at the gate starts growing, getting more and more excited. Eric Magnus sends one of his armored vehicles out onto the lawn, loudspeakers blaring a warning to disperse. The miners throw stones at it. Rademeyer runs to a telephone and calls the mine's general manager. We've got trouble again, he says. The general manager authorizes the use of force. The mine's riot team squares off against a throng of five-hundred-odd dancing, stick-waving black miners, and it's high noon again on Randfontein Estates.

The showdown has started, but Eric Magnus is still thinking in terms of low-key security profiles and defusing the situation. So he gets on the radio again and calls in his secret weapon, a war toy that he has christened Ndlovu, meaning "elephant." A minute or two later, Ndlovu appears in the distance. It's a gleaming, sinister, armor-plated machine, red as a fire engine, with what appears to be a cannon mounted on its turret. Ndlovu comes trundling down the perimeter fence and turns into the compound. The mine workers have never seen this machine before. They gasp as its cannon swings to bear on them, and most of them start backing away. Then Ndlovu opens fire—and water comes spewing out of its gun barrel. Ndlovu is a water cannon.

A great cry goes up from the miners, and then something inexplicable begins to happen. A few men are knocked flying by the jet of water, but the rest "just went mad," in Eric Magnus's phrase. "They were running away, but as soon as the water cannon opened fire, they turned back and attacked us. They came flat out for us, throwing stones and pieces of coal." To Oosthuizen, who is watching the battle from a distance, the black men seem "jubilant." They're ducking and dodging rubber bullets, laughing their heads off. They seem utterly fearless. The security force fires salvo after salvo of rubber bullets, though, and some of the missiles find their mark. More and more of the mine workers go down, howling, clutching injured legs. Eventually the attack wavers, and after that it's all routine—"Good, clean fun," says Magnus. The crowd breaks and runs, and in minutes it's all over.

In the aftermath, in an office papered with pin-studded ordnance maps of his turf, Magnus ponders the curious failure of his new riot-control weapon. He has Ndlovu's user's manual right there in his desk, written by an American counterinsurgency expert whose research has clearly established the water cannon's effectiveness. To intimidate and discourage white rioters, you put green dye in the water. If your rioters are black, the water must be red, or purplish, actually; black South Africans call it purple rain. Magnus did everything by the book, and yet Ndlovu intimidated nobody; on the contrary, its use inspired euphoria.

Magnus is mulling over this mystery when one of his secret agents comes in with a curious report. He says that the workers down at the marsh this morning were members of a rogue faction led by Themba. The union has been urging Themba to cool it, to calm down, but Themba's too angry to listen to reason. He and several other shaft stewards have decided to go it alone. They failed to show up at Blackie's most recent meeting, and when the organizer sent someone to call them they told the messenger to get lost.

According to the secret agent, their plan is to overthrow the mine's white authorities and install Themba on Piet Rademeyer's throne. Toward this end, they imposed a levy on themselves, two rand per man, raising a total of eighteen hundred rand. This sum in hand, they dispatched a representative to the Transkei, homeland of the Xhosa and Pondo tribes, to consult a renowned *inyanga,* or witch doctor. The *inyanga* provided several shoe-polish tins of a very powerful battle medicine called *intsizi,* traditionally made from charred herbs and animal fat. It was black in color, and if you made tiny cuts in your body—on the cheeks, between the eyes, on the shoulder blades—and rubbed it in, it would turn the white man's bullets into water, or so the witch doctor claimed. The medicine arrived at the mine on Friday, and Themba had been holding secret meetings all weekend, administering it to his followers.

Magnus has no idea what to make of all this. He's white, so it sounds incredibly cockeyed to him. Still, it would seem to explain the water cannon's ignominious failure. At the same time, he can't help wondering what's going on in the heads of the dozens of mine workers stung and bloodied by rubber bullets in this morning's riot. He imagines it will be rather hard to convince them this battle medicine is worth the money they paid for it.

It was indeed. Themba and his men held a postmortem the following afternoon. Agent Victor-Victor was there. In his report to mine management, he describes a great grumbling about this lying *inyanga* and his useless battle medicine. The *inyanga* (or maybe it was his representative; Victor-Victor wasn't quite clear on that score) stood up and explained that there had been a misunderstanding. The medicine did not work on the day you took it, he said. You had to wait three days before it worked. What's more, he said, if you took a bath or had a woman in that period, it would not work at all. And finally, he cautioned that the medicine would protect only those warriors who kept their face to the enemy and pressed home the attack. Cowards who turned their backs would be cut down. The miners nodded understandingly and resolved to give it a second chance. They made it clear, however, that if the the magic failed again on the third day, the *inyanga* was a dead man.

In conclusion, Victor-Victor notes that Themba's faction has scheduled a meeting for the following day—the third day, the fatal day. Three hundred fighting comrades from a nearby township have sworn to be there, Victor-Victor says, and they are going to bring guns.

This is not the only alarming report to cross Magnus's desk this night. Golf-Whiskey says a plot is afoot to burn down Cooke 2 compound. Foxtrot-Foxtrot reports talk of a brewing faction fight in Cooke 3, where Xhosa and Pondo tribesmen are at odds with Swazi and Basotho. A neighboring mine reports the discovery of an ominous leaflet in its compounds. "If your heart is weak you can't stand blood," it says, "then go home." And most alarming of all, miners from conservative factions are deserting Randfontein Estates in droves. They are hundreds, even thousands of miles from home, but they are packing their suitcases and just walking off the mine. This is the surest of all portents of coming trouble. Magnus picks up the telephone and calls the South African Police.

Johannes Bernoldus Eksteen is a cheerful little shrimp of a man, sandy-haired, buck-toothed, and barely five feet tall. He's also a former policeman, about twenty-two years old. Unlike Magnus, Eksteen misses his old job—misses it so much he's going back to it in another month or two. Meanwhile, he's taking no chances. He's got a shotgun on his shoulder and a bag of buckshot in one of his pockets, in flagrant contravention of JCI regulations. Mine security officers aren't supposed to carry live ammunition. Eksteen stands to be fired if Magnus finds his bag of buckshot, but he doesn't care. If there's going to be a battle today, Johannes Bernoldus Eksteen intends to take a few of the enemy with him.

Today, on Eric Magnus's orders, he's sitting on top of a man-made mountain of grayish crushed rock, binoculars glued to his eyes. Below him and to his right lies one of Randfontein Estates' worker compounds. A six-foot fence marks the mine's perimeter. Beyond the fence lie two "slimes dams," filled with waste from the gold extraction process, and beyond that, a stretch of open veld, fluorescent green after the rain. On the far side of the veld, about three hundred yards away, lies a sea of small asbestos-roofed houses—the township of Bekkersdal.

A dirt road leads past the compound, through the fence, and out into the open veld. Eksteen has been watching that road since noon, when the morning shift started coming up from underground. Black men are leaving the hostel in a steady trickle. They are walking out into the veld and sitting down in an ever-growing circle, apparently waiting for something to happen. Eksteen has duly reported these developments over his walkie-talkie, and they're being passed on to the South African Police. By and by, a yellow Chevy four-by-four with steel mesh on all its windows appears at the base of Eksteen's rock pile. Eksteen scrambles down to say howzit to the boys in blue. Turns out he knows them.

Sergeant Daniel Pretorius and Constable Frikkie Koekemoer are members of the West Rand Reaction Unit, an elite SAP riot-suppression squad. They are both Afrikaners. Sergeant Danie is twenty-five, blond, sports the regulation white South African mustache and beer belly. Sergeant Danie is, well, you could almost say famous. A few months back, he was on *gatkruip patrollie*, meaning "ass-creep patrol," in a township called Tembisa. Ass-creep patrol is the hearts and minds aspect of riot control in South Africa. A photographer caught him handing out sweets to uniformed black school kids. Danie and the black kids gave the camera a smile and a thumbs-up sign, and the picture made the front page of the *Sunday Times*. "Thumbs up for education," said the caption.

Sergeant Danie's taste in music inclines towards Fleetwood Mac and Van Halen, which sometimes puts him at odds with his partner, Constable Frikkie Koekemoer, aged twenty-seven. Constable Frikkie looks like Buddy Holly, with his long, thin body and black-framed glasses, but he digs the polka beat of *boeremusiek*, traditional Afrikaner concertina music. Constable Frikkie and his eight-months-pregnant wife, Ria, are just crazy about a *boeremusiek* combo called *Dolf en sy Dolfyne*, Dolf and the Dolphins. There was a time when Frikkie and Ria used to go dancing every Saturday night, but these days they never go out anymore. In fact, Frikkie and Danie have had virtually no time off since the black rebellion started, and that's more than a year ago. They're both very tired. Frikkie used to be able to drink a bottle of brandy on his own, or "on his ace," as we say. These days, he has two or three brandies and Coke and passes out exhausted.

On the other hand, let it not be said that Constable Frikkie Koekemoer dislikes his job. It's a swashbuckling, soldier-of-fortune game, and besides, Frikkie rather likes oppressing blacks. "Frikkie hated the kaffirs," his stepfather Danie van Zyl told me. One night, when there was nothing better to do, Van Zyl accompanied Frikkie on one of his patrols. On some dark road, they spotted a vehicle weaving suspiciously in the traffic up ahead. Frikkie pulled it over. It was a Zola Budd, a twelve-seat microbus used as a black taxi. Frikkie yanked the keys out of the ignition and threw them away. When the black driver complained, Frikkie uncorked a tear-gas grenade, chucked it into the bus, then put his shoulder into the door so that the black passengers were trapped inside. "They were jumping around and screaming and banging on the roof," Van Zyl chuckled. "Hoo, boy, you should have seen those kaffirs when we let them out!" This was his and Frikkie's idea of fun.

Frikkie and his sergeant have been in the thick of it since the great uprising began. They have done tours of duty in Sharpeville, in Tembisa, in Kagiso, in places where the toll of black protesters was really heavy. They have probably shot a rioter or two, or five, or ten, and came close to copping it themselves on at least one occasion. Just two weeks ago, a black kid lobbed a petrol bomb into the cab of their Chevy, and they were splashed with flaming gasoline. Sergeant Danie's prematurely receding hairline receded a little farther, and Constable Frikkie's mustache was singed. Their faces turned pink, as if they'd spent a day in the burning sun.

After all they've seen, and all the places they've been, they're not all that impressed by what young Eksteen has to show them. It looks pretty calm to them. Just a knot of mine workers sitting quietly in the veld, fewer than a hundred of them at this stage. Eksteen mentions in passing that these black men have been taking medicine to turn bullets into water. "You should have been here Sunday," he says, "and seen how this *muti* worked. They ran so fast you wouldn't believe it!" They all have a good laugh about that, then the cops drive off casually, promising to look in again later to see if anything interesting has developed.

Sergeant Danie and Constable Frikkie might have been a little less cavalier if they had had a chance to speak to the spy called Victor-Victor, who was out there in the veld with the miners. The crowd was growing. By 4:30, there were four hundred men; by five o'clock, more than six hundred, their ranks swelled by a contingent of comrades from the township of Bekkersdal. Later, in his written report, Victor-Victor will say that many of the black men out there were armed with sticks, iron bars, and pangas. The Bekkersdal comrades had a can of gasoline, a pile of rags, and a stack of empty bottles. They were making petrol bombs, and hiding them in the grass. And finally, there was the man in the balaclava, an ANC insurgent, judging by the gun he carried—a Soviet AK-47 assault rifle. The Bekkersdal comrades were clustering around him, like Secret Service men around an American president, so that nobody got too close a look at him.

The meeting got underway in earnest around five, according to Victor-Victor. It was presided over by Themba and a man identified only as Hlangana. Hlangana was wearing a yellow NUM T-shirt, and Themba was a NUM shaft steward, but both men made disparaging remarks about the union. The union's struggle is going forward too slowly, said Themba. We must take action on our own. He called for five men from each tribe present to step forward and form a delegation to approach the white bosses with the workers' demands. If they were arrested, Themba concluded, steps would be taken to set them free.

While this plan was under discussion, the yellow Chevrolet four-by-four reappeared in the distance and came bouncing across the veld. The police vehicle stopped seventy yards from the crowd, and Sergeant Daniel Pretorius got on his bullhorn. This is an illegal gathering, he said in Afrikaans. You have five minutes to disperse. He repeated the warning in English, and then he and Koekemoer sat back to wait. The mine workers didn't move. After a while, Danie got back on the bullhorn and gave a second warning, the two-minute warning. Themba told his men to stay put, so Pretorius and Koekemoer got out of the truck, carrying grenade launchers. The crowd began to seethe and rumble, but the cops weren't scared. They'd been through this so often before. They lifted their weapons and fired.

As the tear-gas grenades fell hissing in around him, Hlangana leapt to his feet yelling *"Bulala amaBunu!"*—Kill the Boers! "The medicine is strong!" he shouted. And so a great cry arose from the assembled mine workers, and they rose and charged as one. They came out of the cloud of tear gas in the oxhorn formation of nineteenth-century African warfare, the center attacking while the horns rushed to outflank the enemy and close in on him from behind. Sergeant Pretorius unslung his shotgun and shot one of the charging miners in the chest, blew the head off the next at point-blank range. Constable Koekemoer was standing behind the open door of the truck, blasting away with his service pistol. The guns were going off in their very faces, but the miners seemed utterly unafraid. They kept coming.

The watchers on the mine dump saw Pretorius stagger as someone caught him a blow on the head from behind, and then he was overwhelmed and disappeared under a tide of black men. Koekemoer fired until his gun was empty, and then ducked back inside the Chevy's cab. He grabbed the radio and screamed, *"Maak gou,* boys!"—"Hurry, boys, they're killing us." And then the mob grabbed his legs and hauled him out of the cab, and he, too, was stomped, hacked, and kicked to pieces. Literally. Once the cops were dead, the ferocious mob virtually tore their truck apart with their bare hands and overturned it on Koekemoer's corpse. Then they bled some gasoline out of the tank and made a fire on the white man's face, just to be sure he was dead.

In the aftermath, or so it was said at the inquest, Eksteen was white with shock, and shaking so badly that he had to sit down while telling his story. He watched the whole thing from the top of his rock pile, and his account was improbably cinematic; an episode from a war movie, or a hokey Western, maybe. When the smoke started rising, everyone knew the white cops were done for. Eric Magnus went out to retrieve their bodies, but his armored truck was driven back by a barrage of stones. So he deployed his men in a skirmish line between the mine and the township and kept the mob at bay with a "wall of rubber."

At that point a second police vehicle came careening onto the battlefield and drove right up to the crowd. Two white cops leapt out with shotguns and opened fire at point-blank range. The crowd didn't flinch. They just stood there, throwing stones. Someone scored a bull's-eye, and one of the cops staggered back, blood pouring down his face. He and his partner leapt into their van and fled for their lives. Their van jumped a ditch, buried its nose in the far side, and stalled. The van was instantly surrounded, and two more cops seemed doomed. They got the engine going again, however, and shot their way out of the crowd. They'd no sooner escaped than the man in the balaclava opened up from the cover of a blue-gum plantation. Magnus's men hit the dirt, bullets screaming over their heads.

And then there came the sound of a distant droning, and the black crowd looked up to see something terrible—an endless convoy of police vans and armored personnel carriers, converging on the scene. It was the first time this had happened—the first time since the start of the bloody uprising that white cops had been killed in action, and their brother officers were outraged. Every policeman on the West Rand seemed to have heard Constable Koekemoer's dying cry on the radio, and now they were coming in to wreak vengeance. The mob melted away into the township. More than forty blacks had been injured, and eight lay dead or dying on the battlefield.

Half an hour later, helicopters started dropping out of the sky above Randfontein Estates. Convoys of army trucks rolled in from nearby military bases. A grim-faced police brigadier stalked into Piet Rademeyer's office and ordered him to clear out. He set up a command post in Rademeyer's executive suite, threw a cordon of steel around the mine and the adjacent township. And then he sent in his boys to clean up.

It was a very bad night in Bekkersdal. The police kicked every door down and searched every nook and cranny, arresting anyone with razor-blade scratches on his face or shoulders. On the mine, police set up a machine gun on the roof of a compound and ordered black workers to strip and lie face down on the lawn, so that their bodies could be inspected for the telltale markings. By dawn, the cops had 371 prisoners, including the man in the balaclava, plus his rifle and six hand grenades.

By dawn, Themba Ngwazi was also dead. The police apparently worked some of their prisoners over, asking, "Who told you to do this? Who is your leader?" Everyone said, "Themba." There was no escape from Bekkersdal, not that night. The police net was drawn tight and Themba got caught in it. The official version was that he tried to escape, but it was dark, and no one could really see. The prisoner was handcuffed and shackled, and surrounded by heavily armed cops. Some say he ran; some that he was invited to run. All that was really clear, in the end, was that Themba started hobbling away. He had not gone very far before a policeman put a load of buckshot in his back.

A new era of freedom has begun.

—State President P. W. BOTHA, April 1986

And now it comes time to take a coldly scientific look at the sociopolitical scoreboard as it stood on June 12, 1986, another watershed day in the history of South Africa.

The great anti-apartheid uprising of the mid-eighties had been underway for twenty-one months. Hundreds of thousands of blacks had been tear-gassed in clashes with the police, and at least ten thousand injured by rubber bullets, whips, or bird shot. Some 1,650 people were dead. A total of 11,006 had been arrested for "public violence" and similar unrest-related crimes; a further 18,500 detained for varying periods under various state-of-emergency and security regulations.

Almost all detainees were black, of course, and almost all of them were given a rough time—one survey, by a liberal university, found that 83 percent of detainees were subjected to "some form of physical abuse." Most were just beaten up, but some were tortured, too. They were stripped naked and forced to stand on bricks, kept awake for days on end, ordered to sit for hours on nonexistent chairs. Some were given the "helicopter," an ingenious cruelty in which a detainee's wrists were cuffed to his ankles, a broomstick inserted through the loop thus created, and the person suspended for hours in midair. Some had electrodes attached to their nipples or genitals and were subjected to electric shock. This happened to children as young as ten.

In that period, most detainees were released after two weeks and sent home to the townships, which remained as wretched and overcrowded as ever. The nationwide backlog of housing for blacks stood at 487,000 units. The number of homeless black squatters in the industrialized regions was climbing toward the million mark. In white South Africa, schools were standing empty; in black South Africa, they were so crowded that pupils were being turned away. There were empty beds in white hospitals; in black hospitals, patients slept on floors and in corridors. Even the minister of police acknowledged that "appalling" township conditions lay at the root of the political uprising.

The unemployment rate among blacks was officially 7 percent, but academic economists insisted that the true figure was at least four times that and rising rapidly. The population was expanding faster than the economy. About 50 percent of black people were under twenty, and one economist was predicting that up to 44 percent of them would never find a job. A state-financed study of this doomed generation of black teenagers established that one in five suffered from depression, a quarter so severely that they were contemplating suicide. Nine percent were so angry and frustrated that they wanted "to kick and break things," and 12 percent "to hurt and kill."

And so a great deal of hurting and killing had been done. In the townships, the comrades had petrol-bombed 7,700 buses, torched 1,447 schools and 985 black-owned businesses. They had also burned 46 churches, 26 clinics, 60 halls, 3,920 private homes, and untold hundreds of collaborators, rivals, dissidents, and informers.

The rebellion had swept through all four of the country's provinces, and there had been major outbreaks of political violence in several tribal home-lands. Many black schoolchildren and university students had barely seen the inside of a classroom in three years. White business had been hit hard by periodic don't-buy-white and stay-away campaigns, and white industry con-vulsed by strikes—more than four hundred strikes in the first six months of 1986, leading to a cumulative loss of around 500,000 man-days and count-less millions in production.

In many townships, black householders were no longer paying bills for rent, lights, or water, and municipalities were on the verge of bankruptcy. In many townships, black local authorities had resigned or been murdered as collaborators and replaced by "peoples' structures" controlling quasi-liberated zones dubbed Cuba or Azania or Russia. Those black mayors who yet survived had become virtual warlords, kept in power by "blackjacks" or "greenbeans"—young black men who were given guns, uniforms, and three weeks' police training and sent in to shore up the collapsing structures of state. The slogan of the ANC and the United Democratic Front for 1985 was "render South Africa ungovernable," and it had come close to succeeding—in the townships, if nowhere else. White South Africa was losing control of black South Africa.

And then the year turned, and it was 1986, Year of the Armed Struggle for the ANC underground, year of the all-out push against the hated apartheid state. There was a certain mad euphoria on the left as the year turned, a sense that victory was close. As 1986 wore on, the struggle intensified. According to the state Bureau of Information, there were 1,605 outbreaks of political violence in January, resulting in 41 deaths. By April, the number of "unrest incidents" had climbed to 2,293; and in May, it was higher still—2,645 incidents, claiming 157 lives. In the same period, the number of "stone and petrol-bomb attacks" on the white "security forces" increased from 312 to 744, and the extermination rate of black moderates, sellouts, and dissidents rose to alarming levels. During the southern autumn of 1986, 172 blacks died inside the ring of fire, inside the necklace.

And then came June, South Africa's month of destiny. This may sound suspect in light of the grim figures just cited, but South Africa wasn't an entirely totalitarian country on June 11, 1986. In the townships, any black man with a stone in his hand was liable to get a police bullet in his head, yet there remained a measure of freedom in other arenas of life, especially if you were lucky enough to be white.

My high-school buddy Roy, for instance, was a cameraman for *Witness to Apartheid,* a documentary that had excited widespread international attention and was about to be nominated for an Academy Award. Directed and narrated by a New Yorker named Sharon Sopher, *Witness* was the season's most impassioned denunciation of the apartheid tyranny. During her flying visit to South Africa, Sopher was detained for an hour or two by the security forces in Soweto. On the U.S. promotion circuit, and in the documentary itself, she parlayed this into a breathless yarn about risking death to steal the truth from under the guns of apartheid's brutal police.

Moved to anxiety by such tales, my American friends wrote letters asking if "they" were onto me. No, they weren't. They never came anywhere near me, or Roy, or the white guy who produced Sopher's documentary, or anyone else we knew. They were out in the townships, torturing black radicals, presumably. We were sitting around Roy's pool, drinking up the profits of what was privately referred to as "the gold rush." It was a very good time to be a journalist in South Africa. The outside world had suddenly developed an insatiable craving for images of black suffering, and whites of a certain social caste and political inclination were falling over one another in their eagerness to provide them.

Among the items in demand were pictures of and stories about black leaders thunderously denouncing the Botha government as the most evil since Hitler's. There was a measure of truth in that, but anyone who spoke such words in Hitler's Germany would have been in a concentration camp already, along with any reporter who dared quote him. Hitler would also have crushed the militant trade unions, and obliterated the structures of black resistance. Botha had not done that, not yet. Some key black leaders had been rounded up and put on trial for "terrorism" or "treason," but the major organs of resistance—the UDF, National Forum, Azapo, and South African Council of Churches—were still operating more or less openly, and the press remained more or less free, subject to a web of restrictions that kept being overturned or reinterpreted by the courts, which were also functioning more or less freely. Those who compared Botha with Hitler were crying wolf, and the wolves finally came, as is their wont. They came on June 12, 1986, four days short of the tenth anniversary of the bloody Soweto rebellion.

On June 12, at six in the evening, President Botha appeared on TV wagging his authoritarian finger. On television, Botha resembled no one so much as the Soviet Union's Mikhail Gorbachev. They had the same sallow jowls, the same balding pate, and a similar tendency to wag their fingers and deliver lectures. In fact, the similarities went further. Both men had inherited ideologically sclerotic regimes and launched tentative reforms in the teeth of stiff opposition from vested interests and ideological purists.

I dunno, my friend, this is a minority view, but it seemed to me that Botha had tried. He was a cantankerous old bastard, to be sure, but he'd come a long way against the grain, considering that he'd learned his ideological chops from the master, D. F. Malan. Many of the changes he'd made were merely cosmetic, but their cumulative impact was immense, if only on the psyches of whites. "Adapt or die," he ordered. "Tame your hearts with your minds." Botha was signalling that the old days and old ways were over. He seemed to have no clear idea of what came next, but he kept chipping half-heartedly at the edifice of legislation he'd spent the first thirty years of his career enacting.

In the end, he even scrapped the hated pass laws, a move that heralded the end of the deranged Boer fantasy of a pure white South Africa. Shortly thereafter, the National Party took out a series of newspaper ads in which Botha seemed to be begging blacks to take his reforms seriously. "From my heart," said the State President, "I ask you to share in the future." He conjured up a vision of "a new South Africa, where all decent men can look one another in the eye without fear or hatred," and appealed to blacks to help him bring it into being. "A new era of freedom has begun," declared P. W. Botha. As if to convince himself, he added a little postscript, dramatically underlined with a hand-held pen: *"That is the reality!"*

But the overriding reality, the one that really counted, was that it was all too little too late. His policies had set the stage for a black rebellion, and his ruthless attempts to quell it had triggered a furious outcry in the outside world. He had lost the battle for world opinion, and he was losing the fight to stave off sanctions. He was even losing his own right wing. Fractious right-wing elements were forming vigilante groups, demanding shoot-on-sight curfews and throwing government supporters through plate-glass windows at stormy rallies. The white right wanted their government to unglove the iron fist and put blacks back in their place, once and for all. Maybe Botha agreed with them in his heart; maybe they forced his hand. Whatever the truth, his jowly face appeared on my television screen at six in the evening of June 12, 1986, to announce the coming of the wolves.

The sinister forces of revolution, Botha charged, had marked the upcoming Soweto Day anniversary as the moment of final and conclusive uprising. "There comes a time," he continued, "when a nation must choose between war and a dishonorable, fearful peace, and we have arrived at that point." Botha was speaking Afrikaans, to Afrikaners, so the foreign press seemed to miss those words, but they chilled me to the bone. The state president had actually declared war, and now he was launching his opening offensive; another nationwide state of emergency, effective immediately. Even as he spoke, the security forces were moving into the townships in crushing force. They picked up every comrade, activist, and organizer they could lay their hands on, and 24,000 blacks were soon in detention, many of them schoolchildren. The government cracked down brutally on the press, kicking a few foreign correspondents out of the country and forbidding everyone else to film or photograph any "security-force action." The newspapers were no longer allowed to name detainees, agitate for their release, or even quote court testimony about torture during interrogation. On the day of supposed reckoning, June 16, the streets of black South Africa were eerily quiet. Nothing moved save armored cars, and nobody dared breathe too loud.

Beyond that point, the Great Afrikaner Reform of the early eighties came grinding to a halt. Botha unleashed his dogs on the Charterists, abandoned his courtship of the center, and turned his attention to his mutinous right wing. Suddenly, you heard little about "power sharing" or "just and peaceful solutions." Instead, you heard cabinet ministers like F. W. de Klerk saying, "Race remains the basis of National Party policy, and will remain behind lock and key."

On the opposite side of the ideological spectrum, attitudes were equally intransigent. The Afrikaners' most deadly enemy, in this great struggle for power, was not blacks in general so much as the mighty Charterist movement—the UDF–ANC–South African Communist Party axis. It was sometimes hard to say exactly what the ANC stood for, but its journal *Sechaba* offered the occasional clue. In February 1985, *Sechaba* published a document of great import—an essay by Joe Slovo, the influential white Communist who doubled as chief of staff of the ANC's military wing. A great deal of hot air had been expended in debates about which ANC leaders wore what hat, who was Communist and who wasn't, but it all seemed irrelevant to me. The ANC and its Communist allies saw eye to eye on almost everything, and when Comrade Slovo spoke he used the royal *we,* as in "we the movement," the revolutionary alliance.

In his essay, Slovo began by acknowledging that Botha's reforms were having an impact on the lives of blacks inside South Africa, and even on the minds of some comrades in the liberation movement. Indeed, he continued, some "friends and brothers" were taking Botha's talk of "negotiation" so seriously that they had begun to question the ANC's strategy of armed struggle. Such men, Slovo warned, had lost sight of the ANC's true objectives. "In the South African context," he said, "we cannot restrict the struggle objectives to the bourgeois democratic concept of civil rights or democratic rights." Victory would be empty unless the revolution seized the commanding heights of the economy, and Slovo insisted that such an assault had to be carried out by force of arms. Under the circumstances, talk of compromise and negotiation was "nothing but a recipe for submission and surrender."

"We do not believe," Comrade Slovo concluded, "that classes ever commit suicide." The Western press missed this, too, which was a pity. It was the ANC's equivalent of Botha's June 12 declaration of war.

So, race remained under lock and key, and the classes did not commit suicide. To an outsider, F. W. de Klerk and Joe Slovo might appear to have been talking about entirely different matters, but inside South Africa the distinction ultimately vanished. The Botha government's race struggle was the ANC's class struggle. The economic class that would not commit suicide was white South Africa, and white South Africa's "Communist" enemy was rebellious blacks in general.

What then should we do? I found it hard to accept the ANC's assertion that I was still living in "the epoch of world transition from capitalism to socialism," harder still to believe that collectivist policies would feed South Africa's hungry millions and provide roofs for their homeless heads. I mean, it was 1986, not 1916. The Soviet Union, Eastern Europe, and China were emerging from their dark Marxist-Leninist nights, gasping for "bourgeois democratic" freedoms and clutching at capitalist tools to rebuild their crippled economies.

In such an era, Joe Slovo's politics seemed absurd, but so for that matter did Botha's. It was hard to keep a straight face when his government tried to cast itself as the valiant defender of "democratic values" and the Western way. If the white rulers truly wished to thwart the "total Communist onslaught," why didn't they invite black democrats like Gatsha Buthelezi into their camp, and make his followers their equal? Why did they continue to bar blacks from white schools and residential areas, and relegate their putative colored and Indian allies to separate houses of Parliament, where they had no real power? As a hearts-and-minds campaign against Marxism, it was the most stupid conceivable, and it revealed the white state for what it truly was: a ruling racial class. In the end, all South African issues merged into one—the race issue, the issue I had come home to resolve.

WALLS

Man is
a great wall builder
The Berlin Wall
The Wailing Wall of Jerusalem
But the wall
most impregnable
Has a moat
flowing with fright
around his heart

A wall without windows
for the spirit to breeze through

A wall
without a door
for love to walk in.

—*OSWALD MTSHALI,*
Soweto poet

T he murder victim this time was an Afrikaner traditionalist, an elder in the Dutch Reformed Church and a supporter of Dr. Andries Treurnicht's Conservative Party, which stood for a return to the granitic, unyielding apartheid of the Verwoerd and Vorster eras. He made the mistake of driving into a township on a bad day and had an accident in a hailstorm of stones. A black mob hauled him out of his wrecked pickup and trampled him to death.

In the aftermath, I knocked on the door of the dead man's home and found myself facing his widow. She was young and slender and pale with grief. After her children were in bed, I asked her to tell me about her husband. She said she couldn't. She said her family would not like it. She hinted at some terrible secret, something too dark and painful to be aired in public. I pressed her, though, and she finally relented.

She said her husband was brain dead when he reached the hospital, and that doctors told her there was no hope for him. They wanted to turn off the life-support systems and use his organs to give life to others. She thought that that was a good idea, so she gave her blessing. The machines were turned off, and her husband was allowed to die.

And then his heart was transplanted—into a black man. The widow saw no wrong in that at all, because she was not one to hate, but the family in the countryside . . . It tormented them, tortured them. They could not eat or sleep for the thought of their white son's heart beating on inside a black body. They simply could not bear it. *They wanted the heart back.* They wanted the widow to hire a lawyer and sue the hospital to force the doctors to slice that black man's chest open and return their son's heart to them, so that it could be buried with the rest of him. That is why she could not talk to me. It was not a dispute to be aired in public.

And so I left, mesmerized by the appalling power of the story I'd just heard. *They wanted the heart back.* The shelves of my flat were lined with books about apartheid, dozens and dozens of books about apartheid, all dismissing the idea of race as a biological misnomer, rooted in the dubious pseudoscience of the eighteenth and nineteenth centuries. "To speak of race," sniffed the journal *Critical Inquiry,* "is to speak . . . generally in metaphor." That about summed up the conventional wisdom, but the conventional wisdom was incapable of interpreting the widow's tale. I found it hard to see her story as a metaphor for anything. In South Africa, it was reality.

I have a wise friend in Johannesburg who says he knows where the race question lies. "It lies in your heart," he says, "too deep for you ever to find." Not quite, Adriaan, not quite. I found it in mine. When I came home from exile, I was overwhelmed by the feeling that I was seeing South Africa clearly for the first time. The poverty, despair, and injustice were all the more apparent to eyes that had seen the United States, and yet this was not the only curse inflicted by my alien senses. I was accustomed to hearing English and seeing white faces, accustomed to living in a more-or-less homogeneous culture. After all those years away, I felt acutely white back home. I couldn't talk to many Africans, and communicating through interpreters was difficult. Stories got garbled, poetry lost its resonance, and narratives foundered in misunderstanding. The more questions I asked, the more confused I became, especially with regard to the most important question of all: Where do we really stand in relation to one another, *'bra?*

Such things were undiscoverable in the eerie isolation of white suburbia, so I swore a pact with myself: Wherever I went, I would stop for all the black hitch-hikers I saw, to see what they might reveal.

At the outset, I'd fall into a near psychosis of fear whenever I saw a knot of black travelers on the road up ahead. I'd study their clothes and belongings for clues as to who they might be, search their eyes to see whether they were dangerous. Two times out of three, I'd conclude they were, but I'd stop anyway, full of misgivings and visions of my own murder. I'd pull off onto the shoulder and wait for them to catch up to the car. They'd yank the doors open and pile in, five or six black men at a time. I'd swallow hard and think, Oh, shit, now I'm really done for. I'd think, Okay, if they pull knives I'll put my hand in my pocket and pretend I've got a gun, and maybe I'll live to tell the tale. Then the doors would slam and I'd pull off, and the black man in the passenger seat would turn to me and say something like, "What kind of white are you, that you stop for blacks?" Or, "God has sent you to help us." At such moments, I was stricken with remorse, to think I had harbored such ugly suspicions about such kindly people.

Sometimes it was even worse. Sometimes the hitchhikers didn't come at all, and when I turned and looked back I saw heels disappearing into the bush at the roadside, or frightened eyes watching me from behind a distant tree. I was white, they were black, and this was a lonely road. They thought I was going to shoot or rape them.

I began to understand something quite important about South Africa: My fear of blacks was obscuring my understanding of the fear blacks felt for my white skin. On one occasion, I was lost inside a township in the Eastern Cape. The area was aseethe with unrest, and I was scared to get out of the car, but there was no choice. I parked outside a primary school and walked into a quadrangle teeming with tiny black children. They fell dead silent at the sight of me. It was like that brokerage firm ad on American television. Two hundred black children stopped chattering and laughing the instant I appeared. I smiled, but they didn't smile back.

A teacher appeared, shook my hand, and apologized for his children's odd behavior. The only whites who ever came here were policemen, he explained, and the children were scared of them. He was very friendly, though. He deputized a small black boy in a starched white shirt and short pants to guide me on my way. As we left, the teacher warned me to watch out for the white soldiers camped on the township's outskirts. Just last

225

weekend, he said, they captured two teenage comrades and forced them to drink gasoline.

My tiny guide had probably been raised on such stories, and clearly thought he'd been put in a car with the bogeyman. He perched on the edge of the passenger seat, rigid and speechless with terror. Hundreds of minute beads of sweat appeared on his face. I had never seen such a thing. I told him not to be frightened, but he didn't really understand English, so I reached across and tried to put a reassuring arm around his shoulders. He cried out in fear, and cringed into his corner.

To me, such moments seemed to reveal the true tragedy of South Africa. There are so many such moments in our history. In 1510, the Portuguese Viscount D'Almeida came in peace, but the sight of his white skin and strange vessel struck terror in the hearts of Hottentots on the shores of Table Bay, so they killed him, and we've been slaughtering one another in fear ever since. Dawid Malan and the Xhosa slaughtered one another along the Great Fish River for sixty years, and then the Boers trekked into the interior, where they ran into the mighty Zulus. The Voortrekker leader Piet Retief approached the Zulu king Dingaan under a white flag, but Dingaan feared him, and murdered him and all his party. The Afrikaners never forgot Dingaan's treachery. After that, we always shot before we saw the whites of black eyes, and then, in 1948, we invented apartheid, to keep blacks so far away that we couldn't see them at all.

At one point in the fifties, Nelson Mandela's ANC was willing to settle for sixty seats in the white Parliament. The Afrikaners feared black domination, though, and thought they could keep blacks down forever, so they spurned Mandela's humble demands and tried to crush his movement. Three decades later, Botha had second thoughts, and extended a tentative hand of friendship across the racial divide. By then, blacks were also contaminated by fear and hatred, so they struck his hand away, and we spiraled on down toward mutual annihilation. We always seemed to miss each other in the murk of our mutually baffling cultures and our mutually blinding fears.

This is a parable of fear obscuring fear that occurred a long time ago, in a small town called Bulwer, in 1906—the year of the Bambatha rebellion, the last Zulu uprising. Bulwer lay close to Zulu territory, and white farmers in the district feared the local Zulus might join Bambatha's rebel army and butcher their masters in bed. So the whites called a meeting and formulated a plan of action: If the Zulus rose, all whites would rush to Bulwer and barricade themselves inside the stone courthouse.

A few days later, someone cried wolf, and the whites panicked. They loaded their guns and children onto wagons and abandoned their farms, leaving meals on the tables and lowing cows unmilked in the barns. They barricaded themselves inside the courthouse, loaded their guns, posted lookouts, and sat back to await the barbarians. By and by, they saw dust in the distance. Peering out through chinks in the barricade, the whites beheld a vision from their worst nightmares—a horde of Zulus approaching on foot. The crowd halted a few hundred yards away. A deputation detached itself and approached the courthouse. The Zulus knocked on the door. The wary whites opened a window, expecting to hear an ultimatum. Instead, the black men said "Why have you forsaken us? We see there is a terrible danger coming, because our masters have fled into this fort, and we are frightened, for we don't know what it is. So we came to ask if we could also come inside, to be under the protection of our masters' guns."

After several months on the road, it dawned on me that I was behaving rather like the whites in that courthouse. Whenever I ducked into the darkness of an African hut, I felt like Columbus in the New World. There would be chickens roosting in corners, goatskins drying in the dark rafters. The walls would be lined with black men. I couldn't talk to them, and when I looked into their eyes I wasn't quite sure what I was seeing there. Someone would press a bowl of bitter *tshwala* beer into my hands. Then the hut would fall silent, all the men watching to see whether this uninvited white visitor was willing to drink from the communal vessel. When I lifted it to my lips, they murmured approvingly. Then they would begin to discuss me in a language I didn't understand. Some seemed to be saying, "Ah, he's okay; we can talk to him." Others seemed to object to my presence. It was impossible to be sure. It was 1986, but I felt just as my ancestor Hercules Malan must have felt on his first visit to King Dingaan's kraal in 1838: alien, nervous, and paranoid. And yet, on the far side of the racial divide, I was almost always received like a brother.

There is an African tradition called *ubuntu,* which means "largeness of spirit." *Ubuntu* requires a man to show hospitality to travelers and strangers, and it is still strong in some parts of South Africa, especially in the countryside. In the countryside, black people weren't merely friendly; they treated me as if I were a visiting dignitary. The man of the house would dispatch one of his sons into a hut to fetch a comfortable chair for the white man to sit on, another to buy beer or Coke to slake his thirst. No matter how poor they were, they often tried to feed me.

I once interviewed a tribesman outside a mud hut in a desperately poor, drought-stricken homeland. As I arrived, I noticed that there was nothing but dirt in the garbage pile alongside his home. No scraps of plastic, no empty tins, no gnawed bones, no pumpkin rinds, no scrapings from the bottom of the porridge pot—nothing. These black people had nothing to throw away because they were living on the brink of starvation, and yet, in the midst of our talk, the Zulu householder's second wife appeared with a bowl of tripe heaped atop a pile of *putu* (corn porridge). This food was a giant sacrifice, and yet they offered it to me, a white man, and a Boer to boot. The tripe was green, badly cleaned, and swimming in grease, but I ate every last mouthful, forcing it down past the huge lump in my throat.

I carry the memory of many such moments in my heart, and few are finer than my encounter with Spiderman and Halftime. I met them in the Eastern Cape, in the township where the terrified little black boy was given to me as a guide. The boy's instructions were to take me to the UDF, to the lair of the comrades, and if he was scared, I was, too. In those times, the comrades balled their fists when they saw white skin in a passing car and cried, *"Tsa! Tsa, tsa!"*—the sound of mighty blows striking the ruling class. Sometimes they picked up stones and let fly, and I floored the accelerator, praying that my old car would keep going. I used to have bad dreams in which my car sputtered to a halt in a hail of stones, heralding the end of me. In short, I was scared of comrades, and scareder still when Spiderman came out with a hammer in his hand.

Spiderman was eighteen. He had a Grace Jones haircut, the sculpted face and graceful bearing of an Ethiopian prince. He was an office-bearer in the local Youth Congress, in the group that said Mandela—that supported the aims and objectives of the Charterist movement and its parent-in-exile, the ANC. In that strife-torn region, it was essential to reach some sort of understanding with the Mandela comrades if you intended to move around on their turf. You wanted them to know you weren't a cop, and better yet, to act as your guides and bodyguards. So I rolled down my window and made a pitch to Spiderman. "I have come here to find out the truth of the murder of a black man," I said, "and I want you to work with me." Spiderman slapped the hammer into his palm and thought it over. Then he dropped the hammer and said okay. He climbed into the passenger seat, his sidekick,

Halftime, climbed into the back, and we drove off to investigate yet another ordinary murder in this extraordinary country.

We worked together for the best part of a week, and I grew rather fond of Spiderman and Halftime. They ferreted out witnesses, persuaded them to trust me and interpreted their words if they couldn't speak a white language. I had much to thank them for, and so, on my last night in town, I bought two six-packs of beer and took them for a farewell cruise in the dark countryside.

The comrades were socialists, of course, but they didn't really know from Marx. All they really knew was injustice, and the myriad forms it took in their lives. Their township was overcrowded, and their drinking water tasted of piss. Their houses were made of mud and fell down whenever it rained. Their black community councillors were in cahoots with the white authorities. The whites gave liquor and business licenses to their black cronies; the black cronies cut them in on the profits. No competition was allowed, so township dwellers had to pay almost twice the going price for a tin of pilchards. *"Dis 'n smokkel plek hierdie,"* said Halftime: "This is a very crooked town."

In Halftime's hometown, the only available work was picking oranges on white farms. This paid about $2.50 a week. "It's hard work," Halftime told me. "You must carry heavy loads on your shoulder. The thorns, they stick you, and the dust comes in your mouth. But you can't eat an orange. If you eat an orange, you get fired."

As he spoke, we were traveling through orange groves, endless orange groves—so many orange trees in this valley alone that the orange market frequently glutted. When that happened, the local white farmers' cooperative pulped, dumped, and sometimes poisoned the surplus so that blacks could not steal and eat it. Blacks were expected to feed, clothe, and educate an entire family on $2.50 a week, and buy their own oranges to boot. And yet, if a black dared steal an orange off a white farmer's tree, he got six months. "They tell us in school we must eat vitamin C," Spiderman raged. "Where must we get vitamin C?"

Where indeed. I mean, I agreed wholeheartedly; something had to be done about the vitamin C, and about everything else. By now, the first six-pack was finished, and we were feeling downright comradely. We set to work on the second, and by the time it was done we were singing freedom songs—"Rolihlahla Mandela, freedom is in your hands, show us the way to freedom, in our land in Africa." I was absurdly moved to hear that the black brothers held a tune scarcely better than I, the Boer. It was a small thing, but it seemed tremendously encouraging. When I dropped them off in the township, Spiderman and Halftime said they had heard of whites like me, but never yet met one. I was so chuffed that I gave them my beloved cassette tape of *Fosatu Worker Choruses,* a collection of subversive trade union songs. "Can it talk?" Spiderman asked. Then we exchanged the elaborate triple-grip handshake of black power and swore eternal brotherhood, and I drove away with yet another lump in my throat.

It was quite often like that, even in the midst of that bloody uprising. I was desperate to win black trust and friendship, to have done with the absurd bullshit, and often thought I saw an answering yearning in black men's eyes. I hate to inflict yet another contradiction on you, but I think this was a symptom of love. I had been obsessed with blacks all my life, you see, and it was not so different a feeling from that of first love, the truly intense and tragic kind. It was all distance and tension, and I read once that romantic love is a function of those very things. My relations with blacks had always been somehow adolescent, sweaty, and nervous, full of awkward gropings and unrequited yearnings—and what was that, if not love? We all seemed to be groping for one another in the murk of a mutual blindness. Our hands usually missed, so the times when they actually touched seemed heartrendingly poignant.

In Zululand, for instance, I worked for a while with a black man named Ozias. Ozias was a dashing fellow, with huge black eyes and a handsome beard. He was forty-odd years old and boasted of having fathered thirteen children by a wife and an impressive collection of concubines, all somehow supported on his earnings as soccer correspondent and sports photographer for the local white newspaper. Ozias and I got on well, and when our work was done, he refused to accept payment from me. He said I was a friend, and he didn't take money from friends. I invoked his several women and many children, and pressed the cash on him. Eventually he shrugged and took it, but turned right around and blew it on a party in my honor.

On the appointed night, I pitched up at his place in the township of Esikawini. It was a stormy night, with a rain-laden wind blowing in from the sea. I was full of the usual forebodings, and received the usual friendly welcome. It is one of the great ironies of South Africa that it is extremely fashionable in certain circles to have friends of another race. White liberals fell over one another in their eagerness to recruit blacks for their dinner parties, and black men sometimes walked you through every shebeen in the district, just so they could throw a public arm around a white shoulder and say, "Here's Rian. He's a Boer, but he's okay."

Ozias, for instance, seemed to have primed the entire neighborhood with the news that he was having a white over for a *braai*. I had just arrived, and was sitting on Ozias's bed, browsing though his fine collection of American R & B records, when the first of the pilgrims came in to pay his respects. I don't remember his name, but he wore spectacles and taught in a nearby school. He had heard that I was a writer, and wanted to show me the "write to read" computer system that had just been installed at his school. I told him I'd love to, but this wasn't the right time. So he left, and a slim, goateed dude in jeans and an Afro appeared in his place. We exchanged the triple-grip power handshake, and the black man said he was Tiger.

Tiger had heard that I was interested in black music. He had a VCR and a great Teddy Pendergrass tape he wanted me to see. I'll be with you in a moment, I said, I just want to pick out a few records so that Ozias can tape them for me.

A few minutes later, a man named Simon popped his head in the door. I hear you want to tape some music, he said. Come on over to my place, he said. My stereo is state of the art. I didn't know what to say, because I was pathetically eager to please everyone. I was mulling my options when Tiger's ten-year-old son materialized at my side, and started tugging at my sleeve. "Teddy Pendergrass is starting," he said. So I told Simon the kid had a prior claim on my attentions, and let the boy lead me out of the house.

We stepped out of the kitchen door and into a roaring gale. Somewhere in the surrounding darkness, someone was splintering wood with an ax. I walked toward the sound and discovered Ozias hacking up some furniture with a chopper. He suffered a seizure of awkwardness when I appeared. He had forgotten to get wood, he explained, so he was putting some old furniture on the fire. I said, shit, man, don't go to any trouble for me, but he was determined to do things the right way, and brushed my protestations aside. By now Tiger's son had vanished, but Simon loomed out of the darkness, took me by the elbow, and steered me away to see his state-of-the-art stereo. After drinking a beer and listening to a side of jazz, I excused myself and returned to Ozias's yard.

There a harrowing sight awaited. The high wind had turned Ozias's fire into a raging conflagration. Flames were leaping four feet into the air, fat flying, meat charring. Ozias was dancing around this bonfire, trying to douse the flames and save his sausages and steak. A score or so friends and relatives were looking on, anxiously offering advice. I stood around the fire, offering encouragement, but Ozias ignored me and his relatives kept calling me *baas*. Our conversations faltered after a few exchanges, so I was rather relieved when a little boy appeared at my elbow, saying, "Teddy Pendergrass! Teddy Pendergrass!"

Tiger lived just across the courtyard, in a row of fancy duplex apartments. Esikawini was one of the country's newest townships, and it was something of an apartheid showpiece. Tiger taught school, and his lifestyle was middle class. His furniture looked as though it had just come out of a Lubner's display window, and one entire wall was devoted to what Americans would call a "media center"—a fine stereo, a VCR, a large record collection, and a huge color TV. Teddy Pendergrass was standing in the center of the screen, eyes closed, sweating, singing his soul out. Watching from chairs and sofas were Tiger, his brother Lawrence, and their buddies Wiseman and Zee. All four of them were teachers. They offered me a beer, and then another. I thought Ozias knew where I was, and that Tiger was a fellow guest of his. I thought he'd call us when it was time to eat. After an hour, though, I got worried and went outside to see what was happening.

The yard was deserted, and the fire had burned out. Ozias was sitting alone and disconsolate in his house. There had been a misunderstanding. The white guest of honor had disappeared in the midst of the party, and Ozias had been humiliated. His friends and relatives had eaten the meat, drunk the beer, and gone home, no doubt sniggering.

I felt so wretched I wanted to stick knitting needles in my eyes, but that wouldn't have helped. So I just apologized for my stupidity, clapped an arm around his shoulder and suggested we go back to Tiger's place for a few more drinks, at which point I discovered that Tiger wasn't even a friend of his. "I don't like that guy," he said, but he came along anyway. Back in Tiger's living room, I did my best to repair the hurt I had inflicted on Ozias by talking of my high regard for his writing, his skill as an interpreter, and his eye with a camera. I was patronizing him, sure, but what the fuck else could I do?

The evening wore on, and we all got drunk again. And then we started talking politics. You had to be drunk to talk politics in Zululand, because Zululand was teetering on the brink of civil war. South Africa was becoming a country of many conflicts, and the one about to erupt in Zulu-land would be bloodiest of them all, claiming around eighteen hundred African lives to date. This time, the combatants were those who said Mandela, and those who said Buthelezi—who were members of Inkatha, Chief Gatsha Buthelezi's million-strong Zulu "liberation movement." As we sat drinking in Tiger's lounge, the first shots had just been fired, and those men were already wary of one another. If you revealed support for one side, the other might mark you down for eventual assassination, and vice versa.

"You can't trust anyone," Tiger explained. "So if you ask me what I think of Inkatha, I say 'Bleh!' And if you ask me about UDF, I say, 'Bleh!' If you ask me about Azapo, or the Boers, or anyone, I always say, 'Bleh!' It's dangerous to say anything else. They are all around us."

Who were "they"? I could not ask, but I'd guess that Tiger's sympathies lay with the UDF, and that they were Inkatha.

Tiger was drunk by now; we all were. He was waving the dregs of a brandy bottle and waxing somewhat belligerent. "I'll show you how it works," he said. He took two empty beer bottles and set them down side by side on a coffee table. The empty Castle was brown, the spent Amstel green. "This is one side," he said, lifting the first bottle, "and this is the other. You are either on this side, or you are on that side. If you're in the middle you're the worst. The people in the middle are the most dangerous, and they must be killed. If I find out my brother is in the middle, I will kill him. It's people like this who must die," he said, pointing at his brother Lawrence. "He's in the middle." 'Bra Lawrence just laughed at him.

"The end of the world is coming," said Lawrence.

"Well, okay," said Tiger. His head was drooping toward his chest and he was swaying in his chair, but he pulled out of his drunken slump and turned on Ozias.

"Ozias," he said, "I don't trust you." Ozias looked scared and uncomfortable. He said nothing. "If I find out you're a sellout," Tiger continued, "I'm going to kill you, Ozias." And then he lay back in his chair, laughing bitterly. "I know, man, I know," he laughed. "We're all going to kill each other. This country is going to get so bad, man. If only I could get out of here, if only I could get a scholarship, man, I'd take my kids and fuck off and never come back."

He looked up at me. "Hey," he said, "can't you get me a scholarship in America?" I shrugged. "Well," said Tiger, "that's it then. Hey, Ozias," he chuckled, "let's kill each other. Let's do it now, man."

Oh, God, how did I write myself into that corner? I started out to say something entirely different, but all roads somehow led into darkness in the winter of 1986. And that wasn't even my darkness; it was the darkness gathering around Ozias and all the Zulu people. My white darkness was something else entirely. It lay in a thousand places, at the end of a thousand roads, but it always took the same form. I guess I should tell you about the first time I saw it, about a night that changed my life.

One of the first people I looked up when I came home from exile was Mike, my friend from the days when I was *The Star*'s rockspider police reporter and he the crack black writer who'd loll around the newsroom saying, "I'm just a boy around here," as if daring the white liberals to disagree. Mike was the proud black Biko man, the hard drinker who matched me shot for shot in *The Star*'s fourth-floor canteen. I would never have told him this, but our relationship meant a lot to me, and I sometimes imagined the feeling was mutual. He would never have said so, but I sometimes saw something in his cool, challenging gaze—amused tolerance, maybe even affection.

On my first day back in Jo'burg, I called him up, introducing myself as *Speurdersersant Malan van die Veiligheidspolisie*—"Detective Sergeant Malan of the secret police." He chuckled at the sound of my voice and said, "You remembered me," as if touched. He was doing PR for an American corporation in downtown Johannesburg, so we arranged a rendezvous outside a landmark hotel.

I recognized his jaunty tread from a hundred yards away, and my heart came up in my chest. As he neared, I caught a glimpse of white sock between his trouser cuff and shoe. That was unlike the Mike I remembered. The old Mike dressed sharp. The new Mike was eight years older, and eight years closer to defeat. His once-defiant eyes were now hooded, but still he seemed pleased to see me. We shook hands, simultaneously observing that a little jol was called for. So Mike hopped behind the wheel of my rented car, and we roared off toward Soweto.

On the way, he told me that he'd developed something of a drinking problem while I was away. "There came a day," Mike told me, "when I decided I might as well just get drunk. Or die." His cackle was as bitter as ever. As he spoke, we were just entering Soweto, and the first sight of it seemed to kick me in the face. It was so huge, so gray, so dismal, and most of its black people seemed so poor and despairing. I didn't really have to ask Mike why he wanted to obliterate himself. I knew. I knew. I was looking at one of the reasons. Mike went on to say that he'd taken his despairing addiction to a *sangoma,* who had affected a miraculous cure. "I'm exhuming myself from the grave," he said cheerfully. He was technically on the wagon, but he figured that a drink or two on a special occasion wouldn't really hurt anyone.

Life was harder than ever in Soweto, now that the struggle was under-way, but there was still a defiant exuberance in the shebeens, still plenty of beer and laughter and raucous conversation. Mike introduced me to lawyers, gangsters, bespectacled existentialist, and several painted black ladies of questionable virtue. If anyone asked what whitey was doing here, Mike spoke up for me. "He's a liberal rebel of the Afrikaner *volk,* " he said. "I'll go the whole hog for him." That, too, meant a lot to me.

A drink or two became several, and more to follow. Around sundown, we were sitting around a table with five or six black men. They were office workers, truck drivers, and the like, unwinding after work, but they were deeply politicized, like many blacks in South Africa's cities. They were sick of being "slaves and industrial tools," as a garrulous fellow named Panky characterized their lot. They were eagerly looking forward to the day when "all hell breaks loose."

I had forgotten how to comport myself in such conversations. On the one hand, I was white, and dreaded the day that all hell broke loose. On the other, I wasn't prepared to say so. I was still pretending to be the Just White Man, and just white men were obliged to endorse the righteousness of violent revolution. I guess I agreed with Panky a little too enthusiastically for Mike's liking. He was never one to abide hypocrisy. He cleared his throat and said, "There is one small thing Mr. Malán isn't telling you." In Harlem, he would have said, "Tell them your family's in the KKK." In Jerusalem, "Tell them your father was a Nazi." In Soweto, Nat said: "Tell them you're an Afrikaner Malan, of the Malan family."

"Vertel die muntoes, man," he chuckled. "Tell the kaffirs."

The table fell silent.

"Whose country is this?" Mike continued, still jiving me in Afrikaans. I was momentarily at a loss. I had been away for eight years, in a world that was almost entirely white. My jive chops had rusted away.

"It's the white man's land," I said, falsely jocular. *It's the white man's land.* The line flopped. The silence persisted.

"Okay," I said finally. "Now that he's brought it up, how do you feel about drinking with a Boer?"

"The Afrikaner wants the black to be inferior to him," said a man named Sibogang.

"Do you think that's true of me?" I asked.

"I don't think that," he answered. "But a white is a white against the black."

"As long as there's confrontation," Panky chipped in, "you'll vouch for the guy who is your own color. Because there is this hatred beating between us. If we go to one of those integrated hotels, I won't sit with you, man. I want to sit with my own flock. And during the office Christmas party, we will ask you, 'Please sit somewhere away.' We have nothing in common. You stay in the white suburbs; I stay in a shack here. When it's raining, my roof is leaking, but you are sitting comfortably. But you can't be peaceful. You must sleep with a gun under your pillow. You see, this monster is your creation."

"Do you mean," I asked, "that we have to be enemies, because of *this?*" I indicated my white skin. This time the pause was even longer. Stevie Wonder's voice filtered through the wall.

"We won't accept a white man," Sibogang said finally. "Never. Because every white man we see is an enemy to us."

"Unless," he added affably, gesturing around the table, "you sit down with us and make it clear you are with us."

So the truce flags went up, and we resumed our drinking. And when it was time to leave, Mike and I clapped arms around one another's shoulders and staggered out into the night. The darkness was merciful. The towering anticrime floodlights hung like yellow moons in the sky, bathing the streets in a soft yellow benediction. It was easier that way—easier on the eyes, but harder on the psyche. At night in Soweto, you fear what you can't see; you fear the *tsotsis,* the knifemen who ring up a murder rate four or five times higher than New York City's. It struck me that I was possibly the only white man in this vast black city, and I started getting edgy. *Every white man we see is an enemy to us.*

236

The night turned into a blur of stark rooms, naked light bulbs, liquor posters of bikini girls on coral beaches. On our way into one shebeen, a disembodied black face suspended in that weird yellow light muttered something to Mike in a tribal tongue. "He wants to know," Mike chuckled, "if this whitey is ripe for the picking." Inside that shebeen, the black drinkers scowled darkly at the sight of white skin, and even Mike thought it prudent to go elsewhere. The old psychic toxins flooded my brain, and ancient, animal unease started eating at my viscera. I slipped outside myself, and started watching Malan go through the motions, flashing his shit-eating grin, fumbling the black power handshake, saying "Hey *'bra*," "How you, *'bra*"—and, Tell me, *'bra*, is my paranoia showing? I wanted to go home, but Mike wanted another drink, and then another. He had fallen off the wagon, and fallen hard.

Sometime after midnight, we found ourselves sitting at someone's Formica kitchen table, having one for the road. I was drunk. Mike was drunk. The third man at the table was named Judo. He had one eye and no shoes. Mike and I were talking about our fathers. Mike's old man had somehow managed to put five children through high school, a near-miracle in black South Africa. He had a brother at Oxford. I observed that Mike's old man must have been a wonderful father.

"Well," said Mike, "he made his accommodations with the system, for my sake, I suppose. Baas Malan would kick his arse, and he'd say, 'Okay, that's sweet.' Later, I started questioning why we were like this, and the white man like that. I said, 'Why, why, why?' and my father said, 'Boy, you still small; you don't understand.' But today I know. I know why."

"Are you trying to tell me something?" I asked.

"Are you trying to tell *me* something?" he countered.

"Fuck you," I said.

"Fuck *you*," he said.

After a minute or so of uneasy silence, Mike changed the subject, started talking about the politicization of crime. In the old days, ripping off whitey's handbag had been theft. Now it was a revolutionary act, as our drinking buddy Judo could apparently attest. Mike claimed he'd once seen Judo hold up a white man on a Jo'burg street. Judo shook his head and said, "No, couldn't have been me." Mike was adamant, though. He leapt to his feet and started reenacting the robbery, using me as a prop.

"You grabbed him like this," Mike said, throwing an arm roughly around my neck. "You held the knife in his side here, like this—yes! I saw you, *skollie!"* He was laughing, but something wild and violent had entered his mood.

"If Judo saw you in the street in Jo'burg," Mike cackled to me, "he'd rob you, *nê,* Judo?"

A black stranger appeared in the doorway, looked me up and down, and muttered something to Mike and Judo in a language I didn't understand. I started thinking how desirable my shoulder bag must seem to a man with no shoes. I started thinking about murder and robbery, about sharpened bicycle spokes in the heart, a favorite means of dispatch in Soweto.

My shit-eating grin tightened to breaking point and then snapped. I surged to my feet, nodded curtly to Mike, and walked out into the menacing yellow night. A lone white man on foot in Soweto in the middle of the night in the midst of a black uprising, looking for a car parked hundreds of yards away. Maybe it was paranoia, but I figured my chances of reaching the car alive were less than even.

I walked in the middle of the road. I kept my eyes down and moved fast. I passed a group of youths loitering in the surreal yellow glow; their mouths opened, and they spoke to me, but no sound registered. One disembodied foot followed the other. Pebbles leapt off the road in brilliant clarity, casting shadows as stark as shadows on the moon. The night was as silent as outer space. I was walking on the moon. All I could hear was the drumming of blood in my ears, and the rasp of my own breathing. I was out of my mind with terror, and in that moment, in that moment, it came to me: This was *it*—the unseen force that obliterated reason in South Africa; the force that held the white tribe together, and kept our sweating white fists locked in a death grip on the levers of power.

Where did the fear come from? The weight of the human sciences said it was the poisonous fruit of racist conditioning, and I suppose there was truth in that. I grew up in a house where the black servants had to drink from their own cups and eat off their own dishes, which were kept separate from the rest of the crockery. In his dealings with blacks, my father was stiff and formal, my mother somewhat patronizing. She loved blacks, but she loved dogs, too, and I am not sure the distinction was all that clear in her mind. Many of the adults in my life were to varying degrees racist. The old lady next door, for instance, once announced that she needed new glasses because she could no longer tell blacks from whites at a distance. She had caught herself waving to blacks on the street, and that would never do. Such things clearly left their mark on me, but they should surely have inspired contempt, not fear. The fear had another root entirely.

I sometimes think the fear was always with me, even when I was a child and loved all natives, indiscriminately. It is the lot of children to be stalked by amorphous fears and nocturnal terrors, by the feeling that there is something out there in the dark, something threatening. It seems to me that must be true everywhere, but in South Africa's white suburbs, the terror always had a black face. You'd lie with your head under the covers, frozen with fear, listening to the window rattling in the wind, and you knew it was a black out there.

One night when I was maybe twelve or so, my brother and parents went out, leaving me alone in the house. Around nine o'clock, Piet the gardener came banging on the kitchen door. He was my friend, and I would normally have let him in without question, but there was something odd about the banging; he wasn't knocking to be let in, he was trying to batter the door down. So I stuck my head out a window and asked what was going on. I could see straight away that he was half out of his mind. His eyes were flaming red, his breath reeked of brandy, and he was raving incoherently about a woman who had betrayed him, something like that. I couldn't see what this had to do with me, or why he was so determined to come inside, and besides, I was suddenly scared of him. So I refused to open the door.

Piet walked away into the dark garden and stood there silently, staring at Jo'burg's glittering skyline. It was a cold night, and his breath steamed in the air. The dogs were barking nervously. Piet appeared to be deep in thought. And then he spun around and charged the house like a mad bull, smashing his head into the wall so hard that the windows rattled. After that, he started raking his fingernails down the rough Spanish plaster—leaping and twisting high into the night sky and raking the wall on his way down, again and again, until the nails were hanging off his fingers in bloody, fleshy shreds. And then he disappeared into his room and didn't come out again.

The next day Piet was sullenly sober, and his fingertips were knobbly with blood clots. I didn't tell my father what had happened, because I loved Piet and didn't want him to be fired. But I didn't talk to Piet about it either. I couldn't. Something big had come between us, and the words and concepts we had in common were very small, and good only for parsing out the everyday. If he could have spoken, he might have described a seething hell of frustration and impotence. He had a wife and three children to support, but my father paid him a pittance, which is what gardeners got. He was always dreaming up schemes for making more money, but they always fell apart, no matter how hard he tried. If I'd asked, Piet might have told me that he'd reached a point where he just couldn't take it any more. Or he might simply have said, "I wanted to kill you, Rian."

I don't know. He was African, and we white people couldn't really talk to Africans. They lived on the far side of a barrier of language and culture, so when we tried to look into their hearts, all we saw was darkness. Who knows what lurks in darkness? We feared the worst. It was our superstition, I suppose, but it was no less real to us for all that. Anyone who doubted the menacing nature of Africa was sent to see *Africa Addio,* a documentary that appeared on South African screens when I was ten or so. *Africa Addio* was about things that happened in Africa in the early sixties, after the European powers set their colonies free. The work was banned or suppressed in most of the civilized world, but white South Africans were encouraged to see it. And what we saw was this: beaches strewn with corpses in Zanzibar, piles of human hands in the Congo, Alps of dead people in Rwanda, Himalayas of them in Burundi.

I remember my parents discussing these events in hushed tones, so as not to upset the children. We had relatives who lived "up there," you see—in Northern Rhodesia, a British colony that was about to be granted independence. My uncle Bernie was fond of the colonial life-style, the pink gins at sunset and meditative cricket games on the country club's green oval. Many whites left long before independence, but my Uncle Bernie waited until the very last minute. Indeed, he waited too long. By the time he had his family in the car and their belongings on the roof, there was no petrol in Mufulira, and the black masses were rioting in the streets. Uncle Bernie was driving around town looking for an open petrol station when he ran into a crowd that stopped the car and started rocking it. They were chanting, "Independence! Independence!" My aunt and cousins were crying, because they thought they were done for, but my uncle Bernie climbed out and shouted, "Hurrah, independence!" along with the black men, so they let him go.

After that, they drove all the way down to Johannesburg without stopping, and when they got to our house, one of my girl cousins crawled under a bed and started crying because she was terrified of Lena, our black servant. She was littler than me, so I went in after her, stroked her hair, and said, "It's all right, Catherine, it's all right; she won't hurt you." I was amused that she should be so scared of Lena, because I loved Lena and assumed she loved me back. I understood exactly why Catherine was scared, and yet I knew that her fear was entirely, absolutely groundless.

My moonwalk in Soweto ended on a similar note. I heard footsteps behind me, and my terror reached a crescendo. And then a hand tapped my shoulder. I spun around and discovered that the werewolves were phantasms inside my brain. One-eyed Judo was padding along behind me in his bare feet, smiling cheerfully, accompanied by a teenage boy. Mike was straggling along fifty yards behind them, grumbling. "It is not safe for you here," said Judo. "We will walk with you."

I was devastated by their kindness, and utterly ashamed of myself. Even so, my life changed that night. I went on saying that apartheid was stupid and vicious, that racism was ignorant and backward, but in my heart it was no longer simple. I had seen the fear for what it was, and it became my constant companion. It came upon me whenever the black comrades punched the sky at the sight of me, when their stones thundered down on the roof of my car, when I couldn't understand what blacks were saying about me, when I searched the eyes of black hitchhikers, and even when I opened the newspapers. It doesn't help to say that the fear was irrational, or even psychotic. You are what you think, and white men who think blacks pose a mortal danger *are* in mortal danger. After that night, I knew that I had to purge the black fear from my white heart. Unless I did that—unless we all did it—there was no hope for any of us. Whites and blacks would tear one another apart like dogs in a war that left the victor standing in a landscape of graves and ruins. We had to find a way of trusting all the one-eyed black Judos, of giving ourselves into their arms, or we would all wind up like Andries Petrus Hendricks.

When people asked why I was researching murders in the midst of a great racial rebellion, I'd always tell them about the revelatory life and prophetic death of Andries Petrus Hendricks. Alongside the raging struggle, his murder was an inconsequential little drama, but it seemed to illumine the subterranean South African issue more clearly than an entire library of books.

Andries Petrus Hendricks was born in 1910, the younger son of an Orange Free State farmer who expected him to make his own way in life. In the early thirties, young Andries set off to seek his fortune in the Sperrgebiet—the forbidden zone, the nightmarish desert coast of South-West Africa where the beaches were said to be littered with diamonds. Andries and his brother disappeared into the wilderness in a donkey cart. They almost perished out there, but when they came back four months later they were rich men—rich enough, at any rate, for Andries to buy himself a 120-morgen farm just outside a small town named Vredefort, in the flat, featureless mealie fields of the northern Orange Free State.

Andries Hendricks was a strangely gnarled and arid man, incapable of loving or trusting anyone. He didn't trust banks, so he hoarded his money and gold coins in chests under his bed. He didn't trust women, so his only marriage lasted but nine months. He didn't trust men, so he had few friends. And above all, he didn't trust blacks.

In this, he was not so different from his neighbors, rock-solid Boer conservatives for the most part. Very few of them considered blacks to be fully and truly human, but even they were put off by the way Oom Andries treated his black workers. It wasn't that he beat them or anything; he was just meanspirited and devious, always on guard, always trying to cheat them or belittle them, and so riddled with fear and hatred that he denied himself the traditional white luxury of live-in servants. He didn't want blacks anywhere near him. He was so profoundly warped, according to his sister-in-law, that he'd walk out of a movie if a black actor appeared on the screen.

This is a story another of his relatives told about him: "Old Andries showed up on my doorstep at ten o'clock one night. It was harvest time, and he'd been working since dawn to bring in his crop. One of his wagons broke an axle, and he wanted to borrow mine, because there was still another load to be taken to the co-op. He looked as though he'd had a hard day, so I asked him in for a brandy.

"I looked over his shoulder and saw a kaffir sitting in his truck. The boy was covered with dust from head to toe, and he was looking very sorry for himself. So I said to Andries, 'Call your boy to the door, man, and I'll give him a *dop* [a shot of spirits], too.' And Andries said no. Just like that. For no reason. He was just heartless. I said it wasn't very Christian, but he said he didn't care. 'If I'm in heaven,' he said, 'and a kaffir comes walking in through the gates, that's when I walk out the back door.'"

Such spiritual deformity is quite common in white South Africans, but old Andries had a particularly bad case of it, and it ravaged his life. A man who hates cannot expect to be loved, and Andries had no illusions about where he stood in relation to blacks. He hated them and assumed they hated him. He always said, "Those kaffirs will mutilate me one day." As he grew older, his fear deepened into an obsession and, finally, into dementia.

In his late sixties, Oom Andries grew too old and tired to go on farming alone, and he had no sons to take over. So he sold off all his land save for a sliver fifteen feet wide and some three hundred yards long. On this sliver, he built a fort. It was an ugly massif of raw concrete, three stories tall and virtually windowless, rising in the middle of a flat and dreary plain. The reinforced concrete walls were fourteen inches thick, the door a ponderous chunk of steel looted from a demolished bank vault. There were battlements on the roof, and chinks in the walls through which a white man could fire at the encroaching savages. Old Andries sunk a well through the floor for water and stocked the larder with a supply of tinned food. He stashed his three chests of gold under his bed and welded the remainder of his cash into steel pipes in the walls. He brought in his guns (two revolvers, a shotgun, and a rifle) and stockpiled ammunition. And then he locked himself inside his monument to racial paranoia, and sat back to await the apocalypse.

Oom Andries had one weakness, though, a typical white man's weakness. He was prepared to cook and clean for himself, but drew the line at washing and ironing clothes. Twice a week, therefore, the steel door of his fortress swung open, and an old African woman was allowed in to do his drudgery. She was the only black who ever set foot inside Oom Andries's castle. She saw the chests under the bed, and knew about the cash inside the pipes. One day, she brought her two grown sons to work with her, and that was the end of old Andries Hendricks. His body was chopped to pieces and thrown down the well. The old black woman and her sons were caught near the border in his pickup, tried, and hung for murder. By the time I arrived in Vredefort, five years had passed, and no whites could remember their names. They had receded into the anonymous black masses. *"Jussus,"* chuckled one neighbor, "just say the black peril got him."

In his will, this bitter and lonely old Boer bequeathed five English pounds to any relative who attended his funeral; the rest of his money was to be spent on his sarcophagus. He died a fairly rich man, and only one Hendricks showed up at the graveside. So it was quite some tomb that eventually arose in Vredefort's lonely graveyard: six towering columns of marble, swarms of angels and cherubs, a life-sized apostle, and a plinth inscribed with the bitter epitaph Andries Hendricks had chosen for himself: "Gone and Forgotten."

As a tribe, a nation, we are all immured inside a fortress of racial paranoia, jealously hoarding our gold and getting deeper and deeper into a race war we cannot possibly win. We all know that. Our generals have been saying so since 1973. There is no military solution because the enemy is within. He is not beyond a border, where we could machine-gun or shell or even nuke him if it came to it, because we are reputed to have that weapon too. The enemy is inside our cities, inside our very homes, washing dishes and minding children, driving trucks and manning factories. Moral questions aside, we cannot defeat such an enemy without destroying ourselves. If we fail to accept that, we will also be chopped to pieces in a great orgy of bloodletting, obliterated by the forces of history. The ruins of tall buildings will mark our graves, and we, too, will be gone and forgotten.

We must find a way of trusting, but who is there to trust?

We have managed to inflict some casualties on the side of the enemy, eliminating sellouts and stooges . . .

—*Radio Freedom, Voice of the ANC, November 1985*

And here we are on the east side of downtown Johannesburg, the side that is rapidly turning black. Scores of thousands of black office workers flow through this district every morning and evening, on their way to and from Park Station. All the district's white merchants are bent on capturing their share of the passing black trade. Furniture and clothing stores offer attractive hire-purchase deals, allowing economically distressed blacks to secure goods with very low down payments. Hair salons place pictures of exquisitely coiffed black models in their windows. Record bars put loudspeakers on the sidewalk and bombard the crowds with the cool, urban Afro-disco sound of Hotstix Mabuse or *mbaqanga*—township music—from Obed Ngobeni and the Kurhula Sisters.

On Wanderers Street, we turn into the foyer of a rundown office building. The elevators are broken, the corridors dark under smashed light bulbs. The walls are smeared with the grime of decades of commerce. Every third door has a splintered jamb, the work of mysterious nocturnal visitors who jimmy the doors, rifle through desks and filing cabinets, and vanish without being seen. Nobody knows who the visitors are, but the tenants have their suspicions, because they're all enemies of the apartheid state. This is the de facto national headquarters of the BC movement, the network of trade unions and political organizations that carry the standard of Steve Biko, fallen prophet of Black Consciousness. I pass the offices of the building and construction union, the office cleaners' union, the media workers' union, and finally, at the end of a dark corridor plastered with "Don't Buy White" bumper stickers, I find a door marked AZAPO, headquarters of the Azanian People's Organization.

The suite of offices beyond is as dingy as the rest of the building. Springs are busting out of the waiting-room sofa. Cigarettes have been ground out in the threadbare carpet, and bits and pieces of anonymous office machinery lurk in corners under dusty plastic shrouds. On the wall is the Azanian flag, the flag that might have been South Africa's had Biko lived, and BC triumphed. It is divided diagonally into orange and black segments, with a red star in the heart of the orange sector. Alongside the flag are portraits of the BC movement's patron saints: Muammar Qaddafi, Chairman Mao, and Saint Steve Biko the Radiant.

Six thousand miles away, in London, Sir Richard Attenborough is editing a film about Steve Biko and his brave struggle against white tyranny. Biko is about to become a household name in the larger world, but the larger world doesn't seem particularly interested in Biko's surviving friends and comrades, judging from today's turnout. The leaders of Azapo are bitterly cynical about the white-dominated world media. They have seen a draft of Attenborough's script. In their view, it turns Biko into a tame Martin Luther King–like figure, a black liberal acceptable to fastidious white political palates. Attenborough has stolen their martyr, and Bishop Tutu's United Democratic Front has stolen their spotlight. If Bishop Tutu calls a press conference to denounce apartheid, you can scarcely get in for the hordes of foreign correspondents. But when the followers of Biko call one, look who shows up: two black reporters from *The Star,* a cameraless correspondent from ABC, two or three additional stragglers, and me, Malan.

The eight or so reporters crowd into a tiny office, and Azapo's leaders take their seats on the far side of a large desk: Comrade Myeza, Comrade Wauchope, and Comrade Molala. Between them, these three black men have spent a total of almost eighteen years in prison or detention for fighting apartheid. Comrade Muntu Myeza was kicked out of university for political activism, tortured by the secret police, and ultimately jailed for organizing a rally celebrating the downfall of the colonial regime in neighboring Mozambique. He spent eight years on Robben Island, the notorious political prison in Table Bay.

Comrade Nkosi Molala was on the island, too, serving seven years for sabotage. Such experiences are supposed to break a man, but Molala resumed the struggle as soon as they set him free, only to be struck in the face by a police tear-gas grenade and blinded in one eye. The third member of the troika, Comrade George Wauchope, was Steve Biko's main man in Johannesburg in the mid-seventies and played a leading role in the process of political organization and education that culminated in the 1976 Soweto rebellion. These three men have been arrested so often they've lost count, beaten and tortured so routinely that they no longer care to talk about it.

They've spent most of their adult lives running from the white secret police, but now they're running from someone else.

Comrade President Molala opens the proceedings with some general remarks about the BC movement's present predicament. "There are rumors floating in the ghetto," he declares, "that we are going to be eliminated." He goes on to describe a series of attacks recently suffered by members of his movement. Homes have been burned down with firebombs, or blown up with Soviet limpet mines. BC supporters have been attacked on the streets and expelled from schools under threat of death. Members of the BC youth movement have been abducted and murdered. In some instances, the parents and grandparents of these children have been taken hostage and murdered, too. A campaign is underway, Molala concludes, to eliminate Azapo as a political force, and everyone knows who lies behind it: members of Bishop Tutu's supposedly nonviolent United Democratic Front, internal wing of the African National Congress.

Actually, it is a little unfair to mention the bishop's name in this context. Bishop Tutu is a figurehead, not a leader. His truest eminence lies in the eyes of foreign TV cameras. He doesn't control the comrades, and he certainly doesn't write pamphlets of this ilk. Comrade Molala holds up the pamphlet for all to see. It is a two-page document, printed on a UDF letterhead. Just yesterday, thousands of copies of it were scattered in the streets of Soweto. It says, "We are calling all units of our front to war. We have tolerated Azapo for too long. They want to upstage our popularity in the community and they oppose all our campaigns.... WE MUST NOT REST UNTIL WE HAVE HUNTED DOWN EACH AND EVERY MEMBER OF AZAPO FROM SEKHUKUNILAND THROUGH PORT ELIZABETH TO LANGA."

It is hard to be sure, but this particular pamphlet smacks of forgery. It may well be the work of the white secret police, who are old and cunning masters of the art of black propaganda, of dividing the resistance against itself. Even so, as Comrade Molala observes, the state cannot be accused of creating the present crisis, only exploiting it. The bloodcurdling sentiments expressed in this pamphlet bear no relation to the UDF's public positions, but the actions it exhorts are already being undertaken in the streets. The truth of the matter is that followers of Nelson Mandela and Desmond Tutu are killing followers of Steve Biko.

The first question from the press, of course, is why? Why should black radicals, in the midst of a convulsive struggle against a brutally oppressive white supremacist regime, suddenly turn on one another and start killing each other? The query is fielded by Muntu Myeza, Azapo's publicity secretary. "It's not only difficult for people outside to understand why blacks are at each others' throats," he says. "It's difficult for ourselves."

If he doesn't know, what hope of understanding have we? Let us try.

I remember Steve Biko. I never met him, nor saw him speak, but he towered over my Just White Youth like a colossus, a figure who inspired true awe. There are those whites, both leftists and rightists, who dismiss him as a black racist, but I did not see him that way. His writings and court statements seemed to embody the truth, the real truth, not the simpering variant one encountered in the writings of white liberals. White liberals looked down on black victims and said, "Shame." Steve Biko, on the other hand, spoke to the wounded black heart. He said, Rise up; embrace your blackness; be proud of who you are; grow strong. He scorned the sentimental doctrine of mankind's unity, and the white liberals who propounded it, and yet this was not done with hatred. He never sounded like Louis Farrakhan. He slapped away the patronizing hand of whites like me, and yet I was not offended. He seemed to be saying, First this, first the black healing, and then we can talk, when we are all fully men. I don't know, my friend, I am not sure that Steve Biko was really a political figure. I think he transcended politics. I could scarcely believe, in my secret racist heart, that a black man could be so wise and perceptive, and the awe I felt for him had almost religious overtones. I am not mocking when I call him Saint Biko the Radiant. That is how I saw him.

In a way, Biko was a creation of the oppressive white state, in that its own actions set the stage for his inevitable emergence. In 1960, in the aftermath of the Sharpeville massacre, the state crushed Nelson Mandela's ANC and Robert Sobukwe's Pan-African Congress. Both Sobukwe and Mandela later went to jail, and many of their followers into exile. In exile, the ANC was kept alive largely by Moscow, and the PAC by Peking. Both organizations virtually ceased to exist inside South Africa.

Into this absolute vacuum, in the late sixties, stepped Steve Biko. All other leaders had been cut down, and all hope crushed, so Biko was sucked hungrily into the empty, hopeless hearts of hundreds of thousands of black people. In my youth, all the black men I knew supported Biko. All the black reporters with whom I drank in *The Star*'s fourth-floor canteen were Biko men. All the black universities were aseethe with his ideas, and when Soweto's black students took to the streets on June 16, 1976, Steve Biko's name was on their lips. They were shot down, of course, and a year later Biko met his own tragic end in the hands of the secret police.

In the aftermath of his death, revolution again threatened. So the secret police rounded up Biko's followers and smashed his movement, banning eighteen Black Consciousness organizations along with *The World* and *Weekend World*, newspapers that supported the BC line. Forty-eight of the Biko movement's leaders were arrested and detained for up to a year without trial.

When they were finally set free, those men and women regrouped in Azapo, the Azanian People's Organization. The exiled ANC was slow to exploit the climate of anger created by the Soweto riots and Biko's subsequent death, and Sobukwe's PAC was withering away, its Chinese sponsors too preoccupied with their own internal problems to pay much attention to events in distant Africa. So Azapo carried the standard of the black struggle for several years. The BC movement designed a flag for the coming free country and even gave it a name. It would be called Azania, from the ancient Arabic term for the terra incognita that lay south of Zanzibar, and it would be a "black communalist" people's republic, cleansed of the scourge of "racial capitalism." The world's left-wing newspapers took to referring to South Africa as Azania and to black South Africans as Azanians. In the early eighties, Azapo's domination of the internal black resistance was complete.

The ANC was the oldest black liberation movement, however, and in many ways the most politically astute. It was not about to cede its leadership of the struggle to upstarts. In the aftermath of the Soweto riots, the ANC began to woo student leaders away from the Biko movement. A few years later, it started trying to undercut the Biko legend, teaching recruits at its training camps in Angola or East Germany that the martyred BC prophet was a CIA agent. In the early eighties, the ANC began to reestablish a presence inside South Africa. This presence ultimately took the form of the UDF, the United Democratic Front, which hailed Nelson Mandela as its leader and cleaved faithfully to the ANC line.

As a political movement, the ANC-UDF axis had a great deal going for it—a righteous cause, a living martyr as leader, Bishop Tutu as a spokesman, and a line that played well in the West's white-controlled media. This line was "nonracialism." Race was discounted, and the battle for South Africa recast as a struggle between good and evil, or, alternatively, between the working and ruling classes. Whites were welcome to change sides. This analysis appealed to Western journalists and, through them, to Western churches and governments, who poured in funding for salaried organizers, computers, offices, T-shirts, pamphlets, and political campaigns. The UDF was formed in 1983. Within months, it had become a formidable force in South African politics, and Azapo had gone into apparent eclipse.

Azapo had next to nothing in the way of resources. It was so broke that even its leaders were unsalaried volunteers. It had few cars, few telephones, few staff, and its few foreign backers were so distant or powerless that they could offer little but moral support. Its "black racist" line was repugnant to white Western humanists, who couldn't very well endorse an organization that would not accept them as members. Azapo had nothing, in fact, but the memory of Biko, a tradition of brave resistance, and a political line that played rather well in the townships.

That line was that whites were the enemy. Azapo proclaimed that the true aim of the struggle was redemption of the land from the white conquerors. The UDF-ANC axis, on the other hand, cast the "apartheid state" or the "ruling class" as the enemy. Beyond that, it was six of one and half a dozen of another, or so it seemed to me. In South Africa, whites were the ruling class, and race struggle was class struggle. The terms were more or less interchangeable, and besides, both Azapo and the ANC were overtly socialist and overwhelmingly black. There were a handful of whites in the ANC, but they weren't allowed to sit on its ruling council until 1985. It was hard for an outsider to see why the two organizations didn't join forces and set about routing the Boer.

Instead, they became rivals. At first, the rivalry was peaceful, ideological, political. And then, in 1985, Senator Ted Kennedy came to South Africa at the invitation of the UDF's clerical leaders, and the real troubles began. The Reverend Boesak and Bishop Tutu felt that such a visit would focus international attention on the freedom struggle. Azapo was incensed. It wanted to know what kind of black men, not to mention socialists, would go to bed with a white millionaire from Boston. Wherever Kennedy went, Azapo showed up with placards lampooning him, and by extension the UDF, as tools of international capitalism. In radical circles in South Africa, this was the worst insult imaginable. There were angry confrontations, brawls, and fistfights.

Azapo was scarcely visible in the media, but when it came to a showdown it turned out to be extremely powerful. In fact, Azapo had enough clout to keep Kennedy out of Soweto altogether. The liberal senator who had come to South Africa to champion black liberation couldn't set foot in South Africa's largest black city because blacks were threatening to harm him. It was a propaganda debacle, and heralded the onset of open hostilities between Azapo and the UDF.

A few months later, Radio Freedom, clandestine voice of the ANC, broadcasting from somewhere in the heart of Africa, called on its followers inside South Africa to eliminate "the third force." What was the third force? On the streets, it seemed to mean anyone who did not pledge alliance to the ANC and Nelson Mandela—moderates, tribalists, apartheid "stooges" and "sellouts," police informers, but also followers of Steve Biko.

In the Eastern Cape, the region where Steve Biko lived and worked, and where his influence had once been strongest, Azapo "virtually ceased to exist," according to press reports. In Queenstown and Uitenhage, Azapo members were hounded out of town, their homes often burned down behind them. In nearby Port Elizabeth, where Biko sustained fatal brain injuries in a police interrogation cell, the regional secretary of the party that carried his standard was dragged out of a doctor's surgery by a mob and stabbed in broad daylight. In the industrialized Vaal Triangle, townships were divided into rival Mandela and Biko strongholds. It's hard to say how many people died in the Biko versus Mandela war, because their deaths tended to get lost in the general township carnage. Scores, certainly; more than a hundred, possibly. Things had finally reached a pass where even Azapo's top leaders were no longer safe, not even in the hearts of their own strongholds.

And that, ultimately, is why Comrade Molala called a press conference in downtown Johannesburg—to focus the white media's attention on the crisis, in the hope of shaming the UDF into condemning the violence and disciplining the rank and file.

The strategy seemed to have failed, judging from the relatively poor turnout at the press conference. It failed in another respect, too: Nobody offered a convincing explanation as to why the killing was taking place, why it was necessary. That is why I stayed around after the rest of the press had left, and asked the comrades' permission to interview a teenage member of Azasm—the Azanian Students' Movement, youth wing of the BC movement. Azasm members were not supposed to speak to the press without clearance, so I was instructed to come back the following day, to be screened by the youth wing's national executive.

Twenty-four hours later, I found myself sitting in the same conference room, facing six black youths across the same broad desk. They were all in their late teens or early twenties, all passionately sincere and idealistic young people. They genuinely wanted me to understand the roots of their struggle. They explained the history of their movement in great detail and elucidated the points on which they disagreed with the UDF.

The rival organization, they said, was wishy-washy in its commitment to socialism. Furthermore, it was not sworn to reclaim the conquered land. In this, they saw the influence of the white leftists and Communists who occupied some key positions in the UDF and in its mother body, the ANC. The presence of whites in such positions, said these youngsters, had inevitably diluted ANC-UDF doctrines, and blunted its thrust for liberation. Only Azapo, they said, remained true to Biko's vision.

"Our views," concluded Thami Hlekiso, national vice president of the youth wing, "are understood by the black community. That is why we are a force, and that is why they are killing us." He knew whereof he spoke. He had moved out of his parents' home and was living on the run. Some of his fellow executive members had been beaten up or expelled from their schools for refusing to renounce their BC beliefs. All had lost friends in the war against the UDF, and one was soon to lose a brother.

I asked Hlekiso if Azapo would survive the crisis. "We have given our lives to the struggle," he replied, "and if it is necessary to die, I think we will die. That is why I am confident Black Consciousness will survive."

I was glad to hear that, because I was saddened by the thought of a South Africa in which Steve Biko's spirit was extinguished. I said as much, and after that the comrades loosened up somewhat. They had been speaking guardedly, stiffly, but now they relaxed a little. Some even seemed to take a liking to me, in spite of my white skin.

I offered my own analysis of the situation. The ANC's public disavowals of Marxism, I argued, were largely strategic; they were intended to deny conservatives of Ronald Reagan or Margaret Thatcher's ilk a weapon in the struggle for international public opinion. I told them about articles I had read in *Sechaba* in which ANC leaders divided the world into rival "socialist" and "imperialist" blocs, led respectively by the Soviet Union ("the invincible bulwark of peace and mankind's social progress") and USA ("spearhead of the international forces of reaction"). There was no question as to where the ANC stood in this fray: it was "totally and uncompromisingly anti-imperialist," in president Oliver Tambo's phrase. "Anti-imperialists of the world unite!" he declared. Hlekiso and the others found these remarks intriguing. They had never seen *Sechaba* because it was banned in South Africa. We wound up talking for more than an hour. I kept asking why. Why not join forces with the UDF? Why not get on with the struggle and leave the picking of ideological nits for later? In the end, I got an interesting answer.

"The UDF is stealing our struggle," Hlekiso said heatedly. "They have stolen our sign," he said, referring to the clenched fist of black power, "and they have stolen our songs."

"What songs?" I inquired.

"The Zulu song, 'My mother becomes happy when I beat a white,' " he said.

Well, well, I thought. The "nonracial" UDF steals songs about hitting whites, and the doctrinally pure BC socialists get very upset about it. There was clearly more here than met the eye. The national vice president of the Azanian Students' Movement must have missed my raised eyebrows. A few minutes later, he cleared my request to interview a rank and file member of his movement.

If South Africa were a black-run country, Old Potch Road would be a six-lane highway. It's a white-run country, though, so Soweto's motorists crawl to and from town along a potholed two-lane blacktop that is clogged with traffic at almost any hour of the day. About the best thing to be said for Old Potch Road is that you have to travel it slowly—slowly enough to take in the sights, such as they are. We pass a little kid selling bumper stickers at the roadside—"I Love Soweto," they say, or "God Bless and Heal Africa." We pass the cathedral, the squatter camp at Kliptown, and then Moroka Police Station, surrounded by an eight-foot fence.

Inside, laborers are at work on a new apartment complex for black police officers. It is no longer possible, at this stage of history, for black cops to live among fellow blacks. To stay alive, they must stay inside guarded perimeters, behind barbed wire. A little further on, we pass another sign of the times, a gleaming new fast-food joint called Chicken Upeo, fruit of Botha's drive to create a black middle class. And on a transformer housing (itself a sign of "reform," of the recent electrification of Soweto), yet another telling detail—a bloodred *V,* homage to the science-fiction TV series in which freedom fighters battle a cruel race of conquering aliens in the suburbs of Los Angeles.

In the nine years since I was last in Dhlamini, the place has brightened somewhat. Black people have finally been granted the right to permanent residence in "white" South Africa. Many now own the houses they live in, and with ownership has come a measure of pride. Every second or third residence has been expanded or modified in some fashion. There are splashes of color here and there—a house brightly painted, a flowering rose garden, a new car in some lucky man's driveway—but the backdrop remains dreary and depressing. The ranks of matchbox houses run down toward a stretch of reedy marshland, where a rubble-strewn patch of land serves as a makeshift soccer field.

It is deserted today, but in a more innocent time a group of black schoolboys in their early teens might have been playing soccer down there. Those soccer games were a daily after-school ritual for the schoolboys of Dhlamini 1 and its adjoining zone, Dhlamini 2. They took their games seriously and always played to win, but they were good friends off the field. They lived within hailing distance of one another, and often attended the same schools. They were all black, all sons of struggling parents, all victims of apartheid's atrocious Bantu Education, dished out in overcrowded classrooms by teachers barely educated themselves. And they were all to some degree politicized. Some of the boys were members of Azapo, and some belonged to the UDF, but they were still playing soccer together in the afternoons a year or so ago. Today, they're trying to kill each other.

I locate the house I'm looking for and knock on the door. A firebomb has recently exploded on this very doorstep. A month or two hence, a teenaged son of the household within will be waylaid as he's coming home, stabbed with garden forks and burned alive. Right now, however, the street seems peaceful. Even so, I feel apprehensive and cast fearful glances in the direction from which danger will come, if it comes. I usually work with a black interpreter, but nobody would accompany me on this particular mission. They all said it was too dangerous.

The door opens, and I find myself shaking hands with a teenager in a T-shirt and skintight designer jeans. The boy's skin is golden-brown and he's still carrying a little baby fat on his plump face and frame. This is Vuyisele Byron Wauchope, age fifteen. Alongside him stands his friend and ideological mentor, Vuyo Kapa, age nineteen. Through an open doorway I catch a glimpse of Byron's Uncle George, the general secretary of Azapo, sleeping the sleep of the utterly exhausted in a bedroom piled with clothes and other belongings. He is a refugee now. He and his wife and children no longer have a home. Their home has burned down, which means that Byron is homeless too.

Byron leads me through into the dining room, and we sit down at the table to talk. Vuyo joins us. Vuyo is a desperately serious young man. He has a goatee like Trotsky's, and some ideas to match. He is here to keep vigil over the utterances of young Byron, who is too young to have truly mastered the party line. Byron has only just turned fifteen, and he's still inclined to squirm and giggle nervously in the presence of a strange adult. It's hard to see him as a player in the deadly game of township politics, but that's how things were in the great uprising of the mid-eighties. In some ways, it was a Children's Crusade.

Byron is the son of George Wauchope's sister, but he was raised in the BC leader's household and seems to have radical politics in his bones. One of his earliest memories is of visiting his famous uncle in prison during one of George's periodic detention spells. Byron's relatives used to carry him to BC rallies and congresses before he could walk or talk. "I joined politics when I was five," the boy says proudly. Shortly thereafter, he was tear-gassed for the first time, at a rally commemorating Steve Biko's death in detention. At the age of twelve, he became a card-carrying member of the Biko youth movement, and soon rose to be treasurer of the Dhlamini 1 branch of Azasm. His best friend, Fana Mhlongo, was the branch's mascot. Fana was by no means the youngest comrade, but he was one of the smallest, short and fat like a snub-nosed revolver. That's why they called him Gun-man—comrade Gunman Mhlongo, a soldier at the age of fourteen.

Fana lived just up the road, and he'd been Byron's best friend since 1983. The boys were inseparable in all things, not just politics. They attended the same primary school, played on the same soccer team in those afternoon pick-up games. They liked the same TV shows—*Knight Rider, The A-Team* and Bill Cosby—and the same pop groups: Stimela, The Big Dudes, Yvonne Chaka-Chaka. Their favorite film stars were "James Bond" and Chuck Norris. Their favorite movies were *Rambo, First Blood,* and *Wild Geese,* a luridly racist action adventure in which white mercenaries kick hell out of a caricatural African despot. And their favorite game, Byron added, was Monopoly. I thought the next thing to emerge from his young mouth would be some kind words about Ronald Reagan or Margaret Thatcher, but

Byron Wauchope was actually a revolutionary socialist. His friend Fana was one, too.

"We wrote a freedom song," said Byron. It was called, "Strive Tirelessly for a Socialist Azania," and it went like this: "If you can fight fearlessly, I'll meet you on the freedom day. I shall fight for Azania, Azania, my beloved country."

Impressed, I asked Byron why he and Fana had opted to join the Azanians, as opposed to the UDF.

"Well," Byron answered, "the UDF says, 'Mandela it's our father,' but we say, 'Biko it's our father.' "

"Yes," I said, "I understand that, but what I'm really asking is, Why do you prefer BC? What is Black Consciousness?"

He thought about that, and then he said, "Steve Biko was a man, and Abraham Tiro says there is no struggle without casualties."

The late Abraham Tiro was a prominent BC leader in the seventies, but even so, it was not the most illuminating reply. My line of questioning was clearly incorrect, so I tried another tack. Instead of asking what was right about BC, I asked what was wrong with the UDF.

"They are trying to confuse the masses," said Byron.

"How so?" I wondered.

"When they saw we were too powerful," he said, "they said you will get free money and free T-shirts if you join the UDF."

At this point, Vuyo stepped in to offer a more coherent statement on the boy's behalf. "Biko was trying to boost the morale of the exploited masses of Azania," Vuyo began. His discourse lasted ten minutes and touched on several hair-raising conspiracy theories, one of which was that the American CIA was funneling funds through the ANC to the UDF, which was using the money to bribe Biko followers over to the Mandela side. He concluded on a familiar note: Only the BC movement was "fighting for socialism and the total liberation of all blacks and oppressed people" and would not rest until victory was achieved. It was very interesting, but Byron's remark about the T-shirts stood and deserved to be heard.

In the beginning, to hear young Byron tell it, being a comrade was quite exciting. They held meetings and workshops in their homes after school while their parents were away at work. They discussed apartheid and the fight against it. Older members of the organization delivered lectures on ideology and tactics. Once the struggle got underway in earnest, they declared Dhlamini 1 a "liberated zone" and drew up plans to defend it. Every comrade was given a list of names and phone numbers to keep beside his parents' telephone, if they had one, so that he could raise the alarm in the event of an attack. They also devised codes to baffle the system's ubiquitous spies. If a comrade said, "Bring the Kentucky!" for instance, it really meant, "Bring the gun!" Many comrades were so young that they'd stub out cigarettes when they saw their parents coming, but some carried pistols or revolvers in their socks.

The guns were intended for defense against the system, of course, not against people like Paulos Madonsela. Paulos lived three doors down from Byron and often played soccer with him and Fana after school. Paulos was a year or two older, and inclined to play rough. Indeed, he once tackled Byron so hard that he accidently broke his arm, but that was part of the game. The boys remained friends in spite of everything. Even when Paulos succumbed to alleged CIA blandishments and donned the yellow T-shirt of the rival UDF, he and Byron stayed friends. "We all shared a pain for Soweto," Byron explained. But then Senator Kennedy came to South Africa, and nothing was ever the same again.

As the BC comrades saw it, the American senator's visit would only raise false hopes and foster illusions among Soweto's downtrodden people. "The Charterists were telling people who doesn't know anything that someone from the USA is coming to deliver a speech," Byron said. "So people who are not educated thought maybe this man is having good news, coming from the States. But BC said, 'There's nothing like that. Kennedy will deliver nothing. He's out of order. We don't want Kennedy here.' "

Paulos disagreed. He and his fellow Charterists were planning to roll out the red carpet for the famous American. One day Paulos saw Byron in the road and called out mockingly, "Come and listen to this man! Maybe you can be liberated!" Byron just laughed. "Paulos," he replied, "you are still young in politics. You are an amateur."

On the appointed day, all the comrades in Dhlamini marched down the hill to Regina Mundi cathedral, where Kennedy was scheduled to speak. Thousands of people were waiting, plus scores of reporters and TV cameras from all over the world. Paulos and the Charterists stood at the front of the hall. Byron, Fana, and the rest of the BC contingent stood at the back. And Bishop Tutu stood on stage with his hands in the air, begging the seething factions to make peace. It didn't help. The BC comrades were determined not to let Kennedy speak. Indeed, they put on such a show of force and fury that Tutu lost his nerve and advised his friend Kennedy to stay away. It was a humiliation for the UDF, and there would be a price to pay.

One day, not long after, the slogan "One Azania, One Nation" appeared on a transformer housing at the entrance to Dhlamini 1, marking the zone a Zim-zim stronghold. Few whites knew the term Zim-zim, and it seldom if ever appeared in the copy of foreign correspondents. It was becoming an important word in Soweto, though. In Soweto, youngsters who said Biko were dubbed Zim-zims, in honor of all the -*isms* in their ideological arsenal: socialism, racism, capitalism, colonialism. Those who said Mandela, on the other hand, were called Wararas, a corruption of the Afrikaans *waar-waar,* meaning "where-where." In the estimation of Zim-zims, anyone who believed the UDF's nonracial doctrine was very confused. They were groping around in the dark in search of their true enemy, crying, "Where? Where?" Dhlamini 1 became a Zim-zim stronghold, and Dhlamini 2, just across the road, became Warara turf. Much of the rest of Soweto was similarly divided, in preparation for the coming war.

To the best of Byron's recollection, the first casualty was Sipho Mngomezulu, a young man who "preached BC" in a part of Soweto called Emdeni. The Wararas abducted him from his home in full view of his helpless parents, dragged him to a vacant lot and stoned him to death. I tried to ask the Wararas for their version of this event, but I couldn't contact them. They were hiding from the Zim-zims, or on the run from the police. If I had reached them, though, I daresay they might have claimed that Mngomezulu was executed in retaliation for the recent abduction and torture-murders of three teenaged Wararas. The Zim-zims, in turn, denied complicity in those killings, claiming that they were actually carried out by the maKabasa, a criminal gang that just happened to live in a Zim-zim stronghold and probably took orders from the white secret police. Such knots are never unraveled, not in South Africa.

All that is certain is that Sipho Mngomezulu was abducted and killed in broad daylight. To add insult to injury, a mob of Wararas invaded the wake, set fire to Sipho's coffin, and demolished his parents' home with a hijacked bulldozer. The Zim-zims managed to save the coffin and bury it, but there was a second killing after the funeral. This time, the victim was Martin Mohau, age twenty-nine. Mohau was a hero of the struggle against apartheid and another "graduate" of Robben Island, the political prison in Table Bay. He was also a Zim-zim. A mob of Wararas waylaid him on his way home from

Sipho's funeral and necklaced him—put a car tire around his neck, poured gasoline on him, and burned him alive.

"After that," Byron continued, "everyone chose sides." Wararas started "expelling" Zim-zims from schools in their strongholds. Teenagers with dissident politics were threatened or beaten up by their classmates. Some were doused with petrol, put inside car tires and given a choice: "Say Mandela or die." Or: "Say Biko or die."

Fana's school was Ibongho High, a bad place to be BC. One morning, leaders of the dominant Warara faction ordered their teachers and headmaster to go sit in the staff room. Then they summoned the students to an assembly. All Zim-zims were ordered to step to the fore and recant. Several did, but not Comrade Gunman Mhlongo. "He was ready to die for BC," young Byron told me. So Fana and approximately twenty fellow BC stalwarts were banished on pain of death. "If we ever see you here again," the Wararas warned, "tell us what size car tire you wear." Then the Zim-zims were chased away. Fana was a fat boy and couldn't run very fast. He dropped his school bag while making his getaway, and that was the end of his education.

A few days later, a similar incident took place at Byron's school. A group of Wararas led by his old friend Paulos burst into Byron's classroom, looking for him. "Where is he?" the Wararas demanded. "We want to necklace him." Byron was lucky; he'd had a premonition and stayed at home that day.

Appalled by the image of a gang of sixteen-year-olds invading a higher-primary-school classroom to murder a fifteen-year-old, I asked Byron how the teacher responded. "He just shut his mouth," the boy giggled, "because he knew that if he opened it they would kill him, too. But after they left, he phoned my house and told me I must not come back to school."

And so Byron and his best friend Fana stayed home, with nothing to do all day. They listened to Radio Bop, beaming in from the quasi-independent homeland of Bophuthatswana. They played Monopoly, or fooled around on Uncle George's tape, recording themselves singing freedom songs. One day, on their way to the shops, they were attacked by a band of Wararas. Fana fended off a knife-thrust with his bare hand, and one of his fingers was virtually severed. After that, the BC comrades always traveled in a group. They started sleeping in groups too, staying one night at one comrade's house, the next at another's. They wanted to be together in case of an attack.

Outside, the killing continued. A BC comrade's home was damaged by a Soviet limpet mine. In apparent retaliation, Zim-zims hijacked a bus and crashed it into the home of a Warara leader. In counterstrike, the Wararas started kidnapping and killing Zim-zim next-of-kin. A well-known Soweto sports personality and church leader was abducted and murdered by Wararas hunting his son. The aging grandmother of a Zim-zim met a similar fate. A UDF street committee ordered her to produce her grandson; when she failed to comply, she was killed. A few days later, someone from the other side was bundled into a car, shot thrice, and his body dumped in a coalyard. And so it carried on.

In this war, as in all wars, there were no innocent parties and no innocent bystanders, but the Zim-zims were clearly on the losing end. Azapo seemed to be disintegrating, its members resigning in fear of their lives, its leaders driven underground. There came a time when no one was safe anymore, least of all the Wauchope family. George Wauchope had been one of Steve Biko's closest allies, but this did not entitle him to mercy. First there were phone calls, anonymous voices warning George that his time was running out. Then someone rammed a stolen van into the front of his house. A few nights later, a firebomb was hurled at George's home. It smashed against an outside wall, causing little damage, but still, these incidents left him unnerved. George had a family to think about—a wife, two young children, an ailing mother and a teenage nephew. That's why he went into hiding, hoping to draw the Wararas away. And that in turn is why there was no man in the house at 1454 Dhlamini when the Wararas returned to burn it down.

They came at three in the morning, and this time they came in force. Byron was wakened by a great crashing of glass, and the whomp of igniting gasoline. In his estimation, at least twenty Molotov cocktails came in through the windows simultaneously. One landed right on top of his cousin Ephraim, setting his clothes and bedding afire. It was bright as day from the flames, but the house soon filled with smoke. The family milled around in terror. Byron groped his way to the door, but it wouldn't open. Someone was holding it closed from the outside. The flames were mounting, and the Wauchopes thought themselves doomed to burn. They were lucky, though. Their screams roused the neighbors, who came to see what was going on. At that, the Wararas melted away into the night. The door suddenly gave, and the Wauchopes staggered outside, choking and gasping for air.

Nobody was seriously injured in the fire, but the Wauchopes lost almost everything they owned. In the aftermath, young Byron telephoned Uncle

George at his place of hiding and told him to come and see. The BC leader arrived just as the fire brigade was dousing the last flames in the smoldering ruins of his home.

"He didn't say anything," Byron told me. "He just looked down at the ground."

Mrs. Leah Mhlongo is old and tired, and her face is deeply lined with grief. She's sixty-nine years old and wears a *doek* over her iron-gray hair. She sits at a Formica table in her humble kitchen, talking, crying, and punctuating her tales with a curious whooshing sound. The sound signifies something lost and gone—a job here, a certainty there, and all too often, a person. "And where's the boy now?" she asks. *"Whoosh."* The boy is lost and gone.

Mrs. Mhlongo is the grandmother of Fana Mhlongo, Byron Wauchope's best friend. She's a Zulu with roots in the countryside, but she spent most of her adult life in Soweto, working as an office cleaner. She gave birth to three daughters, two of whom—*whoosh*—are dead of heart disease already. Her beloved husband has passed away, too. The sole surviving daughter, Elizabeth, teaches at an Anglican school in Wilgespruit. It's too far to commute every day, so she lives at the school, leaving Granny Mhlongo to raise five grandchildren more or less alone. The old lady has had a hard time of it—especially with Fana and Yvonne, who were fourteen and fifteen respectively when the uprising started.

Mrs. Mhlongo is a conservative person—not a supporter of the apartheid status quo, really; just an old Zulu widow who can't imagine things being any other way. She says she knew from the start that anyone involved in the uprising was bound to meet a sorry end; if the Boers didn't get them, the comrades surely would. "I was not liking this thing," she says. "I saw it's too dangerous."

So she took Fana and Yvonne aside and warned them to stay out of politics and keep their noses clean. They said yes to her face, because they were both dutiful children, but behind her back they did what most other teenagers did—became comrades and threw themselves into the struggle, both on the BC side. When Granny Mhlongo found out about it, she gave them a tongue-lashing, but they weren't prepared to listen. They told her a new world was coming into being, a world where black peoples' lives would be easier and everyone would be free. Mrs. Mhlongo didn't believe it. She clucked angrily to hear such nonsense. Yvonne and Fana just laughed. "Oh, Granny," they said, "you too old. You know nothing because you too old."

The old lady sighs and wipes the tears from her eyes. "Ah," she says, "you know the kids. If we are saying, 'Don't do it!' then they do it. And now where are they? *Whoosh.*" Both gone.

Yvonne vanished at the height of the Biko versus Mandela war, fearing that someone might kill her for being BC. She was fleeing the depradations of the ANC-supporting Wararas, but there was nowhere to run save into the arms of the ANC, and that's where she is today—in some ANC refugee camp in the Botswana desert, an unhappy and lonely fifteen-year-old, desperate to come home. She can't come home, though—not now, maybe never. If she comes home, the South African secret police will take her for one of the people she fled in the first place—a supporter of the outlawed ANC. She'd almost certainly go to jail.

And as for Fana—well, the last time Mrs. Mhlongo saw Fana was a Thursday morning. The boy got up as usual around 7:30 A.M. and helped her with the chores. He ate several slices of bread and jam for breakfast, washing them down with a mug of tea. Then he changed into his oldest clothes—a pair of red shorts and a threadbare sweater—and informed grandma that he was on his way. "Where to?" Mrs. Mhlongo asked. To Comrade George's house, Fana replied. He was going to help his friend Byron clean up the rubble from the fire. Granny Mhlongo frowned disapprovingly, but there was nothing she could do. She just warned the boy to be careful and kissed him goodbye.

Several hours later, the old lady heard a great commotion in the street outside. Peeping through a window, she saw dozens of people running in the streets—some running toward the sound of gunfire, some running away. "The guns were too much that day," she recalled. *Pow! Pow! Pow!* I thought, what's wrong?" Nobody knew. After a while, the streets emptied and the gunfire died away. Mrs. Mhlongo thought no more about it until a boy from the neighborhood came pounding on her door. "Hey, granny," he said breathlessly. "The comrades have taken Fana away."

Mrs. Mhlongo gathered up her skirts and lumbered to the Wauchope's home, several hundred yards away. She found Byron's grandmother Ethel sitting on the ground outside her gutted home, weeping and weak with shock. Several older BC comrades were standing around with guns in their pockets, uncertain what to do. They told Mrs. Mhlongo that her grandson had been kidnapped.

Fana, Byron, and four young friends had been scraping down the blackened walls of the Wauchope's house when someone warned them that Wararas were gathering nearby. Fana and Byron looked outside, and sure enough, there they were—a knot of black teenagers on the far side of the road, among them Paulos Madonsela, their soccer-playing buddy from three doors down. The boys exchanged cold stares. "Never trust a friend," said Fana. There was nothing the Zim-zims could do. They were vastly outnumbered these days. They just went back to work.

A while later, Fana and Byron checked the road again. There were more Wararas now, gathering at either end of the block. The boys grew frightened. Byron decided to go for help. He leapt the backyard fence, strode through the neighbor's property and onto the road beyond. But the Wararas were there, too, an entire platoon of them, armed with knives, guns, and petrol bombs. One lifted a pistol and took aim. Byron dodged out of sight and ran back into his gutted home, shouting, "The enemy is here!"

The Wararas came in behind him, shooting, and Zim-zims ran for their lives. Byron fled into a nearby house and hid under a bed. He heard Fana screaming in the yard outside. Then the Wararas burst in, found Byron's hiding place, and dragged him out into the street. At that moment, a yellow car came around the corner. A police car? Byron's captors were momentarily distracted. He twisted out of their grasp and ran, bullets whistling past his ears.

Fana was less lucky. The last Byron saw of his best friend, he was struggling in the grip of a dozen Wararas, screaming, "What have I done to you? Let me go! Let me go!" The Wararas picked Fana up and set off at a run, firing shots into the air to discourage pursuit. A hundred yards away, a white Nissan panel van drew abreast of the trotting throng. The Wararas bundled Fana into it, and *whoosh,* he was spirited away.

The abduction was carried out in broad daylight. There were scores of witnesses. The identity of Fana's captors was never a secret. Several were boys from the neighborhood, boys who had grown up with Fana and played soccer against him after school. Most were members of the Soweto Student's Congress, an affiliate of the mighty UDF, or so the Zim-zims said. Mrs. Mhlongo gave their names to the cops at Moroka Police Station, but the police didn't seem particularly interested. "Do you think you're the only one who's crying?" they asked her. "Do you think your grandson is the only one missing?"

They opened a docket, but beyond that they dragged their feet. Indeed, there were those who claimed that the list of suspects fell into the hands of the secret police, who returned it to the Zim-zims, hinting that they might want to take the law into their own hands. The cruel white game of divide and rule had become easier than ever to play.

The Zim-zims had a shrewd idea where Fana had been taken—to a house maybe one thousand yards from his own home, in the Warara stronghold on the far side of Old Potch Road. He might as well have been in Moscow. His grandmother actually located his prison. She loitered near the gate and spoke to a schoolgirl who confirmed that the Wararas were interrogating a captive within. Grandma Mhlongo was too scared to go inside, though. "I know they want to hit everybody," she said, "and doesn't care if you are old or young."

We were sitting in Granny Mhlongo's living room by now—the old lady, George Wauchope, and I. The BC leader offered an interpretative remark. "If you go into their stronghold," he explained, "you will surely be killed, because you are outnumbered. Either you are with them, or you are not. There is no middle of the road." He was right. In South Africa's townships, the middle of the road had become a place where nobody dared stand.

Fana's corpse was found on one of Soweto's golf courses ten days later. He had apparently been held over an electric stove at some stage of his "interrogation," because his legs were covered with burns in the shape of concentric circles. There were tiny cuts on his head and on the soles of his feet, where he had been pricked with the point of a sharp knife. Finally, someone had put a bullet in his temple, dumped his body and built a fire on top of it. He was fourteen years old. The body wore short pants. So it goes.

Blessed are the dead

For they will:

> *Never be suspected,*
> *Never be chased,*
> *Never be unmanageable*
> *Never be transformed into firewood*
> *Never be killed*

For they are now:

> *Protected from adversaries*
> *Saved from opponents*
> *Secured from the persecution of this world.*

Blessed are those who are dead.

—*Township Poet B. M. THEMBA*

Last time I saw George Wauchope he'd been drinking, but then lots of people were drinking heavily in those harrowing times. It was a weekday afternoon, and he was sitting in Azapo's dingy headquarters in downtown Jo'burg, telling war stories. A new picture of Steve Biko had materialized on the wall behind him—a painting by some South American revolutionary who had literally beatified the BC martyr, depicting him with a halo around his head. Alongside Saint Biko hung a poster proclaiming, "Our history is written in bloodshed. Our history is written on prison walls." And beneath the poster sat Comrade Wauchope, a lanky, loose-limbed man in an old sportcoat, speaking in an intense monotone. He was filling in the gaps in his background for a white reporter.

George Wauchope's struggle began in the early seventies, when he was a twenty-one-year-old student at the segregated University of Fort Hare. Steve Biko lived in nearby King Williamstown. He was already under a banning order, but he often stole onto the campus under cover of darkness for consciousness-raising sessions. George was something of a moderate at the time, but he attended a few Biko meetings and was won over heart and soul. He became campus coordinator for the BC movement and soon incurred the displeasure of the university's white administrators. In 1972, they expelled him and seventeen others as troublemakers.

George returned to his hometown, Soweto, and went to work for Biko's Black People's Convention, becoming chairman of its Johannesburg Central branch. The BC prophet was confined to a distant country town, so the task of spreading his word through the vast townships outside Johannesburg fell largely to young George Wauchope. He was a widely respected organizer, low-keyed, intelligent, self-effacing, efficient. He organized high school pupils, students, workers—even organized his own family. Under his influence, a sister and a girl cousin "went outside"—jumped the border and joined the exiled ANC. In those days, the Mandela and Biko movements were still on good terms, two fists of the same fighter. His mother, Ethel, and her sister, Joyce, were drawn into the struggle too. Both women eventually wound up in detention under the Terrorism Act, accused of running an underground railroad for young rebels bent on leaving the country for military training.

When the Soweto rebellion broke out in June 1976, George Wauchope's name leapt onto the secret police's most-wanted list. They picked him up on the second day of the troubles and held him—without trial—longer than any other detainee; 297 days in all. One night, at the height of the fighting, some white cops took him out of his cell and into a makeshift morgue. Several black bodies lay on the floor, mangled by bullets from automatic rifles. "This," said the cops, "is what happens when black power comes up against white power." George Wauchope didn't flinch. He knew where he stood, and he was willing to die for it. "If you get into politics in this country," he told me, "you know you're going to wind up in prison or dead."

So he returned to the struggle as soon as they set him free and became the Biko movement's labor secretary. There was a massive upsurge in support for BC organizations in the wake of the Soweto uprising, and the movement became "a state within the state," in George's estimation. That made George himself a virtual shadow cabinet minister, but his exalted office remained largely unsalaried. He had a wife, Nozwakaze, by now, and would soon have two children. Life was sometimes hard. No money would come in for months on end, but George and his family made do. "The struggle must go on," George said. "My wife knew the type of job I was involved in, so she just had to accept the life we lived."

She also had to accept that each day with her husband might be the last. In South Africa, radical black leaders lived from moment to moment. Sooner or later, as George observed, they were likely to wind up in jail or dead. In October 1977, Steve Biko wound up dead, and George Wauchope wound up behind bars again. As far as the white state was concerned, he was too dangerous to be on the loose in a climate of impending revolution. This time, they held him for 281 days, again without trial, but his spirit remained unbroken. "You can't turn back," he said.

Once restored to freedom, George opened a new front in the struggle. The first target was American singer Ray Charles, who toured South Africa in the late seventies. One night there was a knock on Charles's dressing-room door, and there stood George Wauchope, come to do some conscious-ness-raising. The young BC leader told the legendary blind soulman what it was to be black under apartheid, and then demanded to know what Charles was doing in the country. "You're giving comfort to our enemy," George declared. Ray Charles was chagrined and swore never to set foot in South Africa again.

This was the opening gambit in George's so-called isolation campaign, designed to sever cultural ties between white South Africa and the outside world. Pop stars who ignored pleas to stay away reaped a harvest of bad publicity, and touring South Africa soon became more trouble than it was worth, especially after the European Anti-Apartheid Movement intensified its own isolation campaign. The flow of foreign entertainers to South Africa slowed to a trickle and ultimately ceased almost entirely. One of the last acts to defy the boycott, an American R & B band called the O'Jays, found their footsteps dogged by demonstrators wherever they went. And George, who had organized the protests, found himself back behind bars.

That was 1981. Two years later, the United Democratic Front emerged and began to compete with the BC movement for the loyalties of radical blacks. In the beginning, George had the "ambitious and very idealistic" idea that the disparate strains of the resistance movement could be unified, but it didn't work out quite that way. BC ideologues were reluctant to forsake their doctrine of racial exclusivity, and the UDF-ANC axis didn't seem particularly eager to strike a deal. From the very start, the resurgent Mandela movement billed itself as "the only authentic voice" of oppressed black South Africans. One thing led to another, and by mid-1986 the relationship between the rival movements had degenerated into war.

This other civil war in Soweto was a largely subterranean affair, covered desultorily by the press. From time to time the papers noted the violent death of some BC activist at the hands of faceless "groups of youths" or "members of a rival organization," but the killing was seldom if ever attributed to supporters of the UDF—not at the outset, at any rate. "There was a very, very heavy bias," said George. He ascribed this to a "rightist" conspiracy in the media, but a simpler explanation suggested itself to me. The UDF was a supposedly nonviolent, democratic movement, and a fount of hope and righteousness in the eyes of many reporters. It was inconceivable that such an organization should be implicated in a campaign of extermination, so the cutting questions went unasked, which was probably just as well. As far as many UDF leaders were concerned, there was no war at all; the black community was simply cleansing itself of collaborators and right-wing vigilantes.

"They didn't see anything," George said bitterly. "Murphy Morobe, Terror Lekgota, Albertina Sisulu—they never *ever* acknowledged that there was this internecine warfare. They never *ever* tried to stop it." George's movement condemned the violence, but the UDF was slow to follow suit.

And then George's house was burned down, and young Fana Mhlongo abducted from the ruins. George was thirty-six years old on the day it happened, and he'd been a revolutionary for sixteen years. There was nothing else. He had given his entire adult life, every working day, every waking hour, to the cause of BC, the cause of black pride, black power, and total noncollaboration. Azapo did not court favorable coverage in the white-controlled media and disdained the use of the white courts, even for purely strategic ends. There came a time, however, when such pure doctrinairism was no longer affordable.

And so, in the wake of Fana's abduction, George Wauchope took a step that must surely have broken his heart: He appeared, cap in hand, before a white Supreme Court judge, and asked the white judicial system to protect him and his family from further Warara attacks.

The word *Warara* was not mentioned in the pleading, of course. In the pleading, George claimed to be under attack by members of the Soweto Students Council, an affiliate of the UDF. Four individuals were identified by name. They didn't show up to defend themselves, so the judge granted a temporary injunction restraining the Charterists from further violent acts. It made a handy hook for newspaper stories, but otherwise the court order wasn't worth the paper it was printed on—not in Soweto, in 1986. "It just went on and on," the BC leader said.

There were more attempts on George's own life. One of his aunts was kidnapped, another threatened with death. His mother, Ethel, never recovered from the trauma of the firebombing and died within the month of a heart attack. One of his uncles was the target of an attempted assassination. Another uncle was shot dead. One of his nephews was shot in the face, another stabbed in the hand. By the time it was over, George's family was devastated. Most surviving Wauchopes had fled to a township on the far side of the Witwatersrand, and young Byron had been sent to school in a quiet country town. Another relative, seventeen-year-old Ephraim Zitha, was in jail on a murder rap, arising from a killing he maintained was an act of self-defense.

As for George himself, he'd recently stepped down as Azapo's general secretary, and his political career appeared to have come to a tragic end. There were killings on both sides in Soweto's other civil war, and now one was being blamed on him; he was about to stand trial for murder, in a country where convicted murderers were usually hanged.

I asked what had happened, but George just shook his head. "I don't want to talk about it," he said. There was no pain or anger in his voice. Indeed, he seemed curiously dispassionate, as if something inside him was already dead.

There was so much horror in my country, and it came in so many forms. There was the white horror, the horror of black protesters shot down in the streets—412 of them that year. But there was another kind of horror too, the horror blacks inflicted on one another. It was there from the very beginning, from the day it all started, back in September 1984, in the township of Sebokeng. The very first casualty of the great uprising was a black community councillor, a supposed sellout, hacked and burned to death by a black mob. After that, it grew and grew, until it equalled and ultimately eclipsed the white horror. As the grip of the white state weakened, blacks turned on one another in a bloody power struggle that has since claimed close to three black lives for every martyr cut down by apartheid's riot police.

The white state blamed the carnage on a cold-blooded Marxist plot to exterminate the center, and the Mandela Charterists, in a manner of speaking, agreed. Government spokesmen referred to the dead as "moderates" or "law-abiding citizens," Charterists called them "stooges" or "sellouts," but the difference was largely semantic; both sides would have had you believe that there was some sort of overarching logic to the madness, and both sides were talking complete shit.

When that terrible year was done, statisticians in the service of the liberal Institute of Race Relations counted only 79 "perceived collaborators" among 1,302 unrest fatalities. Of the remaining deaths, 265 were attributed to "internecine conflict" among blacks, a further 98 to "unexplained conflict." And beyond that, beyond internecine and inexplicable violence, beyond "accidents" (10 deaths) and "indeterminate" (31), lay the black hole of "burned bodies found"—231 of them in all, the anonymous burned alive by the faceless, under circumstances no one dared examine too closely.

Who on earth were those people? Who ordered their deaths? The ANC initially encouraged the burnings of collaborators, but changed its mind in February 1986, and issued a statement condemning the practice. The sole result was a massive rise in the number of necklacings. Azapo termed the necklace "a crime against humanity," so it was surely not to blame. Bishop Tutu's UDF was supposedly nonviolent. So was Inkatha, Chief Buthelezi's Zulu political movement. So who was doing the killing? Who was telling the truth? Who were the good guys? Who ordered Fana's abduction and execution? Were the UDF comrades who allegedly carried it out disciplined by their nonviolent organization? Indeed, where were the comrades who did it? Where were the police? Who was really in charge—the reasoned and rational black leaders who sat behind the desks, or the teenagers on the streets? There were no clear answers to any of these questions, in the South African winter of 1986.

The only place where the country really made sense was in the pages of the world's enlightened white newspapers, where the struggle was usually portrayed as a rather fastidious affair. In this other, largely imaginary South Africa, "anti-apartheid activists" waged a "nonviolent" and "intensely principled" struggle against white evil in the name of democracy or civil rights. The reality on the streets was so much darker, so much darker. The comrades' ends were just, to be sure, but their means were sometimes as ruthless as the Boers'. They lopped people's ears off for breaking boycotts, forced pacifist Zionists to eat their metal badges. People were dragged behind cars or forced to drink detergent for violating don't-buy-white campaigns. Thousands of moderate, middle-aged blacks were herded to funerals and rallies by young comrades shaking boxes of matches—a not-so-subtle warning of what awaited those who approached the struggle with insufficient enthusiasm. These grim facts of black life tended to undercut the horror of children tortured or shot dead in the streets, so the Western media downplayed them whenever possible, sometimes barely mentioned them at all.

Consider this clipping from the *New York Times,* dated April 15, 1986. At the top of the page is a fourteen-inch story about Desmond Tutu's election as Archbishop of Cape Town, and thus head of South Africa's Anglican Church. It is an elegant piece of writing, intended to evoke a cathedral mood, a reverent silence in which one might hear stirring the most noble aspects of the human spirit, unquenchable in its thirst for freedom and justice. "The doors were suddenly opened. Light poured from the chapel into the darkness . . . and Bishop Tutu stepped into the cool air" to deliver his moving victory speech. He called upon South African churches to transform "religious belief into political code," and rededicated himself to the pursuit of "fundamental change."

Beneath the Tutu story is a minute headline reading, "Eleven Die in Night of Violence," and a squib of copy summarizing the government's overnight "unrest report." The police shot and killed five black people, and six anonymous burned bodies were found. And *beneath* that, unheralded by any headline, are two cryptic little sentences about the discovery, in a place called Sekhukuniland, of something horrible beyond comprehension: the remains of thirty-two African women, hurled alive into pits of flame. This was the worst mass murder in South African history, and it took place in a context that the *Times* clearly could not bring itself to explain. The seventy-six black youths arrested in connection with the massacre were all members or supporters of the UDF—the supposedly nonviolent liberation movement led by the Nobel Peace Laureate at the head of the page. The thirty-two victims were suspected of using sorcery to retard the freedom struggle, and were incinerated in the name of fundamental change.

Looking at this shred of newsprint, my brain yaws at South Africa's amazing reality. I don't intend to deride Bishop Tutu or suggest he was in any way complicit in those killings. I can even find it in my heart to forgive those witch-burning comrades, because I cannot judge an action that lies so far beyond my own understanding. I don't hate any of the black men who appear in this clipping, and yet the sight of it makes me choke with rage. I think I should rest my case right here, for fear that I lose control, leap off the page, and tear out the throat of the nearest enlightened white man.

It is ancient and primordial, this rage of mine; it is the spirit of Slagter-snek—spirit of the futile 1815 rebellion that marked the start of the war of words and the moral recrimination between Boers and other white men. What are we fighting over? Over the doctrine of the brotherhood of man, which holds that all men are born the same and, given the same environment and opportunities, would turn out to be exactly alike. This is a fundamental tenet of the Great Church of Western Thought, and I believe it; I believe it is true. I'm just not sure what it means in a country such as mine. In South Africa, we must evolve a definition of human brotherhood broad enough to embrace an African of Bishop Tutu's stature as well as tribal youths who burn witches in his name; broad enough to grant the justice of black political aspirations and yet ease the fears of whites so apprehensive of Africa that they vow to die rather than accept fundamental change. That's no easy task. It's so much easier for critics to preserve their moral rectitude by looking the other way.

Consider these color photographs, introduced as evidence in a South African trial virtually ignored by the outside world. They show the scarred and mutilated torsos of two teenage torture victims, brothers named Peter and Phillip. (Peter was only sixteen, so the brothers' last name was withheld by the court in accordance with South African law.) Peter and Phillip claim they were roused from their beds in the dead of night by masked gunmen and taken to a prefabricated shack in someone's Soweto backyard, where they were accused of treachery to the struggle and ordered to confess. When they balked, Peter was hanged by the neck from the rafters until the rafters broke. Then the torturers put a plastic bag over his head and half-drowned him in a bucket of water. After that, some women tied Phillip's hands behind his back and forced him to sit in a chair. A man produced a penknife and started carving freedom slogans onto the boy's body: a big "M" for Mandela on his chest, "Viva ANC" on his thigh. And finally, someone fetched a car battery and the wounds were etched into Phillip's flesh with sulphuric acid.

It was just another atrocity in a season of atrocities in most respects save one: It allegedly took place at the home of Mrs. Winnie Mandela, first lady of the Charterist movement and Nobel Peace Prize nominee; subject of ten thousand hagiographic newspaper and magazine profiles, several sycophantic books, at least three prospective Hollywood movies and an on-again, off-again miniseries to be produced by Harry Belafonte. "A woman of extraordinary faith and love of God and of country," gushed Senator

Edward Kennedy, deeply moved by Mrs. Mandela's "gentleness and firmness, in a touching but meaningful way."

As I write, the newspapers are full of tales of another dark deed in Mrs. Mandela's backyard—this time, murder; the murder of Stompie Mokhetsie Seipie, a fourteen-year-old soldier in the anti-apartheid struggle who somehow fell out with his own side. He was allegedly abducted by Mrs. Mandela's bodyguards, tied up, whipped under her supervision, dropped repeatedly on his head until half-conscious, and finally dumped in the veld with a slit throat. The Western media is aghast with shock and dismay at this news, but theirs are crocodile tears. Stompie's murder was the third attributed to members of Mrs. Mandela's entourage, and remarkable only in that the Western media chose to cover it. Two earlier killings and numerous allegations of thuggery and intimidation were resolutely ignored by Mrs. Mandela's media sympathizers—for fear, one assumes, of undermining a myth of their own creation.

Schoolchildren in Mrs. Mandela's neighborhood grew so tired of being bullied by her thugs that they eventually burned her house down in broad daylight while her neighbors looked on indifferently, none bothering to throw so much as a cup of water onto the flames. Every journalist in Johannesburg knew the gory details, but no newspaper that I know of printed them—not at the time, at any rate. Why? I'll tell you why. Because white reporters and editors didn't want to be branded racists, and black reporters were "paralyzed by fear," to use George Wauchope's phrase. If you lived in Soweto, there were some things you dared not say for fear of being labelled a sellout. Sellouts did not live long. One of the township's most prominent black journalists chuckled bleakly when I asked why the full story of the arson attack on Winnie Mandela's home hadn't yet been written. "You write it," he said. "You're white, you might get away with it."

Am I upsetting you, my friend? Good. Do you want to argue? Do you want to tell me about the evil of apartheid? Do you want to talk about democracy and the allied civil and human rights that fall under the umbra of its name? Okay. Let's open my bulging files of tales of ordinary murder. You choose your weapons and I'll choose mine, and we'll annihilate the certainties in one another's brains.

We're in the capital, Pretoria. In the distance stands the Voortrekker Monument, a towering blunt chunk of gray concrete, symbolizing the remorseless resolve of the Boer founding fathers. And here comes a Boer now, strolling down the sidewalk, calmly shooting every black person he passes. The trail of bodies behind him is three blocks long—twenty-nine blacks are down, and six of them are dead. The woman beside us is black, and she says something very strange. She says the terrorist is "beautiful." A Boer holy warrior, with a beatific smile on his face.

We're in Orlando West, Soweto, outside the home of the lovely Masabata Loate, a beauty queen in a more light-hearted era. She's what the Western press would call an anti-apartheid activist. She's just spent five years on Robben Island for agitating for the downfall of the apartheid state. She expected to be welcomed home as a heroine, but her politics are out of fashion these days. Here she comes now, running for her life, with a pack of rival "anti-apartheid activists" on her heels. She falls, is stabbed, rises and runs on again, screaming for help. She pounds on the doors of neighbors, but they're too scared to let her in. She goes down for the last time on her grandmother's doorstep, where she's hacked to pieces with pangas.

We're in Beaufort West in the Karroo, listening to bangs, thuds and screams from inside a black man's humble shack. The door opens and a UDF leader named Kratshi comes staggering outside, blood pouring from wounds in his head. A white cop follows, motioning his brother officers to stand aside. He says something like, "I'm going to shoot this pig." And he does. Dead.

We're in yet another township, at the funeral of a young black boy who became a burned body found. The bereaved father asked the comrades to stay away, but they don't like being told what to do. So they throw the father into his son's grave and hit him with shovels when he tries to climb out again. The old man eventually gives up and sits down on his dead son's coffin, cradling his bloody head in his hands. The comrades bury him alive.

Are you sick and confused, my friend? I'll make you sick yet. I'll hold you down and pound these images into your brain, like Simon pounded white skulls with his hammer, and I'll keep on pounding until they poison you the way they poisoned me.

We're in a forest in the homeland Venda, watching an African father hack off his living daughter's arms. She says, "Please father, let me go, I won't tell anyone," but her father just keeps hacking. A political power struggle is underway in Venda, and he needs her body parts for battle medicine.

We're in a stronghold of the South African Police, discussing the security situation with a Boer colonel. We're speaking the tongue of my tribe, a guttural bastard Dutch in which the r's roll like thunder and the g's grate like a shovel in cold gravel. It is a brutal language, so violent on the tongue that Americans would quail when I tried to teach them the odd word or two. Colonel Viljoen is eyeing us warily. He is thinking, this Malan looks a little weird for a Boer, and he's been out of the country too long to be entirely wholesome, but maybe he's okay. I know the look in his eyes. It is a look of recognition. It says, *maybe I can trust him; maybe he's one of us.* When I fall silent, the colonel says nothing, just takes a card from his wallet and slides it wordlessly across the desk. I pick it up. It is professionally printed and lovingly laminated. It bears a saying of Albert Schweitzer's: "Any white man who comes to work in Africa must understand that these people are subhuman," or words to that effect.

We're on a farm in Bonnievale, witnessing subhuman behavior. An elderly white woman has been raped, and her son has captured a black suspect. The white man puts a shotgun in the black man's face, hands him a pig-castrating tool, and orders him to use it. The black man refuses, so the white shoots him in the leg. At that, the black man unbuckles his blood-drenched trousers and uses the castrating knife on himself. The white man uses a stick to flick the testicles away.

We're in Pietermaritzburg, staring at something the police have seized: a trunk full of human body parts and testes, cut out of corpses by a gang of African holy warriors for use in potions to give their side victory in the struggle for fundamental change.

We're at a roadblock near Soweto, where white soldiers have stopped a car driven by a light-skinned black man. They ask him, "Why are you so white?" Then they beat him to death with their helmets. "They didn't say why," says a witness. "I think they were just doing it for fun."

I could go on, but I'll spare you. Let's stop at this photograph, which appeared on the front page of a black newspaper called *City Press*. The picture was taken on the streets of some sub-tropical township. There are palm trees in the background. In the foreground, in a pool of molten rubber tar, lie the burning bodies of two nameless young black men. The fire has singed all their hair off. Their skulls and limbs are as smooth and shiny as baked ceramic. They look like department store mannequins toppled over on their sides, all twisted and contorted in death. Behind them stands a young black schoolgirl, laughing and clapping her hands. I spent hours staring at this picture, trying to read the girl's avid expression, studying the positioning of her school shoes in relation to her shadow. I can't be sure, but I think she was rising into the air as the shutter clicked. I think she was dancing.

The headline says, "This Is the Face of Today's South Africa."

So I dunno, my friend. I dunno what to say anymore. When I came home to face my demons, I heard a song called "Reggae Vibes Is Cool," as sung by Bernoldus Niemand, "Bernard Nobody," the world's first exponent of Boer New Wave rock and roll. His song was a Boer reggae song, the music of black suffering sung in the vernacular of white supremacy, and its chorus had a line that broke my heart. It ran, "How do I live in this strange place?" That seemed a very valid question to me. I had never learned how to live in my own country. I ran away because it was too strange to bear, and when I came home, it was stranger than ever. Everyone had blood on their hands.

Chief Gatsha Buthelezi's Inkatha movement was trying to crush the Mandela Charterists, and the Charterists were reciprocating. Traditionalists were killing modernists, radicals killing moderates. Those who said Mandela were killing those who said Biko, and vice versa. Conservative vigilantes known as Fathers were killing their comrade sons, and everyone was exterminating those they regarded as traitors. All the blacks were killing each other, and atop the boiling roil sat the Afrikaner tyrants, playing the various forces against one another and killing anyone who survived to challenge them. South African politics had turned into a hall of mirrors in which every reflection was a mockery of itself, and in the center of it all stood a sphinx saying yes: the answer to everything is yes. Yes, the black cause is just. Yes, the Boers are barbaric. Yes, the blacks are barbaric too. Yes, things are bad now. Yes, they can only get worse. The time had come to make choices, but there was nothing on the market but rival barbarities and absurd ideologies.

"A new era of freedom has begun," declared State President Botha, standing atop a pile of corpses.

"The Soviet Union is a torchbearer for all our hopes and aspirations," Winnie Mandela told TASS at the height of what was supposedly a struggle for freedom. "In Soviet Russia," she said, "genuine power of the people has been transformed from dreams into reality."

The time had come to make choices, but there were no rational choices at all.

But that was politics. Beyond politics, there was mythology, and rival myths to live and die by: for some whites, the myth of white supremacy, and for others, the myth of brave and noble Africans in heroic struggle against unspeakable evil. If you were white, you had to embrace one of those two myths, and let it guide your way. If you believed in neither, the paradox fractured your skull and buried its poisonous claws in your brain.

I'm sorry to use such lurid language, my friend, but South Africa calls for strong and sickening words. It has a way of making your brain seethe and your blood boil. South Africans develop antibodies to the poison, they grow numb and blind, but if you leave long enough to detoxify and come back with clear eyes, your skull gets fractured. You see too much, and it makes you sick. God knows what it is like for blacks, but all the white exiles I know fell prey to a disease similar to mine when they returned. My childhood hero, Leon the New Leftist, spent his six weeks back home hiding in a mobile home, afraid of what would happen to his head if he dared venture outside. My childhood sweetheart, Joji, spent seven years in the rational world. When she came home, she took one look, went straight to bed, and wept for weeks. She remembered what it was like. When my own brain started seething she used to hold my hand, and say, "Don't worry. One of these days, you'll be lobotomized. One of these days, you'll go blind again."

Blindness and lobotomy. These were not metaphors, my friend. They were physical conditions in my country, in the winter of 1986. You could not afford to see everything. You could not afford to go from the grave of Simon to the graves of his white victims, from Dennis Mosheshwe's grave to Fana Mhlongo's grave to the grave of Moses Mope. Such pilgrimages made you sick. They forced you to your knees, begging an accommodation with the howling ambiguities; begging for your eyes to go blind.

It was in such a state of mind that I set out for a place called Msinga.

BOOK III

A ROOT IN ARID GROUND

I sell you no phony forgiveness, I'm a desperate man—but too much of your life will be lost, its meaning lost, unless you approach it as much through love as hate.

—RALPH ELLISON, *Invisible Man*

The road to Msinga begins in white South Africa and runs for hours through neat and orderly white farmland, not so different in appearance from parts of central California. Some ten miles beyond the last white town, you cross the border between the First and Third Worlds, between white South Africa and black KwaZulu. The border isn't marked; there is no need. You know you are coming into a different country, a different world. The white centerline vanishes, and the road itself starts rearing and plunging, like a turbulent river rushing toward a waterfall. The very mood of the landscape changes. And then you round a bend, and the tar falls away beneath the wheels, and you're looking down into Africa, into a vast, sweltering valley strewn with broken hills, mud huts, and tin-roofed shanties. From the rim of the escarpment, it looks as though some mad god has taken a knife to the landscape, slashing ravines and gulleys into its red flesh and torturing its floor into rugged hills. This is Msinga, a magisterial district in the self-governing homeland of KwaZulu, the place of Zulus.

As white South Africa fell away behind me, the countryside grew barren and dusty. There were no fences. Goats and cattle strayed into the road. The deeper I drove into Msinga, the worse it got: less grass, less hope, more goats, and more hopeless black people sitting motionless as stones in the roadside dust. The place was an ecological Hiroshima. The last big trees looked like mangroves, stranded high and dry by a receding tide of soil. The earth at their feet had washed away down gaping erosion gulleys and into the river, leaving the first nine inches of root dangling in thin air. In some places, there was no soil at all, just sheets of gray slate and clayey subsoil baked hard as concrete by the sun. Thermals rising from these zones of devastation caused such turbulence at thirty thousand feet that white businessmen jetting between Johannesburg and Durban were losing their lunch over Msinga. South African Airways solved the problem by rerouting its flights. That was white South Africa's usual response to Msinga's problems: Avoid them.

Whites couldn't bear to look at Msinga because its devastation was to some large extent their own fault. Msinga was declared a location, or Zulu reservation, in 1849. As early as 1878, government reports were noting that it was dry, barren, and prone to famine. In the century since, the district's population had quintupled to maybe 120,000, the natural increase augmented in the late sixties by 22,000 "surplus people"—blacks cleared off nearby white farmland and dumped across the border in KwaZulu. The land was carrying at least twice as many humans, cattle, and goats as it could support. That is why it was turning into desert.

Some twenty miles inside the district, a dirt road peeled off the tar and headed north along the banks of the Tugela River. It was a bucking, boulder-strewn abomination of a road, and at the end of it lay an agricultural development project called Mdukatshani, Place of Lost Grasses, where a man named Neil Alcock had done his last good works. As I bounced through the project's gate, a Zulu man wearing tattered overalls and huge colored disks in his earlobes leapt out to challenge me. After checking me out, he set off at a trot down the track, beckoning me to follow. A few hundred yards farther on, he ordered me to park, led me through a wooden gate and into a thicket of thorn trees. Then he saluted and disappeared.

I was left standing on a bluff about twenty feet above the muddy Tugela River. It was dusk, almost dark. A vervet monkey was tethered in the tree above my head. Peering into the surrounding gloom, I realized I was standing in front of a house of sorts. It was made of mud and thatched with grass. A gnarled old tree rose up through the floor, poked its limbs through the walls, and soared into the darkening sky. The house was the color of the landscape, of rock and grass and dust, and virtually invisible in the half-light. Instead of windows, there were holes in the walls, and the doors and shutters were made of raw logs. The walls were plastered with smooth red mud, and the furniture was all stone. Long slabs of gray slate served as benches and tables, and some large boulders, polished smooth by the river, were offered as chairs. It was the Flintstones' living room, save for an incongruous plastic telephone.

The river rushed past this extraordinary structure, turned sharply to the left, and emptied into a still pool at the base of a cliff. Something was moving down there, on a shelf of flat rock beside the pool. At first, I took it to be a troop of baboons drinking from the river, but the creatures scattered and came toward me, revealing themselves to be a woman and her dogs. A white woman, forty-some years old. She came loping up the footpath on powerful calves, a curtain of straight blond hair waving to and fro across her face. She was wearing an old cotton dress and a threadbare cardigan. Her bare calves were crisscrossed with thorn scratches. Her face, when she finally lifted it, was somehow medieval—perfectly oval, with a high, broad forehead and oval eyes, all framed by blond hair that fell to her shoulders from a middle parting. She was spectrally thin. The hand she offered was horny with callus, and the accompanying look was disconcertingly cool.

This was Creina, Neil Alcock's widow, a woman of formidable and fearful repute. Awed Zulus in the surrounding hills whispered that she was a *sangoma,* or witch doctor, and whites in the cities thought she was insanely brave to live the way she did, alone in a lawless and dangerous place. I had been warned that she didn't suffer fools, gawkers, or sensation-seeking reporters, whom she referred to as "looters." When I first called to ask if I could visit, she said, "We have a rule here, Mr. Malan. We only allow visitors who bring tangible benefits to the valley." I offered to bring a pickup-truckful of corn, and she laughed scornfully. "We can't be bought either," she said. In the end, though, she relented, at least to the extent of allowing me to present my case in person.

So Creina Alcock made me a cup of coffee, sat me down outside the door of her hut, and invited me to explain myself. By now, the sun had set, and it was bitterly cold and dark. I suspected she was hoping I'd be so uncomfortable that I'd get into my car and return to white South Africa, but I stuck it out—not that I thought it very likely that she would talk to me. Her late husband was a famous liberal, you see. In Neil Alcock's lifetime, Mdukatshani had been a station on the South African *via dolorosa,* a place where foreign diplomats and journalists came for a firsthand look at the misery of life in the tribal homelands. I had collected a file of newspaper clippings datelined Msinga, and they constituted about as withering an indictment of apartheid as I had ever read. The Zulus of Msinga were desperately poor and downtrodden. There were no jobs, and the ravaged land would no longer yield enough food to support a family. Msinga's men spent their lives in labor barracks in distant cities; its women and children spent their lives waiting. In Msinga, a husband or father was someone you saw once a year, and for that you counted yourself lucky. If your breadwinner got fired, injured on the job, or died, you faced starvation.

In many ways, then, Msinga was the ultimate apartheid horror story, and the Alcocks themselves were always good for a sidebar. They had spent two decades living among Africans, like Africans, trying to undo some of the harm done by apartheid. They lived in mud huts and shat in holes in the ground. They washed their clothes and bodies in the Tugela River and drank its muddy water. Visitors found flies and ants in the sugar bowl and boiled tadpoles in their coffee. The Alcocks were always dusty and disheveled. They endured fire ants in their armpits and rats in their beds, unbearable heat in summer and biting cold in winter. They were as ragged as the black peasants among whom they worked, and thinner to boot. They were the only whites in the country who lived beyond all suspicion of complicity. In a way, Neil Alcock had given his life to his cause, and his death was marked by an obituary in the London *Times*—a rare honor indeed for a South African.

I somehow doubted that the widow of such a man would be receptive to the dark things I was thinking and feeling about South Africa. I thought of lying, and telling her I had come to investigate apartheid atrocities, like all the others before me, but I was tired of lying, so I told the truth. I told her I was searching for a way to live in this strange country—for an alternative, if one existed, to the law of Dawid Malan, as formulated on the far bank of the Great Fish River. I observed that she and Neil seemed to have crossed a similar river and penetrated deeper into Africa than any other whites in our time. "I want to know," I concluded, "what you have learned here." And then I sat back, expecting to be asked to leave.

Instead, Creina fell silent for a long time, so long I thought she'd fallen asleep. When she finally spoke, it was to pose a series of penetrating questions. She asked whether I believed in truth, and sought to serve it honorably. She asked what sins I had committed in my life, and what I understood by the word *love*. She threw out quotes from D. H. Lawrence and T. S. Eliot, and kept asking what I thought. I thought I was hallucinating. I was sitting outside a mud hut on a pitch-dark night in the heart of the Dark Continent being riddled by a sphinx. She seemed to be guarding some secret, some treasure, and testing me to see whether I was worthy of receiving it, whether I understood the gravity of my own question. I answered to the best of my ability, and she lapsed into silence again. In the end, the widow Alcock decided to sleep on it. She produced a flashlight, led me up a dark footpath and into the mud hut kept ready for guests.

It was very cold that night. The chill crept in through the hut's open doorway, through the chinks between the mud walls and the thatched roof. The instant I snuffed out the candle, something came in from outside and started skittering around the floor. Next, it was rooting around inside my bag. It skittered again, and then it was on the bed. A rat, by the weight of it. I flung it off me and relighted the candle, but the creature was nowhere to be seen, so I pulled the blankets over my head and fell asleep. In the course of the night, I was twice woken up by the pitter-patter of tiny feet across my face. I surged up, shouting and yelling, but the rat wouldn't go away. It was utterly fearless, or maybe it was just desperate. In winter, everything and everyone in Msinga grew desperate.

In the morning, there was a pail of water and a washing bowl at my bedside, but I decided I'd rather stink than wash in the bitter cold. A hole in the ground behind my hut led down to an underground chamber, in the center of which stood a "long drop"—a plastic toilet on a wooden platform suspended above a deep pit of shit. This throne was surrounded by cobwebs, and the walls were full of holes and crannies that surely harbored snakes. After pissing, I walked down to the river to brush my teeth. Frost crunched beneath my boots. The muddy water was so cold that it numbed my face, sent shocks racing up my fillings and into my brain. I'd been in Msinga barely twelve hours, and I was already thinking, How the fuck does she stand this?

I found Creina in the open-air kitchen behind her house, boiling water on a gas cooker. She made coffee, and we drank it on a stone patio above the river. The sun rose from behind a twin-humped mountain called Mashunka, and its first rays turned the tawny floodplain across the river into a wash of gold. The river curved away in a series of still pools, each veiled by mist. The valley was very beautiful in the early light. It was a landscape, as Creina put it, of "enormous dramatic potential."

Over the years, she and Neil had often sat here at night, listening to gunfire in the hills and watching tracers arcing across the sky. A few years earlier, the Zulu people living on one of Mashunka's twin humps had fought a war against those on the other. After that, the people on the larger hump went to war against the people of the valley beyond. I drained my tin mug and discovered a dreg of river mud at the bottom. A very strange place indeed.

After a while, the sun acquired some strength, and movement returned to my numb limbs. I guess it must have warmed my cold blood, too, because I just didn't have the heart to ask the first question on my mind. I wanted to ask, Where is it? Where is the agricultural development? What have you accomplished here? What did Neil die for? I was expecting to see tilled fields, fenced paddocks, barns, and tractors. Instead, there was nothing but a cluster of mud buildings, the ruin of a waterwheel, and the lone and level bush stretching far away.

So I alluded and insinuated, and Creina answered with aphorisms about Africa, about how slow it was to change, how the chameleon wavers with each step, how any change is so slow as to be imperceptible, and so deep as to be virtually immeasurable. Eventually, she seemed to lose patience with me. She suggested we take a walk, so I could get a better feel for this place in which she lived.

The project's land began at the river, crossed over a range of hills, and stretched away across the plain beyond. It was dry, rugged country, riven by deep dongas and choked with thickets of thorn trees. I followed Creina along a footpath that led away from the river and up into the hills. She stopped occasionally to exclaim over a rare plant, or to point out a patch of *rooigras*, "red grass." In these parts, she said, there are many grasses, but the red grass is king, so sweet and tasty to cattle that it is the first species to disappear when the land is overgrazed, and the last to return. These few stands of red grass were one step of the African chameleon, one sign that the land was healing. The tendrils of grass growing in the bed of a nearby donga were another. It took nature seventy thousand years to create an inch of soil, she said, so it would take aeons for this land to heal completely.

That was my botany lesson. Its moral was, Be patient. At the top of the hills, my history lesson commenced. Beyond lay an endless plain of grassland and thornbush, so rugged that it took hours to cross the first two miles. This was the plain of Ngongolo, site of the country's last great tribal battle—the Battle of Ngongolo, fought in 1944 by eight thousand Thembu and Mchunu armed mostly with spears and shields. Seventy-six men died in that battle, fighting for land that had belonged to whites, at least on paper, since 1849.

This land had once been a "kaffir farm," you see, a labor farm. Indeed, all the land around us, as far as the eye could see, had belonged to labor farmers—absentee white landlords who usually lived on sugar or wattle plantations in more fertile regions. Such men had need of many laboring hands in certain seasons, so they bought land on the borders of the African tribal reserves and allowed blacks to live on it. In return, they exacted six months' labor from every man on the property, sometimes from his wives and children, too. Otherwise, the blacks were left entirely to their own devices. They lived in the traditional manner, under the rule of tribal chiefs. They worked the land, grazed their cattle on it, and buried the fathers whom they worshiped in its red earth. They even fought wars over it, as in 1944. In their hearts and minds, it was their land.

As far as white liberals were concerned, the six-month system reeked of feudalism, so they agitated for its abolition. In 1969, the apartheid government bowed to mounting pressure and outlawed labor farming, leaving hundreds of thousands of black labor tenants stranded inside "white" South

Africa, making a complete mess of the grand apartheid master plan. Pretoria decided that most of them had to go back to where they "belonged," back to the tribal homelands.

Elsewhere, labor tenants left quietly. In this area, however, the Zulus dug in their heels and refused to go until the police moved in with guns and helicopters. The land on which Creina and I were walking had once been dotted with Zulu huts, but they'd all been burned down and their inhabitants driven into the desolation of Msinga. It was as though a great wave had swept the people off the land and dumped them like hurricane debris on the far side of the border, where there was no free land for them to farm, and no room for their cattle. God knows how they were meant to survive. Perhaps they weren't expected to survive at all. They were officially known as "surplus people," anyway.

When they first came to Msinga, Creina told me, she and Neil had walked this path with an ancient Zulu man, one of the thousands driven off the land in the forced removals. The old one was overcome with emotion. In his heart, this land was his land, and he had never thought to see it again. He greeted every tree by name, Creina told me, and when they reached the largest tree on all the plain, he sat down in its shade, and said, "All my fatigue lies buried under this tree."

Beyond the old man's tree, we turned west, and fought our way down the brush-choked walls of the Skhelenge Gorge. When the Alcocks first came to Msinga, a skeletal black man was living in a cave in its sunless depths. His name was Delanie Mbatha, and he had temporarily lost his sanity when the police drove him off his ancestral land. He thought to himself, This is a terrible country, where white men do such things. I must leave, he thought. So he put his belongings into a sack and set out on foot, looking for another country.

Delanie had never seen an atlas, and had no idea where he was going. He walked all the way to East London, about 700 miles away. In East London, black people spoke a different language, but everything was otherwise the same. It was still South Africa. There was no escape. So Delanie turned around and walked all the way back to Msinga. He wanted to be close to the shades of his forefathers, so he moved into a cave in the depths of the gorge, where he lived on roots, ants, and spiders and waited for the world to end.

Beyond Delanie's cave, Creina and I climbed out of the gorge. Creina sat down on a rock on the brink of a precipice and started peeling an orange.

I was too tired and dusty to ask any more stupid questions, and I suppose that is what she intended. She invited me to sit down beside her, and started talking.

Neil Alcock was born in a stone farm cottage in 1919 and grew up to own a farm of his own. It was called Sunset and lay in the foothills of the Drakensberg Mountains, where the air was cool and streams so cold and clean that trout survived in them. Neil Alcock had some sort of learning disability, and struggled in school. He was a gifted farmer, though. He knew the names of all the plants and grasses, all the animals and birds. He understood the ways of nature and the interdependence of living things. He took good care of his land, and in time prospered greatly. By the mid-1950s, he had built a fine house on Sunset and installed in it a pretty wife, who bore two children, a boy and a girl, both of whom attended the right "public" schools. Neil Alcock was a leading member of the local Farmers' Association and a Freemason to boot.

Outwardly, all that really distinguished him from his white neighbors was his uncanny way with cattle—he could calm a calving cow simply by laying a hand on its head—and the way he treated his "boys," his African laborers. He allowed them to run their own cattle on his range and granted each man eight acres to farm on his own account. If their chiefs or headmen called on him, he fed them at his own table, off his own china, and gave them beds with sheets in his own house, just as if they were white. And then he joined Alan Paton's Liberal Party, and proceeded to sign up all the unwashed "boys" in the district as members. In rural Natal in the 1950s, such behavior was virtually certifiable, but whites tended to accept it as a queer eccentricity in a man they otherwise respected.

Neil Alcock was a liberal, but never soft or sentimental, you see. He never preached or moralized. If anyone asked why he stood for democracy, he muttered, "Everyone has the right to make their own mistakes." Beyond that, he was a man of action. He could run barefoot across mountain ranges, swim swollen rivers, and nurse crippled Land Rovers across trackless swamps. He could fix almost any engine, and make ingenious contraptions from spare parts. "Nothing that can't talk can beat me," he boasted.

Nor could most men. Anyone who crossed the young Neil Alcock got "ten kinds of living shit knocked out of them," in his eldest son David's phrase. He wasn't a bully, though, and his violence was never unjust. He simply hadn't mastered the civilized arts of compromise and appeasement. If something was wrong, it had to be set right, by any means necessary. If circumstances demanded it, Neil Alcock would plant himself in the path of a thundering train. That is exactly what he did when sparks from a passing steam engine set fire to grasslands near his home: chased the train down, parked his car across the tracks, and informed the astounded engineer that he was under arrest.

This is an image of Neil Alcock we must hold in our minds: a man with thunderbolts of anger in his eyes, facing down a train because that was the right thing to do. In a country where so much was wrong, that attitude was a lethal liability. Sooner or later, Neil Alcock was doomed to run into a wrong too profound to be set right. As it turned out, he encountered it in a brimming milk pail in the late 1950s.

At the time, he was still living the sweet life of an ordinary white farmer, cushioned and cosseted by government loans, price supports, and subsidies. His prosperity was based on milk, which he sold—at a heavily subsidized price—to the government Milk Board. In the late fifties, the milk market glutted, and the Milk Board started dumping its surplus into the sea, to keep prices up. Meanwhile, black South Africans had one of the highest mortality rates in the world, largely because they didn't have enough food to eat. Millions of blacks seldom saw milk, because they were too poor to buy it at the retail price.

To Neil Alcock, this seemed wrong. Milk was meant to be drunk, not dumped. So he put a milk can on the back of a bicycle and sent one of his laborers into Pholela to see whether the blacks wanted to buy it at cost. The Zulu returned to say that his people were very grateful, and would the master please send more cheap milk? The next day, Neil put the milk on a truck and drove over to Pholela himself, and that was the end of his first life. He had opened the door into another world, and he was sucked through it, into a vortex of hopelessness and need.

Pholela was a "homeland," and South Africa's homelands were desperately sorry places. When whites first asserted control over the land in the mid-nineteenth century Africans were confined to reservations barely large enough to support existing populations. By 1960, the homelands were overflowing, overgrazed and overplowed to the brink of ecological devastation. Some seven million Africans were still trying to practice traditional subsistence agriculture on their ruined land, and most were close to starving.

In Pholela, as elsewhere, four in ten children died in infancy. Many of those who survived were dulled or deformed by kwashiorkor or rickets. Their mothers were often sickly and dry-breasted, their fathers riddled with tuberculosis.

Under the circumstances, it seemed obscene that surplus milk should be thrown into the sea, so Neil started selling his entire production at cost to the poor people of Pholela. Demand exceeded supply, so he started buying up his white neighbors' surplus, too. Soon, he was calling white dairy farmers all over the province, saying, "I am the sea; dump your milk on me." Eventually, even that wasn't enough, so he went to Johannesburg and persuaded some wealthy white philanthropists to bankroll a nationwide surplus-distribution scheme. He called this new organization Kupugani, Zulu for Raise Yourself, and left his farm to run it. He traveled the country sponging up agricultural surplus in white South Africa and setting up centers to distribute it at cost to hungry blacks.

Wherever he went, Neil encountered misery and hunger—more misery and hunger than he had ever imagined. So he spoke out. Liberal English newspapers started running black-bordered articles headlined "Starvation: A National Disgrace." The secret police started tailing Neil wherever he went, trying to link him to imaginary Communist plots. Some whites accused him of interfering with the balance of nature, arguing that blacks were breeding too fast and that the "surplus" should be allowed to die off. Others were shamed. Beatnik folksingers staged benefits for Kupugani, and guilt-stricken liberals dug deep into their pockets. Flashbulbs detonated, donations poured in, and Neil Alcock became something of a household name. When a white newspaper invited readers to nominate a public figure to go to America and meet Elizabeth Taylor as part of some Hollywood publicity stunt, Neil Alcock came in second.

He wasn't entirely immune to glamour, but he didn't take his new celebrity very seriously. Whatever good Kupugani had done wasn't enough. It was barely even a beginning. Like many whites who achieved consciousness, Neil started choking on the privileges of whiteness. His salary seemed too great in a country where so many had so little, so he gave it away, or plowed it back into Kupugani. Then he shed the white life-style, refusing to sleep in segregated hotels or eat in segregated restaurants. Within a year, he had become a wandering ascetic, sleeping on roadsides, subsisting on milk and army-surplus fortified biscuits. He went into debt and eventually lost his farm. After that, he lost his wife and children, too. By the time Creina met him, he owned nothing but an old Peugeot station wagon, a blackened cooking pot, and a dog named Ulysses, in recognition of his broad travels.

At the time, Creina Bond was in her early twenties and working as a newspaper reporter in the Pietermaritzburg bureau of Durban's *Daily News.* She was one of the more sought-after women in the city's smart young set, the blond and beautiful escort of famous sportsmen and yachtsmen. She was a serious girl at heart, though, with little stomach for the sweet white life. Like many reporters on the English newspapers, Creina was thirsting to strike blows for the cause, to "do something" about apartheid, or at least to write about the suffering it was causing. In 1963, she heard that Kupugani's famous monk penitent was living in the back of his station wagon on the outskirts of her city. She shared Neil's interests in nature and ecology, and in the homeland hunger problem. When her bureau chief suggested that someone accompany Alcock on one of his expeditions into the wounded African heartland, she leapt at the chance.

They set off on a weekday morning, Neil, Creina, and her sister Joey crammed into the front seat of the clattering old Peugeot. In the flesh, Neil Alcock was a striking man—six feet three inches tall, thin, wiry, and balding now that he was in his forties. His head was curiously elongated toward the crown, giving him the look of the African bird called *hamerkop,* or "hammerhead." His face was the face of a bird of prey, long and thin, with a hooked nose, jutting brow, and furiously beetling eyebrows. People who knew him by reputation were surprised to find that he wasn't at all sanctimonious in person. The eyes behind his dusty spectacles were full of humor and kindness. He laughed a lot, made jokes at his own expense, and told spellbinding stories about Africa.

Within hours of their meeting, Creina concluded that Neil Alcock was an extraordinary man, the only white she had ever met who was completely at ease in the world of Africans. That first night, he introduced her to Gatsha Buthelezi, an obscure young Zulu nobleman who was about to start his rise to power and prominence. Buthelezi threw his arms around the white man, greeting him as "my brother." He and Neil sat up late into the night, talking politics in fluent Zulu. The following day, Neil's party pressed on into Tongaland, a wild region near the Mozambique border. Wherever they went, the same thing happened; black leaders threw their arms around the white man and called him brother. In a country where almost all dealings across the racial gulf were poisoned by awkwardness and condescension, Neil's relationship with blacks was loose, easy, and completely natural.

Between stops, Neil talked about Africa and its fragile ecology. He had never made it beyond tenth grade in school, but he was a profoundly wise man, especially when it came to land and soil and the peculiar problems of peasant farmers in Africa. He was convinced that the people of South Africa's tribal homelands would ultimately starve if they were not helped to conserve soil and increase crop yields. "This is our worst problem," he would say. "It is worse than apartheid, because it will be harder to solve." He made Creina think, and he also seemed to have a destiny. For a serious girl, that was an irresistible combination. And so, when Neil asked her to marry him she did, in spite of her family's initially strenuous objections. She was twenty-three; Neil, forty-six.

They wanted to hold the ceremony in the bush, in some wild and African place. South Africa had a law against open-air weddings, though, so they had to get married in a church. They were planning to serve champagne at the reception, but there was a law against that, too. Many of the guests were Africans, and Africans weren't allowed to drink white man's liquor. The law kept a close eye on Neil Alcock, so his wedding reception was dry. The guest of honor was the novelist Alan Paton, and Neil's best man was the Zulu chieftain Gatsha Buthelezi. All this was so wildly unusual, in South Africa in 1965, that the pictures made the front page of newspapers in distant Johannesburg.

The Alcocks spent the first year of their marriage living in a car, and the next ten in an abandoned chicken and rabbit run on a Roman Catholic mission farm, where Neil had set up an agricultural demonstration project. The mission was overgrazed, badly eroded, teeming with hungry people, and perfect for Neil's purposes. He had come to heal it, you see, to show homeland Africans how it could be done.

He began by convincing local Africans to exchange direct ownership of their cows for pieces of paper representing shares in an intangible cattle cooperative. This was no small thing. A piece of paper was not a cow, and in an African cattle culture a man without cows was no man at all. In the end, though, the suspicious peasants agreed to give Neil's plan a try, and black Africa's first cattle cooperative came into being.

Once the cattle were pooled into a single herd, it became possible to fence the communal land and rotate the livestock from camp to camp, allowing the grass to recover. Financed by a grant from the The Chairman's Fund, charity arm of the gold- and diamond-mining Anglo American Corporation, Neil set the jobless to work, blocking dongas with stones and thorn-bushes. In time, the wounds in the land started healing. Grass returned to the hillsides, and dry springs came back to life. As the grazing recovered, the communal herd was able to double in size. On a continent where most development projects failed, all this was something of a miracle. Development workers came from far and wide to stare at the mission's lush pastures and fat cattle, and to replenish their sense of what was possible.

They found the Alcocks still living in a hovel—an abandoned Trappist winery that had been a chicken and rabbit run prior to their arrival. The Alcocks' toilet was a long drop, and there was no running water in their house. They ate vegetables and *putu* and read by lamplight. They owned little but a few books and some changes of clothing. They had two sons by now, G.G. and Rauri, little sandy-haired boys who spoke English with a Zulu inflection, saying "tlee" instead of "three" and "volovolo" instead of "revolver." As managing director of an entity known as Church Agricultural Projects, or CAP, Neil was entitled to a salary of about seventy-five dollars a month, but he never drew it. Creina was editing a small magazine called *African Wildlife* by mail. The job paid fifty dollars a month, about what a domestic servant would earn in one of Johannesburg's better suburbs, but it was enough for a family of four to live on, if they lived like blacks. Neil was widely thought of as a visionary, a guru, even a secular saint.

A saint? Father Barney was not so sure about that. Father Barney was one of the Franciscan priests who ministered to the mission folk's spiritual needs. He was an Irishman, and in his cups was wont to say that apartheid was nothing as compared with the misery the British had inflicted on the Irish. Father Barney and his brethren disapproved of Neil's divorce, and were distressed to learn that Creina was agnostic. When she was caught dispensing birth-control pills to black women, the fathers' worst fears were confirmed. "Some of them aren't even married!" sputtered one clergyman. The priests declared war on the Alcocks, and a long and bitter struggle ensued. The Holy Fathers won. Citing his desire to preserve "the Catholic character of the mission," the archbishop of Natal declined to renew Neil's cooperative's lease when it expired.

And so in the winter of 1975, Neil Alcock and his loyal Zulu lieutenants saddled horses and drove the co-op's cattle off the mission farm. His most generous backer, The Chairman's Fund, had offered to help buy a new home for the project. It was a huge spread, six thousand acres of unfenced, undeveloped, and badly eroded land. It lay sixty miles away, across the river from the place called Msinga.

* * *

Msinga is . . . Oh, God, how do I explain Msinga? Msinga is wild, and yet it is not leaping with buck and lions. There is probably not a single antelope left alive in the entire valley. The district is crisscrossed by tar roads and power lines, packed with tin-roofed shanties and mud huts. It is a place of head-spinning contrasts. In Msinga, you see black men driving goats, and black men driving BMWs. You see Zulu women going down on all fours at the feet of nondescript old men in ill-fitting three-piece suits; they are tribal chiefs or headmen, and must be shown respect. You see bare-breasted Zulu maidens with shaved heads and bodies draped with beads. They seem to have stepped out of *National Geographic,* but if you look closer you see that they're wearing Day-Glo leg warmers and running shoes. You see men in traditional dress carrying briefcases through the bush, and school-uniformed teenagers dancing through the wastelands with ghetto blasters on their shoulders. So Msinga isn't quaint, and it's not storybook Africa. It is a sprawling rural slum, infested with dope smugglers, gunrunners, and bandits. It is the iron age shat squalling and sullen into the twentieth century. Its people look broken as they eat the dust of your passing car, but in their hearts they are proud and untamed, and utterly ungovernable by anyone.

It's easy to blame the apartheid regime for Msinga's misery, but Nelson Mandela or Fidel Castro might not have done any better. The district capital, Tugela Ferry, is an indescribably forlorn and dusty little hamlet on the banks of the Tugela River. From its rooftops, you look out over a broad floodplain. A network of gravity canals comes snaking out down the distant hills and fans out across the plain. These canals draw irrigation water from the Tugela eight miles upstream, carry it across the plain, past the town, and finally return it to the river—unused. There are hundreds of hectares of rich, irrigable land there, enough land to render Msinga agriculturally self-sufficient if it were farmed intensively. But much of it isn't farmed at all. It has lain fallow almost constantly since 1928, its ownership a matter of dispute between subtribes of the Zulu nation. A Thembu who sinks a plowshare into that plain will surely be killed by the Mabaso, and vice versa.

Even the KwaZulu government, a neutral party, cannot use this land. A few years ago, the government assumed direct control of part of the irrigation scheme and invited tribesmen to farm it under government supervision. An official involved in the project was assassinated. After that,

KwaZulu formed a cash-crop consortium with some white farmers and planted strawberries on the disputed land. When the first crop was ripe, someone opened the gates and drove hundreds of cattle and donkeys into the strawberry fields. The consortium disintegrated. The government gave up. The land lay fallow, and the people of Msinga stayed hungry.

So the Thembu and Mabaso are hostile toward one another, but that is only the first order of battle in Msinga. The Zulu nation consists of 250 such subtribes, seven of which call Msinga home. Those seven subtribes are in turn divided into dozens of subgroups called *isigodi,* each three to five thousand strong. An *isigodi* is a neighborhood, for lack of a better word. This hill is Mashunka, the valley beyond Ngubo. The land to this side of that dry watercourse is Ndlela; the land beyond is Mhlangaan. It takes a Msinga man to know the borders between these *isigodi,* and the consequences that await if he crosses them in wartime. There is nothing to distinguish the people on one side from those on the other. They speak the same language, belong to the same nation, suffer the same deprivations. And yet, every now and then, they fight bloody wars against one another.

Why? It's hard to say. There are several theories, but in the end I preferred the word of an old white policeman who said he didn't really know.

Warrant Officer Jurgen Freese was a crusty old militarist who lived in a firearm-squad camp on the outskirts of Tugela Ferry. His superiors posted him to Msinga in 1956, and he'd been there ever since. In 1956, there were few roads in Msinga, and police still patrolled the valley on horseback. The district was administered by old Africa hands, portly colonials with handlebar mustaches, pith helmets, and hides blackened by decades in the sun. The whites played tennis on an old clay court, swam in a pool, and sipped pink gins at sunset on the verandas of quaint colonial bungalows. Tugela Ferry was a lost outpost of the dying British Empire.

Jurgen Freese's mission in Msinga was to stamp out the gun trade and combat "faction fighting," the official term for Msinga's fratricidal wars. In the fifties, Msinga's wars were honorable, manly affairs, fought under the sun on open plains by half-naked warriors. The death toll was light, and the whole thing was over quickly, usually in a single day. If a man fell in battle, every warrior in the opposing *impi* would stab a blade into his corpse, a traditional Zulu battle ritual.

Such killings were not regarded as murder by the white authorities. They were treated as tribal offenses and tried under African law. Whenever someone died in a faction fight, Freese would mount his horse and visit the chief in whose territory the killing had taken place. He would say, "Listen, you fellows know you're not supposed to do this. Now I want the names of those involved." The chief and his headmen would confer with the warring parties. Some warriors were appointed to be the accused, others to give evidence. Such decisions were based less on guilt than on a man's ability to pay a fine. On the appointed day, all the warriors would appear before the white magistrate in the courthouse at Tugela Ferry. Everyone understood that the trial was essentially a farce, a ritual designed to preserve the white man's face and honor. The witnesses told a yarn, the accused tried to look contrite, the magistrate handed down a few two-pound fines, and it was all over.

In the early days, Freese's firearm squad seized the occasional sidearm or hunting rifle, but Msinga's wars were mostly fought with spears and homemade blunderbusses crafted from spare parts and plumbing supplies. As Msinga's migrant laborers were integrated into the white cash economy, however, more and more guns started coming into the district. Battles fought with guns fell outside the legal definition of faction fighting. Warriors who took part in them were supposed to be charged with murder, and tried under white law. "The change was well meant," said Freese, "but I don't know that it was a good thing." Once white law started superseding traditional Zulu law, there was virtually no law in Msinga at all.

Msinga's warriors saw little wrong in these killings, you see. They saw no reason why a man who slew an enemy in honorable battle should be taken away and hanged by the white man, so they stopped cooperating with the police. It became hard to find witnesses. Freese's cosy arrangement with the chiefs gave way to elaborate trials in white courts, where white judges followed white evidentiary rules and white lawyers found it easy to confuse and discredit illiterate witnesses. The state case inevitably fell apart in a welter of contradictions, and the accused went unpunished in those rare cases where they were charged at all.

It was hard to say how many murderers there were in Msinga, or how many victims they had claimed, because nobody was really counting. Suffice to say Msinga's murder rate was ten to twenty times higher than New York City's, and its conviction rate so low as to be almost immeasurable. It was once the practice to post photographs of executed killers on the wall of Tugela Ferry's courthouse. To the best of anyone's recollection, the last time this happened was in 1964.

In the seventies, Msinga's warfare underwent a further evolution, driven this time by soaring sales of the district's chief cash crop, marijuana. Msinga suddenly had money with which to cut big deals on the underground arms market. It was illegal for South African blacks to own guns, but Msinga scoffed at the white man's laws. The latest South African automatic rifles were going into use in Msinga before the South African Defence Force got to test them in combat in Angola. Soviet AK-47s smuggled into the country by brave revolutionaries were sold for beer money on the black market and wound up in the hands of rival factions in the hills above Tugela Ferry.

Msinga's armies dressed to kill in army-surplus combat fatigues and carried deadly modern weaponry, but their campaigns remained curiously archaic. Leaders sought strategic advantage in witchcraft, and most soldiers' marksmanship was erratic. They were reluctant to squint down the sights of a rifle in the heat of battle because they believed that the spirit of a warrior who died with closed eyes was likely to remain trapped inside his body. They shot from the hip instead. In 1978, the Sithole hired a white mercenary sharpshooter to aid them in a war against the Zwane, and a great slaughter ensued. The sharpshooter decimated the front ranks of the Zwane army, which broke and ran. At day's end, there were fifty-six bodies strewn across the plain. Such battles were rare, though. Msinga's wars were mostly furtive hit-and-run affairs. Combatants were ambushed on lonely footpaths, shot in their huts at night, pulled off buses at roadblocks, and executed. Wars that were once over in a day now dragged on for months or even years, unreported even in the South African press. There was always fighting in Msinga, and always had been.

In 1978, black officials of the KwaZulu government took over the district's administration, and most whites left Tugela Ferry. The tennis court disappeared under weeds, and the swimming pool was filled with rubble. Only Jurgen Freese stayed on, alone in his Quonset hut on the river bank, with flies buzzing around his head and sweat trickling down his back. His job was impossible. For every gun his squad seized, another came in, and there were more corpses to account for. In the end, Msinga turned the man into a Graham Greene character. There was a time when he spent most of his day on his back in his hut, contemplating hell through the bottom of a brandy bottle.

After twenty-seven years in purgatory, Freese retired to the suburbs and quit drinking. Msinga was an intoxicant in its own right, though. He found it hard to readjust to normal life, and the South African Police found it equally hard to do without him. And so, when the force asked, Freese returned to Msinga to resume his weary struggle. I found him sitting behind a desk in a prefabricated hut, surrounded by squawking radios and maps festooned with colored pins and pennants, each marking the site of a trouble spot. Over a cup of tea, he told me that he had learned a great deal about Msinga in thirty years—enough to know that he knew virtually nothing. "You will never really find out why a war starts," he said, "and once it has started, you will never stop it."

I asked why, and the old policeman shrugged. "The Zulu is a brave man," he said. "You and I would not go into something looking to be killed, but a Zulu will, if honor demands it. To him, death is of no particular concern. An ox is killed; it's eaten. A man gets killed, and his brothers look after his wives and children. That's it. It's no big thing. If we go out to stop a war, the men know we are coming. They watch us with binoculars watching them with binoculars. So we see no guns, but they're there, hidden within a few hundred feet. They are waiting for us to pass. Once we're gone, they collect the guns and start fighting again. We have postponed some wars by arriving, but we've never stopped one. Not ever yet."

When war was brewing, the police were tipped off by a spy in the dusty post office across the river. The spy knew trouble was coming when women started drifting in to send telegrams to their husbands, fathers, and brothers in the cities. All the telegrams contained a similar message: "There has been a death in the family. Come home."

Those who did not answer this veiled call to arms were expected to make cash contributions to their faction's war effort, but most men came home. You could not avoid war by staying in Soweto, Kimberley, or Pretoria. Disputes rooted in Msinga's dusty hills often bore bloody blossoms in distant white cities. In 1983 in Soweto, one such battle claimed forty-two lives, but slaughter on that scale was unique. Msinga men were more often hunted down singly by hit squads from a rival *isigodi* and killed quietly in their migrant-worker barracks. There was no escape.

So most men came home, dug up their guns, slung greatcoats over their shoulders, and headed for the hills, where they lived for the duration. They slept in the open, in the high ravines, plagued by ticks and heat in summer, freezing cold in winter. There was no respite. The war dragged on until enough blood had been shed to satisfy honor. Then the dead were buried, but never forgotten. In two years, or five, or ten, the war would flare up again.

That's Msinga; that's the way it is. If you ask Msinga's warriors why they fight, they say that someone stabbed someone else's father in 1965, and that the insult must be avenged. White academics, on the other hand, advance a theory that revolves around apartheid-induced land hunger and frustration. In Msinga, life is an appallingly grim business. Most people are hungry most of the time. There are no pipes, so women have to carry water on their heads from distant springs and streams. Even firewood is a luxury. In 1975, there was only one school in Msinga, and one high-school graduate. Eighty-three percent of the populace was illiterate. Msinga's population density is 101 per square kilometer, versus 14 per square kilometer in white South Africa. About 80 percent of Msinga's people have too little land from which to feed themselves.

It makes complete sense that anyone trapped in such a shithole should want to take up arms and fight. All that's odd about Msinga's wars is that Zulus kill one another, instead of joining forces and wiping out the whites across the border.

Oom Flip de Bruin—Uncle Flip—is a great big boulder of a man with a bull neck and prehensile arms that bow out from his muscular body. His face is red from the sun and his hair thinning, now that he's in his fifties. He has a sly smile and chuckle, and a way of looking at you from under his eyelashes that was almost coy, almost shy, almost feline. He is a big sly cat of a man, light on his feet, fast thinking, and probably dangerous—the sort of man to whom violence might come easily and naturally, without passion or anger. On the day I visited, he was wearing shoes but no socks, and a plaid shirt hanging out over faded denims. He looked like a huge overgrown Boer teenager. He told me that he had once been a champion wrestler. "I have terrible power in my body," he said. I believed him.

De Bruin was born on a cattle farm in the far western Transvaal, on the rim of the Kalahari Desert. He wanted to be a farmer himself, but he was a younger son in a poor white family, so he never got the chance. He quit school after the eighth grade and spent most of his adult life working in a factory. He was a Boer at heart, though, so he always owned a little patch of land somewhere and kept a few cattle on it. When blacks were cleared off Msinga's labor farms and the land put on the market dirt cheap, he saw a chance he'd waited his whole life for. So he bought himself a big chunk of it, and became a full-time farmer.

301

Oom Flip's new farm was an old labor farm. The Zulus driven off it in 1969 were now living in huts and shanties on the far bank of the river, simmering in bitter resentment. They did not exactly welcome their new Boer neighbor. In Msinga, it is said that "the only law that counts is the law inside a man's head." In Zulu heads, Flip de Bruin and other whites had taken possession of Zulu land. There were periods of peace along the boundary, but whenever the rains failed, old antagonisms rose to the surface. The Zulus cut white farmers' fences, rustled their stock, stole their crops, hamstrung their cattle, and set fire to their grazing land. Along that frontier, most Zulus obeyed one law, the law inside their heads. Most white farmers lived according to another—the law they wrote with their guns.

De Bruin was one of the district's best-known authors of gun legislation. In just one year, ninety-five of his cattle were butchered or stolen, so the Boer retaliated in kind, developing some novel methods of interrogating suspected rustlers and a trigger-happy reputation. He once called to welcome a newcomer to the district and asked, just by way of small talk, how many blacks the stranger had shot in his time. "None," said the newcomer. "I don't believe it," said Flip de Bruin. "You've been a farmer all your life, and you've never shot a black?" He was never convicted of murder, so it must have been a joke.

Still, the Zulus had reason to hold all manner of grudges against him. One day, he came home to find his watchdogs shot dead and his house on fire. In retaliation, de Bruin and his son burned down the nearest Zulu settlement. A week or two later, a party of Zulu gunmen ambushed de Bruin on a lonely road and tried to kill him. He survived only because he was armed himself and ready to return their fire. Flip de Bruin seldom left home without a rifle slung over his shoulder.

"To live here," he told me, "you must be strong and positive. You must be direct. You can't walk in two directions. You must be straight and strong and hold true to one line. If you're weak, you won't last long here."

I was about to ask his definition of strength when an illustration of sorts unfolded before my disbelieving eyes. A muscular young white man in a sleeveless T-shirt came running into the farmhouse in a state of agitation. This was Oom Flip's nephew. *"Hulle's daar,"* he shouted—"They're there! They're there!" The boy ran to a padlocked gun rack and started rattling it frantically. Oom Flip shot out of his armchair, strode to the kitchen door, shielded his eyes, and peered into the distance, like a pioneer rancher in a Western, scanning the skyline for hostile Injuns. He shrugged. He and the boy disappeared into a bedroom for a whispered conversation. The boy came out looking crestfallen and walked away. Oom Flip sat down to continue our conversation. I asked what was going on. "Ag," he said, "the boy's crazy." He offered no further explanation. He just smiled coyly and grinned like a Cheshire cat.

On the far side of the district, I met a man named Roy Cuff, who had once farmed along Msinga's land boundary. While his wife served tea, Mr. Cuff sat back to spin some yarns about life on the frontier. Once, he said, he allowed some Zulus displaced by a war to take refuge on his farm. The refugees' enemies concluded that Cuff had formed an alliance against them, and he was warned to be ready for an attack. Next thing he knew, his house was full of white cops with machine guns, ordering him to send his wife away, sleep on the floor, and stay away from windows in case an assassin was lurking out there with a high-powered rifle. The attack never materialized. After a few weeks, the war died down, and life returned to normal.

In Msinga, normal was like this: You were white and more or less comfortable; the people on the far side of the fence or river were black and desperate. From time to time, they stole a few of your cattle, or simply killed one, butchering it on the spot, and dragging the bloody haunches back into Msinga. There was no point calling the police. The people of Msinga didn't assist police inquiries. One of them might, however, sidle up to a white farmer and whisper that so-and-so had been selling fresh meat lately.

Such leads could not be passed on to the police. "If that man talks to the police," Cuff explained, "it's tickets for him. He'll be dead within days." So there was still no point in calling the police. Instead, said Mr. Cuff, "You get your friends and go to the suspect's kraal at two in the morning. You give him a little experience, so he remembers it was your cow he ate." I asked what an experience was, but Cuff just shrugged. "It's an ugly way to live," he said. "Both my sons have grown up violent and full of hate. I'm sorry about that."

Cuff's former next-door neighbor, Peter Gill, was a graduate of one of South Africa's better private schools. After finishing high school, Gill went off into the wilds of Angola and hewed a farm out of virgin bush. When the Angolan civil war broke out in 1975, he was wiped out in the cross fire. He left Angola with nothing, walking south by night until he ran into the South African army on the Namibian border. After that, he settled in Ian Smith's Rhodesia, where he bought a cut-rate farm in the war zone. He held onto it until Robert Mugabe's guerrillas blasted several of his neighbors out of their fortified farmhouses with rocket-propelled grenades. He returned to South Africa completely penniless, and worked on a construction site until he'd saved enough money to buy a half-share in a farm on the Msinga border. The first time he drove onto his new land, someone took a shot at him from the back of a bush. Okay, he thought, if that's the way they want it, we'll see who wins.

Most of the whites along that border were blind racists, but Gill was a coolheaded man with a clear understanding of the brutal equation into which he was stepping. He arrived in Msinga at the start of a long and merciless drought. The Zulus had been grazing and watering their cattle on his land, so his arrival threatened their survival. Gill didn't contest that, or advance spurious moral and legal arguments to justify his actions. He knew that the Zulus were desperate, but he was desperate, too. He was rich in Zulu terms, but in white terms he was poor. His house would have blended into the hollows of Appalachia, and he had no running water. He lost a baby daughter in a very Third Worldly accident: She drowned in a bucket of trucked-in drinking water. He understood that the Zulus were suffering, but saw no room for compromise. As far as Gill was concerned, this had nothing to do with racism. "I like blacks," he insisted. He just didn't have enough water or grazing land to share with them. So he took up his gun and secured his boundary.

Any black who set foot on Peter Gill's land was looking for trouble. Even small children stealing water or firewood were likely to find bullets kicking up dust at their feet. Gill had picked up some special-forces skills in the various wars he'd lived through. At night, he blackened his face, donned dark clothing, and patrolled his perimeters on foot. "Basically," he said, "I would say that I defended my land as best I could. I used whatever force was necessary."

Peter Gill was tough. In Msinga, tough was like this: Gill once hired a white farmhand who packed a pistol as he went about his duties. One day, the hired hand strayed a little too close to the Msinga boundary. Some Zulus knocked him out, disarmed him, put the weapon to his head, and pulled the trigger. The gun was on safety, though, so the hired hand lived to tell the tale. As soon as he regained consciousness, however, Gill fired him. "He was weak," Gill told me. "The mere fact that he'd allowed them to flatten his head would have invited more attacks. I was declaring to the Zulus that he wasn't a worthy soldier."

"There's no second prize," Gill concluded. "I'm the fastest gun, and while that lasts I'll survive here. The guy with the bigger stick runs things."

Ask Peter Gill where he lives, and he will say Weenen, which means the Place of Weeping in Dutch. Weenen is the white magisterial district that borders black Msinga, and it was named in remembrance of the 530 Voortrekkers massacred nearby by the Zulus in 1838. Pose the same question to the Zulus on the far side of the boundary fence, however, and they will say that Gill lives in Nobamba, the Place Where We Caught the Whites. What hope of reconciliation is there in such a place? I saw none. That river was just another front in the war without end—the war that started in the 1780s along the Great Fish River and continues to this day. Nothing has been forgiven, nothing forgotten, nothing settled.

Into this churning vortex of hatred and violence, in the winter of 1975, stepped Neil and Creina Alcock. Theirs was the last farm in white South Africa, separated from Msinga in the west by a rusting fence, in the south by the Tugela River. Their land began by the river, climbed over a line of hills, and stretched away across the vast plain beyond. On the day they arrived, Neil and Creina walked the eroded hills, strewing handfuls of wild-grass seed into the wounds of the ruined land. They decided to name the new farm Mdukatshani, the Place of Lost Grasses, but they were already dreaming of another Msinga, a place where grass grew tall and green.

Neil and Creina once set their vision down in a document entitled *Msinga 2000*, less a blueprint for development than a dream of how Msinga might one day be. In the dream, furrows led spring water down Msinga's barren hillsides and into tiny gardens, where Zulu kraalholders grew vegetables in soils enriched by manure and the phosphate-rich ashes of cattle bones. Each Zulu kraal was shaded by fruit trees and surrounded by beehives. Each had its own fish pond and poultry run, its own solar cooker and gas digester—a digester being a low-tech oil-drum contraption designed to transform dung into methane gas. In the dream, this gas replaced wood as Msinga's fuel, allowing the last trees to be spared in order to stabilize the eroding slopes. On the hillsides, the dongas had been blocked with stone packs, and they were slowly silting up. Now that the cattle were communally herded and grazed in rotating camps, grass was returning to the wasteland, and all the cattle were fat again.

The people of this fortunate valley drew their wisdom from Mdukatshani. In the dream, there was a school for children at Mdukatshani, and a "barefoot university" where their fathers studied farming and conservation. Mdukatshani also had a plant nursery, a veterinary clinic, and a cattle stud with prime bulls for injecting good blood into Msinga's scrawny herd. As the dream drew to a close, Msinga's gardens were blooming, its milk pails overflowing, its people plump and healthy. A near-desert had been transformed into Eden, and it had all been accomplished without purchased fertilizer or chemicals, tractors or gasoline. Msinga couldn't afford such things. If it were to survive, and feed itself, it had to do so with existing resources: sun, water, the dung of animals, and the sweat of men. "For the Msingas of Africa," Neil concluded, "and there are many, there is no other way."

Neil's was a new way, a new approach to the problems of a continent where other ways had already failed. It was clear, by 1975, that Africa was heading toward a state of permanent famine. Well-intentioned Westerners were trying to help, but grafts of alien agricultural technology just didn't seem to take in Africa. Development workers would move into the continent's dustbowls with heads full of university theory and pockets bulging with UN or EEC or USAID cash. They'd bulldoze huge dams, plow up plains, install batteries of diesel pumps and center-pin irrigation systems. And then they'd go home, and things would fall apart. Machines broke down and stayed broken down. Few Africans had the skills to maintain complex equipment, and there were no spare parts anyway. Within a year or two, the peasants had returned to scuffling the dust with hoes and donkey plows, and there was little left to see for the new missionaries' efforts save the rusting hulks of imported machinery and futile scratches on the face of the land.

This was often cited, in South Africa and elsewhere, as proof of African incompetence. In Neil Alcock's judgment, it was more likely proof of Western arrogance. It was axiomatic that African peasants were too backward to make plans for themselves, so the new missionaries did it for them. Then they set off for the wastelands in air-conditioned caravans and tried to impose their nostrums on people who had little idea of what they were talking about.

Neil, on the other hand, was something of a peasant himself, a white farmer with a tenth-grade education. He believed in African farmers, and thought they were quite wise enough to devise solutions to their own problems. Such solutions, moreover, were the only ones that would work—African solutions, using African methods and African technologies. As Neil saw it, the role of a Western man, an educated man, was to place himself and his skills at the disposal of the peasantry—to stop dictating and start advising. He also thought some patience was called for. A two-year tour of duty in some famine-stricken African hellhole clearly helped no one. As far as Neil Alcock was concerned, you had to live among Africans, like an African, until you saw through African eyes, until African problems became your own problems and African pain became your pain. It didn't matter whether it took years, even decades. To be effective, a white man had to earn the right of trust and acceptance. Only then could he turn to his black brothers and say, "We are in the dust, my friends; we are lower and less consequential than the white man's dog, but there is a way out, and I will show it to you."

Neil was not so naive as to believe his vision would be easily realized, but he was brave enough to try. A lesser man would have given up on day one. Neil arrived in Msinga with a piece of paper saying that Church Agricultural Projects owned six thousand acres of land. In Msinga, such paper meant nothing. The only land to which Neil could truly lay claim was the few hundred acres visible from his riverside settlement. The land beyond the hills, away from the river, was not really his, and never would be. The Alcocks called it the top country, and it was Zulu country, in terms of the law inside Zulu heads. Zulus cut wood on it, hunted across it, grazed and watered their cattle on it. If anyone controlled the top country, it was the cattle thieves and bandits who lived along its border.

For such men, Neil's arrival was too good to be true. Eight hundred fat cattle, and nobody to guard them but a white man with no guns and a handful of tame Zulu Christians from some upcountry mission. Neil didn't have enough hands to herd the cattle, let alone guard them against human predators. They were easy game. One by one, and then by the dozen, the cattle started disappearing, driven off in the night down the Skhelenge Gorge, across the river, and into the wild heart of Msinga. The police did nothing but take statements, so Neil and his henchmen tracked down some stolen cattle on their own and provided the cops with evidence for a few convictions. If anything, this worsened the rustling, and drew threats of retribution. The mission Zulus were terrified. One by one, they deserted and returned to safer climes. In just two months, seventy of the project's cattle were stolen; almost half as many again died of heartwater, a lowveld cattle disease. "We were hanging on," said Creina, "by the tips of our fingers, on the brink of utter disaster."

And so Neil's dream of continuing the cattle cooperative and ultimately extending it into Msinga came to nothing. It became clear that so long as the project ran cattle, the Zulus would regard Neil as a competitor, not a friend, and he'd have to hold them off with guns, like his white neighbors. Rather than turn Mdukatshani into an armed encampment, the project's directors decided to sell the communal cattle herd and reach an understanding with the people of Msinga. They would henceforth be welcome to graze cattle and collect firewood on the project's land, provided that they cooperated with Neil's conservation schemes. It was an eminently fair deal, and it brought a measure of peace to Mdukatshani's sector of the frontier.

Once the cattle were gone, Neil turned his attention to agricultural development, to the vision contained in the *Msinga 2000* document. He invited Msinga men to a series of *indaba*s, or open-air meetings, where he laid out his plans. The Zulus were too polite to say so, but they thought this white man was mad. He claimed it was possible to grow food in the dust in waterless places without spending any money. Even a child knew that was nonsense.

So Neil and some helpers set out to prove them wrong. They purloined some railroad tracks from an abandoned siding and built a towering scaffold on the riverbank. Then they took a tractor tire, cut it into scoop-like segments, and bolted it spokewise onto the hub of an old tractor wheel. A system of pulleys lowered the wheel into the river. The rubber scoops dipped into the swift brown torrent and spun the tractor hub, which turned the differential from a scrapped Land Rover, which drove a pump, which delivered water to a dry, stony garden site hundreds of yards away. There, in soil fertilized by dung and the ash of cattle bones, some Zulu women planted and reaped a bumper crop of vegetables. Surrounding communities were hugely impressed. From that point, the scheme started moving forward.

Neil organized a committee of tribal elders to run the project, casting himself as their humble servant and technical adviser. The committee was nominally in charge, but it was Neil who really made things happen. He was a man who could stand on a barren, eroded hillside, miles from the nearest water, surrounded by incredulous peasants, and say, "There will be a dam here." And lo, a dam there would be, or a weir across the river, or an irrigation furrow to carry a trickle of precious water from a distant spring to tiny patches of tillable land. Bankrolled by donations from churches, foreign governments, and the Anglo American conglomerate, he hired armies of Zulus to work on a vast iron-age engineering project—laying furrows, stringing fences, blocking dongas with dikes of stone. Dams were dug with shovels, the dirt carried off in buckets on women's heads. Neil drew plans in the dust with sticks, and judged levels with his naked eye. If a boulder lay in the path of one of his furrows, Zulu women built a bonfire under it, heated it until it glowed, then doused it with pails of water. *Voilà.* The rock shattered. Zulu dynamite, they called it.

In the spring of 1977, the first water came trickling down the furrows and into the pioneer gardens, and for a while, the dream seemed to be coming true. In her monthly newsletter to donors and supporters, Creina wrote, "We sense the beginnings of a small revolution." Mdukatshani became a place of pilgrimage for young white volunteers yearning to atone for the sins of their fathers. A steady stream of foreign diplomats and new missionaries came to see the project for themselves.

The man who met visitors at the project's gates was getting on toward sixty now, completely gray, and balding. Neil was always wearing dusty jeans and car-tire sandals, and the first thing he showed off was always his waterwheel; he was immensely proud of his waterwheel. After that, visitors were escorted through a complex of eleven houses, huts, and workshops, all built in the Zulu fashion of mud, stone, and thatch, and costing less than $125 apiece. In the workshops, Zulus were assembling experimental solar cookers and beating old oil drums into prototypical methane digesters. There was a fish pond stocked with bass and *tilapia,* and an earthen cave full of glowing glass beads, the raw materials of a thriving craft project. Under Creina's direction, the beads were turned into Zulu jewelry of astonishing beauty and sold in the distant cities.

As visitors did the rounds, they were introduced to tongue-tied black men who turned out to be the leaders of the project. Mdukatshani's dignified chairman, Petros Majozi, was formerly a cook in a Johannesburg hotel. The resident engineer was Mphephete Masondo, who had never seen the inside of a school. A former police constable, the flamboyant Elijah Mhlongo, was chief of security. The general manager, Bokide Khumalo, couldn't read or write, but he gave orders to white volunteers with impressive university degrees.

At some point, you might have seen Neil scribble his daily love letter to his wife and hand it to a herdboy, who scurried off to deliver it. Creina spent her days in a mud "office" on the cliff top, bashing away on a portable typewriter on a "desk" of river stone. She was still editing *African Wildlife* by mail, and in her spare time writing reports and newsletters to the project's supporters. At the outset, her newsletters were quite dry and factual, but as she and Neil got to know Msinga better they evolved into literature. Fantastic characters moved across her pages, engaged in utterly improbable undertakings. An ancient Zulu gunsmith sat under a thorn tree in the bush, fashioning scrap-metal shotguns with his bare hands. An illiterate dope farmer in the high ravines devised an automatic irrigation system that would have earned a masters in engineering at any Western university. The newsletters were a window into a secret world—the world of rural black South Africans, the country's invisible people. Creina refused to allow them to be published, so they were passed from hand to hand until they fell apart at the staples.

If the visitors were really fortunate, Neil might row them across the river to see the work being done in Msinga itself. They saw irrigation furrows leading water from springs in the hills. They saw the first crops coming up in tiny gardens, fenced against goats with loans from the project's Small Farmer's Trust. They sometimes met ragged black men and women who made solemn statements in broken English. They would declare, "We are weak, but when Neil is with us we feel strong. We cannot write, but he is teaching us to write with grass on the hillsides." Or simply: "God is sending *Numzaan* to help the people." *Numzaan* is a Zulu honorific meaning squire.

Come sunset, visitors met the rest of the Alcock household—the white sons, G.G. and Rauri, and the black sons, seven barefoot Zulu herdboys whom the Alcocks had more or less adopted. Mboma, the eldest, had red hair when he first moved in with the Alcocks—a symptom of the nutritional disease kwashiorkor. He soon recovered, though, and blossomed into an artful dodger, an exceptionally bright child who swiftly mastered English and the allied art of manipulating white volunteers. Creina's sister Kathy wrote a children's book about Mboma's life and hard times, which included a spell as a ten-year-old laborer on a white farm in the district. *The Story of Mboma* became a minor best-seller in the world's progressive bookshops. Mboma Dladla's name was even mentioned in the United Nations, in the course of a debate on "slave labor" in South Africa.

Mboma was G.G.'s best friend. Among Rauri's best friends was a boy named Sensilube, who had been caught milking the Alcocks' cows under cover of darkness. It turned out that his parents had been murdered, leaving Sensilube to fend for his younger siblings and himself. A third boy was Ndudu, a witty little spiv who dreamed of going to Soweto when he grew up and becoming a fancy bootlegger. The black sons and white sons slept in adjoining huts, ate and played together, and explored the surrounding countryside on horseback. In many ways, the white boys were assimilated Zulus. They spoke Zulu like Zulus. They knew how to suck sweet jelly from a hole in the stem of an aloe flower, how to set snares for birds and small game. From Mboma, they learned the best game of all—riding the raging river on driftwood after a summer thunderstorm. It was only in their teens, when they went away to high school, that G.G. and Rauri realized how unorthodox their childhood had been.

And finally, of course, there was Creina. She was the last person you expected to meet in a mud hut. She wore rags and tatters, eschewed makeup, and never shaved her legs, but she remained truly beautiful. She could talk knowledgeably about almost anything—literature, science, the arcana of apartheid legislation, the botany of the thorn veld, agricultural production in the Sudan. There you were in a mud hut, with ants in your food and tadpoles in your coffee, making small talk with a ravishing intellectual who graced her wisdoms with quotes from great philosophers and poets. It all seemed highly improbable.

After supper, Neil sank into the depths of his wicker chair and told stories in the firelight. He'd talk about—oh, the history of the tribes in the region, or the inner workings of the local dope trade, or hapless secret policemen he had known. Some of his best yarns concerned his white neighbors, many of whom referred to him as *die groot terroris*—"the master terrorist," supposedly trained in Red China. It was said that he and his wife had "kaffir" lovers. It was said that Creina stripped naked and washed in the river in full view of any black man who happened to be passing by.

And finally, it was said that the Alcocks were stirring the Zulus to revolt, even arming them. From time to time, the secret police picked up the project's Zulu staff and interrogated them on that score. What did Alcock say? Was he a Communist? Why did he live like a kaffir? What was wrong with him? Was he mad? Lots of whites thought he was mad, living the way he did, in a mud hut, eating "bloody plant soup" or whatever it was that Africans survived on.

Come bedtime, visitors groped their way up a dark footpath and into a mud hut, where they lay under coarse woolen blankets, listening to the river roaring over rapids and staring at the smoke-darkened thatch. Later, many would struggle to describe what they'd experienced that day. They were white, and came from a culture that had lost the ability to discuss matters of the heart without diminishing them inside quotes or disarming them with cynical asides. One such visitor was a former Rhodes scholar who held very high office in a multinational corporation. When I asked what he made of Neil Alcock, he vacillated, coughed embarrassedly, and said, "One was struck by his nonmaterialistic attitude."

Well, that was certainly true. Mdukatshani was arguably the most cost-efficient development project in Africa. At one point, the project's funding level was $1,250 a month—just about enough to cover the salary of a single United Nations development worker. In Neil Alcock's hands, it kept an entire project running, paying the salaries of sixty-nine black and five white staff members. The Alcocks' cut was about $50. On that kind of money, you lived in a mud hut, very simply, and were liable to be mistaken for a saint, a missionary, a man of God, and all sorts of other things that Neil Alcock wasn't.

He was a complete stranger to sanctimony. He mocked self-righteous solemnity and cracked jokes about bearded liberals behind their backs. He didn't mind living in a mud hut. If anything, he liked it. He liked farming, liked cattle, and liked nothing better than sitting under a thorn tree, disputing with Zulu men. There is a Zulu saying "I see you with my heart." Neil saw Zulus that way, and that was the way they saw him.

His arrival in the district, in 1975, had caused fear and consternation on the far side of the boundary fence. Most Zulus had long since ceased to trust whites. When Neil announced that he'd come to help them, they listened impassively, then went home and tried to divine the trick. They spent hours arguing about him, trying to figure out exactly what he was up to, and how he intended to rip them off. Word of his arrival filtered back to Johannesburg's migrant-worker hostels, and the debates continued there. When someone informed Johan Dladla that a white had arrived in Msinga, talking nonsense about working together and sharing the land, he clicked his tongue angrily. "Black and white can never work together," he said.

On his next trip home, Dladla visited the project and told Neil so to his face. "Black and white can never work together," he said. Neil just laughed, and invited Dladla to sit down for a talk. They saw each other's hearts, and

Johan Dladla was won over. He never went back to Jo'burg. He resigned his city job and stayed to work with the white man.

Another man who never went back was Petros Majozi, who eventually became the project's chairman. Majozi sported a giant handlebar mustache and was a man of silent strength, a self-taught philosopher who learned to read under Johannesburg streetlamps. He had always yearned to be a farmer, but that option was closed to a Zulu family man. A Zulu man had to go to the white cities and earn cash, so that his family could "farm at the store." So Majozi spent thirty-six years in Johannesburg, living in some lonely servants' quarters and longing for his home. He had four children back in Msinga, plus a wife and a small herd of beloved cattle, but he saw them only once a year.

January 9, 1975, was the last day of Petros Majozi's annual holiday. He was driving his cattle through the bush, leaden with sadness at the thought of leaving on the morrow, when a white man materialized before him. Majozi's knees turned to water. He was on no-man's-land—land that belonged to whites on paper but to the Zulus in their heads. He thought the white would surely pull a gun, impound his cattle, and maybe arrest him, too. Instead, Neil smiled and said hello in Zulu. They sat down under a tree and talked about land and cattle for a while, and then Neil continued on his way. It was such an insignificant encounter that Neil promptly forgot about it.

Petros Majozi, on the other hand, had seen a white man with his heart. The next morning, he took the bus to Tugela Ferry, joined a queue outside the post office, and telephoned his white boss in Johannesburg. "I'm not coming back," he said.

Majozi was a highly valued employee, so the boss demanded to know why.

"I met a white man who will help me to farm," said Majozi.

"How long have you known him?" asked the boss.

"I have only met him once," Majozi replied.

"And how much is he paying you?"

"Nothing."

"Your family will starve," said the white man.

"I hope not," said Majozi.

"You will lose your pension," said the white man.

"I don't care," Majozi replied. The white man at the other end of the line was at an utter loss to understand how a level-headed and intelligent man could take such a risk on the basis of a chance encounter in the bush, and Majozi was at a loss to explain it. His English was halting, and besides, white men knew little about seeing with the heart. So Majozi just said, "I'm sorry," and put the telephone down.

And then he took the bus back to Mdukatshani, went to see Neil, and told him that he also believed in working together. "We must take this fright in our hearts," he said, "and throw it in the river."

And so Majozi and many others threw in their lot with Neil, and for three years all went well. Mdukatshani became a sort of dusty Camelot, a congenial spot where it was possible to believe, if only for a moment, that South Africa's problems might all be sorted out. It was just a small agricultural project in a forgotten corner of the country, but there was nowhere else quite like it. It lay astride the country's most bitter old frontier, and if love could flourish there it could surely flourish anywhere.

Or so it seemed, at any rate.

Africa is a cruel country; it takes your heart and grinds it into powdered stone—and no-one minds.

—ELSPETH HUXLEY, *The Flame Trees of Thika*

The road linking Mdukatshani to the village of Weenen is as bad as any other in Msinga. It winds along the riverbank, crosses the Bushman's River on a causeway, climbs a rugged hill, and heads on across the plain beyond. It is not a good road to drive in convoy. The wheels of the vehicle ahead raise clouds of choking dust and spray stones into your windshield, and if the vehicle ahead is a bus the journey becomes absolutely intolerable. One morning, Creina got stuck behind a lumbering bus on her way into town and ate dust for several miles. It was hard to overtake another vehicle on Msinga's dirt roads. In the end, though, she saw an opening, shot past the bus, and traveled on toward town.

It was around Christmas 1978. The Alcocks had been in Msinga for three and a half years and were starting to feel less like strangers. Visitors' first impressions to the contrary, their first years in Msinga hadn't been all that easy. They were struggling to control the project's boundaries. A Zulu man who had given evidence on the project's behalf in a goat-theft case had been murdered for his trouble. Indeed, there had been many murders, but that was the nature of Msinga, reflected in its very place names. In Zulu, Tugela Ferry was known as *Mshaya Safa*—Hit Him till He's Dead. In Msinga, you could get killed for almost anything—for having the wrong name, or the wrong address, or plowing disputed land. Mdukatshani's black bookkeeper, Anton Hlongwane, was so scared of being murdered that he refused to send out notices to Zulu debtors. Still, the Alcocks had persevered in spite of all problems, and imagined they had already seen Msinga's worst side. But they had seen nothing, nothing, nothing.

The bus Creina had just passed, for instance, was about to run into trouble. As it rounded a bend, a platoon of black men armed with rifles stepped into the road and forced the driver to halt. The gunmen boarded the bus, pulled five male passengers off it, and executed them. Creina knew

315

nothing of this, of course. She drove on into Weenen, bought supplies, and headed back toward the project. En route, she found the road closed by a line of big boulders. The Zulus traveling with her were too scared to move, so Creina asked one of her sons to get out and roll the rocks aside. She had not been in Msinga long enough to know when to be afraid.

A few miles farther on, at the gates of the project, she came upon a harrowing sight—a Zulu truck driver with a bullet in his abdomen, bleeding to death in Neil's arms. The driver had been ambushed at the line of boulders—the sixth man shot on that road in a single morning. What on earth was this? Where were the police? Where on earth was the ambulance? The fatally injured man had been lying in the sun for hours. An ambulance finally came, and the Alcocks retired to the rocks above the river, to recover from the traumas of the day.

And then they looked up and saw something amazing: a skirmish line of heavily armed black men in military uniforms, advancing toward them on the river's far bank. The Alcocks had been in Msinga for three years, but this was their first sighting of a Zulu *impi*. Most whites would have fled in terror, but not Neil Alcock. He walked down to the water, cupped his hands, and yelled, "Go away! We don't want you here with guns!" The Zulu warriors stood their ground. They had come to escort one of their brothers to safety, and wouldn't leave until he had crossed the river to join them. Then they retreated into the hills.

And so ended the first of many bad days in Msinga. There had been wars elsewhere in the district in the preceding three years, but none near Mdukatshani until now. As Neil and Creina understood it, a young man from the Majola faction, a few miles upriver, had tried to seduce the girlfriend of a rival Madondo. Now young men were killing one another in consequence— killing innocent truck drivers, too. In the ensuing three months, the Majola-Madondo war claimed twenty-seven lives. Just as it was dying down, another war broke out across the river, sparked off this time by a disagreement over the outcome of a tribal dancing competition in a Johannesburg migrants' hostel. Members of the losing team refused to abide by the judges' decision. The argument escalated into violence, so the migrants came home, took up their guns, and settled the dispute in the hills. That war was no sooner over than a third broke out, triggered this time by the murder of a Zulu headman whose testimony put a cattle thief behind bars.

The Alcocks were dismayed. At the outset, they'd believed that all Msinga's problems were rooted in land hunger and apartheid, and would respond to "a little social engineering," as Creina put it. Now it dawned on them that it was not going to be quite that easy. From 1979 onward, Neil and Creina lived amidst constant terror. Bands of gunmen roamed the farm and set up ambushes on the roads that crossed it. There were tracers in the sky at night, and the ravines resounded with gunfire during the day. The wars made development work very difficult. As soon as the first shot was fired, men disappeared, and their wives stopped working, too—they had to carry food and water to their husbands' secret lairs. A war could last months, even years, and while it raged there was little the Alcocks could do save ferry the dead and wounded to the mission hospital in Tugela Ferry. By the end of 1979, a note of despair was creeping into Creina's newsletters. She closed one with a quote from the poet Roy Campbell: "The hurricanes of chaos have begun to buzz like hornets in the shifting sands."

The following year, the rains failed, and the coffin lid started closing on Neil's dream. The grass withered, crops shriveled, and Zulu cattle started dying by the thousand. Atop the drought came two more wars among the Zulus. After war came pestilence—first cholera, then rabies—and after pestilence came famine. As the drought intensified, Zulus started cutting fences along the boundary and turning their starving livestock loose on the project's land. By the end of that first dry winter, more than a thousand cattle and innumerable goats were trespassing on Mdukatshani, and the project was living up to its name: a place of lost grasses, a place of stones and dust.

In 1981, the rains failed again. The fish in Neil's pond went belly up in the foul water. His methane-gas digesters turned out to be impractical and had to be abandoned. The solar cookers tarnished and were thrown out to rust. White volunteers tired of reading their Marx in mud huts and left to find easier ways of fighting apartheid. The irrigation system at Dimbi was spotted by helicopter-borne narcotics cops on a search-and-destroy mission. Taking it for a marijuana farm, they landed and destroyed it. The springs in the hills dried up, and the river dwindled to a turgid trickle.

Beyond a certain point, Neil and Creina's lives seem to assume the quality of a myth or fable; event succeeds event with the random disconnectedness of a dream or nightmare; the plot unfolds according to the caprice of cruel and vengeful gods. The last white volunteer to work on Mdukatshani told me she quit because there seemed to be no end to Msinga's crises and no resolution to any of them. They rolled in like breakers onto a beach, one after the other, with no time between to recover. "Msinga's such a confused and destroyed place," she said. "I felt completely blindfolded and helpless.

There was nothing you could do except rave at somebody." So Neil raved. He raved for years, at anyone with the power to help—the Red Cross, white newspapers, relief organizations, Gatsha Buthelezi, even the apartheid government. He raved so long and so loud that there came a time when even his liberal allies could no longer bear to listen. In 1981, he wrote a series of letters to old friends in the liberal movement, asking why they had abandoned him to his "fatigue, inefficiency and failure." He asked, "Why me alone?" No replies came. He was on his own.

The drought dragged on until 1982, only to break in a raging cloudburst. The canal at Mseleni was buried by a landslide, the dam at Umhlumba washed away by a flood. The river came down in a spate and crippled Neil's beloved waterwheel. After that single thunderstorm, the skies cleared, and the sun beat down more mercilessly than ever.

By September 1982, it was clear that Neil Alcock had met his match in Msinga. After three rainless years, there was little to show for his efforts save some bone-dry furrows, empty dams, a weir across the river, and a single garden in which the two widows of one Philemon Khoza were growing enough vegetables to feed themselves. "Those two women," he said in a heartbreaking report to donors, "must serve as our example of what can be achieved." Otherwise, it was all dust to dust, and chaos to chaos.

Is this beginning to sound like hell to you? It sounded that way to me when I first heard it, and yet it was really a love story, a story about two whites who loved Africa. Love drew Neil and Creina to Msinga, and love kept them there, in their mud hut in the dust, even though staying meant Neil's death. He had leukemia, you see, and he was dying. He'd been advised that he had five years to live and that if he wanted all of them, he had to eat fresh meat, milk, and cheese. There was no electricity on Mdukatshani, and hence no refrigerator. In Msinga's torrid summers, milk curdled in minutes, meat rotted within a day. If Neil wanted to live, he had to leave. He had made a commitment to stay forever, though, and he kept it.

Toward the end, Neil and Creina's life became what life must be for the overwhelming majority of people on this sad continent. They lived from day to day, season to season, with little hope of salvation and no certainties save the certainty of death. Those mute, starving people we see on TV, cradling their dying children in their arms—is that not how life is for them? How else do they see it, if not that way? And yet, to hear Creina tell it, it was often a life of unbearable ecstasy. She did not dwell on the despair and defeat. Instead, she spoke of the hot dust between her toes, and the water of the river cool against her skin. She spoke of men who greeted trees as they walked through the bush, and children who ducked away from the face in the glass because they had never seen themselves in a mirror. She spoke of the nobility and courage of Zulu warriors, and the strength of their widows. She spoke of Christmas Eve, when the migrants came home from the cities and the valley rang with the sound of bugles and hooters and the joyful cries of children who had not seen their fathers in a full year.

And she told me about the time their hut burned down. She and Neil lost what little they had in that fire. As word of their misfortune spread, Zulus started converging on Mdukatshani from miles around. Some were old, some were total strangers, and all were desperately poor, and yet they came to help the white man. Some offered gifts of cash, and those who had nothing offered their muscles, to help with the rebuilding. One ancient man tried to press a tattered banknote into Neil's hand. He must have been hoarding it for decades, and now he was offering it to a white man.

Afterward, if anyone asked Neil why he stayed even though it meant dying, he mentioned that day—the day the poorest black people dug up their buried treasure and offered it to him. He and Creina had yearned all their lives to belong in Africa, and it seemed that Africa had finally accepted them, and returned their embrace. After that, he could not forsake his people, and so he stayed, and Creina stayed with him.

Toward the end of 1982, Neil's end seemed near. His body lost the ability to heal itself. The smallest scratch festered, and soon his face and legs were covered with suppurating sores. He ran a constant fever, and his skin was hot to the touch. He lay down in the windless heat on the flat rocks beside the dwindling river and made ready to die. He didn't die, though; he was too tough. He somehow pulled through. He was too weak to walk, so he had a horse brought to the door, and on its back, he mounted his last crusade.

It was a hot summer afternoon, and the herdboys were watching the sky. There were three of them, all Zulu teenagers, guarding their fathers' cattle on the plain of Ngongolo on the far side of Mdukatshani's hills. Thunder-clouds were building above them, and the boys were worried about lightning. They didn't want to be caught in the open by an electrical storm. And so, when the sky darkened and started spitting, they abandoned their duties and ran home to sit out the storm. After a while, the rain stopped and the sun came out again. The trio of herdboys ventured out onto the rain-swept plain, only to find that their cattle had scattered in the storm. The spoor ran through a hole in the boundary fence, and into white South Africa—into land that belonged to "the soldier."

The soldier's real name was James Christie, but the Zulus didn't know that. When he first bought land on the border, Zulus asked who he was, but Christie wouldn't say. "I come from the world," he said. Then he flipped an eyelid and displayed the white of an eye—a gesture of insult and malevolent intent. In the year or two since, James Christie had become a figure of dread for the Zulus on the far side of the fence. He didn't farm the land himself, but he came by from time to time to make sure that the Zulus weren't grazing their stock on it in his absence. On these patrols, he wore combat fatigues, carried a gun, and allegedly shot any Zulu goats or cattle he came across on his side of the fence. The Africans claimed that he also fired warning shots at them, and in one instance, broke the jaw of a man caught trespassing on his land. The herdboys knew all this, but they had no choice—they had to cross the boundary to retrieve their cattle.

They were not many paces inside white South Africa when the soldier stepped out from behind some bushes with a shotgun in his hands. *"Ja, madoda,"* he said in Zulu, "what are you doing on my land?" And then he pulled the trigger. The boys fled, one limping on a leg full of buckshot, another with a wound in his back. Only when they were safely back in Msinga did the second boy collapse, "breathing bubbles through a hole in his back."

The wounded teenager was rushed to a hospital in Pietermaritzburg, where surgeons operated to remove shot lodged close to his heart. A week or two later, when the boy was well enough to walk again, his father and some relatives took him to the police station in Weenen to press charges against the white gunman. The policeman behind the desk was white. "Is it true," he asked the boy, "that you were walking on a white man's land at the time of the shooting?"

"Yes," the boy replied.

"Well," said the policeman, "if I had been that farmer, I would have put the bullet here." He leaned over the desk and put a finger against the black youngster's temple, and that was just about the end of that, as far as law enforcement was concerned. The shooting was just another skirmish in a very old war—the war of blacks and whites over land.

Men on both sides of the Msinga border kept cattle, and there was too little land to go round, especially for men who were black. The average Msinga cattleman had access to around nine hectares of tribal land. His counterpart in white South Africa owned 598. These were the basic, brutal facts of life along the border, and all else flowed from them. If it rained, the border remained more or less peaceful; if it didn't, there was trouble. In times of drought, Msinga's grazing was swiftly depleted and starving Zulu livestock started piling up along the boundary fence, staring dumbly into white South Africa, where some grass and water remained. For a Zulu, a cow was no mere beast of utility. Each cow had a name, and was spoken to as though she were a member of the family. When a starving cow sank to her knees in the dust and couldn't get up again, her owner sank down and cried alongside her. Rather than see their beloved cattle die, the Zulus started cutting fences and turning them loose on white land. Whites responded with their guns, and the border became a virtual free-fire zone.

Some white farmers simply shot Zulu goats and cattle, but others found a way to profit from the war. They rounded up trespassing livestock and drove it to the government pound. The Zulus had to pay stiff fines for the release of their animals, and most of the money went straight into the white farmer's pocket as compensation for damage to his land. Zulus charged that some whites were actually luring Zulu cattle onto their land with a view to exacting fines. They also alleged that they were routinely assaulted or shot at for trespassing on white land, but the police often turned a blind eye to such complaints. In the case of the herdboys shot by James Christie, for instance, they took some statements and a photograph of the scene of the shooting, but nothing happened after that. More than two years passed, but no charges were filed.

One day, however, a messenger of court showed up at James Christie's place and handed him an official-looking envelope. Christie ripped it open and snorted with indignation. The herdboys were suing him in civil court for attempted murder. A while later, Flip de Bruin received a similar communication. In his case, the plaintiff was a suspected Zulu cattle thief who'd allegedly been subjected to one of de Bruin's novel interrogations—made to crawl through the veld on all fours for half a mile while the Boer prodded him onward with a spear. Soon after that, Peter Gill started receiving inquiries about his habit of using "whatever force was necessary" to defend his land. Neil Alcock's last crusade was under way.

He had two allies in this campaign—the Legal Resources Center, a Durban-based legal services foundation, and a Zulu matron with a seventh-grade education. Mrs. Natty Duma was almost as round as she was tall, and her heart was as big as the rest of her. She was Neil's private eye. Whenever a white man raised his fists or gun to a black man, Natty Duma came sniffing around on his farm, conducting surreptitious interviews with the injured parties. She reported the details to Neil, who passed them on to the Legal Resources Center and encouraged them to sue the bastard.

In all, Neil and Natty investigated some forty allegations of assault and wrongdoing by local whites in the final years of his life. One case involved an eighty-six-year-old black man who was allegedly kicked, beaten, and dragged around by the nose by a white farmer. Another involved a farm laborer who made the mistake of asking his *baas* for his wages. He was beaten up, loaded in a car, dumped in the veld, collected again, and taken to the police, who charged him with trespassing. A third case involved a Zulu woman who claimed she'd been raped by a white farmer and produced a half-breed twelve-year-old daughter to prove it. The white man, Phil Opperman of the farm Darkest Africa, denied all knowledge of the incident. A blood test proved he was lying, though, and he was ordered to start paying child support.

That story made headlines throughout the country and didn't draw Neil Alcock any closer to the hearts of local whites. The lawsuit that completely outraged them, however, was the so-called roads dispute. In the roads dispute, Neil's stated aim was to force the reopening of certain traditional rights-of-way, thus restoring to Zulus the right to travel cross-country from Msinga to Weenen, or down to the river. As far as his white neighbors were concerned, it was something else entirely. The disputed rights-of-way ran across white-owned land; if they were reopened, Zulus would be legally entitled to drive their cattle onto white farms and water them at any point where the path crossed a watercourse. In white minds, the lawsuit raised the specter of huge herds of starving Zulu goats and cattle trekking back and forth between Msinga and their dwindling dams, devouring their last grazing en route. The whites were incensed. They thought Neil was trying to drive them off their land.

White farmers weren't the only target of Neil's final campaign. "Towards the end," a government official told me, "he made life impossible for everyone." He sued the Tugela Ferry police for torturing suspects. He raised a hue and cry about police corruption. He had embarrassing questions asked in Parliament, and twisted the government's arm until it set up a commission to arbitrate Weenen-Msinga border tensions. In the process, he made himself the most hated white man in central Natal. His telephone rang at odd hours, and anonymous Boer voices warned him that his time was coming. The local branch of the ruling National Party passed a resolution imploring the government to remove Alcock from their midst. The secret police sent out a detachment to investigate charges of "racial incitement." Neil didn't falter. If anything, he fought harder as the five years his doctor had allotted him ran out.

In 1983, the rains failed yet again, and the screws on Msinga tightened. Zulu cattle were dying again, but the disputed rights-of-way remained closed. There was no time to wait for justice to run its course, so Neil took matters into his own hands. He and his sons and brother went out one night with picks and ax handles and forced one of the disputed roads open. They broke chains, smashed padlocks, tore the very gates off their hinges and threw them into the nearest gulley. Then they dumped the broken chains and padlocks on a white farmer's doorstep, as if daring him to do something. In rural South Africa, such behavior was virtually suicidal. Neil Alcock was looking for trouble, and there came a time when he seemed likely to get it soon.

Some five miles upriver from Mdukatshani there lived a white man named Tom Uren, a British citizen who'd spent many years in Kenya. He'd recently arrived in Msinga to manage a farm called Sun Valley. Whites regarded Uren as a sound fellow, a good, strict farm manager, but blacks were reputed to hate him, claiming that he docked their wages for infringements of arbitrary rules and put the money into his own pocket. One day, Uren got out of his pickup to open a gate on a lonely road. A shot rang out, and he fell dead with a bullet in his head. Some whites immediately blamed Neil Alcock. "Figure it out for yourself," one told me. "He wanted the kaffirs to have our land, so we had to be chased away. He was encouraging them to attack us."

In the aftermath, Zulu laborers started coming to Mdukatshani at night to warn Neil that their masters were planning murder. One alleged plot was for a sniper to take Neil out on a lonely road. Another was to lure him to a stock sale and start beating up a black in his presence; when Neil intervened in the fight, they'd kill him and claim justifiable homicide. Neil shrugged off the danger, but some of his friends were worried. It was all too easy to see him slain by the bullet from an assassin's gun. Everyone knew, of course, where the danger lay, but when the shot finally rang out, it came from an entirely different direction.

* * *

The house of Qamatha Sokhela stood on a barren plain in the sun-blasted devastation of Msinga, halfway between Mdukatshani and the dusty hamlet of Tugela Ferry. Sokhela was an old man who worked on the railways all his life. It was a good job, and he became very rich, rich enough to afford three wives and a fine house, with five big rooms, brick walls, cement floors, glass windows, and a tin roof. Inside, it was furnished with ancient Victorian armchairs and real beds, just like a white man's home. In Msinga terms, Sokhela's house was a mansion, but that was not why the neighbors envied the old man. They envied him because his roof could not be set alight, and because bullets could not pass through his walls as they could through those of the mud huts of lesser men. In Msinga, Sokhela's house doubled as a fortress, and that is why, at dawn on Christmas morning in 1982, its floors were covered with the sleeping forms of refugees—women and children who were too scared to sleep in their own huts because of the war.

The house of Sokhela overlooked a dry watercourse called the Hyena River. The land on Sokhela's side belonged to an *isigodi* called Mhlangaan. The land on the far side belonged to the Ndlela. In 1982, the Mhlangaan were at war with the Ndlela, and the enemy was strong. The enemy sometimes raided the territory of the Mhlangaan at night, shooting up huts with submachine guns and setting fire to their straw roofs. Women and children were usually considered noncombatants, but they still risked being caught in the cross fire in these nocturnal raids. So dozens of them slept in Sokhela's house for safety. Their fathers, husbands, and brothers were in the hills fighting. They had been up there three months already, living "like baboons" in the ravines. Old Sokhela had been in the hills himself, but he was now too old to fight, too old even to run when it became necessary. Some black policemen from Tugela Ferry caught him and ordered him to reveal the hiding place of the Mhlangaan army. But Sokhela did not trust the police. He feared that they would betray the whereabouts of his brothers to the Ndlela. When he refused to speak, the policemen beat him with their rifle butts, and he was hurt inside. So he came down from the hills on Christmas Eve, and slept in his own house. It was his plan to rise at dawn and flee the district.

Just before the sun rose, however, the slumbering refugees were awakened by the sound of gunfire. One of Sokhela's daughters opened the door and peered outside. She heard shouts. She heard doors kicked open at the neighboring kraal. She heard the wail of an old woman whose husband had been shot dead as he hunted a lost cow in the gray dawn. And then she saw them: "many, many" black men, wearing uniforms and military caps and carrying rifles. It was the Ndlela *impi,* the Ndlela army. By now, the refugees knew there was danger coming. They were streaming out of the house and slipping away into the bush. Sokhela's daughter ran inside and woke her father. "The war has come," she said.

Sokhela hid under his bed. The daughter positioned herself in the doorway to await the enemy. She left the door open behind her, hoping to convey the impression that the house was empty. A Ndlela warrior sauntered toward her.

"Where is the man from here?" he asked.

"There is no man here," she replied.

The soldier glanced through the door behind her, shrugged, and turned to leave. Just then, however, old Sokhela moved in his hiding place, and the bed scraped on the cement floor. The Ndlela soldier turned back. "Come, come," he shouted to his comrades, "there is someone here." Several Ndlela soldiers pushed the daughter aside and stormed into the house, rifles at the ready. "I came away," she told me, "because I didn't want to see. They have come to kill my father, and I don't want to see."

The bullets passed through the mattress and into Sokhela's heart, and he became the fifth casualty in another of Msinga's senseless wars. Why had he died? An ancient elder of Sokhela's faction dimly remembered a land dispute, but he could not say exactly how it originated, or when, because it had happened long before his time. Otherwise, Mhlangaan's warriors said the war arose from an incident that took place in a migrant workers' barracks in the distant city of Kimberley in 1965.

"It all started," said Masithela Mbatha, an elder from Mhlangaan, "when a young man named Ntsele was sitting quietly and drinking his beer. Two men from Ndlela sat down with him and helped themselves to his beer. Ntsele said, 'How can you drink my beer without asking?' And the Ndlela men said, 'How can you stop us?' " Ntsele was from Mhlangaan, and he told his brothers about this rudeness. The insult festered for weeks. "Then Christmas came," Masithela continued, "and all we Zulus gathered for a beerdrink. Everyone was discussing this thing that was done to Ntsele, and the young men wanted to fight. I was there. I fought, too. We fought with sticks and spears and knives. Five men were killed—four of them and one of us."

The men involved in that brawl were arrested but released for lack of evidence. Once set free, they returned to Msinga and continued the war in the hills. "Many" men were killed, but the fires of anger finally burned out, and peace returned to the banks of the Hyena River. By 1982, however, a new generation of warriors had come of age in Ndlela, and they were thirsting for vengeance. They said, "You killed our fathers in Kimberley, so we must kill you."

The new war started quietly, as these wars do. A Mhlangaan man was assassinated in Johannesburg. In Msinga, a Ndlela was killed in retaliation. One night, the Ndlela army came into Mhlangaan and shot up a kraal with machine guns. After that, the men on either side took to the hills with their guns, and the war got underway in earnest. In the ensuing nine months, it claimed twenty-one lives, including Sokhela's. Three men were assassinated in hostels in Johannesburg, one in Dundee. Two were killed in a shoot-out aboard a bus. Stezi Mpungose, a friend of Neil's, was ambushed on a footpath, shot dead, and beheaded. The police made some half-hearted attempts to stop the war. A local chief intervened, but he failed, too.

And then one day in the winter of 1983, two old men came down from the mountain to speak to Neil. Albert Mbatha was a jocular fellow whose trademark homburg was always tilted at a jaunty angle. Thobola Mutwa was a shy, diffident man who had recently retired after forty years in Johannesburg, where he had worked as a security guard. They were both good friends of Neil's, but he hadn't seen them for a long time. They had been on *impi*, on active service in the ravines, for three hundred nights and days. And now they were too old and tired to continue. "Oh, *Numzaan*," cried Albert, "You must help us stop this killing."

This was the truly tragic aspect of Msinga's wars: Nobody wanted them, save the bloodthirsty young hotheads who set them off. Ordinary people thirsted for peace and stability. Hardly anyone wanted to fight, but older men like Albert found it hard to control their sons. "When we tell them this terrible thing must stop," he said, "they reply, 'Watch it, *baba* [father]. We'll hit you too.'" So the youngsters stirred up trouble, and then everyone else was forced to join in by the law of indiscriminate retaliation. Once the slaughter was under way, there was simply no mechanism to stop it. The tribal leaders' power was waning, and the South African Police were entirely ineffectual. Even if a killing took place in broad daylight within sight of hundreds, they could never seem to find witnesses. Maybe they didn't really try. It was said to cost about a hundred dollars to buy yourself out of a murder rap at the police station in Tugela Ferry, a goat or two for a lesser offense.

And now Albert and Mutwa were asking Neil for help. A less courageous man would have said no on the spot. It was terribly dangerous to intervene in Msinga's disputes, but Neil never said no. After the old men left, he contacted the police, the local chiefs and the district magistrate and started organizing a peace conference. At the time, there were two wars under way within a six-mile radius of the project—Mhlangaan versus Ndlela, and Mashunka against Ngubo—and Neil decided to attempt settlements of both simultaneously. The preliminaries took three months. Warriors on all sides were suspicious and had to be convinced that they would not be assassinated if they came out of hiding. To allay their fears, Neil persuaded a police brigadier to give his blessing to the conference and to send some of his men to attend. It was a token gesture, but it strengthened the warriors' confidence, and a date was finally set.

On the appointed day, Bob Frean of Durban's *Daily News* drove out to Msinga. The peace conference was the first of its kind, and his paper thought it would make a fine feature story. Frean arrived at the project just after dawn, and found Neil already waiting, dressed as usual in frayed jeans and car-tire sandals.

In the newsman's estimation, the day got off to an inauspicious start. He and Neil climbed into the project's Japanese microbus and set out for an agreed-upon rendezvous, where a delegation from one of the warring factions was supposed to be waiting. The spot was deserted, so they waited.

Hours passed. The sun rose higher in the sky, and the heat grew suffocating. The dusty hills shimmered and danced in the distance. Half-naked herdboys settled in the shade of nearby thorn trees and stared at the white men. Bony cattle hobbled by. Frean got out and walked around in the dust and desolation. He peered over the wall of a concrete stock dam, and saw a dead dog floating in the scummy water. A crushing sense of enervation descended on his shoulders. Three hours in Msinga, and he already wanted to get out. Alcock had been there eight years, but he still wasn't complaining. In fact, he was sitting behind the wheel of the microbus, scribbling furious letters to newspapers and Members of Parliament about deplorable conditions in Msinga. Frean shook his head. How on earth did the man stand it?

Another person who had his doubts about what Neil was up to was Warrant Officer Jurgen Freese of the firearm squad at Tugela Ferry. He was waiting in the town's sweltering courthouse, fanning himself and yawning.

In Jurgen Freese's opinion, the peace conference was a waste of time. He knew what would happen. The warriors would eventually arrive. Alcock would make a speech. Then the tribesmen would yell at one another about incidents that had taken place in their fathers' and grandfathers' days, and nothing would be resolved.

Freese was more or less right. In due course, all four delegations pitched up, and Neil made some opening remarks. "All of you are suffering," he told the warriors. "For months you have been sleeping in the hills. You have known the pain of having your friends and relatives killed. But the pain has to be forgotten if we are to find a path to stop the blood." With that, he ceded the floor to the warriors.

One by one, they stood up to affirm that they, too, wanted peace, but beyond that, they found no common ground. "A lot was spoken," Freese commented, "but nothing was really said." In the end, the Zulus agreed only to meet again, and the conference broke up on a note of anti-climax.

Outside, the heat was pitiless. Neil sent someone to buy cold drinks at the general store. The conferees waited on the shady porch of the courthouse, watching goats forage through garbage in the dusty marketplace across the street. Mutwa, Albert, and other members of the Mhlangaan delegation stood on one side, the men of Ndlela on the other, not talking or even looking at one another. Later, people would claim to have seen sinister comings and goings around the courthouse, conspiratorial nods and winks, but nobody remarked on them then, and besides, Neil was not really on the lookout for danger. He doubted that the Zulus would harm him. He was their brother, their father. That was what many called him—*uBabawethu,* our father.

After the Cokes were drunk, Albert and the rest of the Mhlangaan delegation clambered aboard an open truck and set off for home, with Creina at the wheel. On the outskirts of town, however, someone started banging frantically on the roof of the cab. "We cannot go down this road," they told Creina, pointing out that it passed through the territory of their Ndlela enemies. "There is danger here," they said. Creina was at a loss to understand why they were so scared; after all, they were travelling under a truce flag. The tribesmen were insistent, though, so she turned back to the courthouse. There, Albert's delegation announced that it was willing to travel the dangerous road only in a closed vehicle, with Neil at the wheel. So Creina drove home alone.

Around four that afternoon, nineteen sweating Zulu men squeezed into

Neil's microbus and set off for home. Neil took the road that peeled off the tar on the far side of the bridge and headed north along the banks of the river, toward the land of the Ndlelas. This was of no particular concern to those of his passengers who were members of the Mashunka faction, for they had no quarrel with the Ndlelas. The Mhlangaan men, on the other hand, fell dead silent as they entered the territory of their enemies. They were right to be afraid. Eyes were watching through binoculars. Word was passing down the line. Rifle bolts were snapping and clips of ammunition clicking into place on submachine guns.

Halfway through the danger zone, the road ahead disappeared into a tumble of huge boulders. As the van neared the spot, some small Zulu boys at the roadside started dancing in a frenzy of excitement. They shouted *Olololo*, a Zulu war cry which means We've got you. The sound filled the passengers with alarm, but Neil didn't seem to notice. His eyes were on the road.

As he turned the corner, some fifty to seventy Ndlela warriors rose from their hiding places among the boulders and started shooting, concentrating their fire on the driver. A bullet from an automatic rifle hit Neil in the neck. Blood spewed into the windshield. The van slowed to a halt. Neil opened the door, staggered out, and fell.

Behind him, Zulus were boiling out of the bus with bullets whistling around their ears. The neutral Mashunka delegation stood to one side with their hands up, screaming, *"Tshwele baThembu!"*—Have mercy! Have mercy! The Ndlela soldiers ignored them and fired at the fleeing Mhlangaan. Several were already injured—one hobbling away on a shattered foot, another trying to run while holding his intestines inside with his hands. The Ndlelas left their hiding places and gave chase, firing as they ran. The screams and gunshots died away in the distance, and there was silence save for the groaning of the wounded. A Zulu man lay dying in the bus, and four others—Mutwa and Albert among them—had been killed before getting very far. And Neil was lying on his face in the dust of Africa, dead.

Once the shooting stopped, crowds of weeping, praying Zulu women converged on the scene. They found an old Zulu man sitting bleakly in the middle of the road, keeping watch over Neil's body. As Neil fell, his briefcase burst open, scattering papers and money. Someone suggested that the old man pick up the papers, but he said no. The police must see it all, just as it happened; nothing must be touched. So he fetched a rock, placed it beside Neil's body, and sat down upon it, waiting.

One or two cars came by, but their black drivers were too scared to help. A big bus thundered over the horizon in a cloud of dust, edged through the crowd, around Neil's body, and drove on without stopping. The sun wheeled and set, and it was nightfall when the police came.

The old man looked up and saw cigarettes glowing in the dark above him. One of the cops stirred Neil's corpse with his toe.

"We don't pick up dogs," he said. "You pick him up. He's your Jesus."

We penetrated deeper and deeper into the heart of darkness. It was very quiet there.

—JOSEPH CONRAD, Heart of Darkness

And so Neil was dead. For many days, it did not seem real to Creina. Zulu women started brewing beer and preparing food for a funeral. Whose funeral? An old black man appeared in the doorway, took off his hat, and held it over his heart. "You're all alone now," he said, "all alone, all alone." It all seemed so unreal.

One morning while it was still dark outside, she heard the clink of shovels and spades as men climbed the hill to dig the grave. Later, she heard the big truck start, and knew her stepson Dave had left to fetch the bodies from Greytown. They had been taken there, forty miles away in white South Africa, because there were rumors of a plot to steal the corpses from the morgue at Tugela Ferry and dismember them for inclusion in a battle-medicine brew. So Dave drove all the way to Greytown, and when he got there the police declined to release all six bodies to him, citing talk of a plot to waylay the truck on its way back into Msinga. And so only Neil's body was taken from the morgue and placed in its coffin, a reject bought cheap from an undertaker in the Place of Weeping. The coffin was loaded on the truck and set out on its last sad journey, bracketed by vehicles bristling with armed police.

Neil had asked to be buried on the cliff top, on a spot overlooking the bend in the river and the sweeping floodplain beyond. A crowd was waiting up there in the burning sun—two prominent black men in suits and a thousand ordinary Msinga people in rags and tatters and vestiges of tribal finery. Many mourners remarked favorably on the coffin, which was made of two shades of wood, one light and the other dark. They said it was a fitting coffin for a man like Neil Alcock, who was half-black and half-white in his heart.

An ancient Zionist prophet said a few words, and the crowd sang "Nkosi Sikalel' iAfrika," "God Bless Africa." And then the coffin was lowered into the grave and covered with stones, and Creina turned and walked away. She sat near the river for a while, watching the male mourners wind down the cliff to the flat rocks at its base, where they stripped off their clothes and washed themselves in accordance with Zulu burial ritual. This is not real, she thought; this is not my river; it looks just like the Ganges.

And so Neil was dead. Why? It seemed so pointless for him to have died in that way. In the distant cities, many whites received the news with disbelief, thinking, No, this just can't be; Neil Alcock cannot have been killed by Zulus. They were certain that there must have been a conspiracy, that if the connections could only be traced, it would emerge that the order for the killing came from somewhere inside the white system, inside the secret police or the apparatus of military intelligence. All the laws of destiny, the rules of poetic symmetry, and the requirements of plot demanded that this be so, but there was little to back the theory save its proponents' longing to believe it. It was hard to believe that any white man other than Neil himself had sufficient influence among the tribes to coax an *impi* to do his secret bidding.

The bad-cop theory was a little more compelling. Shortly before his death, Neil had finally prevailed on the police brass to send an undercover officer to investigate Msinga's hundreds of unsolved murders and the reek of fix that hung over them. In the weeks leading up to the ambush, Neil and a cop named Fires van Vuuren held several secret meetings with Zulus who claimed to have evidence regarding such things. Under the circumstances, certain members of the police garrison at Tugela Ferry had reason to wish Neil dead, and they were in a position to have organized it—most of them were Zulus, several with blood ties to the Ndlela faction.

The mystery was never really solved, although the police seemed to try a little harder than usual. Alcock was a *kafferboetie* and a perpetual pain in their necks, but he remained a white man, and his killing called for swift and certain retribution. So police poured into the district, set up a tent camp on the outskirts of Tugela Ferry, and used helicopters to round up the Ndlela *impi*. Scores of warriors were arrested, and a dozen or so weapons dug up from secret caches in the bush. Ballistics tests proved that some of the guns had been used in the ambush, but the police apparently struggled to establish exactly whom they belonged to, and by whom their triggers had been pulled.

Eventually, thirteen Ndlelas were charged with murder, but there wasn't much of a case against them. Six men were shot dead in broad daylight on an open road in a densely populated area, but nobody saw anything. It was the same old Msinga story. Indeed, the case differed from the thousands before it in only one respect—there was at least one witness, a woman named Buthelezi who stepped forward and broke the law of silence. She told the police she had seen a throng of men with rifles at the ready sitting on the rocks above the ambush site an hour before the killings. She identified eighteen of them by name, and then she vanished. When I went looking for her, some Zulus told me there was no such person, and never had been. A white policeman interpreted this to mean she was probably dead. Without her, there was no case at all; the attorney general declined to prosecute, and the thirteen suspects were set free.

So white man's justice had failed yet again, and to some men in the valley the situation seemed to call for a traditional Msinga solution. Soon after the ambush, the generals of four nearby *isigodi* came to Creina and told her that if she wished, if she was hungry for blood, they would lead their combined armies into Ndlela and burn it to the ground. Creina thanked them, for they were paying her dead husband a great honor, but said no. Neil would not have wanted more war. So the generals went home, and the case was closed in Msinga terms, too. All that was left was for Creina to come to terms with it, and that was the hardest part of all.

She believed in love, you see; not in a sentimental sense, or a religious sense, but just . . . love: giving of yourself and trying to do good for others. Her and Neil's willingness to love had carried them deeper into Africa than any other whites, and she thought love would protect them there. It seemed she had been mistaken. "After Neil's death," she said, "I thought that the whole of my life had been meaningless, and that I had misunderstood every single thing I had ever looked at—that there had never been any meaning from the beginning."

After thinking it through, Creina concluded that she must somehow have failed in love, not loved enough or sacrificed enough to shield her husband from the forces at work in Msinga. It seemed to her that staying was the only way to salvage the meaning of Neil's life, so she refused to abandon the project. Friends, relatives, and the police tried to convince her otherwise, but she refused. "Have you ever planted a tree?" she asked one cop. "Neil and I planted a tree, and I must stay to see it grow." The chorus of white friends and relatives eventually gave up and returned to their cities, leaving Creina and her teenage sons on their own.

She built a rock garden on Neil's grave and planted it with aloes, wildflowers, and grasses. She sat on the grave for hours on end, all through the night sometimes, telling herself that the world had not come to a stand-still, that life and movement remained; that even sitting there, in the hollow she had worn on her husband's grave, she was hurtling through space at nine hundred miles an hour. She grew thin and gaunt, and her friends sometimes feared for her sanity, for she was in the habit, in that extremity of grief, of talking about Neil in the present tense, as if he were still alive. They redoubled their efforts to persuade her to leave, but she would have none of it. "Every time I left the farm, I felt as though I was dying," she said. "It was the only reality there was, and the world outside was so strange."

A year passed, a bitterly hard year for a white woman alone in Africa, and a widow at that, so low on the African social scale that she had virtually ceased to exist. Creina couldn't speak Zulu very well, and knew next to nothing about farming—Neil had always taken care of that. In fact, Neil had taken care of almost everything, and now Neil was gone. "The center pole has fallen," said the Zulus, referring to the pole that kept their structures of mud and thatch erect. They doubted that the project could survive without him, and doubted that Creina had the courage to stay. Believing that Mdukat-shani was doomed, some of them started taking care of their own interests. There was a rash of petty thefts. One of Neil's Zulu lieutenants plowed and planted crops in a sacrosanct conservation camp. Another set himself up in the transport business, ferrying goods and people all over the district in the project's truck. A third man, also a truck driver, took to using the truck for his night-time jaunts. When Creina asked him to stop, he suggested she mind her own business.

And then someone entered Creina's office, which was never locked, and could in fact not be locked, and took the only things of value in it: a broken cassette recorder and a portable typewriter that Neil had given her. When the theft was discovered, everyone thought, Uh-oh, this is Mboma's doing—Mboma Dladla, the little Zulu starveling who'd become part of the Alcock household at the very beginning. Creina had nursed him back to health, and he had become her son G.G.'s best friend, and subject of the best-selling *Story of Mboma*. Mboma and Ndudu and Sensilube—these are names we must resurrect now. They were among the herdboys who had once lived in her household and been her sons' best friends—members of her family, virtually. Sensilube was the boy who milked the cows in secret so he could feed his orphaned brothers and sisters. Ndudu was the spiv, the boy with wit and sparkle, and Mboma was the clever one, the ingenious kid of whom

Neil joked, "This boy will either be prime minister, or wind up on the gallows."

Several years had since passed, and Mboma, Ndudu, and Sensilube were now in their late teens or early twenties. Ndudu and Sensilube were still living nearby, but Mboma had been cast out, and it looked as though he was fulfilling the darker half of Neil's prophecy. He had been caught stealing from fellow Zulu workers and was kicked off the project at their insistence. Mboma's version was that he'd been framed, and that the others had put a witchcraft on him because they were jealous of his closeness to Neil and the white boys. Whatever the truth, Mboma left the Alcocks and went to live with his father. The Alcocks heard that he'd dug up the old man's gun and sold it, then stolen his clothes and sold them, too. After that, Mboma was banished again, and vanished into the maw of Soweto.

A few months after the ambush, though, he turned up in Msinga again. He'd grown into a heavy-set young man, moon-faced and slow moving, with a chiseler's winning smile. The farm committee seemed to have forgotten that it had declared the project off-limits to him, and Creina lacked the authority to enforce the rule herself. Whenever she drove out of the project's gates, there was Mboma, peering at her through his scholarly bifocals, thumb in the air for a ride. She always picked him up, but she had grown wary of him from long experience. He was hanging around on the day her typewriter disappeared, and the evidence pointed to him as the one who'd taken it.

Creina didn't think it worth calling the police, but the typewriter was of sentimental value, so she asked Mboma's community to help. A day or two later, two of Msinga's toughest guys showed up at the project, announcing that they'd come to solve the case of the missing typewriter. Kunene was a professional car thief, and Zwane a famous warrior, with many killings to his name. "A most enchanting man," said Creina, and not at all sarcastically; if you were prissy about choosing friends in Msinga, you were likely to have no friends at all. The two tough guys borrowed one of the project's vans, and set out in search of Mboma.

That evening, Creina was flagged down in the bush by a crowd of shouting Zulu men. They told her they'd caught Mboma and Sensilube, another of her Zulu "sons," in possession of something in a suitcase. Was this the missing machine? It was indeed. Creina burst out crying. The Zulu men stood around beaming. It was just a small thing, but it gave Creina a tremendous surge of hope and confidence. By rallying around her, the Zulu men seemed to be saying that she, too, was an insider now, in the way that Neil had been.

Even as the hand-over ceremony was under way, however, Mboma and Sensilube were on their way to the police station at Tugela Ferry, to report that the warrior Zwane had leveled a revolver at them. Next thing, the police were out looking for him, investigating a firearms charge. Zwane fled to Johannesburg. As soon as he was out of the way, Mboma and Sensilube came swaggering back into the project, not in the least put out. When next Creina passed through the farm gates, Mboma was there as usual, smiling and chattering as though nothing had happened. There was little Creina could do but smile back, and stop to pick him up.

Another year passed. One day, South Africa's minister of justice passed overhead in a helicopter and landed at Tugela Ferry, where a press conference was held. The minister made noises about cleaning up the district and ameliorating its suffering, but the killings continued, as did the hunger and hardship. Lacking Neil's command of Zulu and his male authority, Creina found it hard to negotiate the tortuous tribal politics on the far side of the river. She and the farm committee thus decided to expand the community gardens that lay on Mdukatshani itself. Several hundred additional plots were laid out alongside the river, dams built, a pump installed, and the women of the valley invited in to till and hoe and plant. The gardens were a great success, and Creina's bead business was doing better than ever. Orders were pouring in from the great fashion houses of Europe. Msinga beads were to be seen in the display cases of Yves St. Laurent, around the necks of *Vogue* models, and on the wrists of Hollywood stars.

Bead day came once a month. On its eve, Creina drove into Greytown and drew the proceeds of sales from a bank. The following morning, Zulu women in purple cloaks and ocher headdress came out of the hills, and, folding their stiff leather skirts beneath their thighs, settled in a great chattering flock in the shade of a big thorn tree. Creina sat down among them with a pair of scales and bags of ruby-red and aquamarine and emerald-green glass beads. Then loose beads were exchanged for finished articles, and other things exchanged, too: gossip and rumors of war, obituaries and requiems for newly dead fathers, husbands, and sons. Creina loved her bead women, and assumed they loved her back.

On the eve of one bead day, Creina's sons came home from town with a vanload of bread and groceries, and a satchel containing two thousand dollars in cash—the bead women's wages. It was dark by the time they arrived, so they left the money and goods in the van overnight. In the morning, the gas tank was empty, and so was the vehicle itself: All the groceries had vanished, along with the satchel of cash.

Creina couldn't figure out how the thief or thieves had carried off an entire vanload of loot on foot. She was standing there, puzzling it over, when some staff members mentioned that they'd just seen Mboma Dladla and some of his cronies on the road, pushing a broken-down pickup piled with cardboard cartons and grocery bags. Creina put two and two together and called the police. It turned out that Mboma's pickup had been stolen in a nearby white town, and as for the missing groceries, some were discovered stashed away in his grandmother's kraal, along with about one hundred and eighty dollars in cash. The rest of the money had vanished. "What money?" said Mboma. "I don't know what you're talking about."

So Mboma was taken away, protesting his innocence, and Creina was left in a quandary. Forty or fifty Zulu women were sitting under the thorn tree outside her hut waiting to be paid for their beadwork. Creina felt rotten. She felt she'd been negligent, and blamed herself for the theft. So she drove back into town, borrowed money to cover the wages, and resigned herself to the long and hard struggle of repaying the loan out of her own wage of seventy-five dollars a month.

There was some consolation to be drawn from the fact that Mboma was behind bars, and presumably on his way to jail, but it didn't last long. One Sunday, six weeks after his arrest, he came back home, laughing his head off again. Creina was outraged. She called the police, who explained that Mboma had been released because he had "a sore eye." Such were the mysterious processes of law enforcement in Msinga.

Mboma hadn't held a steady job in his life, but he suddenly seemed to have plenty of money. He tossed coins to adoring young herdboys, donated groceries to the poor. Indeed, someone claimed to have seen him root under a rock near his family's kraal and emerge with fistfuls of cash, which he threw into the air, singing and dancing and blessing his ancestors for bringing him luck. When asked where the money came from, Mboma reportedly laughed. "If you are walking to water," he said, "and find something in your path, it is yours to keep."

Creina tried not to count betrayals. She'd virtually raised that boy. She provided a steady income for one of his grandmothers, who did beadwork, and Neil had lied to help his grandfather obtain a government old-age pension. She and Neil had done several good works in Mboma's community, which was Ndlela—the community whose army had ultimately murdered Neil. Indeed, one of Mboma's uncles was in the *impi* that carried out the killings, and when the police came hunting in helicopters, relatives used Creina's telephone to arrange a hiding place in the city for him. Only one woman in Ndlela had come forward to testify about the ambush, and now nobody would testify about the bead-money theft—not even Creina's beloved bead women. Worse yet, Mboma emerged from the affair as something of a hero. Little Zulu boys would come to Creina and say, "Oh, Mboma's so nice; he's giving us presents," while their mothers stood around beaming. What could Creina do? She forgave, as she'd always forgiven.

From a criminal point of view, the theft of the bead money was inspirational. In Msinga, two thousand dollars was a fortune. Nobody in the valley had had any idea that there were such riches on Mdukatshani, to be had more or less for the taking. In Msinga, anyone who owned anything worth stealing had guns, guards, and barbed-wire fences, but Creina was alone and defenseless.

One night, she was awakened by a torch in her face. Two young black men were standing over her bed, leveling a revolver at her. "We want money," they said. "We kill you." Creina got up and opened the safe where the bead women's wages were kept. She was a little too slow for the robbers' liking, so they clubbed her to the ground with the butt of the gun, then hauled her to her feet, bleeding and half-conscious, and warned her to be quick about it. So she handed over the package of bank notes, and they vanished into the night.

She didn't know who had done it, of course, and Ndudu was the last person she suspected. Ndudu was one of her younger son's best friends. He was no longer working on the project, but he almost always came to lunch on Sunday. He was there as usual after the robbery, full of solicitude, and wondering aloud who could have done such a vile deed. He knew more than he was letting on, though. He knew when Creina went to get the money, how much it was, and where she hid it. He also knew her dogs. A day or two later, he was in police custody, confessing that it was he who led the robbers to the house, he who calmed the barking dogs and held them while his accomplices went inside to pistol-whip his white mother.

After Ndudu's robbery, the darkness seemed to close in on Creina. If Mboma, Sensilube, and Ndudu were not loyal to her, was there anyone in the valley whom she could trust? Suddenly, every sign seemed ominous.

Strangers approached the project's staff asking curious questions about her dogs. The telephone kept ringing in the dead of night, and a black voice would ask for people she'd never heard of. For the first time in her life, Creina grew afraid. She came to dread the sunset. She often lay awake long into the night, listening for footfalls on the path outside her hut, and praying that if they came again, they would at least not hit her, please not hit her. Half of her face was left nerveless after Ndudu's robbery, and she'd almost lost an eye.

And then the year turned, and it was 1985. The winter was a bad one, as brutal as any in recent memory. By August, it had not rained in ten months. The grass was all eaten, and cattle started dying again. Even the rats grew desperate—so desperate that they lost their fear of humans, and started invading Msinga's houses. At night, when Creina doused her lamp, they invaded her hut and skittered over her face as she lay waiting for the next Ndudu.

When the sun rose, the sky was blue and cold and cloudless, and puffs of powdery dust hung in the wake of bony cattle moving on the hillsides. And then the goats started coming, huge swarms of hungry goats, pouring through holes in the project's cut fences and devouring every last shred of vegetation on Mdukatshani's dusty, eroded hills. The goat owners lived along the project's boundaries, and Creina regarded them as friends. She begged them to keep their animals out, and they were only too eager to oblige. For a day or two, there would be no goats on the project, but promises were soon forgotten, and the goats would start coming again, scavenging along the riverbank and right into Creina's mud-walled living-room. She'd come home at night to find dung on her windowsills, dung all over the floor.

Creina was so weary of talking. She and Neil and their Zulu allies had talked nicely for more than a decade, but nothing ever seemed to change. It had always been like this, you see, even in Neil's day, even in the time of his last crusade, when he was smashing gates on white farm roads and accompanying the Zulus in midnight raids on his white neighbors' dwindling springs. Zulus knew their animals wouldn't be shot or impounded if they were turned loose on Mdukatshani, and a lawless few took advantage of that fact. They cut the project's fences to ribbons and there was little anyone could do about it, short of resorting to force. Neil's two closest Zulu allies, his blood brothers Majozi and Nxongo, had become the chief *induna*s, or prime ministers, of their respective Zulu subtribes. Both men urged

Msinga's outlaws to cooperate with the project; both were warned to mind their own business or die. As if to underscore the threat, a Zulu appointed to make sure that no green trees were felled on Mdukatshani was waylaid and beaten to within an inch of his life.

Neil had understood why these things happened. He knew the depths of desperation that drove people to such acts, so he forgave, as he'd always forgiven. That grew harder as the years went by and grazing piracy intensified, and he and his Zulu allies eventually decided to strike back. They rounded up all the goats and cattle trespassing on Mdukatshani and started driving them towards the kraal of the nearest Zulu chief, planning to ask him to try and punish their owners under traditional African law. The posse never reached its destination, though. It was waylaid en route by a mob of irate Zulus who waved sticks in the air and howled with outrage, accusing the white man of stealing their cattle. They threatened violence, and a very ugly scene ensued. Neil wound up firing warning shots into the air to keep the peace, and had to let the trespassing goats and cattle go.

"There are two theories of fence maintenance," Creina observed in her next newsletter. "Shoot or negotiate. Our neighbors live by the first theory, we live by the second. Our neighbors have their fences cut, but Mdukatshani's fences are severed too. If guns, threats and talks have failed, what's left? Something formidably slow."

Formidably slow indeed. In the final year of his life, Neil was reduced to pleading with the local Zulu chiefs to support the project and uphold some semblance of law. This put the chiefs in a very difficult position. Their own authority was growing tenuous, and they were reluctant to be seen as acting against their own people on behalf of a project run by a white man. Shortly before his death, Neil asked the Msinga's Regional Authority, or council of chiefs, to put the sensitive livestock trespass issue on the agenda for an upcoming meeting. On the appointed day, he spent four hours waiting at the meeting place, but no chiefs came, and Neil didn't live long enough to find out why. A week later, he was dead, shot down in broad daylight by Zulus, within earshot of hundreds of Zulus who heard nothing.

And now, in the winter of 1985, the situation was worse than ever. Whenever Creina raised her eyes to the horizon, goats were swarming across it. After they'd eaten everything else, they started on Neil's grave, stripping it of its flowers and grasses and defiling it with their droppings. "I just felt desperate," Creina said. "We had meeting after meeting with everyone. I said, 'For God's sake, can't you just make sure the goats don't get into the gardens?' They had finished my garden. They finished everybody's gardens. Day after day, we'd see them coming from almost everywhere, advancing. I'd say to people, 'Can't you just post children, just let them swim in the river and shoo the goats away?' " Small boys would be posted for a day or two, but then they'd vanish, and the invasion would begin again.

Early one winter morning, Creina set out from her home with a pack of mongrels at her heels. One of the dogs was Insiswa, a tawny brute with the look of a jackal and an instinct to go for the throat. As a puppy, he'd attacked goats, but the habit had been thrashed out of him. He was a good dog these days. Creina led the dogs across the dirt road and up into the foothills, to a barren, sheet-eroded field she was trying to reclaim. She was working alone, laying rocks in anti-erosion contours, when the first flock of goats appeared. She waved her arms, shouted, and threw pebbles at them. The goats scattered, but as soon as Creina turned her back they returned. She chased them off several times, but they always came back again.

Soon, two more flocks appeared. While she was chasing one, another would dash into the field behind her. The goats were pitiless, relentless. The skirmish went on all morning, and it was slowly driving Creina mad. She thought she'd lost the ability to feel anger when Neil was murdered, but she was suddenly seething with rage. She thought, Well, maybe the only way anybody will understand anything is if I do things the way Msinga does.

Msinga's way was violence and killing, and Msinga's rules, as Creina saw them, were "an eye for an eye, and then an arm for an arm, and a leg for a leg." That was the law on the black side of the frontier, and on the white side of the frontier, too. If black-owned goats invaded a white man's land, the white man shot or impounded them, and threatened to do likewise to their owners—to put a bullet between their eyes and throw their black bodies in a thorn thicket so dense that their rotting corpses would be traced only by the smell. This was an old Afrikaner philosophy called *kragdadigheid*, the act of power: You took what you wanted, and held it with your gun and fists. Creina and Neil Alcock had spent their entire lives fighting against whites who lived according to that barbaric philosophy, but now Creina decided to try it their way.

It was August 1985, almost two centuries since Dawid Malan crossed the Great Fish River. Like him, Creina entered Africa an enlightened creature. Her head was full of reason and rationality, of D. H. Lawrence and T. S. Eliot. She was a gentle person, moved easily to tears. She was so sickened by violence that she could not bear to sit through an ordinary Hollywood action-adventure movie. She had always tried to love, but now it was time to kill.

When the next flock came, she whistled for Insiswa and took off running alongside the goats, inciting the dog to attack. Insiswa had been whipped for attacking goats, so he was bewildered and uncertain at first. Creina kept goading, though, and the dog finally took off on the hunt. Creina lost sight of him, but she heard a terror-stricken bleating in the bushes, and knew he'd caught and killed a goat. Insiswa returned, tail wagging, and Creina was coldly pleased.

She set the dog on another goat, and then another, and another. Two goats were killed, two injured too badly to walk, before Creina decided that she'd shed enough blood to make herself clear. Then she stalked over to the community gardens and told the Zulu women what she'd done. "Insiswa has just killed your goats," she shouted. "It was not an accident. I wanted to kill them and will go on killing your goats until they stop coming onto the farm. Go home and tell your men!"

The following morning, Creina returned to the site of her killings and found one of the dead goats still lying there, half-eaten by some scavenging beast. She set to work, carrying rocks to and fro. The smell of death hung in the air around her. An old Zulu woman—a relative of Mboma's—came up to her, asking for blankets and food. Creina screamed, "Go away, you horrible old woman!" She worked furiously all morning, entirely untroubled by goats. There wasn't a single goat on the project. Not one.

"I thought I had won," Creina said. "I had beaten Msinga. I had found a language Msinga could understand."

She had indeed, and Msinga replied in a similar tongue.

Three weeks later the owner of one of the goats she'd killed sent Creina a death threat. It brought home to her what she had done. It was like waking up from a bad dream, a nightmare in which some foul excrescence had come bubbling up out of some uncharted reach of her brain. She felt defiled. She had behaved like a savage, like a Boer—like all those white men along the border who shot or impounded trespassing Zulu livestock and threatened to do likewise to their owners. She felt as though she'd betrayed everything she lived for, and all Neil had died for. So she prostrated herself before the aggrieved goat owner, begging forgiveness for her uncontrollable temper and promising to make restitution.

It was a mistake. It merely revealed another vulnerability, another avenue of exploitation. Not long after, Creina received a second letter in the post. In it, a Zulu man accused her of killing eight of his goats, in a place where she had never been. He demanded compensation, and added a little postscript, entirely in keeping with the traditions of a brutal continent. "If you don't pay," he wrote, "I will kill you."

Creina had been talking into my tape recorder every night for almost a week, and her voice was growing hoarse. Her tale was not yet done, but she fell silent for a while, and I lowered my head into my hands. I didn't want to hear any more. I was thinking about Afrikaners—about Dawid Malan and the Doppers, the frontiersmen who extinguished the light of the Enlightenment because they found themselves in a place of darkness, where loving made for weak and doubtful men. Creina's willingness to love, to bear light, had carried her deeper into Africa than any other white I had ever heard of, and she seemed to have discovered that the Doppers were right. If you loved you were vulnerable, and if you were vulnerable you were weak, and if you were weak in Africa, you got fucked, and fucked again, and again, until you could no longer stand it.

It was late winter, and the Zulus were burning the grass across the river to ensure a swift sprouting of green when the first rains fell. The wind was laden with the acrid smell of smoke, and there was an orange glow in the sky. We sat there in the dark, this otherworldly woman and I, our faces bathed in the light of the fires, the hot wind stirring our hair, and for me, it was like standing in the mouth of some diabolical furnace, like staring into hell.

And then Creina resumed her tale, and finally answered the question I put to her on the night of my arrival, the night she'd riddled me like a sphinx. I had asked, "How do you live in this strange place?" and now she was about to tell me. "I put the second death-threat letter aside," she whispered, "and looked out the door, and I was suddenly terribly afraid. I had this sense of utter blackness, worse than when Neil had died. I thought, Well, I can't actually live in Msinga, because I haven't got what it takes to live by Msinga rules. I could manage two goats once, but I would never be able to keep it up. I felt utterly betrayed by loving. All the things I had ever been told about love just weren't true. It was all full of false promises. I understood that love was a safety and a protection, and that if you loved you would be rewarded by someone loving you back, or at least not wanting to damage you. But it wasn't true, any of it. I knew that if I stayed, this was how it was going to be: It would never get any better; it would stay the same, or get worse. I thought, If you're really going to live in Africa, you have to be able to look at it and say, This is the way of love, down this road: Look at it hard. This is where it is going to lead you.

"I think you will know what I mean if I tell you love is worth nothing until it has been tested by its own defeat. I felt I was being asked to try to love enough not to be afraid of the consequences. I realized that love, even if it ends in defeat, gives you a kind of honor; but without love, you have no honor at all. I think that is what I had misunderstood all my life. Love is to enable you to transcend defeat.

"You said one could be deformed by this country, and yet it seems to me one can only be deformed by the things one does to oneself. It's not the outside things that deform you, it's the choices you make. To live anywhere in the world, you must know how to live in Africa. The only thing you can do is love, because it is the only thing that leaves light inside you, instead of the total, obliterating darkness."

I'm so very tired, my friend. This all started so long ago, so long ago, and I'm so deeply enmeshed in half-truths and fictionalizations of myself that I'll never escape until I simply tell the truth. This is not the book I was contracted to write, long ago by someone in New York, and I am not sure I'm any of the men I have pretended to be. The book that was to be was very different from the book you have just read. It was supposed to be about the Malan clan, and our bloody trajectory across three centuries of African history; a book that began with Dawid Malan and traced apartheid from its roots to poisonous fruits. But I am a reporter and a muckraker, so I started raking the muck in my own brain, and discovered a story more telling than the one I had in mind.

This other story begins long ago in a cave on the banks of a nameless river, on the shores of a nameless green sea. In this cave lived creatures unlike any ever seen before. They were tall, clean-limbed, dark-skinned, and almost hairless. They used tools, hunted with weapons, painted their bodies with ocher, and buried their dead—a sign that they were self-aware. You could have taken one of them and put him in a suit and turned him loose in Manhattan, and nobody would have turned a hair, because they looked just like us. In fact, they were us; they were *Homo sapiens sapiens,* the very first modern man. Some of these men stayed in and around their cave, and some set out to conquer new lands. They walked out of the continent we call Africa, and nothing was ever heard from them again.

And then one day, maybe forty-five thousand years after their brothers had vanished, the dark-skinned Africans living in the cave's vicinity looked up and saw two riders crossing the horizon, a black woman and a white man. It was August 1788, and Dawid Malan was coming home, not that he saw it that way. How was he to know? Nobody knew it, not then. For Dawid Malan, the nameless stream was just another obstacle to be forded in his headlong flight from the law, so he and Sara just rode on by. Two more centuries would pass before archaeologists discovered the cave at the mouth of the Klasies River, and in it, the oldest relics yet found of the species we call mankind.

A few days later, the riders came to another river, the Great Fish River, on the far side of which lay Africa. Dawid Malan had been away from Africa for a very, very long time. His skin had been blanched white by aeons in the mist and snow, and he carried the coldness of the northern winter in his heart. All those aeons of whiteness behind him, those aeons of ethnocentricity, in which whites were "us" and all others "them," and the relationship between the two was one mostly of war. As he spurred his horse across the river, Dawid Malan surely thought, What now? If I lower my gun and open my arms, will the Africans embrace me as a brother? Or will they take advantage of my position to plunge their spears into my chest?

The South African tableau remains frozen in that moment. Dawid Malan and his generation found no grounds for trusting Africa, so they put the black man down and evolved the law of keeping him that way, forever and ever and ever. Very little had changed between that day and the day I came home to my country, after eight years of running away. My people were still standing guard with guns at the ready and jackboots on Africa's back, and I was one of them. I didn't have to dig in the archives for Dawid Malan; I looked in the mirror and there he was. His frontier had moved inside my head, and travelled with me wherever I went. I thought of him whenever I crossed the border into the riot-torn black townships, and my guts started gnarling with dread. I thought, What now? If I lower my guard and approach these people with open arms, will they embrace me like a brother? Or will they pick up stones at the sight of me, and throw them at my speeding car? Two centuries had passed, but the question remained essentially the same. If Dawid Malan had a disease of the soul, then Rian Malan had it too.

So I threw away the book that was to be—the book about the Malans—and set out to confront this thing in a place where I thought it lay: in stories of the way we killed each other. It was the time of death and dying, the season of stark choices in the winter of 1986. I wandered from grave to grave, but the stories I gathered revealed meanings that ultimately annihilated one another.

"A mouth that talks like yours is asking for a hiding," said Augie de Koker.

"*Ek het vokol*," said Samuel Mope. "I am black, and I have fuck-all."

"A white is a white against the black," said Sibogang, drinking in a Soweto shebeen. "Every white man we see is an enemy to us."

"There is no fairness on this earth," said Simon the Hammerman.

"Oh, baby," said Allen Pizzey of CBS News, "when the day comes you'll still be whitey."

"Frikkie hated the kaffirs," said the stepfather of a slain white policeman.

"Themba was hating the whites," said Blackie Mshotshiza, trade unionist.

"Those in the middle are the most dangerous," said Tiger, juggling empty beer bottles in Zululand. "Those in the middle must die."

"If you go into their stronghold you will surely be killed," said George Wauchope, in the midst of Soweto's other civil war. "There is no middle of the road."

In the end there was no middle anywhere, no refuge from choice, not even in my own mind. I had always been two people, you see: A Just White Man appalled by the cruelties Afrikaners inflicted on Africans, and an Afrikaner appalled by the cruelties Africans inflicted on each other, and might one day inflict on us. There were always these two paths open before me, these two forces tugging at my traitor's heart.

The first path led into the deep cold and darkness of ideological outer space, a vantage from which the earth was tiny, blue, and silent, and South Africa a speck on its face, populated by beings so antlike and inconsequential that they could be sacrificed if the need arose. Blacks rebelling? In that case, kill them. Lock them up, thirty thousand of them at once. Jail or ban their leaders. Muzzle their newspapers. Obliterate their organizations. Send death squads into the townships. Blow up trade union and church buildings. Assassinate black leaders in exile. Put out your eyes and do what's necessary in darkness, that the white rock may stand in the turbulent African sea.

That passage in Conrad's *Heart of Darkness* where Kurtz rears up on his deathbed and croaks, "The horror! The horror!"—you remember it, don't you? Critics have always wondered what Kurtz was looking at as he spoke those words, but I know, I know, I know. I was out there for a while in the winter of 1986. I contemplated the totalitarian absolute, but it didn't work for me. It's a little late in the game to say that some of my best friends are black, so I'll just say this instead: I closed my eyes and imagined putting a gun to an African's temple in the name of Boer supremacy, but I didn't have it in me to pull the trigger. I had lost my blood, as Colonel Red Russian Swanepoel once put it over tea in the Blue Hotel. Maybe I never had the blood in the first place. Maybe the Red Russian was an animal, and I something just slightly more.

That being the case, there was only one path left for the likes of me—the path that led into Africa, the path of no guarantees. There were no guarantees of safety for Dawid Malan in 1788, and there were none for white South Africans in 1986. The place where we were going was clearly very different from the whites-only moonbase where I was born. Strange terrors and ecstasies awaited us in Africa, but that was the choice we faced: Either we stayed as we were, trapped inside our fortress of paranoia, deformed by fear and greed, or we opened the door to Africa and set forth into the unknown.

There were other roads into the unknown, I suppose, but the one I took was the road to Msinga, the road that carried me across an invisible boundary and into another world, where a strange, mystical woman lived in a house of mud. Creina and Neil Alcock were pioneers in the country South Africa will one day become—a truly African country, where whites have no guarantees. They arrived in Africa years ahead of the rest of us, and I have told you what befell them there. It was a tale of appalling violence and betrayal ... and yet, and yet, and yet: It was not entirely bereft of hope. There was light beyond the darkness—a tiny pinprick of dawning possibilities, casting just enough of a glow to show the rest of us the way.

As I write, Creina is still living in Msinga, in a place where the ravines echo with gunfire and tracer bullets arc across the night sky. The wars continue as always, unreported by anyone. The village across the river was burned down one night, and the view from Creina's bluff in the morning evoked Berlin at the end of World War II. The drought of the early eighties gave way to a season of floods, one of which obliterated her home under a fifteen-foot-deep glacier of mud.

A while ago, gunmen came to the project to kill a Zulu headman staying there. They surrounded Creina's house, cut the telephone line, and opened fire on the night watchmen. Creina crawled out of a window and fled. In the darkness, she ran into a warrior who raised his rifle and pulled the trigger, twice. Hearing all this gunfire, the project's Zulu staff thought Creina was surely dead, but they found her alive in the morning, shivering in a hiding place on the river's bank. Again, people who loved her tried to persuade her to leave, but she remained determined to stay. "Trust can never be a fortress," she said, "a safe enclosure against life. Trusting is dangerous. But without trust there is no hope for love, and love is all we ever have to hold against the dark."

And it cannot be said that the Alcocks' love has gone unrewarded, in spite of all that has happened. The long years of struggle against desertification appear to be bearing fruit. There is grass where there was no grass before, and the dongas are slowly silting over. Little Zulu children build anti-erosion contours with pebbles on footpaths. Their fathers have visions of a green valley not so different from the one Neil once saw. There is less tension along the border now. White farmers say it is because Alcock is no longer around to stir things up, but who knows—perhaps it is the memory of Neil's last crusade that stays their hands. There is a line of T. S. Eliot's that Creina is fond of quoting: "Be satisfied that ye have enough light to secure another foothold." She has held onto a foothold in Africa, and her husband's investment of love would seem to have been redeemed.

Early one morning in the winter of 1988, two aging Zulu men who'd loved and honored Neil climbed into a pickup and drove to the bend in the road where he was killed. What they were about to do had never been done before, and there were those Zulu traditionalists who thought it should not be done at all. They asked, "How can you do this thing?" and the two men answered, "Because Neil, he was same like a black man. The skin was white, but the heart it was same like a black."

One of the Zulus was Petros Majozi, the man who'd given up his job and pension on the basis of a single glimpse into a white man's heart. The other was Majozi Nxongo, the tribal warrior–statesman who once helped a floundering white reporter unravel the secrets of Simon the Hammerman. They stood over the spot where their white brother was slain, and invited his spirit to enter their sacred stick. *"Numzaan,"* they said, "we come to fetch you. Come, let us go to home." Then they placed the stick in a plastic bag and returned in solemn silence to the mud house by the river, bringing Neil's spirit back home.

The following day, a huge crowd of Zulus gathered outside Creina's house, looking more ragged and pitiful than ever in honor of this great occasion. At such a ceremony, Zulus wore their oldest clothes, to ensure that the returning spirit would recognize them and not be startled by unfamiliar sights. There were several *sangoma*s in the crowd, draped in beads and totems, with inflated pig bladders in their hair, and, right beside them, an old friend of Neil's from the townships—a black man in a jacket and tie, as fascinated by the strange goings-on as any of the whites present. Two cattle were brought forward and slaughtered with knives, in such a way that their bellowing might awaken and summon Msinga's shades. Then the carcasses were butchered and hung in great bloody chunks in Creina's bedroom, which looked like a charnel house by the time the ceremony was done: blood on the walls, blood on the floor; blood to wash the sins and sorrows of the past away.

After that, the ceremony became a celebration, and Zulus came from far and wide to join in. Two thousand liters of beer were drunk, mountains of food consumed, and the dancing carried on for two days. It was a stirring spectacle indeed. Feet thundered in unison, sweat glistened on black skin, and dust rose into the sky. The Zulus heaved and ululated joyously, carrying a lone white woman along with them, teaching her how to dance. Creina was smiling shyly and moving stiffly, but you had to start somewhere; in coming to terms with Africa, as in learning how to dance.

In the end, the sun went down and the celebrants went home, leaving the horns of the sacrificial cattle nailed to the roof of Creina's home. The horns were a reminder of the ceremony performed that day, a sign that the household within had honored its shades. In a continent where people worship their ancestors, Neil Alcock had become a god—the first white god in Africa, as far as anybody knows. Aeons after our ancestors walked away, the first white man had come home to Africa to stay.